Financial Management in the Sport Industry

Financial Management in the Sport Industry

Edited by Terry Webb

Larsen & Keller
www.larsen-keller.com

Financial Management in the Sport Industry
Edited by Terry Webb
ISBN: 979-8-88836-068-2 (Hardback)

Larsen & Keller
Published by Larsen and Keller Education,
5 Penn Plaza,
19th Floor,
New York, NY 10001, USA

Cataloging-in-Publication Data

Financial management in the sport industry / edited by Terry Webb.
p. cm.
Includes bibliographical references and index.
ISBN 979-8-88836-068-2
1. Sports--Finance--Management. 2. Sports administration.
3. Sports--Economic aspects. 4. Sporting goods
industry--Finance--Management. I. Webb, Terry.
GV716 .F56 2023
338.477 96--dc23

Table of Contents

Preface

It is often said that books are a boon to mankind. They document every progress and pass on the knowledge from one generation to the other. They play a crucial role in our lives. Thus I was both excited and nervous while editing this book. I was pleased by the thought of being able to make a mark but I was also nervous to do it right because the future of students depends upon it. Hence, I took a few months to research further into the discipline, revise my knowledge and also explore some more aspects. Post this process, I begun with the editing of this book.

Sports financial management is a management function that deals with planning, raising, controlling and administering the funds of a sports organization. This function allows the organization to measure and monitor its expenditure and the impact it has on the sports organization. It gives the management the much-needed flexibility to make adjustments in their budgets. In sports industry, efficient financial management is significant for the success of any sports program. The most crucial aspects of financial administration are funds management, resolution of budget issues, and knowing the most important area within a particular program. The first step in sports financial management is to decide what resources are available and how to distribute them. Furthermore, it involves reviewing prior financial records for existing programs and developing a new budget and strategy for new programs, which necessitates collaboration with important stakeholders to determine the optimum allocation of financial resources. This book contains some path-breaking studies on sports financial management. Those in search of information to further their knowledge will be greatly assisted by it.

I thank my publisher with all my heart for considering me worthy of this unparalleled opportunity and for showing unwavering faith in my skills. I would also like to thank the editorial team who worked closely with me at every step and contributed immensely towards the successful completion of this book. Last but not the least, I wish to thank my friends and colleagues for their support.

Editor

1

The Impact of College Athletic Success on Donations and Applicant Quality

Benjamin Baumer [1] and Andrew Zimbalist [2,*]

[1] Program in Statistical and Data Sciences, Smith College, Northampton, MA 01063, USA; bbaumer@smith.edu
[2] Department of Economics, Smith College, Northampton, MA 01063, USA
* Correspondence: azimbali@smith.edu

Abstract: For the 65 colleges and universities that participate in the Power Five athletic conferences (Pac 12, Big 10, SEC, ACC, and Big 12), the football and men's basketball teams are highly visible. While these programs generate tens of millions of dollars in revenue annually, very few of them turn an operating "profit." Their existence is thus justified by the claim that athletic success leads to ancillary benefits for the academic institution, in terms of both quantity (e.g., more applications, donations, and state funding) and quality (e.g., stronger applicants, lower acceptance rates, higher yields). Previous studies provide only weak support for some of these claims. Using data from 2006–2016 and a multiple regression model with corrections for multiple testing, we find that while a successful football program is associated with more applicants, there is no effect on the composition of the student body or (with a few caveats) funding for the school through donations or state appropriations.

Keywords: college sports; finances; economics

JEL Classification: C4; I2; H7; Z2

1. Introduction

Intercollegiate athletics is in a turbulent period. Recruiting and academic scandals along with antitrust litigations are erupting with unprecedented frequency. The Rice Commission on reforming college basketball called for a panoply of structural reforms.

Meanwhile, the financial outcomes of college athletic departments remain bleak for the vast majority of institutions. NCAA reports consistently show that in recent years only about 20 out of roughly 130 athletic departments in FBS (the Football Bowl Subdivision of Division I, the most commercial subdivision in the NCAA) run an operating surplus. FBS itself is subdivided into the Power Five or Autonomous Conferences (Pac 12, Big 10, SEC, ACC and Big 12) with 65 schools and the five Non-Autonomous Conferences with 64 schools. The Power Five command the large television contracts, control the football championship playoff and enjoy much larger attendance at their games.

During the 2015–2016 school year, the median reported operating deficit at all FBS athletic programs was $14.4 million. At the Power Five schools, the median reported operating deficit was $3.6 million. There were 24 Power Five schools during 2015–2016 that experienced an operating surplus—the median surplus for these schools was $10 million (NCAA 2017).

Because of accounting irregularities, however, it appears that most FBS athletic departments do not include significant shares of their capital costs in their reports to the NCAA. According to one NCAA study, capital costs, properly reckoned, exceed $20 million annually at the average FBS school (Orszag and Orszag 2005). If these and other indirect costs were included, most estimates suggest that no more than a half dozen programs would have a true surplus.

To be sure, there is an active debate about the underlying economic reality of intercollegiate athletic programs. For instance, many economists assert that it is improper to include the cost of athletic scholarships in the financial reports because they do not represent the actual marginal costs to the school. That is, even though the school may charge $50,000 tuition, the incremental cost of educating an additional student is close to zero. Put differently, an economics professor will get paid, say, $150,000, whether she has 120 or 121 students in her introductory macroeconomics class and there are no additional facility costs incurred by the extra student.

While this is a fair point, it is also reasonable to note that fielding an FBS football team requires 85 scholarships. If the relevant alternative is having no football team, then it is no longer true that the incremental cost of educating 85 students is zero. Indeed, it is misleading to think that the marginal cost of educating a single football player is zero. The school expends considerable resources on tutoring centers and academic support to keep players eligible.

It might also be relevant to consider the opportunity cost of a football scholarship. If low income and highly qualified students do not get scholarships, and thus do not attend the school, then the school may suffer from lower graduation rates, fewer serious students in the classroom and a lower profile for its student body in terms of standardized test scores and school rank.

Further, even if all athletic aid were eliminated from the financials, it would only amount to a median savings of $4.6 million—well below the median operating deficit of $14.4 million in FBS. Moreover, standard athletic accounting does not include a host of indirect expenses, such as a share of the school president's time, travel, office, and administrative assistants' salaries.

The reality is that intercollegiate athletic departments are not profit maximizers. They do not have shareholders who demand quarterly profits to boost stock prices or corporate dividends. Instead, they have stakeholders who want victories. Subject to some constraints, athletic directors are win maximizers. The conventional method for maximizing wins is to hire well-known coaches at multi-million dollar salaries, invest lavishly in athletic and tutoring facilities and spend freely on recruitment. Thus, when revenues rise, the athletic director finds more than enough ways to spend the bounty. And even if the football or men's basketball team yields a surplus, much of it is drained by the deficits experienced by the 15 or more "non-revenue" men's and women's sports. The consequence is that the vast majority of programs run in deficit.

How, then, can these hyper-commercialized, massive athletic programs be justified? One line of defense holds that while the programs might run financial deficits, they provide invaluable exposure and advertising for the university. This branding value, in turn, produces an increase in applications. These applications fill empty beds in the dormitories and enable the college to be more selective in its admissions policies, yielding an improvement in the quality of the student body (usually measured in standardized test scores). Additionally, alumni and athletic boosters become excited by team success or media prominence and open up their wallets, leading to increased donations and endowment growth. And, in some cases, this line of reasoning goes, state legislators also become enthused and allocate more budgetary assistance to the university.

Of course, even if it could be verified that athletic success leads to these salutary outcomes, it would not justify the tens of millions of dollars of investment that most FBS universities make annually. This is because only roughly half of all teams have a winning record and only a handful of teams achieve top ranking. If regression analysis shows that winning is positively correlated with applications, this implies both that applications tend to go up when wins increase and that applications tend to go down when wins decrease. Further, many, if not most, FBS universities bend the rules or cheat in order to promote athletic success. Some of these schools get caught and scandals ensue. The resulting ignominy may have negative enduring effects on applications, donations and legislative appropriations. The lowering of admissions' standards for athletes and the creation of sham courses also serve to dilute the educational experience and intellectual spirit on the campus.

In this paper we endeavor to expand upon, clarify, and update the existing scholarly literature on whether athletic success in football and men's basketball leads to increased applications, enhanced quality of the student body, more donations and greater state support. This updating is important because the organization and rules affecting college sports have been in flux in the 21st century.

We consider evidence from 2005–2006 through 2015–2016 for the 65 Power Five schools in the FBS. These schools are athletically the most successful and best known by a considerable margin and, therefore, the most likely to garner the positive publicity effects from athletic success.

In what follows we review the existing scholarship, describe our data sources and our data profile, discuss our models and results and draw conclusions. The evolution of the literature is not linear and the current state of knowledge remains ambiguous.

2. Review of the Literature

2.1. Athletic Success and the Quantity and Quality of Applications

One of the first and most frequently cited studies on the impact of athletic success on admissions is McCormick and Tinsley (1987). They gather data on 150 schools for 1971. On the basis of a multiple regression test with several control variables, they estimate that a school with a "big-time" athletics program had 3% higher SAT scores than schools without such a program. They identified 63 of the schools in their sample to have a big-time program. A difficulty with this cross-sectional analysis is that characteristics not identified by the control variables of a school lead to an incomplete model specification. In an attempt to rectify this deficiency, McCormick and Tinsley test a second model with data from 1981 to 1984, focusing exclusively on schools with big-time programs. They explore the link between changes in SAT scores and changes in athletic performance over this period. None of the estimated coefficients are statistically different than zero at standard confidence levels.

Bremmer and Kesselring (1993) essayed a retest of the McCormick and Tinsley hypotheses, using data from 1989 for 132 schools and from 1981–1989 for 53 schools. They find no evidence that basketball or football success led to increased SAT scores of matriculated students.

Tucker and Amato (1993) adapt the McCormick and Tinsley model by using a new metric of athletic success—whether the school was in the Associated Press top twenty ranking in football or basketball. They find no relationship between basketball success and SAT scores, but that a football program ranked in the top twenty for ten consecutive years (1980–1989) would attract a freshman class with 3% higher average SAT scores than a program which never ranked in the top twenty.

Murphy and Trandel (1994) construct a ten-year panel, 1978–1987, and use team win percentage as the measure of athletic success. They use school fixed effects and, thereby, control more effectively for unobserved differences among institutions. Murphy and Trandel find that a 50% increase in a team's win percentage results in a rather small increase of only 1.3% in the number of its applicants.

Mixon (1995) employs a different measure of basketball success—the number of rounds through which the school's team advanced in March Madness in the spring before the applications were filed the next fall[1]. Mixon's estimate was positive and statistically significant, suggesting that the average SAT score in the entering class increased by 1.7 points for each additional round the school's team was in the tournament.

Toma and Cross (1998) examine the records for the thirteen different universities that won the FBS football championship between 1979 and 1992 and the eleven different universities that won the NCAA men's basketball tournament over the same period. They track the quantity and quality of undergraduate applications for five years preceding and succeeding their championship for each of these schools. They find a clear correlation between winning a championship and the number of applicants, but are unable to identify any measurable impact of a championship on the quality of admitted or entering students.

Zimbalist (2001) uses data from 86 FBS colleges from 1980 through 1995 and performs a variety of fixed effect multiple regressions, using different measures of athletic success. The tests reveal

1 Mixon also co-authored two cross-sectional studies based on data from 1990 and 1993 that found a relationship between athletic success or prominence and the attraction of a school to out-of-state residents (Mixon and Hsing 1994; Mixon and Ressler 1995).

that, while there is some tendency for athletic success to increase applications, there is no significant relationship between athletic success and average SAT scores.

In a study under commission from the NCAA, Litan, Orszag, and Orszag (Litan et al. 2003) use a fixed-effects model for 1993–2001 and are unable to find a statistically significant relationship between football winning percentage and SAT scores of the incoming class.[2]

Tucker (2005) considers evidence from 1990, 1996, 2000, 2001 and 2002 from 78 Division I schools. He finds that after 1996 football success has a positive impact on the average SAT scores of the incoming class. He argues that the perfection of the Bowl Championship Series played a central role in bringing increased attention and, hence, advertising exposure to the top football programs.

Smith (2008), in contrast, considers data from Division I schools during 1994–2005 and finds little evidence to support a link between different measures of men's basketball success and four measurements of student quality. The one exception was that schools that had a "breakout" year (lagged two years) experienced an 8.86 point average increase in the SAT scores of the 75th percentile of the entering class. Breakout was defined in various ways, but basically denoted that a school went from a perennial losing record to a strong winning record.

Pope and Pope (2009), using a data set from 330 Division I schools during 1983–2002, find that certain types of athletic success appear to increase interest in a school from applicants with high, medium and low SAT scores, but that the increase in enrollments from the students with SAT scores above 600 in English and in Math is weaker and less reliable. Indeed, for some of the athletic performance variables the relationship between athletic success and the log of enrollment is significantly negative. Further, any impact tends to be in the next year with no significant effect after two or three years. In the end, Pope and Pope conclude that "the summary data . . . would suggest that athletically successful schools actually saw slightly lower long-run growth in applications and enrollments." One important caveat in interpreting these results is that Pope and Pope test fixed effect multiple regressions with control variables and thirty-two athletic performance variables. At a 0.10 level of significance, one would anticipate that 3.2 variables would achieve statistical significance randomly. The authors should have, but did not, control for the multiplicity problem.[3] Multicollinearity among the performance variables presents another challenge in interpreting the coefficients.[4]

Pope and Pope (2014) use a Division I data set of 332 schools during 1994–2001 to test the impact of men's basketball and football on the propensity of high school applicants to send their SAT scores to a school. They find that a school with stellar results in either sport receives on average up to 10% more SAT scores. They also find that the relationship is stronger for some demographic subgroups, such as males, people of color, out-of-state students and high school athletes. They do not test for actual applications to the school or for eventual enrollments. Pope and Pope model one to three year lags and find that the statistical significance of sports success "decays very quickly across time."

In sum, the various studies lend some support to the notion that robust athletic success can lead to an increase in applications to a school. The correlate of this proposition is that poor athletic performance can lead to falling applications. There is only weak support, if any, for the claim that sport success leads to an increase in the quality of students. The increase in applications in some cases, however, may assist a school in filling empty beds in its dormitories. These conclusions are supported anecdotally by a self study done at the University of Massachusetts following its ascent to basketball fame in the mid-1990s under John Calipari.

---

2 For a summary of the literature through 2004, see Frank (2004).

3 See, for instance, Benjamini and Hochberg (1995).

4 Castle and Kostelnik (2011) examine 14 Division II schools in Pennsylvania during 1995–2004 and find weak evidence that some measures of athletic success were correlated with an increase in applications and the SAT scores of the entering class. Three studies found that football success was associated with lower student grades; see Clotfelter (2011); Lindo, Swensen, and Waddell (Lindo et al. 2012); and Hernández-Julián and Rotthoff (2014).

> The period from fall 1988 to fall 1990 did not include outstanding basketball years. In 1991, UMass was a semi-finalist in the NIT and in the four years since has been featured consistently on national television, has been ranked consistently in the top twenty and has gone to the NCAA tournament ... It is clear that after double digit declines in out-of-state applications from fall 1988 to fall 1991, we experienced two years of double digit increases in fall 1993 and 1994. It has been suggested that this bump in applications might be related to, among other things, the greater awareness of the university beyond Massachusetts, at least partially as a result of the success in basketball.
>
> It has been reported that the University of Connecticut experienced a similar application increase after their very successful Elite Eight season in 1991, with a 26% increase in out-of-state and 6% increase of in-state applications. Despite the growth of applications correlated with UConn basketball success, the conclusion was that there was no impact on yield (enrollment divided by admittances). With the numbers of applications up, it would also be expected that the quality of students enrolled might increase because of a larger pool on which to draw. The Connecticut experience indicates no changes in the quality of students. In the UMass figures there was a decrease in the SAT scores of applicants and enrolled students for both in- and out-of-state students. In fact, this [1995–1996] was the first year that the SAT scores of out-of-state students fell below in-state. None of this suggests that team success carries beyond the application stage. In fact, in the year following the "Dream Season," UConn applications dropped back to earlier numbers. Their conclusion was that there was no lasting impact on the admission numbers. (Massachusetts Football Task Force 1996)

2.2. *Athletic Success and Alumni Giving*

Studies on alumni or other giving are less numerous and less complete. The primary reason for this is that the availability of data on alumni giving is spotty. Sigelman and Carter (1979) assemble data from the Council for Financial Aid to Education (CFAE) from 1966–1967 to 1975–1976 and test the relationship between the yearly change in total giving to the annual fund and athletic success, measured by win percentages in football and men's basketball and a dummy variable indicating whether the team participated in the post-season. Sigelman and Carter do not find any statistically significant relationships between giving and athletic success, and even note that some of the coefficients were negative.

Brooker and Klastorin (1981) critique the Sigelman and Carter study on the grounds that it does not control for institutional heterogeneity. They adjust for this by using institutional fixed effects and find some positive and some negative relationships between athletic success and giving. Together, they run tests on 1740 coefficients and find only 1.7% of them to be significant at the 0.10 level, which is fewer than the number that would be expected by chance. The authors do not report the magnitude of the effects.

Sigelman and Bookheimer (1983) introduce a fixed effects model and break down alumni contributions into two components, restricted gifts to the athletics department and unrestricted gifts to the annual fund. They find that the two types of giving are uncorrelated with each other and that only gifts to the athletics department are correlated with sport success (football, not basketball). More precisely, they estimate that a 10% increase in football win percentage over the previous four years leads to a $125,000 increase in donations to the athletics department (measured in 1983 dollars).

Grimes and Chressanthis (1994) focus on one school, Mississippi State, over a 30-year period between 1962 and 1991. They considered success of the football, basketball and baseball teams. Winning success in football had a negative coefficient that was not statistically significant. Basketball's coefficient was significant at the 0.05 level and positive, but extremely small.

Baade and Sundberg (1996) construct a data set from Division I schools during 1973–1979. They employ both winning percentage and bowl or March Madness appearances as measures of sport success. They find no impact on giving from increased winning percentages, but a modest effect for postseason appearances. They do not distinguish between athletic and academic giving.

Rhoads and Gerking (2000) follow the modelling of Baade and Sundberg with data for 1986–1987 to 1995–1996.[5] They run their tests first without institutional fixed effects and find impact very similar to those of Baade and Sundberg. They run the tests again with fixed effects and none of the athletic success variables are statistically significant predictors of giving. Rhoads and Gerking also estimate that being placed on NCAA probation for a basketball violation reduces total giving by $1.6 million (measured in 1987 dollars).

Turner, Meserve, and Bowen (Turner et al. 2001) consider a data set of 15 private schools during 1988–1989 to 1997–1998. Using a fixed effects model, they find that football win percentage has no significant effect on the *rate* of giving among alumni in FBS programs, but that it has a highly significant (at 0.01) and negative effect on the giving *amount* among alumni. Specifically, an increase of 12 wins is associated with a *decrease* in giving by $270 for an average person.

Humphreys and Mondello (2007), based on 320 Division I schools from 1976 to 1996 find that postseason play was positively correlated with giving to athletics, but not to giving to academics. Stinson and Howard (2008) investigated 208 institutions from Divisions I-AA and I-AAA and found no correlation between giving to athletics and giving to academics.[6]

2.3. Athletic Success and State Budgetary Support

Three scholarly articles have explored the impact of university athletic success on legislative appropriations. Humphreys (2006) estimates a reduced form model with data from 1975 to 1996 that controls for state and institution specific characteristics.[7] He finds that state appropriations are 8% higher for institutions in FBS (formerly Division IA), other things equal. The presence of an increase in state support for having an FBS football team of $2.6 million on average (in 1982 dollars) may do little more than offset the additional net costs of fielding the team. Humphreys, however, does not find that either appearance in a bowl game or achieving a national ranking in the top 25 had a statistically significant impact on state appropriations.

Alexander and Kern (2010) consider 117 schools from FBS, FCS and Division II for the period 1983–1984 to 2006–2007. They do not explain why their sample is more heavily weighted to FBS or why certain schools were omitted. They find that increases in basketball and football win percentage for schools in FBS do produce a statistically significant increase in state appropriations, but appearances in major bowl games or in the NCAA Final Four does not. The three models that they test yield R-squares of 0.05, 0.05 and 0.08, suggesting that they are underspecified and calling into question the reliability of their coefficient estimates.

Jones (2015) uses a difference-in-difference model that focused on six universities that transitioned from FCS to FBS between 2000 and 2010. Jones finds that when the six schools were compared to all

---

5 Goff (2000) also considers the impact of sport success on the endowment. Goff, however, only looks at endowment data only for two schools, Georgia Tech and Northwestern. While he finds no statistically significant relationship between sport success and donations at Georgia Tech, Goff does find one at Northwestern. However, Goff notes that the finding for Northwestern may have been affected by an accounting change at the school (moving a substantial amount of cash into long-term equity during the period studied.) In any event, the data base is much too thin to assign much importance to these results.

6 Koo and Dittmore (2014), based on an unexplained sample of 155 schools from Divisions I, II and III during 2002–2003 to 2011–2012, purport to find a positive correlation between athletic giving lagged one year and current academic giving. They conclude that athletic giving does not crowd out academic giving. They do not offer an explanation of why they lag athletic giving; any crowding out would presumably happen in the same year. It is also not clear what their full model is and whether, for instance, they detrended their data or used time fixed effects. Walker (2015) uses a sample of between 954 and 1052 schools during 2002–2011 and finds that appearances in the Final Four are significantly associated with increases in private donations, but, again, he does not break out athletic and academic donations and does not provide a full description of his model.

7 There was a prior study to Humphreys, but is was based on only one year (1980–1981) and 52 DIA schools (Coughlin and Erekson 1986).

other FCS schools, there is no significant correlation between FBS affiliation and state appropriations. When the six schools are compared only to other FCS schools in the same region, there is still no significant correlation. Only when the comparison is made between FCS schools in the same region and within the same propensity score range[8] did the move to FBS yield a significant relationship with state appropriations. Jones concludes that this result provides some support for the hypothesis of a positive effect between NCAA subdivision and state support.

2.4. *Anderson on Athletic Benefits*

Anderson (2017) deploys the most sophisticated econometric treatment of the relationships between athletic success and various school outcome variables in the extant literature, uses the most recent data, and has been cited numerous times as representing the state of current knowledge on these matters; hence, this paper warrants a separate and more detailed discussion. He considers a data set for FBS schools from 1986 to 2009 and employs a propensity score model to estimate these relationships. Anderson's motivation for adopting this framework is the difficulty of unraveling causality from observational data, especially given that selection bias (e.g., recruiting skill of coaches and administrators), reverse causality (e.g., athletic success begets donations, which are in turn spent to achieve greater athletic success), and confounding variables are likely present.[9]

Anderson's basic approach is to use bookmaker spreads for individual football games to establish (via a fifth order polynomial logistic model) a probability of winning (the propensity score). Actual wins are then conditioned on the propensity score and used as the independent variable (or treatment). This method depends on the assumption that gambling is efficient (the bookmaker spread represents full and rationally-processed information to determine the likelihood of contest outcome; put differently, all the relevant variables that impact a game's result are subsumed into the point spread.[10]) Anderson then essentially runs school applications, SAT scores and donations on the difference between the actual and the expected wins during a season. Thus, Anderson is estimating the effect of unexpected wins (losses) on his school outcome variables.

While it is interesting to know what the effect of unexpected wins is, it is likely a different effect than wins or general athletic success. Few would question, for instance, that a football or men's basketball team that rises from sport oblivion to prominence in one year will experience an uptick in applications, donations or state appropriations (see previous discussion of UMass/UConn.)[11] This is a different matter than a team perennially appearing in March's Elite Eight or Final Four or in the Football Championship Playoff.

Anderson does indeed find that unexpected wins are associated with increased applications, higher SAT scores and increased donations to the athletics department (but not to the general fund). Notably, Anderson's strongest result is for donations to the athletics department, but this finding

---

8 Jones' propensity score includes a number of school characteristics, including size, percentage of full-time students, percent of graduate students, degree of institutional urbanization, freshmen retention rate, and total education expenditures.

9 Reverse causality would not appear to a significant issue when considering applications or SAT scores and athletic success. That is, while it may be logical to expect athletic success to increase applications or SAT scores, it does not seem plausible that more applications or higher SAT scores would engender greater athletic success. Top football and basketball players in FBS are recruited and, by all accounts, base their decisions on factors related to the athletics program. The effects of confounding variables, such as the managerial talent of a school president or provost, along with other unquantifiable attributes, could be accounted for by team fixed effects. Reverse causality may be an issue with athletic success and donations. In such a case, however, one would expect that the presence of reverse causality would strengthen the estimated correlation between the variables. Since Anderson's use of a propensity score is intended to mitigate the impact of reverse causality, other things equal, one would expect his model to imply a weaker correlation between athletic success and donations, contrary to his findings.

10 For this crucial assumption to be statistically valid, the R_2 from this equation must be very high, approaching 1. Anderson, however, does not mention what the R_2 is in this test. It is nonetheless true that the literature on sports betting markets indicates that they operate efficiently. See, for example, the discussion in Lopez, Matthews, and Baumer (Lopez et al. 2018).

11 Such a finding would be consistent with the empirical work of Smith (2008), op. cit., and his "breakout" variable.

relies on a very incomplete data set on donations (495 observations for BCS[12] athletic donations versus 1560 observations possible for 65 schools over 24 years). He also runs tests separately for the Power Five conferences within FBS and for the remaining FBS (or "Group of Five") conferences and finds that his relationships only hold for the Power Five schools.

Three other points from Anderson are worth noting. First, he finds little evidence that the positive effect of unexpected wins lasts more than one year. Second, his positive results appear to be considerably weaker than he claims. Thus, after correcting for multiple testing, none of his treatment variables are significant at the 0.05 level. His Alumni Athletic Operating Donations variable comes closest with significance at the 0.053 level, but this variable is missing more than two-thirds of its possible observations, creating a possible selection bias.[13] Third, in his conclusion, Anderson misrepresents his own results when he states: "Consider a school that improves its season wins by three games . . . . This school may expect alumni athletic donations to increase by $409,000 (17%), applications to increase by 406 (3%) . . . ." But Anderson is not looking at the net benefit of three wins; he is looking the net benefit of three wins over expectation. That is, if a team wins three more games but the betting markets expected the team would win three more games, there would be no net benefit.

2.5. Summary of the Existing Literature

Overall, the literature on the impact of college sport success on the quantity and quality of applications and enrollments, donations to the athletics department and general fund, and state appropriations is mixed and somewhat inconclusive. When significant results have been found, they have tended to be small in practical magnitude. Much of the existing scholarship is limited by methodological issues and data availability and most studies have not considered evidence from the 2000s. Each new study appears to use a new set of schools, conferences or divisions, a different set of athletic success variables, distinct issues with missing data, and different modelling of the relationship between the treatment and outcome variable. Given the restructuring of the NCAA subdivisions and conferences, the emergence of conference-owned RSNs and attendant spurt in television revenues, the increased autonomy of the Power Five conferences and the enhanced role of athletics in university finances and governance since 2000, it makes sense to examine the stability of the relationships between success in sports and possible indirect benefits for the school with more recent data. In what follows, we attempt to overcome some of the methodological issues of previous work and to construct a more up-to-date data set.

3. Our Data

Anderson (2017) found that for 1986–2009, the Power Five conferences are the most athletically prominent and the most likely to experience benefits from athletic success. As an update, our data covers the eleven academic years from 2005–2006 through 2015–2016 (plus the three preceding years for lagged variables) for the 65 schools that were members of Power Five conferences in 2015–2016[14]. Our data sources are the Council for Advancement and Support of Education annual Voluntary Support of Education (VSE) surveys, Integrated Postsecondary Education Data System (IPEDs) surveys, the National Center for Education Statistics for high school graduates, the US Census Bureau for demographic information, and Sports-Reference.com. The data are available through the colleges package for R, available on GitHub (Baumer 2018).

---

12 BCS stands for Bowl Championship Series and refers to universities prior to 2014 in today's Power Five conferences plus the former Big East conference. The BCS conferences were sometimes referred to as the AQ or Automatic Qualifying conferences.

13 Anderson, Table 3, p. 127. In his conclusion (p. 132), Anderson suggests that school investments in athletics may have net revenue payoffs, but to conclude this he misleads because the NCAA definition of revenue includes athletic donations, and, indeed, is a major share of athletic department revenues for FBS schools.

14 Conference alignment was retroactively fixed to the 2015–2016 alignment. A school like the University of Utah, which moved from the Mountain West Conference to the Pac-12 in 2012, is considered to have always belonged to the Pac-12 for the purposes of this study.

Our school benefit response variables—summarized in Table 1—include the number of applications (*Applied*, measured in thousands), the average 75th percentile SAT score across three portions of the exam (*SAT75p*), the admissions rate (*Admit*) and yield (*Yield*), donations to athletics by alumni (*Athletics*, in millions of dollars), total donations by alumni (*Alumni*, in millions of dollars), total non-athletic donations by alumni (*NonAthletics*) and total state appropriations to the school (*State*, in millions of dollars), also computed per student (*StatePC*, in thousands).

Table 1. Data profile, response variables.

Statistic	N	Mean	St. Dev.	Pctl (25)	Pctl (75)
Applied	711	21.786	11.470	13.058	28.030
SAT75p	675	661.211	50.828	630.000	696.667
Donations	605	178.522	152.569	85.672	230.596
Athletics	356	20.128	14.453	11.939	26.523
NonAthletics	356	154.485	159.349	66.488	197.043
State	558	279.541	137.115	174.574	371.532
StatePC	557	58.073	26.899	39.911	71.806
Yield	711	0.408	0.111	0.338	0.459
Admit	711	0.591	0.214	0.453	0.762

We note that for variables derived from IPEDS (acceptance rate, number of applicants, yield, and 75th percentile SAT score), we have nearly complete coverage with only one school (Maryland) failing to report in multiple years. Notably, as is the case with Anderson's data set, the extent of the missing data for donations is much larger. We have athletic donations data for only 356 school-years and total donations data for 605 school years out of a total possible 715 observations. The pattern of missing data in donations suggests a possible bias, as certain schools (mostly private, notably Notre Dame, Boston College, Miami (FL), Syracuse, Wake Forest) simply did not report donation data (the data is certainly not missing at random). Hence, our findings for the athletic donations response variable should be interpreted with caution. Of course, private schools do not receive state funding, but this does not fully account for the missing data for that variable—state-related schools like Penn State and Pittsburgh also did not report state funding. Many of these variables are strongly right-skewed, and in these cases we have fit the model to their logarithm.

Our athletic success treatment variables—summarized in Table 1—include measures of being good, great, and the best at both basketball and football. Specifically, for both sports we record the cumulative winning percentage over the previous three seasons (*BBWpct*, *FBWpct*), as well as any Final Four appearances[15] and national championships in any of the three preceding seasons. Thus, we consider one, two, and three year lags on the Final Four (*BBFF*1, *BBFF*2, *BBFF*3, and *FBFF*1, *FBFF*2, *FBFF*3, respectively) and championship variables (*BBChamps*1, *BBChamps*2, *BBChamps*3, and *FBChamps*1, *FBChamps*2, *FBChamps*3, respectively). The choice to include cumulative winning percentage over three years—as opposed to say, winning percentage in each of the previous three years—was designed to smooth out year-to-year noise in winning percentage, while still reflecting relevant recent history.

Our control variables include median income per capita in the state (*Income*, in thousands of dollars), number of high school diplomas issued in the state in the previous year (*HSDiplomas*, in thousands), and state funding, both overall and per student (*State* and *StatePC*, respectively). These variables help account for variation in the income and population of each state, in addition to the support from state government (only relevant for public schools). While it may be the case that state household income is less relevant for private schools, such schools often draw regional interest

15 Final Four appearances in basketball are measured by performance in the NCAA Tournament. Final Four appearances in football are measured by end-of-season national ranking by the Associated Press.

and represent only about one-fifth of the schools considered. Further, to control for the unobserved heterogeneity of the 65 institutions we tested both school (*School*) and year (*Year*) fixed effects, with both variables treated as categorical.[16] The fixed effect for *School* should capture the effect of the long-term branding value of the school's athletic program (i.e., Duke basketball), as well as many other attributes. The fixed effect for *Year* should capture changes due to inflation and other economic conditions.

The data in Table 2 come exclusively from Sports-Reference and the US Census Bureau, and there is no missing data. As the number of high school diplomas awarded is right-skewed, we use the logarithm of this variable in our models.

Table 2. Data profile, explanatory variables.

Statistic	N	Mean	St. Dev.	Pctl (25)	Pctl (75)
HSDiplomas	715	106.500	100.914	39.227	127.515
Income	715	26.349	3.709	23.797	28.351
BBFF1	715	0.046	0.210	0	0
BBFF2	715	0.045	0.207	0	0
BBFF3	715	0.045	0.207	0	0
BBWpct	715	0.599	0.124	0.514	0.694
BBChamps1	715	0.013	0.112	0	0
BBChamps2	715	0.011	0.105	0	0
BBChamps3	715	0.013	0.112	0	0
FBFF1	715	0.060	0.238	0	0
FBFF2	715	0.060	0.238	0	0
FBFF3	715	0.060	0.238	0	0
FBWpct	715	0.570	0.175	0.444	0.700
FBChamps1	715	0.015	0.123	0	0
FBChamps2	715	0.015	0.123	0	0
FBChamps3	715	0.015	0.123	0	0

4. Our Models

We tested a wide variety of models, including semi-logs, different lag patterns and interactive effects, and focus here on the most important results (please see our data Appendix A for additional information).[17] Unless otherwise indicated, our standard errors are robust (using the HC1 sandwich variance-covariance matrix (Zeileis and Hothorn 2002)) and our p-values are corrected for multiplicity via the Benjamini-Hochberg method (Benjamini and Hochberg 1995)[18], which controls the false discovery rate. All computations were performed in R version 3.4 (R Core Team 2018).

Our general regression model for each response variable y_j is:

$$\begin{aligned}
y_i &= \beta \cdot X + \varepsilon_j \\
&= \beta_{j0} + \alpha_j \cdot Year + \gamma_j \cdot School + \beta_{j1} \cdot \log(HSDiplomas) + \beta_{j2} \cdot Income \\
&+ \theta_{j1} \cdot BBWpct + \theta_{j2} \cdot BBChamps1 + \theta_{j3} \cdot BBChamps2 + \theta_{j4} \cdot BBChamps3 \\
&+ \theta_{j5} \cdot BBFF1 + \theta_{j6} \cdot BBFF2 + \theta_{j7} \cdot BBFF3 \\
&+ \lambda_{j1} \cdot FBWpct + \lambda_{j2} \cdot FBChamps1 + \lambda_{j3} \cdot FBChamps2 + \lambda_{j4} \cdot FBChamps3 \\
&+ \lambda_{j5} \cdot FBFF1 + \lambda_{j6} \cdot FBFF2 + \lambda_{j7} \cdot FBFF3 \\
&+ \varepsilon_j
\end{aligned}$$

16 We also collected many variables that were not included in our regression models. For example, cost of attendance, state population, etc. These variables are included in the colleges package (Baumer 2018), but are often incomplete and/or strongly correlated with our other explanatory variables.

17 None of the models we explored but are not reporting offered substantially different or contradictory results to the ones offered here.

18 All reported p-values were adjusted using the p.adjust() function in the stats package.

where each α_j is a vector of length 10 containing the fixed effects associated with each academic year (relative to 2005–2006), each γ_j is a vector of length 64 containing the fixed effects associated with each school (relative to the University of Alabama, which comes first alphabetically[19]), β_{j1} and β_{j2} are control variables associated with the number of high school diplomas granted in the previous year and the per capita income in the corresponding state, the θ's are associated with the school's recent success in basketball, the λ's are associated with the school's recent success in football, and the error terms $\epsilon_j \sim N(0, \sigma_{\epsilon_j})$, for some fixed value of σ_{ϵ_j}.[20] For readability we omit the $j$subscripts in what follows.

5. Our Results

In each of the models we fit, *School* and *Year* (which is treated as a categorical variable) were statistically significant. For clarity of presentation we relegate these results to our data Appendix A, but these effects capture much of the variability in the data. There are obvious broad trends, such as a general increase in the number of applications over time, and obvious school-specific effects for which these variables control. Multicollinearity among the explanatory variables of interest—as measured by generalized variance inflation factors (Fox and Monette 1992)—does not appear to be problematic in these models.[21]

5.1. *Athletic Success and the Quantity and Quality of Applications*

Our first model, shown below, tests the effect of athletic success on school applications,

$$y_1 = log(Applied) = \beta_1 \cdot X + \epsilon_1.$$

Results from this model are shown in Table 3.

19 The success of the University of Alabama's football team impacts our interpretation of the football-related variables. However, using Alabama as the reference group has no impact on any term's statistically significance, since we consider only the significance of the *School* variable as a whole.

20 Note that our models do not directly account for the possibility that a school is not simultaneously investing in competitive athletics and other areas of school achievement or marketing. That is, if a school hired a new football coach for $10 million, leading to an appearance in the national football playoffs, at the same time that it hired two nobel prize winning professors and began a multimillion dollar marketing campaign, then attributing an increase in applications, in entering students SAT scores or in alumni donations to football success would be spurious. There are two caveats to such an endogeneity concern. First, we do employ institutional fixed effects that may attenuate or eliminate such a problem. Second, we do not know of any evidence that such behavior occurred. In any event, we are not attributing causality to the treatment variables in our models; rather, we are noting the presence or absence of statistically significant relationships and the magnitude of such relationships.

21 We computed generalized variance inflation factors raised to the $1/(2 \cdot df)$ power, as recommend by Fox and Monette (1992) for all explanatory variables in all models. Those factors were only above 2 for the control variables number of high school diplomas (ranging from 20.8 to 23.9) and per capita income (8.9 to 10.0).

Table 3. Models for Applicants.

	Dependent Variable	
	Log(Applied) **(1)**	**Admit** **(2)**
log(HSDiplomas)	0.127 (0.124) $p = 0.440$	−0.086 (0.075) $p = 0.399$
Income	0.012 (0.011) $p = 0.424$	0.003 (0.006) $p = 0.763$
BBFF1	−0.014 (0.022) $p = 0.676$	−0.002 (0.013) $p = 0.954$
BBFF2	−0.030 (0.019) $p = 0.209$	−0.001 (0.020) $p = 0.990$
BBFF3	0.018 (0.024) $p = 0.593$	−0.008 (0.017) $p = 0.826$
BBWpct	0.067 (0.059) $p = 0.412$	−0.009 (0.036) $p = 0.919$
BBChamps1	0.059 (0.033) $p = 0.145$	−0.008 (0.020) $p = 0.857$
BBChamps2	0.095 (0.035) $p = 0.016$ **	−0.003 (0.023) $p = 0.094$
BBChamps3	−0.010 (0.046) $p = 0.855$	0.018 (0.022) $p = 0.605$
FBFF1	0.031 (0.022) $p = 0.270$	−0.008 (0.009) $p = 0.596$
FBFF2	0.010 (0.021) $p = 0.778$	0.004 (0.008) $p = 0.810$
FBFF3	0.023 (0.020) $p = 0.412$	−0.005 (0.008) $p = 0.713$
FBWpct	0.144 (0.044) $p = 0.004$ ***	−0.053 (0.024) $p = 0.077$ *
FBChamps1	0.013 (0.042) $p = 0.832$	−0.021 (0.015) $p = 0.322$
FBChamps2	0.045 (0.042) $p = 0.424$	−0.009 (0.017) $p = 0.763$
FBChamps3	0.042 (0.043) $p = 0.459$	0.004 (0.018) $p = 0.919$
Constant	1.810 (0.571) $p = 0.005$ ***	0.930 (0.336) $p = 0.020$ **
Observations	711	711
R^2	0.955	0.920
Adjusted R^2	0.949	0.909
Residual Std. Error (df = 620)	0.115	0.065
F Statistic (df = 90; 620)	147.817 ***	79.434 ***

Note: * $p < 0.1$; ** $p < 0.05$; *** $p < 0.01$.

Out of the 14 athletic performance variables, only two are statistically significant at the 0.10 level: *BBChamps*2 and *FBWpct*. *BBChamps*2 is significant at the 0.05 level and its coefficient (θ_3) indicates a national championship two years earlier is associated with a 10% increase in applications.[22] *FBWpct* is significant at the 0.001 level and its coefficient (λ_1) indicates an additional win per year on average over the previous three seasons is associated with a 1.1% increase in applications.[23]

These results are consistent with the bulk of previous literature that big-time football and men's basketball success does provide an advertising (and/or anticipated quality of life) effect which boosts applications to a university. Two additional observations are in order. First, the effect for increasing win percentage in the regular season does not apply to basketball (after controlling for football) and for football the magnitude of the effect is rather modest. Thus, direct advertising of a school's academic programs and campus life might be more effective in generating applications than investing in its basketball or football success. Second, the other observed impact occurs only for the rarest of accomplishments (1 out of 65 in each year): a national championship. Investing in creating a national championship basketball or football team entails very high risk for rather ordinary returns. Further, the returns in the form of increased applications appear to delay for one year and then dissipate by year three.

Table 3 also shows the results for a model for the rate of admissions. These results are highly consistent with the previous ones, due to the obvious functional dependence between the rate of admission and the number of applicants (the number of students is largely fixed at most schools). The negative coefficient for football winning percentage—the only variable to achieve statistical significance at the 0.10 level—implies that greater success in football is associated with higher selectivity.

Albeit tenuous, the existence of a statistically significant link between athletic success and applications leads to the next question: whether athletic success improves a school's admission yield (the percent of admitted students who enroll.) We ran the following equation to test this relationship.

$$y_3 = Yield = \beta_3 \cdot X + \epsilon_3$$

Results for this model as shown in Table 4. Of the 14 athletic performance variables, only one is statistically significant at the 0.10 level. *FBWpct* is significant at the 0.05 level with an association between an extra regular season win on average over the previous three years and an increased yield of 0.476 percentage points; that is, a yield of 30% would increase to 30.476%. While football's impact appears to be statistically significant but small, performance of the men's basketball team does not have a statistically significant impact on yield.

If athletic success may lead to an uptick in applications, even with a steady yield, the school may become more selective. Greater selectivity, in turn, may lead to an improvement on the quality of the student body, often represented by a school's SAT scores.

In the following equation we test what impact athletic success has on the 75th percentile of SAT scores across the three sections of the exam (Math, English, Writing) for the 65 Power Five schools in our sample.

$$y_4 = SAT75p = \beta_4 \cdot X + \epsilon_4$$

The results from this model are also shown in Table 4. Only one of the 14 athletic performance variables achieve statistical significance at the 0.10 level: *BBWpct*. The coefficient of *BBWpct* (θ_1) implies that every regular season win on average over three years is associated with a 0.6 point increase in the average across the English, Writing and Math portions of the SAT for the 75th percentile of the school's student body—a statistically significant effect with no practical impact.

---

22 The coefficient was 0.095 and $exp(0.095) = 1.1$.

23 The coefficient was 0.144 and $exp(0.144/13) = 1.011$ (divided by an average of 13 regular season games).

Table 4. Models for Admissions.

	Dependent Variable	
	SAT75p **(1)**	**Yield** **(2)**
log(HSDiplomas)	17.070 (14.516) $p = 0.397$	0.082 (0.059) $p = 0.255$
Income	−1.457 (1.033) $p = 0.286$	0.001 (0.005) $p = 0.880$
BBFF1	0.108 (3.459) $p = 0.980$	0.003 (0.012) $p = 0.902$
BBFF2	−0.100 (3.914) $p = 0.980$	0.015 (0.022) $p = 0.627$
BBFF3	1.963 (3.631) $p = 0.741$	0.0002 (0.013) $p = 0.887$
BBWpct	17.937 (7.451) $p = 0.041$ **	−0.002 (0.013) $p = 0.987$
BBChamps1	−7.067 (6.423) $p = 0.418$	0.0003 (0.017) $p = 0.987$
BBChamps2	−0.140 (5.528) $p = 0.980$	−0.019 (0.022) $p = 0.512$
BBChamps3	−2.869 (6.094) $p = 0.787$	−0.001 (0.015) $p = 0.980$
FBFF1	−9.598 (7.237) $p = 0.327$	−0.001 (0.009) $p = 0.944$
FBFF2	1.231 (3.781) $p = 0.874$	−0.005 (0.007) $p = 0.573$
FBFF3	−7.317 (6.818) $p = 0.426$	−0.011 (0.008) $p = 0.241$
FBWpct	−4.963 (6.418) $p = 0.600$	0.062 (0.023) $p = 0.019$**
FBChamps1	7.934 (9.794) $p = 0.589$	−0.002 (0.014) $p = 0.944$
FBChamps2	−1.843 (4.135) $p = 0.798$	−0.012 (0.016) $p = 0.586$
FBChamps3	−0.445 (9.155) $p = 0.980$	−0.020 (0.011) $p = 0.139$
Constant	580.580 (55.642) $p = 0.000$ ***	0.152 (0.265) $p = 0.698$
Observations	675	711
R^2	0.925	0.803
Adjusted R^2	0.914	0.775
Residual Std. Error (df = 620)	14.941 (df = 585)	0.053 (df = 620)
F Statistic (df = 90; 620)	81.070 *** (df = 89; 585)	28.153 *** (df = 90; 620)

Note: * $p < 0.1$; ** $p < 0.05$; *** $p < 0.01$.

5.2. Athletic Success and Alumni Giving

Our next test explores the relationship between alumni donations and athletic success. As was the case with Anderson (2017), who also relied on data from the annual survey of the Council for Aid to Education, there is a substantial problem with missing data. Many of the respondent schools simply do not answer the survey questions on alumni donations or do not do so completely or on a regular annual basis. In Anderson's data set, approximately two-thirds of donation data is missing, in ours approximately 15% of overall donations and about half of athletics donations are missing (359 out of 715). Accordingly, although there is no obvious pattern to which schools did not report, our results must be interpreted with caution. The following equation examines the relationship between alumni donations to athletics and athletic performance, with the standard control variables. Its results are shown in Table 5.

$$y_5 = log(Athletics) = \beta_5 \cdot X + \epsilon_5$$

Table 5. Models for Donations.

	Dependent Variable	
	log(Athletics) (1)	**log(NonAthletics)** (2)
log(HSDiplomas)	−0.453 (1.144) $p = 0.932$	0.508 (0.331) $p = 0.269$
Income	0.040 (0.090) $p = 0.919$	0.068 (0.029) $p = 0.058$ *
BBFF1	−0.118 (0.307) $p = 0.932$	0.123 (0.085) $p = 0.292$
BBFF2	0.014 (0.151) $p = 0.978$	−0.027 (0.068) $p = 0.887$
BBFF3	0.113 (0.137) $p = 0.919$	0.010 (0.058) $p = 0.929$
BBWpct	0.331 (0.510) $p = 0.919$	−0.020 (0.183) $p = 0.952$
BBChamps1	−0.092 (0.290) $p = 0.932$	−0.052 (0.171) $p = 0.893$
BBChamps2	−0.153 (0.254) $p = 0.919$	0.036 (0.080) $p = 0.876$
BBChamps3	−0.349 (0.194) $p = 0.629$	0.020 (0.075) $p = 0.893$
FBFF1	0.027 (0.328) $p = 0.978$	−0.087 (0.086) $p = 0.584$
FBFF2	0.349 (0.333) $p = 0.919$	−0.046 (0.067) $p = 0.759$
FBFF3	0.203 (0.269) $p = 0.919$	−0.120 (0.071) $p = 0.201$
FBWpct	0.321 (0.273) $p = 0.919$	0.250 (0.111) $p = 0.071$ *

Table 5. *Cont.*

	Dependent Variable	
	log(Athletics) **(1)**	**log(NonAthletics)** **(2)**
FBChamps1	−0.310 (0.589) $p = 0.919$	−0.053 (0.103) $p = 0.838$
FBChamps2	0.045 (0.408) $p = 0.978$	−0.141 (0.094) $p = 0.274$
FBChamps3	0.365 (0.382) $p = 0.919$	−0.027 (0.123) $p = 0.917$
Constant	3.079 (5.783) $p = 0.919$	1.039 (1.559) $p = 0.759$
Observations	356	356
R^2	0.709	0.939
Adjusted R^2	0.636	0.924
Residual Std. Error (df = 284)	0.589	0.213
F Statistic (df = 71; 284)	9.725 ***	61.789 ***

Note: * $p < 0.1$; ** $p < 0.05$; *** $p < 0.01$.

None of the 14 athletic performance variables is statistically significant at the 0.10 level.[24]

$$y_6 = log(NonAthletics) = \beta_6 \cdot X + \epsilon_6$$

This equation examines the relationship between donations to the school's general fund minus athletic donations (Non-Athletic Donations) and athletic performance.

Only one of the 14 athletic performance variables is statistically significant at the 0.10 level: *FBWpct*. However, the effect size—an expected increase of 1.94% for each additional victory per year—is small. Nine of the 14 coefficients had negative signs.

5.3. Athletic Success and State Budgetary Support

Our final model was on the relationship between academic performance and state funding for public universities. The results are shown in Table 6.

$$y_7 = State = \beta_7 \cdot X + \epsilon_7$$

Three of the 14 athletic performance variables were significant at the 0.10 level: *BBFF1*, *FBFF1*, and *FBFF2*.

The nominal interpretation of the first coefficient (θ_5) is that a Final Four appearance in the previous basketball season is associated with a 5.3% increase in state funding. However, this is nearly offset by a −3.9 decrease associated with actually winning the championship, although this effect is not statistically significant. It is hard to square the idea that teams that reach the Final Four tend to receive greater increases in state funding than teams that win the championship.

[24] The high adjusted p-values for the coefficients in the *Athletics* regression are a result of the unadjusted p-values being relatively uniformly distributed with a large mean (0.48).

Table 6. Models for Funding.

	Dependent Variable	
	log(State) (1)	**log(StatePC)** (2)
log(HSDiplomas)	−0.103 (0.198) $p = 0.705$	−0.024 (0.177) $p = 0.905$
Income	−0.028 (0.031) $p = 0.471$	−0.032 (0.023) $p = 0.214$
BBFF1	0.052 (0.023) $p = 0.044$ **	0.049 (0.030) $p = 0.154$
BBFF2	0.032 (0.029) $p = 0.377$	0.037 (0.034) $p = 0.338$
BBFF3	−0.005 (0.041) $p = 0.937$	−0.011 (0.050) $p = 0.870$
BBWpct	0.042 (0.117) $p = 0.800$	0.059 (0.095) $p = 0.623$
BBChamps1	−0.040 (0.043) $p = 0.471$	−0.071 (0.058) $p = 0.296$
BBChamps2	−2.869 (6.094) $p = 0.787$	−0.058 (0.052) $p = 0.334$
BBChamps3	−0.016 (0.052) $p = 0.823$	−0.017 (0.069) $p = 0.867$
FBFF1	−0.064 (0.031) $p = 0.073$ *	−0.079 (0.031) $p = 0.019$ **
FBFF2	−0.059 (0.029) $p = 0.079$ *	−0.039 (0.031) $p = 0.276$
FBFF3	−0.035 (0.027) $p = 0.286$	−0.028 (0.025) $p = 0.338$
FBWpct	−0.159 (0.155) $p = 0.411$	−0.023 (0.109) $p = 0.870$
FBChamps1	0.073 (0.041) $p = 0.129$	0.094 (0.056) $p = 0.151$
FBChamps2	0.057 (0.052) $p = 0.387$	0.041 (0.067) $p = 0.623$
FBChamps3	0.011 (0.034) $p = 0.823$	0.006 (0.045) $p = 0.905$
Constant	5.863 (1.225) $p = 0.00001$ ***	4.190 (0.966) $p = 0.00005$ ***
Observations	558	557
R^2	0.949	0.942
Adjusted R^2	0.941	0.933
Residual Std. Error (df = 481)	0.216	0.177
F Statistic (df = 76; 481)	117.728 ***	103.449 ***

Note: * $p < 0.1$; ** $p < 0.05$; *** $p < 0.01$.

Further muddying the waters is the fact that the effects on the football side show the same offsetting pattern, but in the opposite direction (negative for reaching the Final Four, positive for winning the championship).

When we consider the state funding per capita (as in Table 6), the statistical significance of all variables save for *FBFF*1 disappears, and the direction of the effect remains negative.

6. Conclusions

Previous literature on the effect of athletic success on applications, quality of the student body, donations and state funding has been inconclusive. Researchers have employed different methodologies and models and most have been limited by incomplete data. We develop a recent data set for the Power Five conferences during the eleven years from 2006 through 2016 and use fixed effects linear regression models to retest these relationships. We report robust standard errors and control for multiple testing. We find that certain measures of football success have a modest positive and short-lived impact on student applications, but no clear impact on admission yield or on the quality of the student body. Although hampered by incomplete data, we also found that athletic success did not have a statistically significant effect on donations. Final Four appearances in both basketball and football showed some statistical significance associated with state funding, but the direction and robustness of these findings is unclear.

Author Contributions: The authors contributed equally to this article.

Acknowledgments: The authors would like to thank Junzhou Liu, our data collection assistant, as well as Michael Lopez, Roger Noll, Brad Humphreys, Ann Kaplan, Nick Horton, Dennis Coates, the reviewers and the associate editor for helpful comments and suggestions.

Appendix A

ANOVA tables

Below we present the ANOVA tables for all models discussed in the paper. Note the persistent statistical significance of the Year and School terms.

Table A1. ANOVA table for log(Applied).

	Df	Sum Sq	Mean Sq	F Value	Pr(>F)
Year	10	26.197	2.620	198.729	0.000
school_name	64	148.990	2.328	176.601	0.000
log(hs_diplomas_lag1)	1	0.008	0.008	0.578	0.447
per_capita_income	1	0.008	0.008	0.602	0.438
bball_avg_wpct_lag3	1	0.020	0.020	1.5474	0.214
bb_champs_lag1	1	0.011	0.011	0.867	0.352
bb_champs_lag2	1	0.056	0.056	4.278	0.039
bb_champs_lag3	1	0.008	0.008	0.613	0.434
fball_avg_wpct_lag3	1	0.288	0.288	21.859	0.000
fb_champs_lag1	1	0.016	0.016	1.241	0.266
fb_champs_lag2	1	0.023	0.023	1.777	0.183
fb_champs_lag3	1	0.036	0.036	2.749	0.098
Residuals	626	8.252	0.013		

Table A2. ANOVA table for SAT75p.

	Df	Sum Sq	Mean Sq	F Value	Pr(>F)
Year	10	12,802.322	12,802.322	5.654	0.000
school_name	63	1,591,052.696	25,254.805	111.543	0.000
log(hs_diplomas_lag1)	1	417.541	417.541	1.844	0.175
per_capita_income	1	400.511	400.511	1.769	0.184
bball_avg_wpct_lag3	1	1199.903	1199.903	5.300	0.022
bb_champs_lag1	1	278.781	278.781	1.231	0.268
bb_champs_lag2	1	8.558	8.558	0.038	0.846
bb_champs_lag3	1	20.627	20.627	0.091	0.763
fball_avg_wpct_lag3	1	865.252	865.252	3.822	0.051
fb_champs_lag1	1	0.010	0.010	0.000	0.995
fb_champs_lag2	1	7.444	7.444	0.033	0.856
fb_champs_lag3	1	394.777	394.777	1.744	0.187
Residuals	591	133,810.192	226.413		

Table A3. ANOVA table for log(Donations).

	Df	Sum Sq	Mean Sq	F Value	Pr(>F)
Year	10	9.510	9.510	33.107	0.000
school_name	59	241.490	4.093	142.499	0.000
log(hs_diplomas_lag1)	1	0.176	0.176	6.141	0.014
per_capita_income	1	0.302	0.302	10.500	0.001
bball_avg_wpct_lag3	1	0.000	0.000	0.011	0.918
bb_champs_lag1	1	0.005	0.005	0.180	0.671
bb_champs_lag2	1	0.015	0.015	0.510	0.476
bb_champs_lag3	1	0.028	0.028	0.988	0.321
fball_avg_wpct_lag3	1	0.204	0.204	7.100	0.008
fb_champs_lag1	1	0.016	0.016	0.573	0.450
fb_champs_lag2	1	0.001	0.001	0.027	0.870
fb_champs_lag3	1	0.030	0.030	1.033	0.310
Residuals	525	15.080	0.029		

Table A4. ANOVA table for log(Athletics).

	Df	Sum Sq	Mean Sq	F Value	Pr(>F)
Year	10	10.467	1.047	3.028	0.001
school_name	45	225.721	5.016	14.513	0.000
log(hs_diplomas_lag1)	1	0.051	0.051	0.147	0.702
per_capita_income	1	0.071	0.071	0.204	0.652
bball_avg_wpct_lag3	1	0.125	0.125	0.362	0.548
bb_champs_lag1	1	0.045	0.045	0.129	0.720
bb_champs_lag2	1	0.002	0.002	0.005	0.941
bb_champs_lag3	1	0.078	0.078	0.226	0.635
fball_avg_wpct_lag3	1	0.647	0.647	1.8722	0.172
fb_champs_lag1	1	0.446	0.446	1.289	0.257
fb_champs_lag2	1	0.150	0.150	0.433	0.511
fb_champs_lag3	1	0.4360.	0.436	1.263	0.262
Residuals	290	100.232	0.346		

Table A5. ANOVA table for log(NonAthletics).

	Df	Sum Sq	Mean Sq	F Value	Pr(>F)
Year	10	8.851	0.885	19.548	0.000
school_name	45	188.907	4.198	92.717	0.000
log(hs_diplomas_lag1)	1	0.066	0.066	1.457	0.228
per_capita_income	1	0.316	0.316	6.979	0.009
bball_avg_wpct_lag3	1	0.000	0.000	0.001	0.977
bb_champs_lag1	1	0.006	0.006	0.140	0.708
bb_champs_lag2	1	0.001	0.001	0.016	0.898
bb_champs_lag3	1	0.010	0.010	0.226	0.635
fball_avg_wpct_lag3	1	0.157	0.157	3.462	0.064
fb_champs_lag1	1	0.024	0.024	0.523	0.470
fb_champs_lag2	1	0.066	0.066	1.459	0.228
fb_champs_lag3	1	0.023	0.023	0.517	0.473
Residuals	290	13.130	0.045		

Table A6. ANOVA table for log(State).

	Df	Sum Sq	Mean Sq	F Value	Pr(>F)
Year	10	1.997	0.200	4.294	0.000
school_name	50	414.854	8.297	178.446	0.000
log(hs_diplomas_lag1)	1	0.003	0.003	0.066	0.798
per_capita_income	1	0.094	0.094	2.013	0.157
bball_avg_wpct_lag3	1	0.006	0.006	0.125	0.724
bb_champs_lag1	1	0.004	0.004	0.096	0.756
bb_champs_lag2	1	0.003	0.003	0.067	0.796
bb_champs_lag3	1	0.000	0.000	0.004	0.950
fball_avg_wpct_lag3	1	0.075	0.075	1.607	0.205
fb_champs_lag1	1	0.003	0.003	0.063	0.801
fb_champs_lag2	1	0.001	0.001	0.019	0.891
fb_champs_lag3	1	0.004	0.004	0.086	0.770
Residuals	487	22.644	0.046		

Table A7. ANOVA table for log(StatePC).

	Df	Sum Sq	Mean Sq	F Value	Pr(>F)
Year	10	5.056	5.056	16.124	0.000
school_name	50	240.754	4.815	153.543	0.000
log(hs_diplomas_lag1)	1	0.002	0.002	0.061	0.804
per_capita_income	1	0.106	0.106	3.387	0.066
bball_avg_wpct_lag3	1	0.022	0.022	0.690	0.407
bb_champs_lag1	1	0.000	0.000	0.004	0.953
bb_champs_lag2	1	0.006	0.006	0.202	0.653
bb_champs_lag3	1	0.004	0.004	0.139	0.710
fball_avg_wpct_lag3	1	0.027	0.027	0.861	0.354
fb_champs_lag1	1	0.005	0.005	0.167	0.683
fb_champs_lag2	1	0.001	0.001	0.042	0.838
fb_champs_lag3	1	0.003	0.003	0.083	0.774
Residuals	486	15.241	0.031		

Table A8. ANOVA table for Yield.

	Df	Sum Sq	Mean Sq	F Value	Pr(>F)
Year	10	0.823	0.082	29.646	0.000
school_name	64	6.200	6.200	34.880	0.000
log(hs_diplomas_lag1)	1	0.007	0.007	2.608	0.107
per_capita_income	1	0.000	0.000	0.151	0.698
bball_avg_wpct_lag3	1	0.000	0.000	0.117	0.732
bb_champs_lag1	1	0.001	0.001	0.395	0.530
bb_champs_lag2	1	0.000	0.000	0.021	0.884
bb_champs_lag3	1	0.000	0.000	0.001	0.976
fball_avg_wpct_lag3	1	0.022	0.022	7.883	0.005
fb_champs_lag1	1	0.000	0.000	0.057	0.812
fb_champs_lag2	1	0.002	0.002	0.825	0.364
fb_champs_lag3	1	0.008	0.008	2.791	0.095
Residuals	626	1.739	0.003		

Table A9. ANOVA table for Admit.

	Df	Sum Sq	Mean Sq	F Value	Pr(>F)
Year	10	0.364	0.036	8.796	0.000
school_name	64	29.422	0.460	111.044	0.000
log(hs_diplomas_lag1)	1	0.009	0.009	2.088	0.149
per_capita_income	1	0.002	0.002	0.494	0.482
bball_avg_wpct_lag3	1	0.001	0.001	0.257	0.612
bb_champs_lag1	1	0.002	0.002	0.367	0.545
bb_champs_lag2	1	0.001	0.001	0.256	0.613
bb_champs_lag3	1	0.000	0.000	0.017	0.896
fball_avg_wpct_lag3	1	0.034	0.034	8.164	0.004
fb_champs_lag1	1	0.007	0.007	1.604	0.206
fb_champs_lag2	1	0.001	0.001	0.321	0.571
fb_champs_lag3	1	0.000	0.000	0.000	0.990
Residuals	626	2.592	0.004		

References

1. Alexander, Donald L., and William Kern. 2010. Does Athletic Success Generate Legislative Largess from Sports-Crazed Representatives? The Impact of Athletic Success on State Appropriations to Colleges and Universities. *International Journal of Sport Finance* 5: 253–67.
2. Anderson, Michael L. 2017. The Benefits of College Athletic Success: An Application of the Propensity Score Design. *Review of Economics and Statistics* 99: 119–34. [CrossRef]
3. Baade, Robert A., and Jeffrey O. Sundberg. 1996. What Determines Alumni Generosity? *Economics of Education Review* 15: 75–82. [CrossRef]
4. Baumer, Benjamin S. 2018. Colleges: Data About College Enrollments, Donations, and Athletics. Available online: http://github.com/beanumber/colleges (accessed on 1 November 2018).
5. Benjamini, Yoav, and Yosef Hochberg. 1995. Controlling the False Discovery Rate: A Practical and Powerful Approach to Multiple Testing. *Journal of the Royal Statistical Society. Series B (Methodological)* 57: 289–300. [CrossRef]
6. Bremmer, Dale S., and Randall G. Kesselring. 1993. The Advertising Effect of University Athletic Success: A Reappraisal of the Evidence. *The Quarterly Review of Economics and Finance* 33: 409–21. [CrossRef]
7. Brooker, George W., and Theodore D. Klastorin. 1981. To the Victors Belong the Spoils? College Athletics and Alumni Giving. *Social Science Quarterly* 62: 744–50.
8. Castle, Joshua, and Robert Kostelnik. 2011. The Effects of an Institution's Athletic Success on the Future Freshmen Application Pool at Ncaa Division Ii Universities. *Journal of Issues in Intercollegiate Athletics* 4: 411–27.
9. Clotfelter, Charles T. 2011. *Big-Time Sports in American Universities*. New York: Cambridge University Press.
10. Coughlin, Cletus C., and O. Homer Erekson. 1986. Determinants of State Aid and Voluntary Support of Higher Education. *Economics of Education Review* 5: 179–90. [CrossRef]

11. Fox, John, and Georges Monette. 1992. Generalized collinearity diagnostics. *Journal of the American Statistical Association* 87: 178–83. [CrossRef]
12. Frank, Robert H. 2004. *Challenging the Myth: A Review of the Links among College Athletic Success, Student Quality, and Donations*. Miami: Knight Foundation Commission on Intercollegiate Athletics.
13. Goff, Brian. 2000. Effects of University Athletics on the University: A Review and Extension of Empirical Assessment. *Journal of Sport Management* 14: 85–104. [CrossRef]
14. Grimes, Paul W., and George A. Chressanthis. 1994. Alumni Contributions to Academics: The Role of Intercollegiate Sports and Ncaa Sanctions. *American Journal of Economics and Sociology* 53: 27–40. [CrossRef]
15. Hernández-Julián, Rey, and Kurt W. Rotthoff. 2014. The Impact of College Football on Academic Achievement. *Economics of Education Review* 43: 141–47. [CrossRef]
16. Humphreys, Brad R. 2006. The Relationship Between Big-Time College Football and State Appropriations for Higher Education. *International Journal of Sport Finance* 1: 119–28.
17. Humphreys, Brad R., and Michael Mondello. 2007. Intercollegiate Athletic Success and Donations at Ncaa Division I Institutions. *Journal of Sport Management* 21: 265–80. [CrossRef]
18. Jones, Willis A. 2015. High-Level Football and Appropriations to Universities: Are Sports-Crazed Representatives Responsive to Ncaa Divisional Affiliation? *Journal of Education Finance* 40: 438–55.
19. Koo, Gi-Yong, and Stephen W. Dittmore. 2014. Effects of Intercollegiate Athletics on Private Giving in Higher Education. *Journal of Issues in Intercollegiate Athletics* 7: 1–16.
20. Lindo, Jason M., Isaac D. Swensen, and Glen R. Waddell. 2012. Are Big-Time Sports a Threat to Student Achievement? *American Economic Journal: Applied Economics* 4: 254–74. [CrossRef]
21. Litan, Robert E., Jonathan M. Orszag, and Peter R. Orszag. 2003. *The Empirical Effects of Collegiate Athletics: An Interim Report*. Washington, DC, USA: Sebago Associates.
22. Lopez, Michael, Gregory J. Matthews, and Benjamin S. Baumer. 2018. How Often Does the Best Team Win? A Unified Approach to Understanding Randomness in North American Sport. *Annals of Applied Statistics* 12: 2483–516. [CrossRef]
23. Massachusetts Football Task Force. 1996. *Final Report of the I-a Football Task Force*. Boston: University of Massachusetts.
24. McCormick, Robert E., and Maurice Tinsley. 1987. Athletics Versus Academics? Evidence from Sat Scores. *Journal of Political Economy* 95: 1103–16. [CrossRef]
25. Mixon, Franklin G., Jr. 1995. Athletics Versus Academics? Rejoining the Evidence from Sat Scores. *Education Economics* 3: 277–83. [CrossRef]
26. Mixon, Franklin G., Jr., and Yu Hsing. 1994. The Determinants of Out-of-State Enrollments in Higher Education: A Tobit Analysis. *Economics of Education Review* 13: 329–35. [CrossRef]
27. Mixon, Franklin G., Jr., and Rand W. Ressler. 1995. An Empirical Note on the Impact of College Athletics on Tuition Revenues. *Applied Economics Letters* 2: 383–87. [CrossRef]
28. Murphy, Robert G., and Gregory A. Trandel. 1994. The Relation between a University's Football Record and the Size of Its Applicant Pool. *Economics of Education Review* 13: 265–70. [CrossRef]
29. NCAA. 2017. *Revenues and Expenses of Division I Intercollegiate Athletics Program, 2004–2016*. Indianapolis: NCAA.
30. Orszag, Jonathan M., and Peter R. Orszag. 2005. *The Physical Capital Stock Used in Collegiate Athletics*. Indianapolis: NCAA.
31. Pope, Devin G., and Jaren C. Pope. 2009. The Impact of College Sports Success on the Quantity and Quality of Student Applications. *Southern Economic Journal* 75: 750–80.
32. Pope, Devin G., and Jaren C. Pope. 2014. Understanding College Application Decisions: Why College Sports Success Matters. *Journal of Sports Economics* 15: 107–31. [CrossRef]
33. R Core Team. 2018. *R: A Language and Environment for Statistical Computing*. Vienna: R Foundation for Statistical Computing.
34. Rhoads, Thomas A., and Shelby Gerking. 2000. Educational Contributions, Academic Quality, and Athletic Success. *Contemporary Economic Policy* 18: 248–58. [CrossRef]
35. Sigelman, Lee, and Samuel Bookheimer. 1983. Is It Whether You Win or Lose? Monetary Contributions to Big-Time College Athletic Programs. *Social Science Quarterly* 64: 347–59.
36. Sigelman, Lee, and Robert Carter. 1979. Win One for the Giver? Alumni Giving and Big-Time College Sports. *Social Science Quarterly* 60: 284–94.
37. Smith, D. Randall. 2008. Big-Time College Basketball and the Advertising Effect: Does Success Really Matter? *Journal of Sports Economics* 9: 387–406. [CrossRef]
38. Stinson, Jeffrey L., and Dennis R. Howard. 2008. Winning Does Matter: Patterns in Private Giving to Athletic and Academic Programs at NCAA Division I-AA and I-AAA Institutions. *Sport Management Review* 11: 1–20. [CrossRef]
39. Toma, J. Douglas, and Michael E. Cross. 1998. Intercollegiate Athletics and Student College Choice: Exploring the Impact of Championship Seasons on Undergraduate Applications. *Research in Higher Education* 39: 633–61. [CrossRef]

40. Tucker, Irvin B. 2005. Big-Time Pigskin Success: Is There an Advertising Effect? *Journal of Sports Economics* 6: 222–29. [CrossRef]
41. Tucker, Irvin B., and Louis Amato. 1993. Does Big-Time Success in Football or Basketball Affect Sat Scores? *Economics of Education Review* 12: 177–81. [CrossRef]
42. Turner, Sarah E., Lauren A. Meserve, and William G. Bowen. 2001. Winning and Giving a Study of the Responsiveness of Giving to Performance on the Field. *Social Science Quarterly* 82: 812–26. [CrossRef]
43. Walker, Adam G. 2015. Division I Intercollegiate Athletics Success and the Financial Impact on Universities. *SAGE Open* 5: 1–13. [CrossRef]
44. Zeileis, Achim, and Torsten Hothorn. 2002. Diagnostic Checking in Regression Relationships. *R News* 2: 7–10.
45. Zimbalist, Andrew. 2001. *Unpaid Professionals: Commercialism and Conflict in Big-Time College Sports*. Princeton: Princeton University Press.

2

The Long-Term Game: An Analysis of the Life Expectancy of National Football League Players

Ruud Koning [1], Victor Matheson [2,*], Anil Nathan [2] and James Pantano [2]

1 Department of Economics and Econometrics, Faculty of Economics and Business, University of Groningen, PO Box 800, 9700 AV Groningen, The Netherlands; r.h.koning@rug.nl

2 Department of Economics and Accounting, College of the Holy Cross, One College Street, Worcester, MA 01610, USA; anathan@holycross.edu (A.N.); JFPANT13@g.holycross.edu (J.P.)

* Author to whom correspondence should be addressed; vmatheso@holycross.edu

Abstract: The National Football League (NFL) has recently received significant negative media attention surrounding the safety of its players, revolving largely around the long term health risks of playing the sport. Recent premature deaths and instances of suicide associated with chronic traumatic encephalopathy and other football related injuries have brought the sport under increased scrutiny. By comparing mortality rates of the general population to mortality rates of players using publically available data from the 1970 and 1994 NFL seasons, we test whether participation in football is significantly harmful to the longevity of the players. We conclude that, in total, players in the NFL have lower mortality rates than the general population. However, there is evidence that line players have higher mortality rates than other players and that those who played more games have higher mortality rates than those who played fewer games.

Keywords: National Football League; premature deaths; survivability; injuries

---

1. Introduction

The National Football League (NFL) has recently been scrutinized about the impact of playing the game on mortality and quality of life. High profile cases such as the suicides of Atlanta Falcons safety Ray Easterling, Chicago Bears defensive back Dave Duerson, and San Diego Chargers linebacker Junior Seau, as well as the tragic premature death of long-time Pittsburgh Steeler Mike Webster, have certainly pushed these issues to the forefront of media attention. Cantu [1] and Samson [2] confirm that both Webster and Seau had chronic traumatic encephalopathy (CTE), and Mecham [3] confirms evidence of CTE in both Duerson and Easterling. CTE is most often caused by severe and repeated head injuries and leads to brain degeneration and dementia [4].

In August 2013, the NFL attempted to settle a lawsuit brought by former players claiming that the league downplayed the risks of concussion-related brain injuries. The NFL agreed to provide $765 million to compensate victims, pay for medical exams for 4500 plaintiffs and other retired players, and engage in medical research [5]. Due to questions regarding the adequacy of the payout, however, the settlement was not granted initial approval by Judge Anita Brody who noted that, " ... it is difficult to see how the Monetary Award Fund would have the funds available over its lifespan to pay all claimants ... " [6]. A better understanding of risk factors relating to premature deaths are of interest both to the teams individually, and the NFL collectively.

However, the financial implications go much further than just settling the grievances of past players. The future of the NFL could be at stake through two channels. First of all, the perception already exists that the NFL is a guilty pleasure where spectators enjoy the game at the long-term expense of the health of the participants [7]. Mounting evidence that playing in the NFL causes serious health problems or shortens life could cause a drop in the NFL's popularity similar to what has happened to the sport of boxing [8]. Secondly, due to health concerns there has already been a drop in football participation rates at the youth level. Between 2010 and 2012, a period of heightened awareness of head injuries in the NFL, there was a 6.7% drop in the number of players ages 6 through 14 playing Pop Warner Football, the largest decline in the long history of nation's biggest youth football program [9]. A continued drop in participation would impact the pipeline of players into the NFL as well as future interest in the sport in general.

While anecdotal evidence of players dying prematurely is both alarming and the subject of considerable attention in the popular press, can it be statistically shown that playing in the NFL leads to a lower life expectancy for ex-players? This paper will examine whether NFL players have a higher mortality rate than the general population and will look at which factors affect the mortality of NFL players.

Baron and Rinsky [10] show that former NFL players have a much lower mortality rate than the general population, as well as some other interesting patterns. For example, defensive linemen have higher rates of cardiovascular disease than the general population, and black players were more likely to develop cardiovascular disease than white players. Lehman *et al.* [11] also find that NFL players have lower mortality rates than the general population while having a higher incidence of neurodegenerative mortality. These papers show evidence that high profile deaths can skew the perception of the risk of playing in the NFL.

This paper is related to other papers that examine (excess) mortality in professional sports. Related literature is discussed in Koning and Amelink [12], who show that Dutch professional soccer players have a lower mortality rate than the general Dutch population. Sanchis-Gomez *et al.* [13] and Marijon *et al.* [14] show that mortality among French professional cyclists who participated in the Tour de France is lower than that of the French population. These studies suggest that professional athletes have better health than the average population, increasing longevity.

Our paper adds to the literature by using a flexible probability model developed in Koning and Amelink [12] that can be used to compare NFL mortality rates to those in the general population. In addition, we also use Cox hazard rate models [15], to estimate survival of players at an individual level and to determine the impact of games played, position, and race on player mortality.

Our results show that NFL players have a lower mortality rate than the general population (by race and overall) in both the 1970 and 1994 seasons. In the 1970 season, offensive and defensive line players have higher mortality rates than those in the other positions, and non-white players have higher mortality rates than white players. Most importantly, players who played more than 2 seasons worth of games have higher mortality rates than those that have played less. In the 1994 season, line players have higher mortality rates than those who are in the skilled positions, but other factors are not statistically significant.

Sections 2 and 3 describe the data and models used in the study, while Section 4 displays the results. Section 5 concludes and discusses some more potential research.

2. Data

We examine player cohorts for two seasons, 1970 and 1994, and include all players who appeared in at least one game during either of those seasons. The 1970 cohort consists of 1244 players, and the 1970 cohort has 1600 players. The 1970 season was chosen for two reasons. First, using an older season ensures that survival probabilities in the general population become sufficiently low and observational data with the players have enough natural attrition to be meaningful. Second, 1970 was the first season after the National Football League-American Football League merger effectively doubling sample size of players and also ensuring that players in the sample had relatively standardized equipment and playing conditions. It should be noted, however, that the data set includes all players who played during the 1970 season, not just who started their careers in the 1970 season, so the player statistics may include games played prior to the merger. The 1994 season included to see whether changes in the game, including better equipment as well and stronger and faster players, has had an effect on player mortality. In addition, the 1994 cohort has, anecdotally, experienced an abnormally large number of premature deaths.

Most of the player data for the 1970 and 1994 NFL seasons was collected on "Pro-Football-Reference.com" [16] which has season-by-season statistics for every player to have appeared in an NFL game as well as dates of birth and death for all players. Data on race was revealed through online picture searches of the players. Players were placed into one of three positional categories: skill positions, which include wide receivers, tight ends, quarterbacks, and running backs; line positions, which include players on the offensive and defensive lines, who tend to be much larger and heavier than other players; and other, which includes mostly defensive players who are not linemen plus some punters and kickers.

Table 1 lists summary statistics for the 1970 and 1994 seasons. There were 1244 total players who participated in the 1970 season and 1600 players in the 1994 season with identifiable race data. Approximately two-thirds of the players who played in the 1970 season are white, but by 1994 only one third of the players are white. Across both whites and non-whites, the percentage of players still alive is very similar. This survival rate equality is not reflective of the survival rates of whites and non-whites in the general population where non-whites have experienced significantly higher mortality rates than whites. For both seasons, the average age was in the mid-twenties at the relevant time. The split between positions was generally even in 1970, with a shift towards line players and away from skill players in 1994. Players in 1994 participated in more games over their career than those in 1970, at least in part due to the regular season being extended by two games. In 1970, whites played about a season's more worth of games over a career than non-whites, but in 1994 non-whites played more than two-and-a-half more seasons than whites. This fact is also reflected in the percentage of whites and non-whites that played at least two season's worth of games in 1970 compared to 1994.

Table 1. Summary Statistics.

Season	Variable	All	White	Non-White
	Alive in 2012	1091	690	401
1970	Alive in 2012 (%)	87.7	88.35	86.61
	Dead in 2012	153	91	62
	Dead in 2012 (%)	12.3	11.65%	13.39%
	Age in 1970	25.1	25.45	24.52
	White (%)	64.98	-	-
	Line (%)	33.2	36.24	28.08
	Skill (%)	33.92	32.01	37.15
	Other (%)	32.88	31.75	34.77
	Games Played	95.73	100.12	88.35
	Long Career (%) (27+ career games played)	88.1	91.66	82.07
1994	Alive in 2012	1559	523	1036
	Alive in 2012 (%)	97.44	97.03	97.64
	Dead in 2012	41	16	25
	Dead in 2012 (%)	2.56	2.97	2.36
	Age in 1994	25.79	27.13	25.11
	White (%)	33.69	-	-
	Line (%)	38.12	35.99	39.21
	Skill (%)	26.12	27.83	25.26
	Other (%)	35.75	36.18	35.53
	Games Played	108.18	80.68	122.16
	Long Career (%) (27+ career games played)	88.62	74.03	96.04

3. Models

The following survival model is an adaptation of the one developed in Koning and Amelink [12] for Dutch soccer players. The idea is to compare the expected survival of individuals based on the general population at the appropriate time to the observed survival of NFL players. Let x be the age of an individual, t be the base (or starting) year, and let s be the number of years after t. Also, let N (x, t) be the number of individuals of age x alive at time t. Therefore, N (t), which is the number of individuals (regardless of age) that are alive at time t is as follows.

$$N(t) = \sum_x N(x,t) \tag{1}$$

Let $(x, t, t + s)$ be the probability that an individual of age x at time t survives to time $t + s$ (or in other words, survives s years from time t). So, for example, an individual survives one year from time t with a probability P $(x, t, t + 1)$. As such, the probability that an individual of age x at time t survives to time $t + s$ can be represented by the product of successive one-year probabilities.

$$P(x,t,t+s) = \prod_{n=1}^{s} P(x,t+n-1,t+n) \tag{2}$$

The expected number of individuals of age x alive at time t that are still alive at $t + s$ can be represented as follows.

$$N(x + s, t + s) = N(x, t) * P(x, t, t + s) \tag{3}$$

Using equation (1) above, the total number of individuals alive at time t that are expected to be alive at time $t + s$ is the following.

$$N(t+s) = \sum_x N(x+s,t+s) \tag{4}$$

N $(t + s)$, the expected number of individuals that survive to time $t + s$ can then be compared to the actual number of players that survive to time $t + s$ to see if these players experience different longevity than the general population of a similar age composition.

This approach compares mortality between the population of NFL players, and the US population in general. Besides that, we also examine whether observable risk factors influence the individual risk of mortality within the population of NFL players. To do so, we estimate a Cox proportional hazard model was also constructed to determine factors that impact mortality with the following equation.

$$\lambda(t) = \lambda_0(t)e^{(\beta' x)} \tag{5}$$

The covariates used are games played, position played, and race. In this case, the baseline hazard ($\lambda_0(t)$) captures mortality among NFL players in general. In this specification, we do not allow for time-varying covariates. That is, we only allow for individual specific covariates. The relevant time scale is the age of the player, and we allow for censored observation using the usual start/stop approach as in Therneau and Grambsch [15] and Fox [17].

4. Results

The expected number of survivors, classified by age, based on population probabilities of survival and the model above can be calculated in order to make a comparison with the actual numbers of players (also classified by age) surviving. Tables 2 and 3 list the comparisons overall and by race for 1970 and 1994.

Table 2. Actual Survival and Expected Survival (1970 Season).

Age	All				White				Non-White			
	Number	Alive	Expected Alive	*P*-value	Number	Alive	Expected Alive	*P*-value	Number	Alive	Expected Alive	*P*-value
21	116	107	94.97	0	64	60	53.41	0.03	38	34	25.46	0
22	186	176	150.28	0	110	107	90.65	0	71	64	46.42	0
23	168	156	133.71	0	94	87	76.36	0	67	62	42.67	0
24	150	126	117.35	0.09	90	81	71.92	0.02	53	39	32.82	0.09
25	154	137	118.18	0	97	85	76.09	0.03	52	48	31.23	0
26	100	89	75.11	0	64	58	49.18	0.01	35	30	20.35	0
27	104	87	76.29	0.02	64	54	48.07	0.11	37	30	20.79	0
28	75	63	53.61	0.01	56	46	41.02	0.17	19	17	10.29	0
29	60	50	41.68	0.02	43	35	30.63	0.18	16	14	8.34	0
30	47	34	31.62	0.54	28	22	19.33	0.31	19	12	9.48	0.26
31	32	29	20.76	0	24	22	16	0.01	7	6	3.33	0.06
32	18	12	11.21	0.81	15	10	9.61	1	3	2	1.35	0.59
33	14	10	8.33	0.43	13	9	7.96	0.78	1	1	0.43	0.43
34	10	9	5.66	0.05	9	8	5.24	0.09	1	1	0.4	0.4
35	4	4	2.14	0.13	4	4	2.2	0.13	-	-	-	-
36	4	1	2.01	0.37	4	1	2.07	0.36	-	-	-	-
38	1	1	0.44	0.44	1	1	0.45	0.45	-	-	-	-
42	1	0	0.3	1	1	0	0.31	1	-	-	-	-

Table 3. Actual Survival and Expected Survival (1994 Season).

Age	All				White				Non-White			
	Number	Alive	Expected Alive	*P*-value	Number	Alive	Expected Alive	*P*-value	Number	Alive	Expected Alive	*P*-value
19	1	1	0.97	1	1	1	0.97	1	-	-	-	-
20	7	7	6.79	1	-	-	-	-	7	7	6.62	1
21	66	66	63.97	0.27	14	14	13.61	1	52	52	49.09	0.12
22	163	163	157.78	0.01	37	37	35.93	0.63	126	126	118.68	0
23	255	249	246.46	0.49	62	61	60.12	1	193	188	181.28	0.05
24	202	195	194.85	1	43	42	41.62	1	159	153	148.88	0.25
25	175	170	168.41	0.69	49	48	47.32	1	126	122	117.54	0.15
26	154	149	147.79	0.84	48	44	46.23	0.1	106	105	98.45	0.01
27	135	130	129.16	1	44	43	42.26	1	91	87	84.1	0.32
28	116	113	110.62	0.38	50	47	47.88	0.47	66	66	60.66	0.01
29	87	87	82.68	0.02	48	48	45.82	0.17	39	39	35.62	0.05
30	58	57	54.92	0.37	32	31	30.44	1	26	26	23.59	0.17
31	70	68	66.02	0.44	45	44	42.66	0.73	25	24	22.5	0.51
32	44	41	41.31	0.75	20	19	18.88	1	24	22	21.41	1
33	30	28	28.03	1	18	17	16.92	1	12	11	10.6	1
34	14	12	13.01	0.26	9	8	8.42	0.45	5	4	4.37	0.49
35	7	7	6.47	1	6	6	5.59	1	1	1	0.86	1
36	4	4	3.67	1	4	4	3.7	1	-	-	-	-
37	9	9	8.22	1	7	7	6.44	1	2	2	1.68	1
38	1	1	0.91	1	1	1	0.92	1	-	-	-	-
39	2	2	1.8	1	1	1	0.91	1	1	1	0.82	1

For the 1970 cohort for almost all ages, the actual number of NFL players still alive in 2013 is statistically significantly higher (at the 5% level) than what is predicted by the population survival model. In 1994, the actual numbers of players surviving by age is also generally higher than expected, but the observed number of survivors is typically not statistically significantly larger than the expected number of survivors. There are two possible explanations for this result. First, most of the players from the 1994 cohort are still alive and therefore the statistical power of this test to uncover differences in survival rates is lower than statistical tests for the 1970 cohort. Second, it is possible that the increasing size, speed and strength of players in the modern game subjects more recent players to higher long-term risks. Thus, the much higher survival rates of older NFL veterans may not be replicated in more recent age groups. That being said, it is still notable that the number of deaths in this cohort is below the number of deaths that would be expected in the general population, which goes against the popular notion that this cohort had a particularly high mortality rate.

Figure 1a–f charts overall survival by year *versus* the number expected to survive by year. For both the cohorts, the actual survival plot is above the expected survival plot. In fact, the only time when the actual survival plot is even within the 95% confidence interval of survival is for white players who played in the 1994 season. Perhaps this reflects the unusual mortality of that particular season, but the confidence interval is very wide due to the fact that one would not expect there to be many deaths for such a young cohort.

Table 4 reports the results of the Cox hazard rate model. In both seasons, the baseline hazard is that of non-white line players with a career length in the bottom 10% of their respective cohort. For both 1970 and 1994 this means career lengths of approximately two NFL seasons or less. A negative coefficient implies a lower hazard rate of death (compared to the baseline hazard) and a positive coefficient implies increased risk. The results are quite striking in for the 1970 cohort. White players have a 33% lower hazard rate (which is the odds ratio reported in Table 4 subtracted from one) than a non-white players. Skill position players and other players have a 38% and 46% lower hazard rate, respectively, than the baseline. Both of these results are in line with the findings of Baron and Rinsky [10] who found that defensive linemen and black players both experienced high rates of cardiovascular disease. It is acknowledged, however, that individuals with body types similar to line players are more susceptible to ailments such as cardiovascular disease solely due to their body mass alone. Of most interest, however, is that the players with more than 2 seasons of experience have a striking 347% higher hazard rate than those players who played in the NFL in 1970 but had only a short NFL career. Other specifications of games played are also robust to this analysis.

Table 4. Cox Hazard Rate Model Results.

Attribute	1970 Season			1994 Season		
	Coeff.	**Odds Ratio**	***P*-Value**	**Coeff.**	**Odds Ratio**	***P*-Value**
White	−0.4	0.67	0.02	0.03	1.03	0.93
Skill	−0.48	0.62	0	−1.65	0.19	0.01
Other	−0.63	0.54	0.01	−0.34	0.71	0.3
Long career	1.5	4.47	0.01	−0.3	0.74	0.6

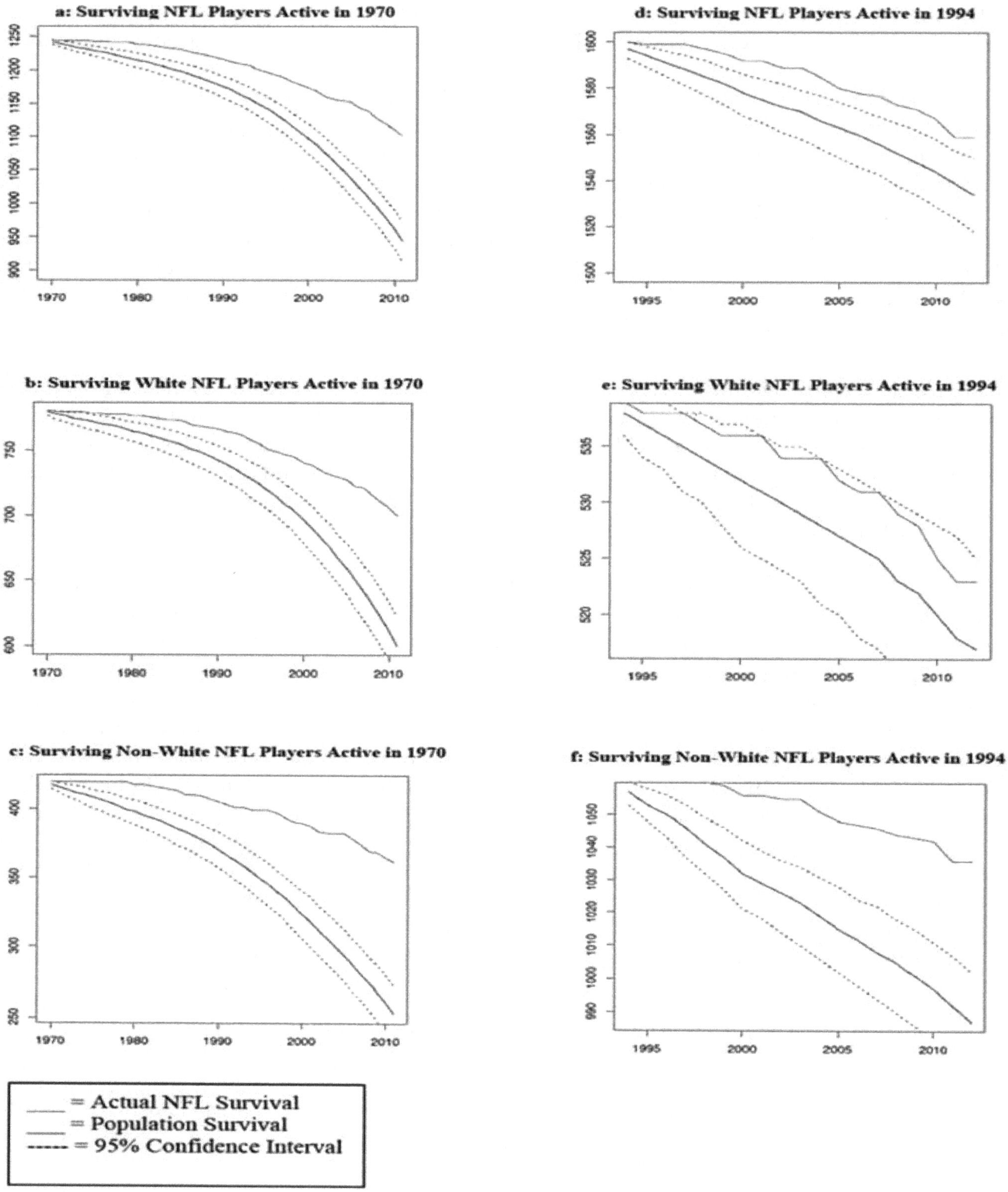

Figure 1. Surviving NFL Players by Year and Date.

The 1994 cohort produces substantially different results. White players no longer exhibit lower mortality than non-white players. In addition, only skill position players have a significantly different hazard rate than linemen. Here, skill position players have an 81% lower hazard than the baseline, but other players are not statistically significantly different. Players with short NFL careers no longer exhibit lower mortality than players with longer careers. However, as discussed previously, not enough time has elapsed since that season to estimate effects with a high degree of precision.

5. Conclusions

It has been popular recently, based on anecdotal evidence and a few very high profile cases, to conclude that players in the NFL may have higher mortality rates than the general population. Using data on the actual survivability of NFL players and comparing it to the expected population survival of individuals in a similar time period, it seems that NFL players have higher survivability (lower mortality) rates than the general population. However, there is evidence that mortality rates are higher for line players, who may take more abuse or have different physical characteristics than other players. There is also evidence that those players who play more than two seasons worth of games also face higher mortality rates than other players. So, compared to the overall population, NFL players survive longer, but when compared with their peers who do not play many games, those that play more do not survive as long.

There are some limitations to this study. For example, a claim may be made that the difference in expected *versus* actual survivability may be overestimated due to the fact that players in the NFL may be healthier (they are elite athletes, after all) or have better access to quality health care in general [18,19]. Income differences could also lead to differential health effects, and Weir *et al.* [20] show that NFL player earnings are substantially higher than that of the general population. If it can be assumed, however, that players with longer careers have similar general background characteristics (such as innate health, body mass index, life circumstances, *etc.*) as those without career longevity, then this study provides clear evidence that the rigors of the NFL may actually shorten life expectancy, but not to an extent that NFL players have a higher mortality rate than the general population.

We have also not touched on any specific ailments or any injury history (such as concussions), which could cause quality of life issues that differ from the general population. This issue is often conflated with mortality, but may be even more important and need elucidating. In terms of purely examining life expectancy, however, our results suggest that this is another example of confirmation bias in the NFL, where a presupposition is backed by strong anecdotal evidence but no statistical backing [21].

The NFL, however, has cause to be alarmed by the variation in the mortality rates between players at different positions. This study provides some evidence that certain types of players (*i.e.*, linemen) die faster than others, potentially cutting into the future pipeline of these types of players. Even more concerning is the evidence that players with the shortest careers have the longest life expectancy. A general public distaste of knowing that a source of entertainment may actually shorten the lives of those who participate in it the most, may hurt interest in the NFL in the long term, which will subsequently negatively impact the NFL's bottom line.

Acknowledgments: We thank James Hamilton for his excellent research assistance. We also thank the College of the Holy Cross for funding the Holy Cross Economics and Accounting summer research assistant program.

Author Contributions: All listed authors contributed equally in all aspects of the paper including writing, editing, literature review, data collection and analysis.

References

1. Cantu, R.C. Chronic Traumatic Encephalopathy in the National Football League. *Neurosurgery* **2007**, *61*, 223–225. [CrossRef]
2. Samson, K. Former NFL Player Junior Seau Had CTE. *Neurol. Today* **2013**, *13*, 12–15.
3. Mecham, M. Paul Oliver: Latest in a string of NFL suicides. Available online: http://fox13now.com/2013/09/26/paul-oliver-latest-in-a-string-of-nfl-suicides/ (accessed on 26 September 2013).

4. McKee, A.C.; Stein, T.D.; Nowinski, C.J.; Stern, R.A.; Daneshvar, D.H.; Alvarez, V.E.; Lee, H.-S.; Hall, G.; Wojtowicz, S.M.; Baugh, C.M. The Spectrum of Disease in Chronic Traumatic Encephalopathy. *Brain* **2012**, *136*, 43–64.
5. Smith, S. NFL and ex-players reach deal in concussion lawsuit. Available online: http://www.cnn.com/2013/08/29/health/nfl-concussion-settlement/ (accessed on 30 August 2013).
6. Farrar, D. Judge Anita Brody denies preliminary approval for NFL concussion settlement. Available online: http://nfl.si.com/2014/01/14/nfl-concussion-lawsuit-settlement-2/ (accessed on 14 January 2014).
7. Reilly, R. Football Getting Harder to Watch. Available online: http://espn.go.com/nfl/story/_/id/9932209/nfl-becoming-guilty-pleasure (accessed on 6 November 2013).
8. Donnelly, P. On boxing: Notes on the past, present and future of a sport in transition. *Curr. Psychol.* **1988**, *7*, 331–346. [CrossRef]
9. Fainaru, S.; Fainaru-Wada, M. Youth Football Participation Drops. Available online: http://espn.go.com/espn/otl/story/_/page/popwarner/pop-warner-youth-football-participation-drops-nfl-concussion-crisis-seen-causal-factor (accessed on 13 November 2013).
10. Baron, S.; Rinsky, R. *NIOSH Mortality Study of NFL Football Players: 1959–1988*; HETA 88-085; Centers for Disease Control, National Institute for Occupational Safety and Health: Cincinnati, OH, USA, 1994.
11. Lehman, E.J.; Hein, M.J.; Baron, S.L.; Gersic, C.M. Neurodegenerative Causes of Death Among Retired National Football League Players. *Neurology* **2012**, *79*, 1970–1974. [CrossRef]
12. Koning, R.H.; Amelink, R. Medium-Term Mortality of Dutch Professional Soccer Players. *Econ. Lab. Relat. Rev.* **2012**, *23*, 55–68. [CrossRef]
13. Sanchis-Gomar, F.; Olaso-Gonzalez, G.; Corella, D.; Gomez-Cabrera, M.C.; Vina, J. Increased Average Longevity among the "Tour de France" Cyclists. *Int. J. Sports Med.* **2011**, *32*, 644–647. [CrossRef]
14. Marijon, E.; Tafflet, M.; Antenero-Jacquemin, J.; El Helou, N.; Berthelot, G.; Celermajer, D.S.; Bouhouin, W.; Combes, N.; Hermine, O.; Empana, J.-P.; *et al.* Mortality of French participants in the Tour de France (1947–2012). *Eur. Heart J.* **2013**, *34*, 3145–3150. [CrossRef]
15. Therneau, T.M.; Grambsch, P.M. *Modeling Survival Data: Extending the Cox Model*; Springer: New York, NY, USA, 2000.
16. Pro Football Reference. Available online: http://www.pro-football-reference.com/ (accessed on 1 June 2012).
17. Fox, J. Cox Proportional-Hazards Regression for Survival Data—Appendix to *An R and S-PLUS Companion to Applied Regression*. Available online: http://cran.r-project.org/doc/contrib/Fox-Companion/appendix-cox-regression.pdf (accessed on 31 January 2014).
18. Andersen, L.B.; Schnohr, P.; Schroll, M.; Hein, H.O. All-Cause Mortality Associated With Physical Activity During Leisure Time, Work, Sports, and Cycling To Work. *Arch. Int. Med.* **2000**, *160*, 1621–1628. [CrossRef]
19. Lee, I.-M.; Paffenbarger, R.S. Associations of Light, Moderate, and Vigorous Intensity Physical Activity with Longevity: The Harvard Alumni Health Study. *Am. J. Epidemiol.* **2000**, *151*, 293–299. [CrossRef]
20. Weir, D.R.; Jackson, J.S.; Sonnega, A. *National Football League Player Care Foundation Study of Retired NFL Players*; University of Michigan Institute for Social Research: Ann Arbor, MI, USA, 2009.
21. Bursik, P.B. Behavioral Economics in the NFL. In *The Economics of the National Football League*; Springer: New York, NY, USA, 2012; pp. 259–276.

3

Performance Bonuses and Effort: Evidence from Fight Night Awards in Mixed Martial Arts

Paul Gift

Pepperdine Graziadio Business School, Los Angeles, CA 90045, USA; paul.gift@pepperdine.edu

Abstract: This paper investigates the role of fight night bonus awards on fighter behavior in the Ultimate Fighting Championship (UFC) and World Extreme Cage (WEC) fighting mixed martial arts (MMA) promotions. Behavior is analyzed using detailed fighter performance statistics, exploiting variation in bonus size across events and over time. Findings suggest that fighters are not meaningfully influenced by bonus levels within the range observed in the sample period and possible explanations are discussed. Fight night bonuses appear to serve as a lottery compensation mechanism to ex post reward performances consistent with an MMA promotion's desires rather than ex ante incentivize such performances. Findings have implications for strategic MMA promoter decisions and contribute more broadly to the personnel economics literature on incentives and compensation.

Keywords: bonuses; effort; fighter performance; mixed martial arts (MMA); Ultimate Fighting Championship (UFC); World Extreme Cagefighting (WEC); Zuffa LLC

JEL Classification: J33; M52; Z22

1. Introduction

A tournament occurs when economic agents compete for rewards on the basis of relative rank. The non-linear compensation structure of tournament rewards is designed to induce optimal effort levels and tournament theory predicts that more effort will be put into production when there is a large difference between winning and losing payouts (Lazear and Oyer 2012). Sports contests can be an ideal laboratory to test aspects of tournament theory, such as the incentive effects of bonuses or various compensation structures, as athlete performance is typically rigorously tracked, monetary incentives well documented, and the goal of production (winning, scoring, defending, etc.) is also generally well defined.

Much of the existing sports economics literature on monetary incentives and performance comes from less frequently examined sports. Ehrenberg and Bognanno (1990a, 1990b) analyze performance and prize money data from the PGA tour and find that larger total money prizes and marginal returns to effort in the final round each lead to lower golfer scores. Becker and Huselid (1992) examine two car-racing panels (NASCAR and IMSA) and find that larger tournament spreads have a positive impact on performance, and drivers undertake more risky behavior as the spread increases. In foot racing, Maloney and McCormick (2000) find that larger average prize sizes and prize spreads lead to lower race times. Lynch and Zax (2000) also study foot racing and appear to find evidence supporting the incentive effects of larger prize spreads. However, once controls for runner ability are included, most of their significant effects disappear. They argue that race times appeared faster with larger prizes because they attracted faster runners.

In mixed martial arts (MMA), much of the literature has examined the determinants of pay-per-view (PPV) demand or event attendance (Tainsky et al. 2012; Watanabe 2012; Tainsky et al. 2013; Watanabe 2015; Reams and Shapiro 2017), while Collier et al. (2012) and Gift (2018) analyzed MMA judges with Gift finding that judges tend to show favoritism towards larger betting favorites, those with insurmountable leads, and the fighter who won the previous round. Finally, in boxing, where fighter compensation is contracted in advance and performance and win bonuses are not utilized, Tenorio (2000) found suggestive evidence, through examination of successful title defenses, to argue for a moral hazard in effort exertion.

The present paper examines the incentive effects of fight night bonus awards in MMA. The sport of MMA is an intriguing non-experimental laboratory to examine bonus incentives because fighter performance statistics are meticulously and rigorously tracked by a statistical agency, FightMetric LLC, and fight night bonuses can be substantial, often 300 percent or more of a fighter's guaranteed show money compensation. During the sample period of the present study, bonuses were typically awarded following the conclusion of each event for Fight of the Night (FOTN), Knockout of the Night (KOTN), and Submission of the Night (SOTN). FOTN was awarded to "each of the fighters in the best fight of the night" (Ultimate Fighting Championship (UFC) 2014). Precise definitions of KOTN and SOTN were not made explicit but presumably were awarded to the fighters with the best knockout/technical knockout (KO/TKO) and submission finishes of the night, respectively.[1]

MMA bonuses essentially define a tournament-within-a-tournament compensation structure. Competition within an MMA promotion over time can be considered one long, continuous rank-order tournament. The current "winner" is the champion of each weight class and there is a constant stream of challengers. Consistent with tournament theory, there is a large disparity in the pay of highly-ranked fighters relative to their low-ranked counterparts. Champions and top-tier fighters can earn hundreds of thousands or even millions of dollars per fight while newly-signed fighters earned as little as $2000 to show and $2000 to win as recently as 2006, increasing to $8000 to show/win by the end of the sample period.

Within the continuous tournament for rankings and champion status in each weight class is a separate tournament that takes place within each event—a tournament for bonus awards. Thus, there can be conflicting incentives between exerting effort towards winning the fight and exerting effort towards obtaining a bonus, possibly to the detriment of winning.

In the remainder of the paper, I examine the effect of changes in monetary rewards on observable performance outcomes such as fight finishes, action, and positioning. I find no evidence that fighters are meaningfully influenced by bonus levels within the observed range and argue this is likely due to auxiliary incentives such as the non-linear compensation structure as fighters progress up the rankings, the potential effect of win bonuses, and the critical importance of winning for maintaining a roster spot in elite MMA.

2. MMA/UFC Background

Television critic Howard Rosenberg is credited with the first documented use of the term "mixed martial arts" (U.S. House of Representatives Committee on Energy and Commerce 2017) after UFC 1 matched a variety of martial arts styles against each other in a no-holds-barred competition.[2] MMA has since become a legalized[3] and regulated combat sport involving striking and grappling in standing positions or on the ground. MMA bouts may be held in either a ring or cage enclosure, but all bouts in the present study took place in an octagon-shaped cage.

In early 2001, Zuffa LLC purchased the UFC and soon grew into the largest MMA promotion and live PPV event provider in the world (UFC 2019). In December 2006, Zuffa purchased rival promoter World Extreme Cage (WEC) fighting and quickly transitioned the new acquisition to lighter weight divisions. Zuffa did not use the WEC as a feeder to the UFC, but rather an extension of the UFC into

1 FightMetric does not separately record whether a fight ended by knockout (KO) or technical knockout (TKO), so they will collectively be referred to as KO/TKO for the remainder of the paper.

2 There were only two fouls at UFC 1: Eye gouging and biting. By 2017, there were 26 fouls under the Unified Rules of MMA.

3 In the U.S., MMA is now legal in all 50 states following New York's legalization of the sport in 2016 (Bieler 2016).

the lower weight classes. Eighty percent of Zuffa's bouts with the WEC took place in the lightweight, featherweight, and bantamweight divisions. The dataset for this paper encompasses UFC and WEC events during the times they were owned by Zuffa and operated using the Unified Rules of MMA.

Bonuses were not part of the fighter pay structure in the early days of the UFC and Zuffa's ownership. Fighters received their contracted show money (and win money should they be victorious) as well as possible side-letter payments, PPV points, and any discretionary "locker room" bonuses the promotion decided to pay the fighter.

The first fight night bonus award was given at UFC Fight Night 3 on 16 January 2006. Throughout that year, most, but not all, events included fight night bonuses. Since UFC 66 on 30 December 2006, every UFC event has included such performance bonuses. The amount of the awards varied over time until March 2013 when the UFC standardized its bonuses at $50,000 for all future events (MMA Junkie Staff 2013).[4] The WEC offered performance bonuses for every event in the sample from January 2007 through December 2010. Its bonuses were typically smaller than those of the UFC. In December 2010, the WEC was shuttered and its fighters were absorbed into the UFC and its higher bonus structure.

Two long-time UFC fighters confirmed in private interviews that bonus amounts were communicated to all fighters during the pre-fight meeting on the day of weigh-ins.[5] Thus, it appears fighters are ex ante aware of the monetary prize they will receive should they win a fight night award.

Following UFC 169 in February 2014, the UFC substituted two Performance of the Night (POTN) bonuses for KOTN and SOTN, partially to provide more flexibility in rewarding top fight finishes. If an event had no submissions, SOTN could not be awarded (likewise for KOTN), but there may have been two deserving KO/TKO finishes. POTN provides a more flexible mechanism to reward desired fight finishes no matter the type: KO/TKO or submission. However, from a research perspective it may influence the incentive mechanism examined in this paper. Thus, the sample period of the present study ends at UFC 169 on 1 February 2014, the final UFC event with KOTN and SOTN awards.

3. Data

The dataset for the present study encompasses the Zuffa-owned and operated UFC and WEC promotions from 4 May 2001—when the Unified Rules of MMA were first implemented in the UFC—through 1 February 2014. Data on fight night bonuses were collected using publicly-available reports from major MMA media outlets such as *MMA Fighting* and *MMA Junkie*.

3.1. FightMetric LLC

Fighter performance statistics were obtained from FightMetric for all UFC and WEC events promoted under the Zuffa banner from UFC 31 on 4 May 2001 through UFC 169 on 1 February 2014.[6] For each bout, FightMetric tracks over 100 fighter performance statistics covering striking, knockdowns, takedowns, grappling, submissions, and time spent in different positions. The statistics are documented and verified using frame-by-frame analysis of the bout video, if need be (Genauer 2013).

For the purposes of the present study, FightMetric does not distinguish between punches, kicks, knees, and elbows. They are all classified as "strikes" with their type being "jab" or "power." A jab is a non-power strike and FightMetric uses physical cues to determine if a strike has power or not. Submissions include chokes, where blood is cut off to the brain or breathing impaired, and joint locks, where pressure is applied to large joints such as elbows, shoulders, wrists, ankles, or knees in a manner in which they are not intended to bend. FightMetric also tracks the amount of time each fighter spends

---

4 There were four exceptions to the UFC's standardized bonus policy through the end of the sample period in February 2014 resulting in bonuses of $60,000 (twice), $65,000, and $75,000. In one case, a fighter reportedly convinced UFC President Dana White to increase the bonus to $65,000 during the pre-fight meeting, which suggests fighters are cognizant of bonus sizes leading up to an event (Marrocco 2013).

5 Weigh-ins took place one day prior to each event.

6 FightMetric is the official statistics provider of the UFC.

at distance, in the clinch, and on the ground.[7] Table 1 contains complete descriptions of the variables employed in the present study.

Table 1. Variable descriptions.

Variable Label	Description
Dependent	
FINISH	Indicator variable equal to one if a fighter won by KO/TKO or submission, and zero otherwise.
KOTKO	Indicator variable equal to one if a fighter won by KO/TKO, and zero otherwise.
SUBMISSION	Indicator variable equal to one if a fighter won by submission, and zero otherwise.
STRIKERATE	Total strikes attempted per five minutes.
PSTRIKERATE	Total power strikes attempted per five minutes. FightMetric uses various cues such as whether a strike is a kick, knee, elbow, or punch, how the strike is thrown, the effect on the opponent, etc. to determine if a strike has power.
DISTANCEPCT	Percent of total fight time a fighter is standing and not touching the opponent (0–100 scale).
GROUNDPCT	Percent of total fight time a fighter is on the ground (0–100 scale).
Independent	
BONUS	Monetary amount of any FOTN, KOTN, or SOTN awards for each event (in thousands).
REALBONUS	Inflation-adjusted BONUS using the Consumer Price Index.
AGE	Age (in years).
HEIGHT	Height (in inches).
REACH	Reach (in inches).
LEFTVSRIGHT	Indicator variable equal to one if a fighter is left-handed (i.e., a southpaw) fighting against a right-handed opponent, and zero otherwise.
EXPER	The number of Zuffa bouts a fighter has in the FightMetric database.
SNPROB	Standard normalization win probability of Sauer (2005).
MAINEVENT	Indicator variable equal to one if the bout headlined the event, and zero otherwise.
5ROUNDS	Indicator variable equal to one if the bout was scheduled for five rounds, and zero otherwise.
TITLE	Indicator variable equal to one if the bout was a title fight, and zero otherwise.
PPV	Indicator variable equal to one if the bout took place on a PPV event, and zero otherwise.
KOTKOPCT	A fighter's prior percentage of wins by KO/TKO.
SUBPCT	A fighter's prior percentage of wins by submission.
WEIGHT	Weight class. Used for fixed effects.

7 Fighters are "at distance" when they are standing but separated, "in the clinch" when they are standing and touching each other, and "on the ground" when at least one of them is not standing.

3.2. Descriptive Statistics

Descriptive statistics for the events, bouts, and bonus awards included in the sample are presented in Table 2. The full dataset includes over 250 events and more than 2500 bouts. When events contained bonus awards, the vast majority of the time one award of each type was allocated at the end of the night (93 percent for FOTN, 92 percent for KOTN, and 87 percent for SOTN). In the rare situations where no KOTN or SOTN was awarded, the event usually did not experience any qualifying KO/TKOs or submissions.

Table 2. Event size and award statistics by promotion.

	UFC		WEC		Total	
All Events						
Events	227		29		256	
Bouts	2315		274		2589	
Fighter-Bouts	4630		548		5178	
Events with Bonus Awards						
Events	192		29		221	
Bouts	2035		274		2309	
Fighter-Bouts	4070		548		4618	
FOTN Awards per Event with Bonus						
Zero	3	2%	1	3%	4	2%
One	180	94%	25	86%	205	93%
Two	8	4%	3	10%	11	5%
Three	1	1%	0	0%	1	0%
Total	192	100%	29	100%	221	100%
KOTN Awards per Event with Bonus						
Zero	8	4%	1	3%	9	4%
One	176	92%	28	97%	204	92%
Two	7	4%	0	0%	7	3%
Three	1	1%	0	0%	1	0%
Total	192	100%	29	100%	221	100%
SOTN Awards per Event with Bonus						
Zero	19	10%	2	7%	21	10%
One	166	86%	27	93%	193	87%
Two	7	4%	0	0%	7	3%
Total	192	100%	29	100%	221	100%

Note: For all Zuffa-owned Ultimate Fighting Championship (UFC) and World Extreme Cage (WEC) bouts from 4 May 2001 through 1 February 2014.

The first 35 UFC events in the dataset did not have bonus awards. In total, 192 UFC events had bonus awards ranging in value from $25,000 to $129,000. For the WEC, all 29 events had bonus awards ranging in value from $7500 to $10,000, with one exception.[8] Figure 1 presents the time trend of bonus awards showing their variation event-by-event and over time, as well as the more recent period with bonuses standardized at $50,000.

8 The promotion's sole PPV event, WEC 48, had bonus awards of $65,000.

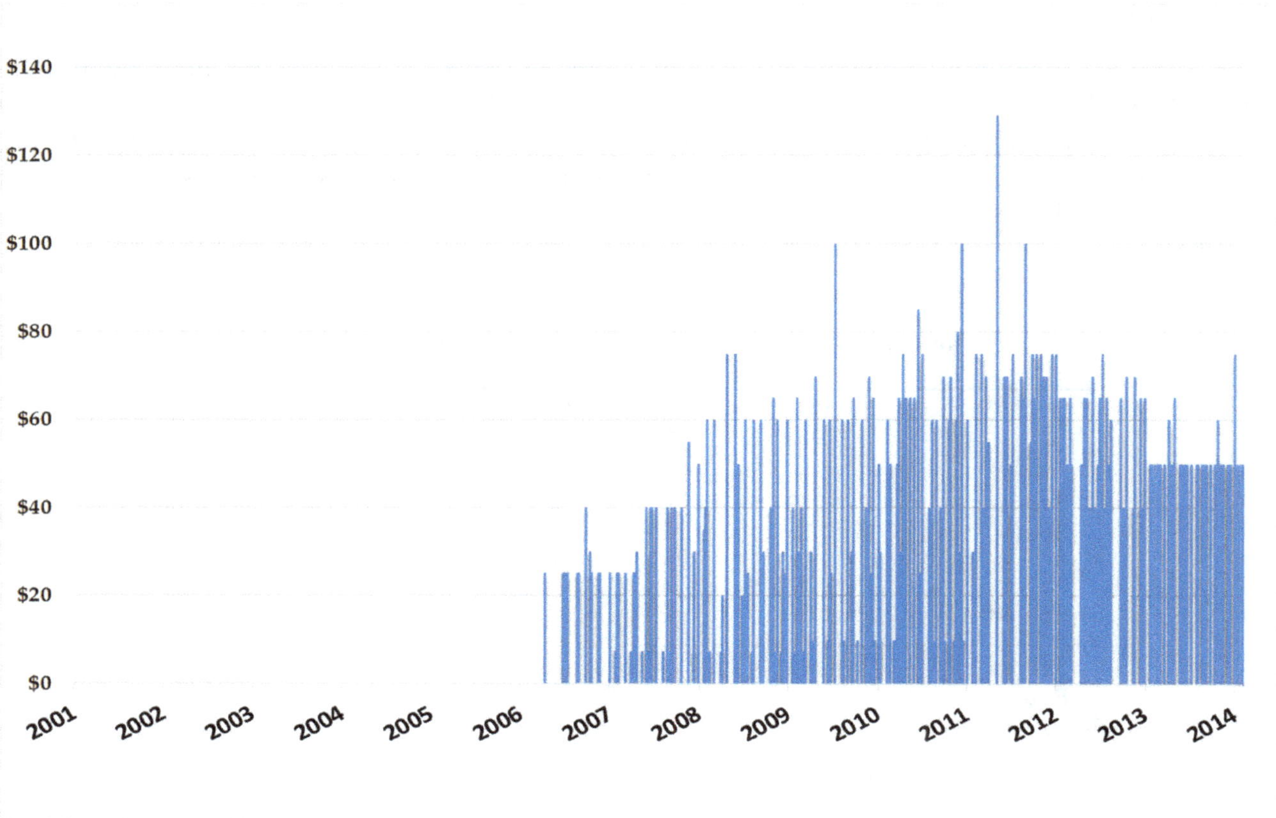

Figure 1. Fight night bonuses over time. Note: For all Zuffa-owned UFC and WEC bouts from 4 May 2001 through 1 February 2014. Data in thousands.

Table 3 presents summary statistics of the variables used in the analysis. The top panel contains potential performance variables of interest relating to fight finishes (FINISH, KOTKO, and SUBMISSION), action (STRIKERATE and PSTRIKERATE), and fight positioning (DISTANCEPCT and GROUNDPCT). The bottom panel contains bonuses and controls for fighter characteristics tracked by FightMetric (AGE, HEIGHT, REACH, and LEFTVSRIGHT), experience, and win probability; bout characteristics that may explain differences in performance variables such as whether the bout was a main event, title, or five-round fight; and an event characteristic for whether the event was on PPV. When regression analyses are performed, AGE, HEIGHT, REACH, LEFTVSRIGHT, and EXPER are the difference in values between the fighter in question and the opponent.

Table 3. Summary statistics.

Variables	Mean	S.D.	N	Min	Max
Dependent					
FINISH	0.29	0.45	5178	0	1
KOTKO	0.17	0.38	5178	0	1
SUBMISSION	0.11	0.32	5178	0	1
STRIKERATE	44.92	22.07	5178	0.0	416.7
PSTRIKERATE	22.01	13.52	5178	0.0	416.7
DISTANCEPCT	45.84	27.69	5178	1.0	100.0
GROUNDPCT	37.90	26.94	5178	0.0	97.2

Table 3. *Cont.*

Variables	Mean	S.D.	N	Min	Max
Independent					
BONUS	42.35	25.20	5178	0	129
REALBONUS	45.09	26.58	5178	0	136
AGE	29.17	3.99	5120	18.5	47.9
HEIGHT	70.80	3.16	5174	61.0	83.0
REACH	72.71	3.65	4443	62.0	84.5
LEFTVSRIGHT	0.15	0.36	5062	0	1
EXPER	5.39	4.45	5178	1	24
SNPROB	50.00	18.88	4912	7.0	93.0
MAINEVENT	0.10	0.30	5178	0	1
5ROUNDS	0.08	0.27	5178	0	1
TITLE	0.07	0.25	5178	0	1
PPV	0.51	0.50	5178	0	1
KOTKOPCT	0.32	0.35	4161	0	1
SUBPCT	0.23	0.32	4161	0	1

Note: For all Zuffa-owned UFC and WEC bouts from 4 May 2001 through 1 February 2014. Bout-level observations for each fighter. STRIKERATE, PSTRIKERATE, DISTANCEPCT, and GROUNDPCT means are weighted by total time. REALBONUS is the inflation-adjusted BONUS using the Consumer Price Index (CPI).

4. Model

The identification strategy in this paper exploits the variation of fight night bonus awards over time and across events. Two models were employed to explain fighter performance outcomes (Y). The first directly examines the role of inflation-adjusted bonuses, REALBONUS, and is specified as:

$$\begin{aligned} Y_{fbwt} = \beta_0 + \gamma_t + \gamma_w + \beta_1 \cdot REALBONUS_{bwt} + \beta_2 \cdot AGE_{fbwt} + \beta_3 \cdot HEIGHT_{fbwt} \\ + \beta_4 \cdot REACH_{fbwt} + \beta_5 \cdot LEFTVSRIGHT_{fbwt} + \beta_6 \cdot EXPER_{fbwt} \\ + \beta_7 \cdot SNPROB_{fbwt} + \beta_8 \cdot MAINEVENT_{bwt} + \beta_9 \cdot 5ROUNDS_{bwt} \\ + \beta_{10} \cdot TITLE_{bwt} + \beta_{11} \cdot PPV_{bwt} + \varepsilon_{fbwt} \end{aligned} \quad (1)$$

where *fbwt* denotes fighter f in bout b in weight class w in time period t. λ_t and γ_w are fixed effects for 14 time periods from 2001 to 2014 and nine weight classes, respectively. The parameter of interest is β_1, the marginal effect of *REALBONUS*.

The second model includes an interaction term allowing the marginal effect of REALBONUS to vary by pre-fight characteristics KOTKOPCT or SUBPCT. It is specified as:

$$\begin{aligned} Y_{fbwt} = \beta_0 + \gamma_t + \gamma_w + \beta_1 \cdot REALBONUS_{bwt} + \beta_2 \cdot X_{fbwt} \\ + \beta_3 \cdot REALBONUS_{bwt} \cdot X_{fbwt} + \beta_4 \cdot AGE_{fbwt} + \beta_5 \cdot HEIGHT_{fbwt} \\ + \beta_6 \cdot REACH_{fbwt} + \beta_7 \cdot LEFTVSRIGHT_{fbwt} + \beta_8 \cdot EXPER_{fbwt} \\ + \beta_9 \cdot SNPROB_{fbwt} + \beta_{10} \cdot MAINEVENT_{bwt} + \beta_{11} \cdot 5ROUNDS_{bwt} \\ + \beta_{12} \cdot TITLE_{bwt} + \beta_{13} \cdot PPV_{bwt} + \varepsilon_{fbwt} \end{aligned} \quad (2)$$

where X is either KOTKOPCT or SUBPCT depending on the performance outcome examined. The equation of interest is the marginal effect of REALBONUS ($\beta_1 + \beta_3 \cdot X$), which will be examined at the 10th, 25th, 50th, 75th, and 90th percentiles of X.

Equations (1) and (2) were estimated using logit and OLS regressions for binary and continuous performance outcomes, respectively. Standard errors were cluster-corrected at the event level as some performance outcome error terms were correlated across fighter-bout observations. For example, if one fighter's FINISH indicator is "1," the opponent's will be "0," leading to a negative correlation of error terms within bouts.

5. Empirical Results

Table 4 presents results for five performance outcomes relating to finishing the fight and action. Results suggest that older fighters earn fewer finishes, due to reduced wins by KO/TKO, and tend to have lower overall and power striking rates. Fighters with a longer reach and southpaw's fighting orthodox fighters appear to earn more finishes, again through KO/TKOs. More experienced fighters saw an increase in submission finishes while fighters with higher betting odds had significant increases in all performance outcomes. However, changes in REALBONUS did not have a significant impact on fight finishes or striking activity.

Table 4. Effect of fight night bonuses on performance variables of interest.

Variable	(1) FINISH		(2) KOTKO		(3) SUBMISSION		(4) STRIKERATE		(5) PSTRIKERATE	
	Beta	S.E.	Beta	S.E.	Beta	S.E.	Beta	S.E.	Beta	S.E.
REALBONUS	0.000	0.002	−0.001	0.003	0.003	0.003	0.010	0.025	−0.007	0.018
AGE	−0.039 ***	0.010	−0.049 ***	0.011	−0.009	0.013	−0.196 ***	0.072	−0.154***	0.039
HEIGHT	−0.011	0.023	−0.038	0.025	0.030	0.031	0.481 **	0.189	−0.107	0.095
REACH	0.039 **	0.018	0.032 *	0.018	0.035	0.024	0.202	0.138	0.008	0.073
LEFTVSRIGHT	0.176 **	0.077	0.193 **	0.085	0.096	0.102	1.498 **	0.619	0.339	0.320
EXPER	−0.002	0.010	−0.022 *	0.012	0.033 ***	0.011	0.065	0.074	−0.004	0.038
SNPROB	0.028 ***	0.003	0.024 ***	0.003	0.024 ***	0.003	0.139 ***	0.021	0.082 ***	0.010
MAINEVENT	−0.167	0.135	−0.015	0.157	−0.377 *	0.225	1.207	1.790	0.710	1.168
5ROUNDS	0.624 ***	0.217	0.642 **	0.275	0.166	0.514	−1.164	2.952	−3.160	2.106
TITLE	−0.283	0.208	−0.343	0.274	0.072	0.521	−3.934	2.748	0.527	1.915
PPV	−0.217 ***	0.074	−0.092	0.108	−0.336 ***	0.131	1.024	0.994	−0.141	0.752
N	3720				3720		3710		3710	

Note: Regressions 1 to 3 utilize a logit model while regressions 4 to 5 utilize OLS and are weighted by total time. AGE, HEIGHT, REACH, LEFTVSRIGHT, and EXPER are the difference in values between the fighter in question and the opponent. All regressions contain year and weight class fixed effects. Standard errors were cluster-corrected at the event level. ***, **, and * indicate significance at the 1, 5, and 10 percent levels, respectively.

It is possible that certain types of fighters may have different motivations when bonus levels change. Those with a history of knockout finishes may devote more effort towards obtaining a KO/TKO, throwing heavy strikes, or remaining in the best position to win a KOTN award. Those with a history of submission finishes may devote more effort towards obtaining a submission or being in the best position to win a SOTN award. To that end, the next two figures show the distribution of fight positions from which fighters won KOTN awards relative to all other KO/TKO finishes (Figure 2) and SOTN awards relative to all other submission finishes (Figure 3). Figure 2 supports the notion that KO/TKOs from the distance position (i.e., the big knockout blow) are more likely to be perceived as higher quality by promotion executives than "ground and pound" finishes on the canvas. If fighters are aware of this, those attempting to win KOTN may be incentivized to try to keep the fight at distance.

Figure 3 suggests that submissions are different. A particular fight position doesn't appear more likely to win SOTN, but the vast majority of submissions (87 percent) took place on the ground. A fighter incentivized to win SOTN will surely take a submission wherever he or she can get it but may apply extra effort to take and keep the fight on the ground knowing most submissions occur from that position.

Table 5 presents results when interactions were included to control for potential differences in fighter types. The first four columns show that fighters with a greater history (i.e., percentage) of KO/TKO finishes tended to be more likely to earn a KO/TKO finish in their current bout, had higher overall and power striking rates, and tended to spend more fight time at distance. The final two columns suggest that those with a greater history of submission finishes were more likely to achieve a submission in their current bout and tended to spend more fight time on the ground, where the majority of submissions occur. The interaction of REALBONUS with either KOTKOPCT or SUBPCT allows the marginal effect of bonus levels to vary by a fighter's prior history with KO/TKOs or submissions. These marginal effects are examined at the 10th, 25th, 50th, 75th, and 90th percentiles in

Figure 4 and are presented with 95 percent confidence bands. All marginal effects of REALBONUS were insignificant, suggesting that while fighters of various types may strike and position themselves differently with different likelihoods of obtaining KO/TKO or submission finishes, their performances do not appear to be meaningfully influenced by the level of fight night bonuses.

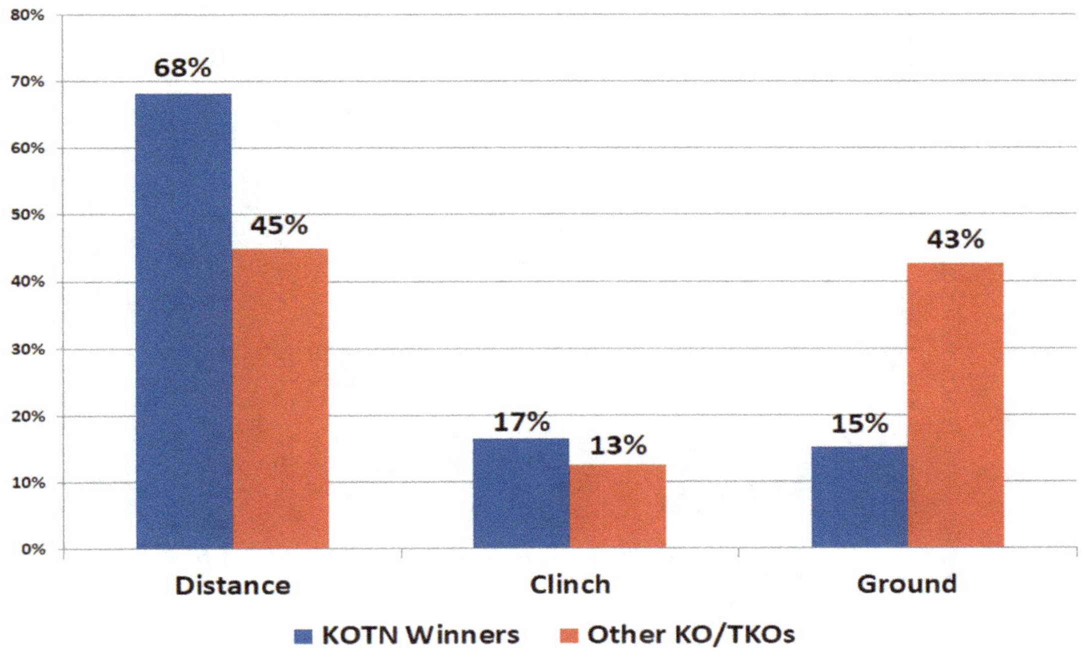

Figure 2. Fight ending positions for Knockout of the Night (KOTN) finishes and other KO/TKOs. Note: For all Zuffa-owned UFC and WEC bouts from 4 May 2001 through 1 February 2014.

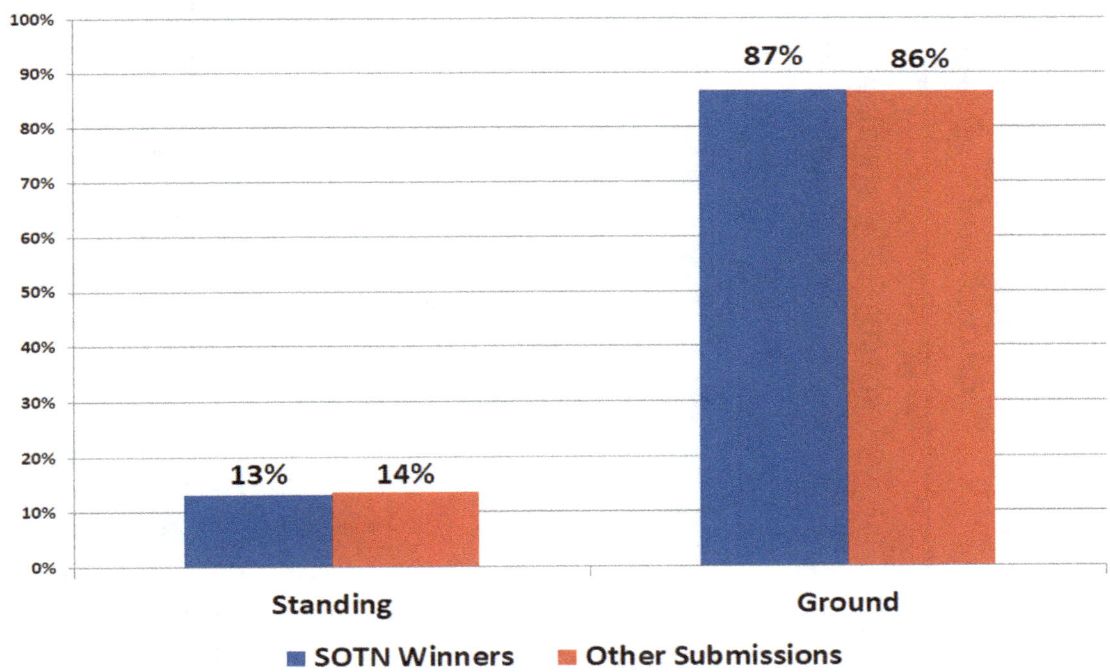

Figure 3. Fight ending positions for Submission of the Night (SOTN) finishes and other submissions. Note: For all Zuffa-owned UFC and WEC bouts from 4 May 2001 through 1 February 2014. Standing position is when fighters are either at distance or in the clinch.

Table 5. Effect of fight night bonuses with KO/TKO or submission interaction effects.

Variable	(1) KOTKO		(2) STRIKERATE		(3) PSTRIKERATE		(4) DISTANCEPCT		(5) SUBMISSION		(6) GROUNDPCT	
	Beta	S.E.	Beta	S.E.	Beta	S.E.	Beta	S.E.	Beta	S.E.	Beta	S.E.
REALBONUS	0.001	0.003	0.022	0.026	−0.015	0.018	−0.023	0.048	0.002	0.004	0.055	0.051
KOTKOPCT	0.829 ***	0.308	4.535 **	2.183	2.701 **	1.329	6.650 *	3.396				
REALBONUS × KOTKOPCT	−0.004	0.005	−0.076 **	0.038	0.006	0.023	0.018	0.061				
SUBPCT									1.240 ***	0.337	7.794 **	3.628
REALBONUS × SUBPCT									0.004	0.006	−0.002	0.069
AGE	−0.054 ***	0.013	−0.213 ***	0.078	−0.158 ***	0.043	−0.060 *	0.036	−0.013	0.013	0.056	0.037
HEIGHT	−0.051 *	0.028	0.435 **	0.206	−0.144	0.105	−0.024	0.071	0.003	0.034	0.005	0.075
REACH	0.039 **	0.020	0.236	0.150	0.029	0.083	−0.054	0.054	0.041	0.025	−0.001	0.061
LEFTVSRIGHT	0.177 **	0.088	1.656 **	0.660	0.353	0.354	−0.151	0.184	0.157	0.111	0.258	0.184
EXPER	−0.018	0.012	0.038	0.078	−0.018	0.040	−0.003	0.033	0.040 ***	0.013	0.000	0.033
SNPROB	0.023 ***	0.003	0.133 ***	0.023	0.078 ***	0.011	−0.015 *	0.008	0.027 ***	0.004	0.010	0.009
MAINEVENT	−0.014	0.160	1.124	1.918	0.445	1.236	7.621 **	3.028	−0.298	0.237	−9.033 ***	2.813
5ROUNDS	0.630 **	0.279	−1.323	2.947	−3.349	2.086	−3.146	6.160	0.171	0.506	5.541	4.508
TITLE	−0.361	0.280	−4.408	2.680	0.173	1.831	5.566	6.033	0.097	0.516	−4.886	4.259
PPV	−0.083	0.108	1.157	1.014	−0.125	0.743	2.535	1.839	−0.368 ***	0.135	−1.511	1.775
N	3313		3313		3313		3313		3305		3313	

Note: Regressions 1 and 5 utilize a logit model while regressions 2 to 4 and 6 utilize OLS and are weighted by total time. AGE, HEIGHT, REACH, LEFTVSRIGHT, and EXPER are the difference in values between the fighter in question and the opponent. All regressions contain year and weight class fixed effects. Standard errors were cluster-corrected at the event level. ***, **, and * indicate significance at the 1, 5, and 10 percent levels, respectively.

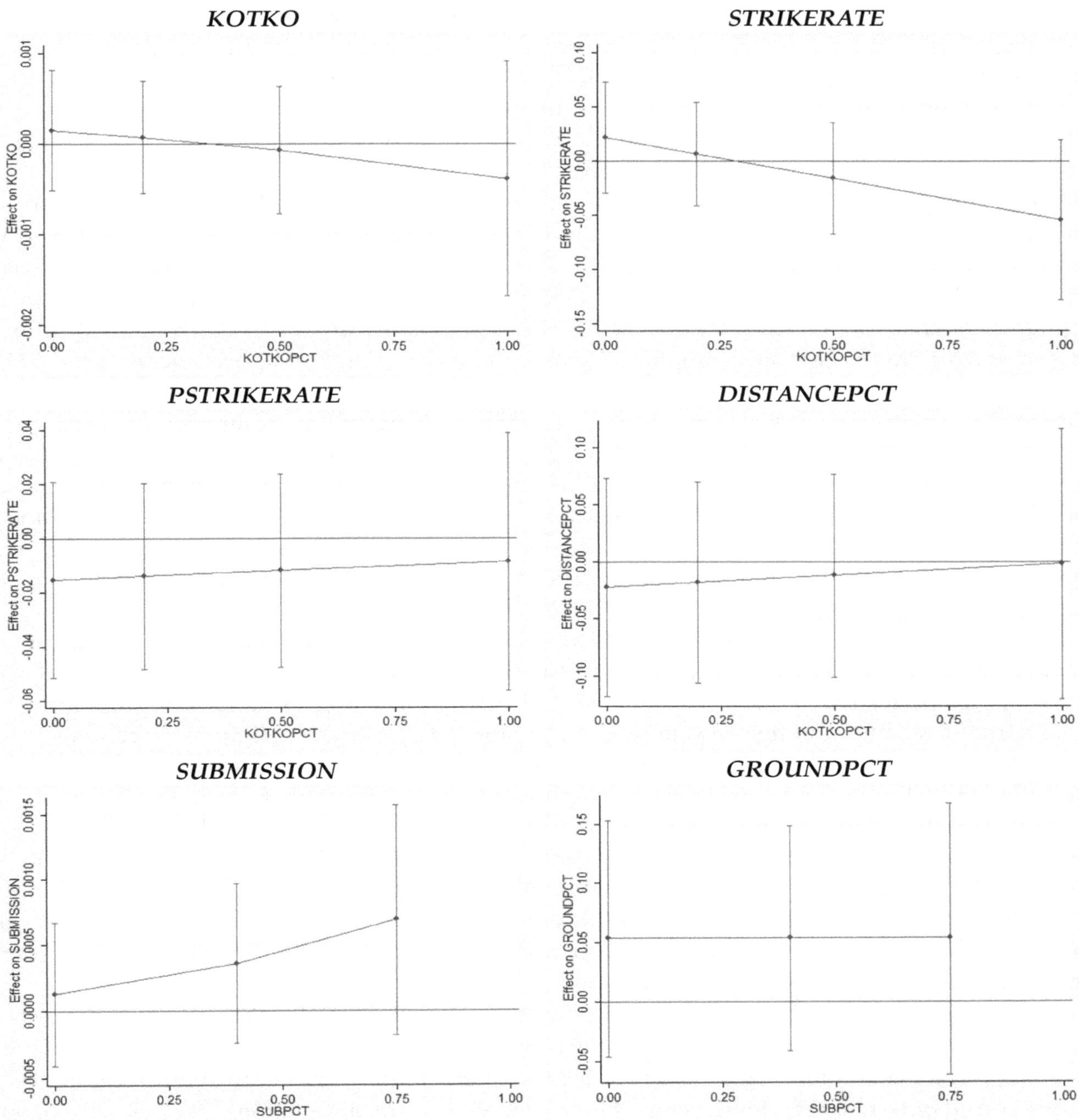

Figure 4. Marginal effects of REALBONUS with KOTKOPCT or SUBPCT interactions. Note: For all Zuffa-owned UFC and WEC bouts from 4 May 2001 through 1 February 2014. The 10th and 25th percentiles of *KOTKOPCT* and the 10th, 25th, and 50th percentiles of SUBPCT were identical at zero percent.

6. Discussion

Fight night bonuses in MMA are not unique to Zuffa (under the UFC and WEC promotions). Other promotions have utilized KOTN, SOTN, and FOTN bonuses or variants such as a special bonus for specific finishing moves, a bonus for every finish, or bonuses for making an "impression" on the CEO. To my knowledge, this is the first study to examine the incentive effects of particular MMA bonuses on fighter performance.

Tournament theory predicts that more effort will be put into production when there is a large difference between winning and losing payouts. Zuffa fighter payouts are known to take a variety of different potential forms, per court documents (Le et al. 2018). All fighters receive their contractual show money. Most fighters, but not all, earn a win money bonus for winning their bout, and it is often an amount equal to their show money. Some fighters receive contractual side-letter compensation, some earn PPV points, and "locker room" bonuses are sometimes paid to fighters at the discretion of UFC management. The latter three forms of compensation are private information between fighters and the UFC. However, show and win money payments are occasionally disclosed by the state or tribal athletic commissions regulating the event.

Since every fighter is, at minimum, guaranteed their show money, such data were collected from the Nevada State Athletic Commission for UFC events promoted in the state from 2001 to 2014 as well as 49 events in other states from public media reports. In all, show money data were collected for 2860 of the fighter-bouts in the sample period (55.2 percent). While an inherently incomplete picture of fighter compensation, Figure 5 shows the distribution of show money as one might expect in the tournament over time to become champion. Eighty-one percent of fighter appearances earned $25,000 or less in guaranteed show money while 3.1 percent, generally champions or otherwise popular fighters, earned $150,000 or more. The figure also allows for a visual distributional comparison of show money relative to fight night bonus amounts. For 76.1 percent of fighter appearances, a fight night bonus was worth more than their guaranteed show money and, on average, those bonuses were 269 percent larger than show money. Additionally, fighters can potentially win KOTN or SOTN in conjunction with FOTN to further increase their monetary compensation.[9] Hence, relative to contracted show money compensation, Zuffa fight night bonuses should theoretically serve as a substantial monetary inducement to influence fighter behavior inside the cage.

While fighters are aware of bonus sizes before an event and have even lobbied UFC President Dana White to increase them (Marrocco 2013), the evidence in the present study does not suggest that MMA fighters' in-cage performances are affected by such monetary incentives. All findings suggest that fight finishes, striking activity, and fight positioning are unaffected by the size of fight night bonus awards.

While it is beyond the scope of this paper to perform an in-depth analysis on the mechanisms contributing to such a benign effect, fighter perceptions and the possibility of conflicting incentives may offer plausible explanations. First, marginal changes in effort levels from what they otherwise would have been without fight night bonuses may be perceived as only trivially affecting one's probability of finishing the opponent or generating excitement. When fighters are locked in the cage, not only are their livelihoods be on the line, but also their health and, potentially, their lives. Fighters may thus already be sufficiently incentivized to exert effort, not only to win the fight, but to keep from absorbing too much physical damage in the process.

Second, the marginal cost of additional effort may be substantial when opportunity costs are considered. As supported earlier by Figure 5, the compensation structure is heavily skewed in favor of champions, former champions, and those near the top of the rankings, not only in terms of salaries but also in-cage and out-of-cage endorsements. If marginal effort towards obtaining a bonus is detrimental to the probability of winning (e.g., hunting for a knockout), these non-linear future earnings would be further at risk.; and more immediately, a fighter's win bonus would be at risk. While win bonuses are often identical to a fighter's show money and therefore smaller than fight night bonuses, they are a guaranteed payment to all victorious fighters who have them in their promotional contract.

Third, the structure of fighter contracts may be another explanatory factor behind the findings of this paper. As a private company, the terms of Zuffa's fighter contracts were not public knowledge until a 2013 legal dispute led to disclosure of the promotion's standard contract.[10] Examination of its terms reveals another potential incentive for devoting effort towards winning the bout instead of obtaining a bonus. Fighters typically sign multi-fight, exclusive contracts with the UFC, but they can

---

9 For example, Pat Barry won $120,000 in bonuses (KOTN and FOTN) at UFC 104 while his contracted show and win money were $7000 each.

10 In December 2012, Bellator's former lightweight champion, Eddie Alvarez, signed with the UFC. Bellator exercised its right of first refusal and sued Alvarez to enforce its contractual matching rights.

be released any time they are "not declared the winner" of a bout (Snowden 2013). Thus, not only does a win progress a fighter up the rankings and towards higher future non-linear rewards, it also ensures the maintenance of their roster spot in the top MMA promotion in the world.

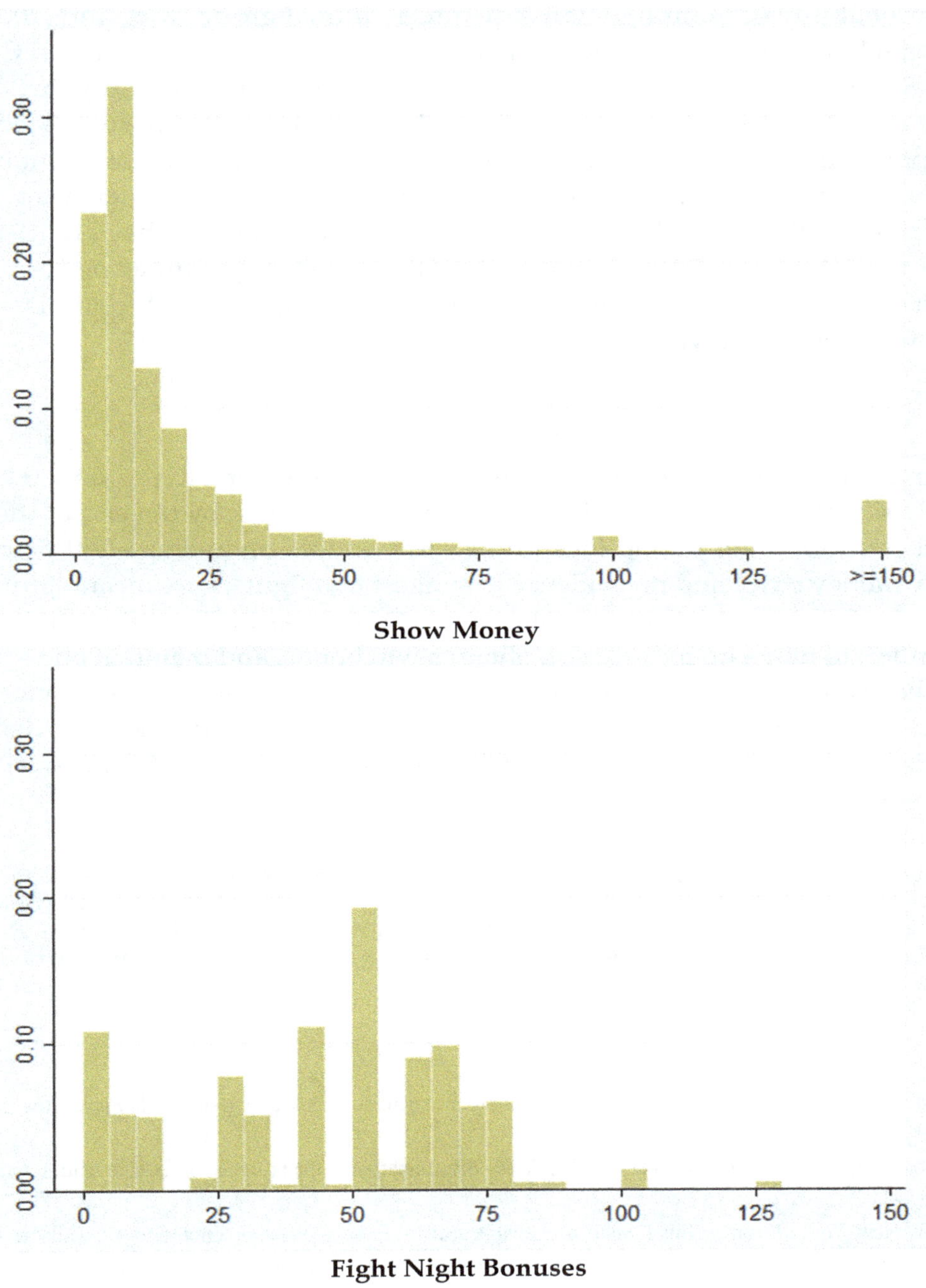

Figure 5. Distribution of fighter show money and fight night bonuses. Note: UFC and WEC combined. Data in thousands of dollars.

In Berri et al. (2015) study of salary determination in the presence of fixed revenues, they found evidence that players in the Big 4 sports leagues were substantially overpaid by the logic of the traditional model of wage determination. They noted that owners were unlikely to systematically make errors of such magnitudes and argued that salaries reflect a combination of expected performance and bargaining power. With respect to the present study, if the sole purpose of fight night bonuses were to ex ante incentivize fighter performance, it seems unlikely UFC management would continue such a practice with a benign effect, especially considering that the next-largest competitor, Bellator MMA, does not utilize bonuses.

One possibility is that fight night bonuses serve as an additional form of compensation via lottery and Zuffa's fighters exhibit risk seeking behavior. Optimism bias can lead to the overweighting of small probabilities and give rise to risk seeking (Kahneman and Tversky 1982). Bleichrodt et al. (2018) studied field hockey players and found that professional players were more optimistic and over weighted their probability of winning relative to a recreational group. McCann (2006) documented potential optimism bias in incentive-laden athlete contract negotiations. In the UFC, an anecdote is suggestive that fighters may prefer a portion of their compensation via lottery. In 2013, following a large amount of complaints about fighter pay, UFC President Dana White suggested the promotion could raise the pay of fighters on the lower end of the pay scale and eliminate fight night and locker room bonuses. Not long after, White stated, "I got a lot of feedback. The fighters want the (fight-night) bonuses and they want the discretionary bonuses to stay the same. So that's that" (Erickson 2013). Thus, while fight night bonuses do not appear to influence in-cage fighter performance, they may serve as a preferred method of additional compensation for fighters with optimism bias regarding their chances of winning such awards.

7. Conclusions

Fight night bonuses can be a powerful means to supplement living and training expenses, especially for a UFC fighter earning $8000 to show and $8000 to win by the end of the sample period. Yet even with these seemingly strong incentives and bonuses on average 269 percent larger than guaranteed show money pay, I find no evidence to suggest that fighters are meaningfully influenced by bonus levels within the observed range. Fighter perceptions regarding marginal changes in effort and conflicting incentives to move up in rankings, obtain a win bonus, and maintain one's Zuffa roster spot may offer plausible explanations. Fight night bonuses instead appear to serve as a lottery compensation mechanism to ex post reward performances consistent with an MMA promotion's desires rather than ex ante incentivize such performances and may be a preferred method of compensation for fighters with optimism bias.

Acknowledgments: I am grateful for helpful comments and suggestions from Rami Genauer, Michael Gift, seminar participants at Pepperdine University, conference participants at the Western Economic Association, and excellent research assistance from Willis Clow and Dai Shiheng. I would like to thank Rami Genauer and FightMetric LLC for providing the fighter performance data. Any remaining errors are my own.

References

1. Becker, Brian, and Mark Huselid. 1992. The incentive effects of tournament compensation systems. *Administrative Science Quarterly* 37: 336–50. [CrossRef]
2. Berri, David, Michael Leeds, and Peter von Allmen. 2015. Salary determination in the presence of fixed revenues. *International Journal of Sport Finance* 10: 5–25.
3. Bieler, Des. 2016. New York Becomes Final State to Legalize MMA Events. Washingtonpost.com. Available online: https://www.washingtonpost.com/news/early-lead/wp/2016/03/22/new-york-becomes-final- state-to-legalize-mma-events (accessed on 12 February 2018).
4. Bleichrodt, Han, Olivier L'Haridon, and David Van Ass. 2018. The risk attitudes of professional athletes: Optimism and success are related. *Decision* 5: 95–118. [CrossRef]
5. Collier, Trevor, Andrew L. Johnson, and John Ruggiero. 2012. Aggression in mixed martial arts: An analysis of the likelihood of winning a decision. In *Violence and Aggression in Sporting Contests: Economics, History, and Policy*. Edited by R. Todd Jewell. New York: Springer, pp. 97–109.
6. Ehrenberg, Ronald, and Michael Bognanno. 1990a. Do tournaments have incentive effects? *Journal of Political Economy* 98: 1307–24. [CrossRef]
7. Ehrenberg, Ronald, and Michael Bognanno. 1990b. The incentive effects of tournaments revisited: Evidence from the European PGA tour. *Industrial & Labor Relations Review* 43: 74S–88S.

8. Erickson, Matt. 2013. Dana White Makes It Official: UFC Fight-Night Bonuses Staying. Mmajunkie.com. Available online: https://mmajunkie.com/2013/07/dana-white-makes-it-official-ufc-fight-night-bonuses-staying (accessed on 12 May 2018).
9. Genauer, Rami. 2013. Interviewed by Paul Gift, Los Angeles, CA, January.
10. Gift, Paul. 2018. Moving the Needle in MMA: On the Marginal Revenue Product of UFC Fighters. Manuscript submitted for publication.
11. Kahneman, Daniel, and Amos Tversky. 1982. The psychology of preferences. *Scientific American* 246: 160–73. [CrossRef]
12. Lazear, Edward, and Paul Oyer. 2012. Personnel economics. In *The Handbook of Organizational Economics*. Edited by Robert Gibbons and John Roberts. Princeton: Princeton University Press, pp. 479–519.
13. Le, Cung, Nathan Quarry, Jon Fitch, Brandon Vera, Luis Javier Vazquez, Kyle Kingsbury, and Zuffa, LLC. 2018. Case No. 2:15-cv-01045-RFB-PAL. Zuffa, LLC's Opposition to Plaintiffs' Motion for Class Certification. ECF No. 540, Exhibit 92 (D. Nev. April 6, 2018).
14. Lynch, James, and Jeffrey Zax. 2000. The rewards to running. *Journal of Sports Economics* 1: 323–40. [CrossRef]
15. Maloney, Michael, and Robert McCormick. 2000. The response of workers to wages in tournaments: Evidence from foot races. *Journal of Sports Economics* 1: 99–123. [CrossRef]
16. Marrocco, Steven. 2013. Bryan Caraway Haggles for Bigger Fight-Night Bonuses at UFC 159. Mmajunkie.com. Available online: http://mmajunkie.com/2013/04/bryan-caraway-haggles-for-bigger-fight-night-bonuses- at-ufc-159 (accessed on 15 May 2018).
17. McCann, Michael. 2006. It's not about the money: The role of preferences, cognitive biases and heuristics among professional athletes. *Brooklyn Law Review* 71: 1459–528.
18. MMA Junkie Staff. 2013. All UFC Fight-Night Bonuses Now Capped at $50,000. Mmajunkie.com. Available online: http://mmajunkie.com/2013/03/all-ufc-fight-night-bonuses-now-capped-at-50000 (accessed on 15 May 2018).
19. Reams, Lamar, and Stephen Shapiro. 2017. Who's the main attraction? Star power as a determinant of Ultimate Fighting Championship pay-per-view demand. *European Sport Management Quarterly* 17: 132–51. [CrossRef]
20. Sauer, Raymond D. 2005. The state of research on markets for sports betting and suggested future directions. *Journal of Economics and Finance* 29: 416–26. [CrossRef]
21. Snowden, Jonathan. 2013. The Business of Fighting: A Look inside the UFC's Top-Secret Fighter Contract. Bleacherreport.com. Available online: https://bleacherreport.com/articles/1516575-the-business-of- fighting-a-look-inside-the-ufcs-top-secret-fighter-contract (accessed on 15 May 2018).
22. Tainsky, Scott, Steven Salaga, and Carla Almeida Santos. 2012. Estimating attendance for the Ultimate Fighting Championship: A demand theory approach. *International Journal of Sport Management and Marketing* 11: 206–24. [CrossRef]
23. Tainsky, Scott, Steven Salaga, and Carla Almeida Santos. 2013. Determinants of pay-per-view broadcast viewership in sports: The case of the Ultimate Fighting Championship. *Journal of Sport Management* 27: 43–58. [CrossRef] Tenorio, Rafael. 2000. The economics of professional boxing contracts. Journal of Sports Economics 1: 363–84. [CrossRef]
24. UFC. 2014. UFC Statement on Fight Night Bonuses. Ufc.com. Available online: http://www.ufc.com/news/UFC- Statement-on-Fight-Night-Bonuses (accessed on 19 May 2018).
25. UFC. 2019. About UFC. Ufc.com. Available online: https://www.ufc.com/about (accessed on 9 January 2019).
26. U.S. House of Representatives Committee on Energy and Commerce. 2017. Perspectives on Mixed Martial Arts: Background Memo. House.gov. Available online: https://docs.house.gov/meetings/IF/IF17/20171109/ 106604/HHRG-115-IF17-20171109-SD003.pdf (accessed on 15 December 2017).
27. Watanabe, Nicholas. 2012. Demand for pay-per-view consumption of Ultimate Fighting Championship events. *International Journal of Sport Management and Marketing* 11: 225–38. [CrossRef]
28. Watanabe, Nicholas. 2015. Sources of direct demand: An examination of demand for the Ultimate Fighting Championship. *International Journal of Sport Finance* 10: 26–41.

4

Market Efficiency and Behavioral Biases in the WNBA Betting Market

Rodney J. Paul [1,*] and Andrew P. Weinbach [2]

[1] Department of Sport Management, David B. Falk College of Sport and Human Dynamics, Syracuse University, 810 Nottingham Road, Syracuse, NY 13224-8165, USA
[2] E. Craig Wall Sr. College of Business Administration, Coastal Carolina University, P.O. Box 261954, Conway, SC 26195, USA; aweinbac@coastal.edu
* Author to whom correspondence should be addressed; rpaul01@syr.edu

Abstract: The betting market for the Women's National Basketball Association (WNBA) is a thin financial market, which does not attract much interest from sports bettors. Given these characteristics, it is possible that profitable wagering strategies could exist for informed bettors of the WNBA. Using betting data on the WNBA from 2007–2012, we find that simple betting strategies do not earn statistically significant returns. WNBA bettors are like NBA bettors; however, in that they strongly prefer the best teams, particularly when they are on the road. Despite this clear bias, betting against the most popular public wagers is not found to earn statistically significant profits.

Keywords: efficient markets; gambling; behavioral biases

JEL Classification: G14; G10; G02

---

1. Introduction

Most of the betting on professional basketball in the United States is tied to National Basketball Association (NBA) games, the dominant men's league which offers the greatest exposure and highest salaries in the world of basketball. Women's basketball also has a professional league in North America, the WNBA. A wagering market also exists for the WNBA, but the betting market for the WNBA is quite small and attracts little interest relative to the NBA. According to records of data from [1], for participating sportsbooks, the average betting volume for a WNBA game is under 1200 bets per game, which is extremely small compared to the average betting volume in men's professional and college sports. In comparison, NBA games attracted roughly 10,000 bets per game during the same period. In terms of dollars bet, although [1] does not directly provide this information, Humphreys *et al.* [2] obtained dollars bet from an online sportsbook and found that the [1] information on the number of bets are highly correlated with the dollars bet on a game (correlation coefficient of 0.85).

Given the thin nature of this betting market and the apparent general lack of interest it generates among most male bettors, it is possible that profitable opportunities may exist in betting the WNBA which would not exist in betting the NBA or other mainstream sports. The nature of the thin market may make it exploitable if sports book managers do not spend the resources to update their information on teams and players. The possibility of market inefficiencies existing in thin betting markets has been explored in horse and dog racing (*i.e.*, Gramm and Owens [3] and Weinbach and Paul [4]). A thin betting market where market efficiency was rejected in team sports was found for the Arena Football League (Borghesi *et al.* [5]), where betting volume is quite low compared to other North American sports.

If informed bettors do exist within the WNBA betting market, it may be possible to determine their existence through tests for market efficiency and unbiasedness and betting simulations based on simple wagering strategies. If the sports book sets point spreads that are accurate, however, these profitable opportunities may not exist even within the context of this thin market.

To examine this betting market, we obtained WNBA betting data from [1] for the 2007–2012 seasons. The data obtained from [1] not only includes the standard pointspread and game outcome information, but it also includes information on betting percentages. The betting percentages note the percentage of the betting action on favorites and underdogs in this market.

Levitt [6] used data from a betting tournament to illustrate that sportsbooks do not adhere to the balanced book hypothesis. In his study of the NFL, Levitt [6] showed that bettors prefer favorites (in particular road favorites) in that more bets accrue on favorites, and the sportsbook appears to allow unbalanced betting action to maximize profits. Paul and Weinbach [7,8] used data from actual on-line sportsbooks and similarly reject the balanced book hypothesis for the NFL and the NBA. The difference between the NFL and NBA betting markets is that in the NFL, the sportsbook appears to shade the pointspread toward the favorite using their knowledge of the biases of the betting public to earn additional profits. In the NBA, however, the sportsbook does not appear to shade the pointspread, even in the presence of significant imbalances, but appears to price more as a forecast of game outcomes. This difference is likely due to the larger volume of betting which occurs in the NFL compared to the NBA, where sportsbooks may have a greater incentive to undertake the transactions costs to shade the point spread in NFL games compared to NBA games (Paul and Weinbach [8]).

Given the relatively smaller size of the WNBA betting market, does the WNBA market work in the same fashion as the NBA betting market? To examine this question and to explore if there is any evidence of informed betting actions by the wagering public, we explore a few avenues with the gambling data available through [1]. First, we run a simple test for market efficiency based on a regression model of pointspreads and game outcomes. Then, we test if big underdogs and home underdogs win more than implied by efficiency through simple betting simulations. In the NBA, big underdogs and home underdogs were shown to outperform favorites (Paul and Weinbach [8]) as the null hypothesis of a fair bet (win percentage is equal to 50%) could be rejected but the null hypothesis of no profitability (win percentage is equal to 52.4%—the percentage needed to break even given the bet $11 to win $10 rule in sports wagering) could not be rejected.

We then use the WNBA betting percentage data to test the null hypothesis of a balanced book (equal betting action on both sides of the wagering proposition). After examining this relationship with respect to the size of the favorite based on the pointspread and a road favorite dummy variable, we explore simple betting simulations based upon wagering with or against the public when a certain threshold of bets accrue on the favorite (*i.e.*, 70% or more, 60% or more, *etc.*). We compare these results to the research performed on the NBA betting market and conclude the paper with some thoughts as to the similarities and differences between these basketball betting markets.

2. Market Efficiency Tests and Betting Simulations—WNBA

To begin our analysis, we will test the WNBA betting market under the null hypothesis of market efficiency using standard regression analysis outlined in Zuber *et al.* [9] and Sauer *et al.* [10]. Data for the WNBA gambling market was purchased from [1], a website specializing in sports gambling information. The years included in our sample are 2007 through 2012. Games for which no betting action was reported, or in cases where pertinent information was missing, were removed from the sample. Summary statistics for games with home favorites and games with road favorites are shown in the summary statistics below (Table 1).

Table 1. Summary Statistics for Women's National Basketball Association (WNBA) Home and Road Favorites 2007–2012.

	Home Favorites	*Observations = 978*	
	Pointspread	Score Differential	% Bet on Favorite
Mean	5.98	5.25	53.50
Median	5.50	6.00	54.00
Standard Deviation	3.26	11.58	15.29
	Road Favorites	*Observations = 305*	
	Pointspread	Score Differential	% Bet on Favorite
Mean	4.71	3.85	68.09
Median	4.00	6.00	69.00
Standard Deviation	2.91	12.55	12.33

The basic regression model to test market efficiency in this simple financial betting market takes the form:

$$\text{Score} = \alpha_0 + \beta_1 \text{ Line} + \varepsilon_1 \tag{1}$$

Score is the scoring differential between the favorite team and the underdog team, Line is the pointspread on the game, and ε_1 is the error term with its normal properties. To test for market efficiency, the joint hypothesis is tested that $\alpha_0 = 0$ and $\beta_1 = 1$. Results are presented in Table 2 below.

Using a simple regression-based test, market efficiency in the WNBA betting market is rejected at the 10% level. The f-test that the intercept is equal to zero and the coefficient on the pointspread is equal to one takes a value of 2.82 and rejects market efficiency at the 10% threshold. Although the basic test for market efficiency is rejected, this does not imply that profitable wagering strategies exist. Further tests are necessary to examine if this market offers potential positive betting market returns.

Table 2. Regression Results—Efficiency Test—WNBA. Dependent Variable: Score Differential (Favorite Score—Underdog Score).

Variable	**Coefficient** **(T-Statistic)**
Intercept	−1.01 (−1.59)
Pointspread	1.05 *** (10.72)
F-Test—Intercept = 0 and Pointspread = 1	F-statistic (Probability Value) 2.82 (0.06)

***: statistical significance of the t-test at the 1% level.

To test for possible profitable betting strategies in the WNBA, we use a simple betting simulation, observing the win-loss record of favorites and underdogs during our sample of the 2007 through 2012 seasons. We break the sample into home and road favorites, due to previous findings of successful wagering strategies based on betting on home underdogs. Research on betting markets have found profitability in wagering on home underdogs in the NFL in studies by Dare and McDonald [11], Golec and Tamarkin [12], and Dare and Holland [13] with similar findings in the NBA in studies such as Paul and Weinbach [8]. It appears across sports using point spreads that there is the tendency for bettors to underestimate the home field advantage of inferior teams (or overestimate the abilitiesof the superior road teams), which could help to explain the favorable results found in wagering on home underdogs.

We choose various thresholds of favorites, denoting big favorites where there is a large enough sample of games to yield potentially meaningful inferences. For home favorites, we present the results for favorites of 10 points or more, 9 points or more, *etc.* and for the overall sample of home favorites (all). For road favorites, where the implicit home court advantage leads to fewer large road favorites, we choose thresholds of 7 points or more, 6 points or more, *etc.* and for the overall sample of road favorites (all).

Results related to home favorites are presented in Table 3 and road favorites are presented in Table 4. In each table, favorite wins, underdog wins, pushes (game outcome equals pointspread), win percentage, and log likelihood ratio tests for a fair bet (win percentage equal 0.500) and for no profits (win percentage equal 0.524) are presented. The null of a fair bet is a test for unbiasedness of the pointspread. The null of no profits tests if any bias in the pointspread is exploitable compared to transactions costs within the market (overcoming the bookmaker commission).

The log likelihood test statistics have a chi-square distribution with one degree of freedom. Critical Values are 2.70 (for an $\alpha = 0.10$), 3.84 (for an $\alpha = 0.05$), and 6.64 (for an $\alpha = 0.01$).

Table 3. Betting Simulation Results—WNBA—Home Favorites.

Pointspread greater than or equal to:	Favorite Wins	Underdog Wins	Pushes	Underdog Win Percentage	Log Likelihood Ratio Fair Bet	Log Likelihood Ratio No Profits
10	51	60	2	54.05%	0.73	0.12
9	74	85	2	53.46%	0.76	0.08
8	109	121	4	52.61%	0.63	0.00
7	156	180	5	53.57%	1.72	0.19
6	219	231	7	51.33%	0.32	NA
5	289	300	8	50.93%	0.21	NA
ALL	491	472	15	49.01%	0.37	NA

Table 4. Betting Simulation Results—WNBA—Road Favorites.

Point spread greater than or equal to:	Favorite Wins	Underdog Wins	Pushes	Favorite Win Percentage	Log Likelihood Ratio Fair Bet	Log Likelihood Ratio No Profits
7	42	29	1	59.15%	2.39	1.32
6	55	41	2	57.29%	2.05	0.93
5	70	59	2	54.26%	0.94	0.18
4	82	78	4	51.25%	0.10	NA
3	99	97	4	50.51%	0.02	NA
ALL	155	145	5	51.67%	0.33	NA

The log likelihood test statistics have a chi-square distribution with one degree of freedom. Critical Values are 2.7 (for an $\alpha = 0.10$), 3.8 (for an $\alpha = 0.05$), and 6.6 (for an $\alpha = 0.01$).

With respect to home favorites, underdogs were found to win slightly less than 50% of the time in the overall sample. These results, however, were not found to be statistically different from 50% from the log likelihood ratio test. For big home favorites, road underdogs were found to win in excess of 53% at the various thresholds examined. The null hypothesis of a fair bet (and therefore the null hypothesis of no profitability) could not be rejected at normal significance levels. These results are similar to what was found for the NBA betting market in Paul and Weinbach [8] in that underdogs outperformed favorites, but returns were not great enough to earn statistically significant profits.

Table 3 presented the results for road favorites. In the case of road favorites, the favorite was shown to win more than 50% of the time overall, with some high win percentages at the highest thresholds observed. In all cases, however, the null hypothesis of a fair bet (and therefore also the null of no profitability) could not be rejected. These results are similar to the NBA (Paul and Weinbach [8]), where statistically significant results were not found in the sample of road favorites.

To test for robustness, we divided the sample in half and did the same tests for the games played early in the sample compared to late in the sample. Large road favorites (7+, 8+, and 9+ point favorites) did perform slightly better in the early part of our sample (2007–2009), rejecting the null hypothesis of a fair bet for these years. In the more recent sample (2010–2012), statistically significant results were not found. Therefore, there is some evidence that the simple strategy of wagering on the road underdogs has become less profitable over time. In relation to the sample of road favorites, no statistically significant results were found in either subsample.

Given that road favorites win more than 50% of the time in the WNBA, it is possible that the home court advantage is slightly overstated (although not statistically significant) in the WBNA betting market. Given that home field advantage incorporates a variety of factors in most sports (unique stadium attributes, being able to sleep at home rather than in a hotel, the intensity of the home crowd); the home field can be a potent factor. In the WNBA, however, home court may not be as pivotal as basketball courts are uniform in nature and small crowds for WNBA games may not affect opponents as much as lively sold-out arenas for sports such as the NBA. In any case, although favorites won more often than underdogs, the returns were not great enough to earn statistically significant results.

3. Betting Percentage Regression and Betting Simulation Results

In this section, we examine the determinants of betting percentages for the WNBA in the same manner they were examined for the NBA in Paul and Weinbach [8]. The source of our data, [1], reports the percentage of bets on the favoriteand the underdog. As noted in the introduction, however, Humphreys *et al.* [2] found that the dollars bet on a game are highly correlated with the number of bets reported by [1]. Therefore, the percentage of dollars bet on the game are highly correlated with the percentage of bets reported in our data set. A very simple regression model is tested, which illustrates the actions of the sportsbook. The model to be estimated is as follows for the sides (pointspread) market:

$$(\text{\% Bet on the Favorite})_i = \alpha_0 + \beta_1(\text{Pointspread})_i + \beta_2(\text{Dummy for Road Favorite})_i + \varepsilon_i \quad (2)$$

The dependent variable is the percentage of dollars bet on the favorite. The independent variables include an intercept, the pointspread on the game (presented as a positive number—greater favorites have larger pointspreads), and a dummy for teams which are road favorites. Road favorites have been shown to be commonly overbet in wagering market studies such as Golec and Tomarkin [12], Gray and Gray [14], and Levitt [6].

A couple of simple propositions can be tested from this regression model. First, if bettors overbet favorites and stronger favorites are bet more heavily than weaker favorites, the coefficient β_1 should be positive and significant. If bettors overbet road favorites, the coefficient on the dummy variable, β_2, should also be positive and significant. Under the balanced book hypothesis of sportsbook behavior, the intercept should be equal to 50 and the other coefficients should be equal to zero. The balanced book hypothesis has been rejected in similar studies for the NFL (Levitt [6]; Paul and Weinbach [7]), NBA (Paul and Weinbach [8]), College Basketball (Paul and Weinbach [15]) and other sports using data from [1] or similar data. Regression results are shown in Table 5 below.

As is the case for the NBA and other sports, the regression results for the WNBA soundly reject the null hypothesis of a balanced book. Although the intercept is found to be slightly under 50%, the percentage bet is found to increase with the magnitude of the favorite (by about three-quarters of a point for each point of the pointspread—significant at the 1% level) and road favorites are found to be heavily bet in this market, with an additional 15.5% bet on home favorites in this sample. In short, WNBA bettors, like bettors of other sports, appear to favor the best teams, particularly on the road.

Table 5. Regression Results—Determinants of Favorite Betting Percentage—WNBA. Dependent Variable: Percentage Bet on Favorite.

Variable	Coefficient (T-statistic)
Intercept	49.07 *** (55.02)
Pointspread	0.74 *** (5.81)
Road Favorite Dummy	15.56 *** (16.13)

***: statistical significance of the t-test at the 1% level.

To determine if the betting public finds a way to exploit the WNBA betting market, we run simple betting simulations observing results where one particular side of the betting proposition receives a disproportionate share of the betting action. We choose thresholds of 70% or more, 65% or more, 60% or more, and 55% or more for both home favorites (Table 6) and road favorites (Table 7). As with Tables 3 and 4 in the previous section, favorite wins, underdog wins, pushes, win percentage, and log likelihood ratio tests are presented. If the betting public can successfully pick winners, the more popular side of the proposition should win more than 50% of the time. In this scenario, the sportsbook would be losing money to bettors as the sportsbook is not balanced.

Table 6. Betting Simulations—Betting with the Public—Home Favorites.

Betting Percentage on Favorite greater than or equal to:	Favorite Wins	Underdog Wins	Pushes	FavoriteWin Percentage	Log Likelihood Ratio Fair Bet	Log Likelihood Ratio No Profits
70	77	67	2	53.47%	0.70	0.07
65	110	106	2	50.93%	0.07	NA
60	167	160	3	51.07%	0.15	NA
55	247	226	5	52.22%	0.93	NA

The log likelihood test statistics have a chi-square distribution with one degree of freedom. Critical Values are 2.71 (for an $\alpha = 0.10$), 3.84 (for an $\alpha = 0.05$), and 6.63 (for an $\alpha = 0.01$).

Table 7. Betting Simulations—Betting with the Public—Road Favorites.

Betting Percentage on Favorite greater than or equal to:	Favorite Wins	Underdog Wins	Pushes	Favorite Win Percentage	Log Likelihood Ratio Fair Bet	Log Likelihood Ratio No Profits
70	74	70	2	51.39%	0.11	NA
65	101	86	4	54.01%	1.20	0.20
60	126	105	4	54.55%	1.91	0.44
55	135	123	5	52.33%	0.56	NA

The log likelihood test statistics have a chi-square distribution with one degree of freedom. Critical Values are 2.71 (for an $\alpha = 0.10$), 3.84 (for an $\alpha = 0.05$), and 6.64 (for an $\alpha = 0.01$).

For the sample of home favorites (Table 6), when the favorite is significantly overbet compared to the underdog, no statistical significance is found as the null of a fair bet (and no profitability) cannot be rejected. Win percentages are slightly above 50% in each threshold case studied. For the sample of road favorites (Table 7), win percentages are found to be slightly higher than for home favorites in the thresholds studied for relatively small samples (compared to home favorites). The null of a fair bet and the null of no profitability cannot be rejected in any of the groupings. As in the previous section, we also tested for robustness by dividing the sample in half for the market efficiency tests based upon unbalanced betting. Statistically significant results were not found in either subsample.

Unlike other sports, where either underdogs do slightly better than favorites when the favorites attract a high percentage of the betting action or the results are closer to an even 50/50 split, betting with popular road favorites in the WNBA wins more often than underdogs. If these results were to persist in a larger sample, it they could indicate the existence of some informed WNBA bettors, who are taking advantage of possible mispricing of the home court advantage in WNBA games. In this current sample, however, even though the percentages lean toward some inclination of informed bettors in this thinly-bet market, statistical significance cannot be found.

4. Conclusions

The betting market for the WNBA was examined both in terms of game outcomes compared to the pointspread and the preferences of the betting public, using betting percentages on favorites and underdogs. For the most part, the betting market for the WNBA is quite similar to other betting markets, with bettors exhibiting a tendency to wager on the better teams. This tendency to bet on the best teams is consistent with the idea that bettors are often fans, and betting on games may be viewed as a consumption activity, rather than strategic investment. Although market efficiency was rejected using the simple regression model approach, simple betting simulations did not reveal statistically significant results.

Studying the betting percentages on favorites and underdogs revealed a rejection of the balanced book hypothesis. Like other sports, the percentage bet on the favorite increases with each point of the pointspread by a statistically significant margin. In addition, road favorites attract a large (15%) and statistically significant increase in bets. Road favorites, however, were found to win more often than home underdogs. This is contrary to what is generally observed in other sports, where home underdogs have been shown to win more often than implied by efficiency and, in some cases, earn statistically significant profits (*i.e.*, Levitt [6], Paul and Weinbach [7]). Although favorites outperformed underdogs, statistically significant results were not found. The success of road favorites could reflect a possible overstating of home court advantage in the WNBA by sportsbooks, with smaller crowds at games providing less of an advantage.

With the relatively light volume and lower betting limits (limits of 10%–50% of NBA limits are common in the industry), it may also be the case that sportsbooks choose to invest fewer resources in setting and adjusting the lines in this market, or treat WNBA betting not as a money making proposition, but as a service offered to keep customers actively engaged in between seasons. Mayer [16] indicated that as an illegal bookie, he made little money on baseball betting, but provided it as a service to bettors to retain their loyalty and keep customers coming back for the football season. This type of behavior by the sportsbook could attract informed bettors into the market.

To determine if bettors of the WNBA are exploiting the sportsbook for profits, we performed some basic betting simulations based on different threshold levels of percentage bet on the favorite. When favorites, both home and road, attract a disproportionate share of the betting action, the null of a fair bet cannot be rejected with win percentages hovering around 50% for favorites and underdogs. One finding that was different from the NBA was that popular favorites outperformed their underdog opponents, as road favorites who received a disproportionate share of the betting activity won more than 50% of the time. As noted above, however, they did not win often enough to earn statistically significant returns.

Overall, the WNBA betting market appears similar to the betting market of the NBA, despite low overall bettor interest. Bettors of the WNBA prefer to bet on the best teams (big favorites), particularly when they are on the road. Even with the thin market and the biased views of bettors, simple betting strategies of wagering against the most popular public wagers did not win often enough to earn statistically significant profits. It appears book makers for the WNBA act in the same fashion as they do in other sports, essentially pricing as a function of expected game outcomes despite clear public preferences for one team over the other. There are either few (if any) informed bettors within the WNBA betting market or their presence (or perceived presence) leads the sportsbook to price as a forecast of game outcomes to discourage their participation. In any case, there does not appear to be easy profits to be made for informed traders within this market.

Author Contributions: Rodney J. Paul and Andrew P. Weinbach split the research work on this paper. Andrew P. Weinbach found and gathered the data on the WNBA and did background research on the topic. Rodney J. Paul ran the statistical models, and wrote the manuscript, with insight, editing, and help from his co-author.

References

1. Sportsinsights. Available online: http://www.sportsinsights.com (accessed on 22 April 2014).
2. Humphreys, B.; Paul, R.; Weinbach, A. Consumption Benefits and Gambling: Evidence from the NCAA Basketball Betting Market. *J. Econ. Psychol.* **2013**, *39*, 376–386. [CrossRef]
3. Gramm, M.; Owens, D. Determinants of Betting Market Efficiency. *Appl. Econ. Lett.* **2005**, *12*, 181–185. [CrossRef]

4. Weinbach, A.; Paul, R. The Link between Information and the Favorite-Longshot Bias in Parimutuel Wagering Markets. *J. Gambl. Bus. Econ.* **2008**, *2*, 30–44.
5. Borghesi, R.; Paul, R.; Weinbach, A. Market Frictions and Overpriced Favorites: Evidence from Arena Football. *Appl. Econ. Lett.* **2009**, *16*, 903–906. [CrossRef]
6. Levitt, S. Why are gambling markets organized so differently from financial markets? *Econ. J.* **2004**, *114*, 223–246. [CrossRef]
7. Paul, R.; Weinbach, A. Does Sportsbook.com Set Pointspreads to Maximize Profits? Tests of the Levitt Model of Sportsbook Behavior. *J. Predict. Mark.* **2008**, *1*, 209–218.
8. Paul, R.; Weinbach, A. Price Setting in the NBA Gambling Market: Tests of the Levitt Model of Sportsbook Behavior. *Int. J. Sports Financ.* **2008**, *3*, 2–18.
9. Zuber, R.; Gandar, J.; Bowers, B. Beating the spread: Testing the efficiency of the gambling market for National Football League games. *J. Polit. Econ.* **1985**, *93*, 800–806.
10. Sauer, R. The Economics of Wagering Markets. *J. Econ. Lit.* **1998**, *36*, 2021–2064.
11. Dare, W.; McDonald, S. A Generalized Model for Testing the Home and Favorite Team Advantage in Point Spread Markets. *J. Financ. Econ.* **1996**, *40*, 295–318. [CrossRef]
12. Golec, J.; Tamarkin, M. The degree of inefficiency in the football betting market: Statistical tests. *J. Financ. Econ.* **1991**, *30*, 311–323. [CrossRef]
13. Dare, W.; Holland, S. Efficiency in the NFL Betting Market: Modifying and Consolidating Research Methods. *Appl. Econ.* **2004**, *36*, 9–15. [CrossRef]
14. Gray, P.; Gray, S. Testing market efficiency: Evidence from the NFL sports betting market. *J. Financ.* **1997**, *52*, 1725–1737. [CrossRef]
15. Paul, R.; Weinbach, A. Investigating Allegations of Pointshaving in NCAA Basketball using Actual Sportsbook Percentages. *J. Sports Econ.* **2011**, *12*, 432–447. [CrossRef]
16. Mayer, G. *Bookie: My Life in Disorganized Crime*; J.P. Tarcher, Inc.: Los Angeles, CA, USA, 1974.

5

The Impact of Union of European Football Associations (UEFA) Financial Fair Play Regulation on Audit Fees: Evidence from Spanish Football

Mercedes Mareque [1], **Angel Barajas** [2,*] **and Francisco Lopez-Corrales** [3]

1 Department of Financial Economics and Accounting, Faculty of Business and Tourism, University of Vigo, Campus Universitario, s/n, 32004 Ourense, Spain; chedesmareque@uvigo.es
2 Department of Finance, School of Economics and Management, National Research University Higher School of Economics, 194100 St. Petersburg, Russia
3 Department of Financial Economics and Accounting, Faculty of Social Sciences and Communication, University of Vigo, Campus A Xunqueira, s/n, 36005 Pontevedra, Spain; corrales@uvigo.es
* Correspondence: balonso@hse.ru

Abstract: This paper analyzes whether the Financial Fair Play (FFP) regulations set by Union of European Football Associations (UEFA) have influenced the auditing fees charged to football clubs. In addition, it explores the determinants of audit fees. We used a two-sample t-test with equal variances to determine whether differences are present. After this, we carried out a panel data regression with the clubs fix effect to estimate the determinants of audit fees in football clubs. Our findings revealed an increase of audit fees after the implementation of FFP regulations. On top of that, audit fees were explained by the presence of foreign investors if the audit firm was one of the Big 4 and if the auditor was a woman. The regulation change has had an impact on the audit fees charged by auditors for their services. However, this increase may be compensated over future years given the improving financial situation of clubs; therefore, the auditors' risk diminishes and subsequent audit fees may be reduced. UEFA should monitor audit fees as well as the quality of the audit reports, which have become crucial to obtaining the license to participate in UEFA competitions.

Keywords: football; audit fees; audit shopping; Financial Fair Play; UEFA; Z2; M41; M42

---

1. Introduction

Increasing debts and persistent deficits have characterized the financial situation of most of the European football clubs (Ascari and Gagnepain 2006; Barajas 2004; Barajas and Rodríguez 2010; Boscá et al. 2008; Deloitte 2014; Gammelsæter 2010; García and Rodríguez 2003; Gay 2009a, 2009b; Robinson and Simmons 2014; Storm and Nielsen 2012). Serious financial problems due to the imbalance between revenues and expenses and the subsequent increase in debt have affected European football; for this reason, some clubs are or have been on the edge of bankruptcy. Numerous clubs have been under administration. Kuper and Szymanski (2009) pointed out that 40 professional English football clubs were involved in processes of insolvency between 1992 and 2008. Beech et al. (2010) indicated that over half of the clubs in the Premier League and the English Football League Championship in season 2008–2009 had been insolvent over the last years. In Spain, at the end of 2011, 22 clubs were or had been under administration (Barajas and Rodríguez 2014).

Concerned with the financial health of the clubs, the Union of European Football Associations (UEFA) approved the Financial Fair Play (FFP) Regulations in 2010, subsequently updated in 2012 and 2015. Since 2011, all clubs taking part in competitions organized by UEFA have had to fulfill the requirements of the FFP. These regulations aim to ensure the long-term financial viability and the sustainability of the clubs. They should be managed in break even, avoid reporting negative equity changes, set overdue payables, and finally prove their going concern ability (Morrow 2014; UEFA 2010).

The FFP Regulation stipulates that an independent external auditor must audit clubs' financial statements. UEFA assesses the content of the auditing report and can deny the license if (i) the report has a disclaimer of opinion or an adverse opinion, (ii) the auditor's report either has an emphasis of matter or a qualified 'except for' opinion in respect of going concern, and (iii) the auditor's report has, concerning a matter other than going concern, either an emphasis of matter or a qualified 'except for' opinion, but they are significant in expressing the true and fair image of the equity and financial results of the club.

Failure of the clubs to meet the criteria established by the FFP Regulation may lead to sanctions and the denial of the license for participation in UEFA competitions. This could lead to serious losses for the sanctioned club, since competitions, such as the Champions League or the Europa League, provide clubs with significant revenues, thus potentially jeopardizing their financial viability (Dimitropoulos 2016).

Therefore, the role of auditors will become even more relevant. In many countries, when the football clubs presented their audited accounts, the opinion of the auditors had no repercussions on sporting. However, as previously explained, the implementation of the FFP has converted the opinion of the auditor into a crucial factor. In this way, auditors will increasingly become responsible for expressing their opinion. Along with this, audit efforts will have to be greater given the current financial problems of the clubs. The relevance of having an unqualified opinion can exert pressure on the auditor. Ruiz-Barbadillo (2016) asserts that an unqualified opinion for the users may generate an extra cost for the company and its managers. This fact implies pressure on the auditor to provide a positive opinion, which is a threat to the independence of the auditor. This possible attitude, on top of being fraud, could actually damage the interest of the shareholder and affect stakeholders using the financial information (De Angelo 1981; Archambeault and DeZoort 2001; Ruíz-Barbadillo and Gómez-Aguilar 2007).

On the other hand, the weak financial position of numerous football clubs—some of which have serious on-going problems—will increase the risk of the auditors and affect their work. The studies of Simunic (1980), Simunic and Stein (1996), Seetharaman et al. (2002), Choi et al. (2008), and Francis and Wang (2008) support the theory that auditors increase their effort in high risk environments. If the perception of business risk is higher, the auditors increase the audit procedures. This implies more evidence to be gathered, more time, more personnel, and consequently, higher fees (Mautz and Sharaf 1961; Davis et al. 1993; Bell et al. 2001; Bell et al. 2008; Bedard et al. 2008; Asthana et al. 2009; Redmayne et al. 2010).

Previous studies show that audit risk will be determined for the client business risk as well as for the financial reporting risk. In this regard, football clubs operate in a very competitive context. Part of their business is the transfer of players for huge amounts of money in comparison with their revenues. Moreover, those players receive extremely high salaries in order to maintain them. This leads to the fact, that, in many cases, club finances are affected by increasing debts and persistent deficits, leading to some clubs having real continuity problems (going concern problems), some of them operating on the verge of bankruptcy (Barajas and Rodríguez 2010; Dimitropoulos et al. 2016). In this environment, auditors must increase their audit procedures in order to evaluate the club's compliance with the going concern principle. They have to reduce the risk of issuing an inadequate opinion (for example, issuing a more favorable opinion than the client deserves and then the company goes bankrupt). Brumfield et al. (1983) assert that when an audit firm accepts a client with high business risk the auditor reacts to that risk increasing the time for audit work. Auditors face higher chances to be sued if their clients go into bankruptcy or if they have extremely high losses (Rittenberg et al. 2012). Bell et al. (2001) also found a positive relationship between business risk and audit fees. They sustain that the increase in the audit fees is solely due to the higher number of working hours needed and that the auditor will try to be on the safe side with an additional audit effort when bigger losses are expected.

When auditors carry out their work in entities experiencing financial problems, the audit risk of issuing an inappropriate opinion will increase and subsequently the litigation risk will be higher. The relationship between litigation risk and increment in audit fees has been studied by Badertscher et al. (2014), Choi et al. (2009), Venkataraman et al. (2008). Abbott et al. (Abbott et al. 2017, p. 1104) affirm that these studies obtain evidence that 'as the imposition of expected auditor losses from legal liability increases, ceteris paribus, audit fees will increase because auditors exert more effort to reduce audit firm litigation risk, charge a pure premium for bearing increased exposure to litigation risk, or both'. Seetharaman et al. (2002) and Venkataraman et al. (2008) found evidence on the relation between litigation risk and audit fees as well. In particular, they observed that auditors raise their fees when their exposure to litigation increases. Badertscher et al. (2014, p. 307) assert that auditors respond to the eventuality of litigation by increasing their fees in order to '(i) to cover the cost of increased audit production effort, (ii) to reduce the audit firm's risk of failing to detect material misstatement, or (iii) to add a risk premium for higher expected future litigation costs'.

Aware of the financial reporting risk in football clubs, UEFA has set strict financial rules in the FFP Regulations to ensure clubs' financial sustainability. These regulations affect the audit work because changes or new regulations usually imply a higher auditing effort. This is due to the additional time for learning the rules and the additional time (working hours). Subsequently, the audit fees will be affected. In this sense, previous studies, such as Griffin et al. (2009), Vieru and Shadewitz (2010), Kim et al. (2012), De George et al. (2013), De Fuentes and Sierra-Grau (2015), Higgins et al. (2016), and Lin and Yen (2016), have studied the impact of new rules or changes in regulations on audit fees in several countries from an accounting perspective. Menon and Williams (2001), Oxera Report (2006), Raghunandan and Rama (2006), Griffin and Lont (2007), Ghosh and Pawlewicz (2009), Huang et al. (2009), Salman and Carson (2009), Charles et al. (2010), and De Fuentes and Sierra-Grau (2015) have analyzed the impact of changes in auditing standards on audit fees. However, no paper has analyzed the impact of FFP Regulation implementation on audit fees charged by football club auditors. Dimitropoulos (2016) pointed out the need for future research on audit fees paid by clubs before and after FFP implementation. This paper aims to fill this gap in the literature. To this end, we have used the Spanish clubs in First Division during the period 2007 to 2016 as the sample to be tested. FFP regulation was inexistent from 2007 to 2010, the period from 2010 to 2013 was a transition period, and FFP regulation was totally implemented throughout 2014 to 2016. Additionally, this paper also studies the factors that determine audit fees.

This paper makes two main contributions; firstly, it examines one of the economic consequences of implementing FFP regulations and analyzes its effect on audit fees. Secondly, it analyzes the behavior of audit fees within a particular context, namely the football industry.

The methodology that is employed is in line with previous studies. After a t-test to determine the presence of significant changes in audit fees, we use an OLS to test the hypothesis that the change in regulation and other variables affects the audit fees. The model includes features that are related to both the auditor and the clubs.

As aforementioned, this paper analyzes the clubs in the Spanish First Division. These clubs can qualify for the UEFA competitions (Champions League and Europa League) and they would need the UEFA license to do so. The period under study began in 2007–2008 and spanned until 2015–2016. The study divides this period into three periods: Pre-FFP, the time before the regulations were set (from June 2007 to 2010); trans-FFP, a transitory period (from June 2010 to 2013); and, FFP, when the regulations fully apply (from June 2013 to 2016). Dimitropoulos (2016) and Dimitropoulos et al. (2016) have employed similar divisions. Financial data have been deflated. We have therefore worked with real (not nominal) prices.

The results show that the new FFP rules have increased audit fees in real terms. Moreover, audit fees are explained by the presence of foreign investors if the audit firm is one of the Big 4 and if the auditor is a woman.

The remainder of this paper is organized, as follows; Section 2 provides an overview of the relevant literature and introduces the hypotheses, while the model and data are described in Section 3 and the results are presented in Section 4. Section 5 summarizes the main findings and discusses some implications.

2. Literature Review and Hypotheses Development

The literature evidences that the implementation and changes in rules of both accountancy and auditing have driven to increased audit fees. Changes in account rules affect the audit fees because auditors will need to invest in acquiring the necessary knowledge on the new rules, which will subsequently increase their cost. Moreover, the inherent risk of the financial statements will increase, and in turn, the audit risk. According to De Fuentes and Sierra-Grau (2015), IFRSs implied a significant change for most European countries. Their results show that, between 2004 and 2006, audit fees increased for the group accounts of Spanish listed companies given the incremental costs that are associated with the mandatory adoption of IFRS. On the other hand, they also reflect an increase for parent audit fees in 2008 with the new domestic accounting rules.

Griffin et al. (2009) found that the audit fees increased significantly in the year prior to IFRS adoption, the year of adoption, and in subsequent years in New Zealand. Higgins et al. (2016) confirm the results of Griffin et al. (2009), indicating higher audit fees post-IFRS, but they extend the prior analysis by considering a longer sample period (2002–2012).

Vieru and Shadewitz (2010) indicate that IFRS adjustments, as a measure of the disparity between Finnish Accounting Standards (FAS) and IFRS, positively and significantly affect total audit fees paid to statutory auditors. Additionally, Kim et al. (2012) conclude that mandatory IFRS adoption leads to an increase in audit fees, which suggests that the increase in audit task complexity is the driving force behind the IFRS-related audit fee increase. In the same line, De De George et al. (2013) provide evidence of a directly observable and significant cost of IFRS adoption. Their results imply an overall increase of approximately 9 percent in the average level of audit fees in the year of IFRS adoption.

For a sample of the Shanghai and Shenzhen stock exchanges, Lin and Yen (2016) found that auditors with IFRS experience charged significantly higher audit premiums in the initial years of IFRS adoption. They also found that audit clients with IFRS experience paid significantly lower incremental fees. In the UK, the Oxera Report (2006) identified high audit fees between 2002 and 2004 due to changes in regulation and accounting rules.

Regarding auditing rules, Menon and Williams (2001) observed increased audit fees between 1980 and 1997. In particular, they noted a significant increase in 1988, when the Auditing Standards Board issued the "expectation gap" standards. Most of the research focuses on the implementation of the Sarbanes Oxley Act (Sarbanes Oxley-SOX 2002), which revealed high audit fees that were charged to customers during the post-SOX period in relation to the pre-SOX period as consequence of the increased auditing procedures, increased liability litigation, and a more highly regulated audit environment.

Thus, for the United States, Raghunandan and Rama (2006) examine the association between audit fees and internal control disclosures pursuant to section 404 of the SOX Act, which requires management and the auditor to report on internal controls over financial reporting. They found that audit fees for the firms were on average 86 percent higher for fiscal 2004 than the corresponding fees for 2003.

Huang et al. (2009) hypothesized that initial-year audit fee discounts would be less likely in the post-SOX period than in the pre-SOX period. They examined the audit fees for clients changing auditors in 2001 and 2006 and found that there was a significant initial-year audit fee discount in 2001 for clients of the Big 4 audit firms. The new clients paid, on average, about 24 percent less than continuing clients. In contrast, a significant premium for new Big 4 clients was present in 2006. Initial-year client premiums were, on average, 16 percent higher than those of continuing clients.

Charles et al. (2010) found a positive statistically and economically significant relationship between financial reporting risk and audit fees that were paid to Big 4 auditors. The relation between financial reporting risk and audit fees strengthened significantly in 2002 and 2003. This is consistent with a shift in the way auditors priced risk in likely response to the events surrounding the Sarbanes-Oxley Act of 2002.

Regarding football, as mentioned in the introduction, the FFP regulations implemented by UEFA will imply a more influential role on the part of the auditors in this process. One way to see this is to consider audit fee changes. Silva et al. (2016) highlight the relevant role of independent audits in the reduction of informational asymmetry in the football industry. The perception is that a special role can bring about changes in auditor service charges. Moreover, Dimitropoulos et al. (2016) evidenced that club managers became more inclined towards aggressive Earning Management after the FFP regulation was established. They additionally found that club managers tended to move from big-4 company auditors to local auditors. Moreover, these authors consider that regulatory monitoring that is related to accounting data will inevitably lead to a deterioration in accounting quality. Nevertheless, financial statements must be audited by independent auditors and the reports must be 'clean'; new tensions are thus likely to appear and may be reflected in the audit fees. For this reason, studying audit fees sheds light on a wider debate than just auditor earnings; audit fees point to a deeper effect in the changes brought about by FFP regulation.

Therefore, according to the previous evidence, audit fees are expected to increase with the establishment of the FFP regulation given the greater auditing effort and risk with higher exposure of their responsibility when the auditors send opinion. The weak financial situation of many football clubs implies a greater audit effort due to the higher perception of auditor risk. This perception of risk usually represents more working hours and therefore higher fees. The FFP regulation emphasizes the going concern. If auditors perceive symptoms of going concern, they will modify the audit processes to investigate the impact of risk factors in depth. Consequently, we propose the following hypothesis:

Hypothesis 1 (H1). *Auditors increase their audit fees after implementing Fair Play regulation.*

3. Methodology

3.1. Data

The study conducts the empirical analysis for the football teams of the Spanish First Division. It uses the information included in the individual annual accounts and their corresponding audit reports. Financial Statement are reported according to Spanish GAAP, rather than using the IFRS. We have gathered this information from several sources: websites of football teams, Spanish Professional Football League (La Liga), House of Companies, and the Amadeus database. Therefore, the initial sample consists of data from 20 football teams with a nine-year follow-up for each of the seasons between 2007/08 and 2015/16, that is, 180 records. We have only analyzed the first division teams as they are the ones that have the chance to qualify for UEFA competitions (Champions League and Europa League). Finally, the data for Osasuna (from 2009/10 to 2012/13), Xerez (2009/10) and Levante (2007/08) are missing. Therefore, the database contains 174 records. None of the Spanish football clubs were listed on the stock exchange. As there is promotion and relegation, we have an unbalanced panel.

As shown in Table 1 and Figure 1, the audit fees paid by Real Madrid and Barcelona (group 1 in the graph) are much higher on average than those that are paid by the rest of the clubs (group 0 in the Figure 1). This is why Real Madrid and Barcelona have been excluded from the sample.

Table 1. Descriptive statistics for Real Madrid (RM) and Barcelona audit fees and those of the rest of the clubs. (Data in Euros corrected for inflation).

	Obs.	Mean	Std. Dev.	Min	Max
Rest of the clubs	156	18,449.25	9,804.43	3,705.00	50,500.00
RM and Barcelona	18	144,333.30	23,069.59	104,000.00	170,000.00

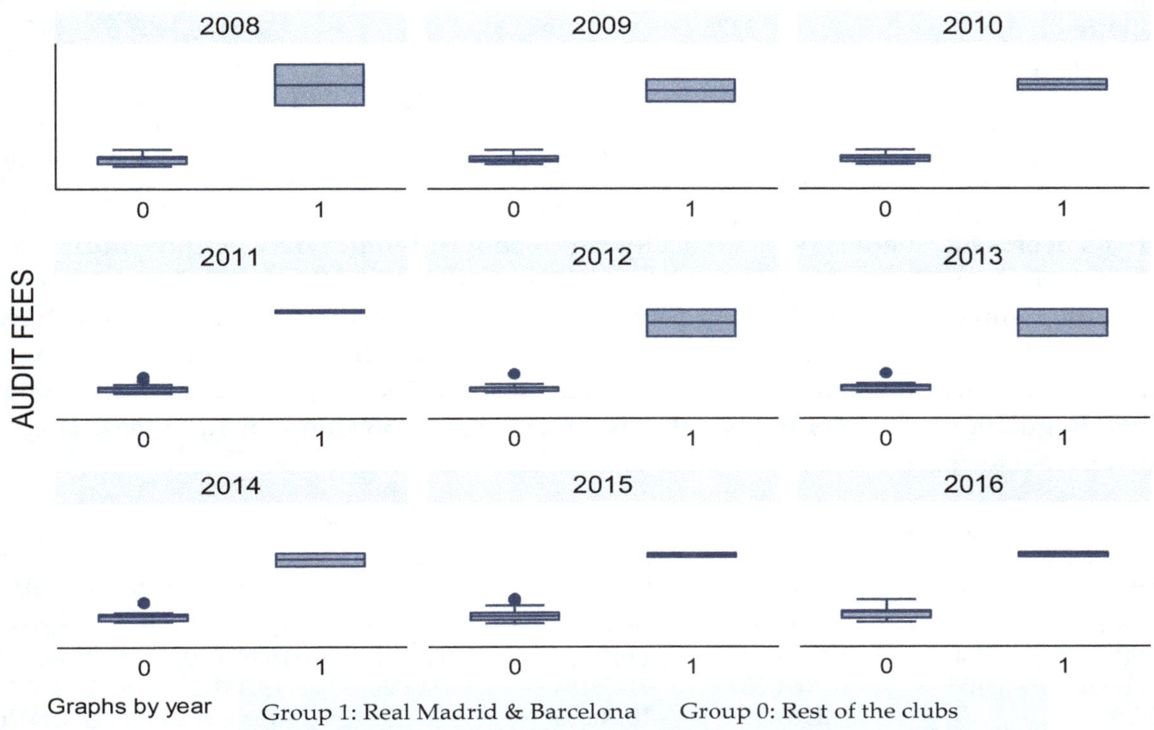

Figure 1. Differences, on average, between the Real Madrid and Barcelona audit fees and those of the rest of the clubs.

Before analyzing the factors that explain the audit fees, we conducted different t-tests for the two samples to detect significant differences among the three periods. First, the comparison is between each of the periods and the rest (Tables 2 and 3). We do this on the sample without Real Madrid and Barcelona and when comparing real values to avoid problems with inflation.

Table 2. Two-sample t-test with equal variances (pre-FFP).

Group	Obs.	Mean	Std. Err.	Std. Dev.	[95% Conf. Interval]	
Trans-FFP + FFP	105	17,499.07	931.671	9546.787	15,651.54	19,346.61
Pre FFP	51	15,329.05	1016.084	7256.292	13,288.18	17,369.91
combined	156	16,789.64	712.4386	8898.355	15,382.3	18,196.98
diff		2170.025	1513.627		−820.1261	5160.177
diff = mean(0) − mean(1)				t = 1.4337		
Ho: diff = 0				degrees of freedom = 154		
Ha: diff < 0			Ha: diff ! = 0		Ha: diff > 0	
Pr(T < t) = 0.9232			Pr(|T| > |t|) = 0.1537		Pr(T > t) = 0.0768	

The audit fees in the period before the FFP are slightly lower than the two other periods. However, the transition period showed no significant difference in audit fees. Secondly, the audit fees in the period of full FFP implementation are significantly higher than those of the two previous periods (Table 3).

Table 3. Two-sample t-test with equal variances (Financial Fair Play (FFP)).

Group	Obs	Mean	Std. Err.	Std. Dev.	[95% Conf.	Interval]
Pre-FFP + Trans FFP	102	15,673.23	746.4224	7538.497	14,192.53	17,153.93
FFP	54	18,898.43	1467.803	10,786.1	15,954.39	21,842.47
combined	156	16,789.64	712.4386	8898.355	15,382.3	18,196.98
Diff		−3225.198	1479.733		−6148.392	−302.0034
diff = mean(0) − mean(1)				t = −2.1796		
Ho: diff = 0				degrees of freedom = 154		
Ha: diff < 0		Ha: diff ! = 0			Ha: diff > 0	
Pr(T < t) = 0.0154		Pr(|T| > |t|) = 0.0308			Pr(T > t) = 0.9846	

As it has been said, there is no statistically significant difference between the audit fees in the transition period regarding the fees before the implementation of FFP and the fees when the FFP was fully implemented. As it could be expected that rational clubs and auditors could have used the transition period to adapt the fees, we have also compared the fees before FFP and when the regulations are fully implemented. Table 4 presents the results. The difference is significant, and clubs with the FFP Regulation implemented pay that is, on average, €3569 more in audit fees. This amount is presented in real terms.

Table 4. Two-sample t-test with equal variances (pre-FFP vs. FFP).

Group	Obs	Mean	Std. Err.	Std. Dev.	[95% Conf.	Interval]
Pre-FFP	51	15,329.05	1016.084	7256.292	13,288.18	17,369.91
FFP	54	18,898.43	1467.803	10,786.1	15,954.39	21,842.47
combined	105	17,164.73	914.5184	9371.025	15,351.2	18,978.25
Diff		−3569.38	1804.694		−7148.562	9.808026
diff = mean(0) − mean(1)				t = −1.9778		
Ho: diff = 0				degrees of freedom = 103		
Ha: diff < 0		Ha: diff ! = 0			Ha: diff > 0	
Pr(T < t) = 0.0253		Pr(|T| > |t|) = 0.0506			Pr(T > t) = 0.9747	

3.2. *Regression Model and Variable Definitions*

The model proposed by Simunic (1980) is the starting point for literature on the study of fees. In this seminal work, audit fees are considered to be a cost in the client's accounting system, which clients attempt to minimize.

The research conducted so far in different countries signals a set of independent variables that are linked to the determination of audit fees for both the audited company and the auditor. The variables related to the audited company are fundamentally size, complexity and risk.

Following Simunic (1980), the model used to explain audit fees and test the stated hypothesis presents the following expression:

$$\begin{aligned} AUDITFEES_{it} = \; & \beta_0 + \beta_1 TRAN_{FFP} + \beta_2 FFP + \beta_3\, NON_{AUDITFEES_{it}} + \beta_4 TA_{it-1} \\ & + \beta_5\, \mathrm{FOWND_{it}} + \beta_6\, REPORTLAG_{it} + \beta_7 ROA_{it-1} \\ & + \beta_8 LEV_{it-1} + \beta_9 LIQ_{it-1} + \beta_{10} LOSS_{it-1} + \beta_{11} GCO_{it-1} \\ & + \beta_{12} BIG\,4_{it} + \beta_{13} AUDITCHANG_{it} + \beta_{14} GENDER_{it} \\ & + \beta_{15} POINTS_{it-1} + \beta_{16} ATTENDANCE_{it-1} + \beta_{17} \mathrm{UCL\_EL}_{it-1} + \varepsilon_{it} \end{aligned} \quad (1)$$

Table 5 presents the variables included in the model. The dependent variable is the amount of money paid for audit services. As well as the other financial variables, this variable has been taken in real terms adjusted for inflation. In the model, three dummy variables reflect the different periods that are under scrutiny in this paper. They are related directly to FFP. The seasons before the FFP (PRE_FFP) are considered as a basis. The total assets variable has been included to control for size. We have considered whether the owner of the club is a foreigner as a factor that may increase the audit fees. We have also included other variables to analyze the impact of risk, these being ROA, leverage, liquidity, whether the club had losses in the previous season, and whether the auditing report presented going concern opinion. The features of the auditor are included to analyze the effect of the auditor being one of the Big 4 and whether choosing to change the auditor and selecting an auditor of another gender affects the fees and the perception of non-audit fees by the auditor. Our work includes the report lag in the audit report to capture the potential existence of more complex audit work. Finally, we introduce the possible effect of sporting factors in the model through the points that were obtained in the previous season, the average attendance to the stadium and whether the club participated in the previous season UEFA competitions. The following subsections explain all of these variables.

Table 5. Description of the variables included in the model and expected sign (financial variables in real terms).

Variables	Definition	Sign
	Dependent variable	
AUDITFEES	Amount paid for auditing fees (in Euros)	
	Independent variables	
PRE_FFP	1 seasons when FFP regulations were not applied (2007/08, 2008/09 y 2009/10); 0 otherwise.	(base)
TRAN_FFP	1 seasons of transition to the full implementation of the FFP (2010/11, 2011/12 y 2012/13; 0 otherwise.	+
FFP	1 seasons when FFP regulations are fully implemented (2013/14, 2014/15 y 2015/16); 0 otherwise.	+
NON_AUDITFEES	Expenses on non-audit services (in Euros)	+/−
L.TA	Total Assets in the previous fiscal year	+
FOWND	1 if the main owner is foreign; 0 otherwise	+
REPORTLAG	Days between the close of the accounts and the auditing report.	+
L.ROA	Return on Assets in previous fiscal year	−
L.LEV	Leverage in previous fiscal year	+
L.LIQ	Current Assets divided by Current Liabilities in previous year	−
L.LOSS	1 if the club had losses in previous season; 0 otherwise.	+
L.GCO	1 if the report in the previous year included going concern opinion; 0 otherwise.	+
BIG 4	1 if auditor is one of the big 4 auditing companies; 0 otherwise.	+
AUDITCHANG	1 if the auditor has changed; 0 otherwise.	−
GENDER	1 if the auditor who signs the report is a woman; 0 otherwise.	+
L.POINTS	Points obtained by the club in the previous season	−/+
L.ATTENDANCE	Average attendance to the stadium in the previous season	−
L.UCL_EL	1 if the club participated in the previous season UEFA competitions; 0 otherwise.	−

Table 6 presents the values of the sample variables. The first thing to remark is that upon using lagged variables to avoid problems of lag causality, the number of observations drops considerably. However, when using the variables of the same year, the results of the regression are similar. In that sense, we consider that it is better to maintain the lag variables. Audit fees in real terms vary notably from the fees that are paid by SD Eibar in 2015—a promoted team with healthy ratios of liquidity (1.73), leverage (0.47), ROA (0.31)—and the fees paid by Valencia CF in 2015, a club struggling with huge financial problems (losses over 1.7 million Euros, low liquidity and high leverage). Many clubs (42.95%) do not contract non audit services. RCD Espanyol and Valencia CF spent €45,320.98 and €55,362.68, respectably in 2016. The amount paid that year by Valencia CF was higher than the maximum amount paid for audit fees in the whole period. Two clubs—CD Osasuna and Hercules CF—had a delay of more than two years in presenting the audit report for season 2011. Some figures on financial ratios may sound odd. However, studies on the finances of Spanish football show that these values have not been very uncommon (see for example Ascari and Gagnepain 2006; Barajas and Rodríguez 2010; 2014). ROA is negative in 37.74% of the observations. In the case of Hercules CF, in 2011 its operating losses were higher than its total assets. That season, the club had returned to First Division after more 14 years and made a big effort to be competitive by hiring well-known players. However, at the end of the season the team ended second to last and was relegated. This fact meant huge losses, further relegation to Second B Division, and it is on the brink of disappearing. On the other hand, there are also cases with high ROA. Having entered under administration in 2011 and attaining its best league position in 2013 while simultaneously qualifying for the UEL (the club did not receive the UEFA license due to its financial situation), Rayo Vallecano SAD made a remarkable profit in 2014. Clubs with high values in Leverage ratio usually benefit from having been under administration. That is the case of RC Deportivo de La Coruña in 2015 and 2016 (4.5 and 3.6, respectively). It is also worth noting that the audit reports of the clubs presented ongoing concerns in 53% of the cases. Almost 40% presented losses in the previous year. This situation is improving in the period of fully implementation of FFP regulations (29.6%). In only 9% of the cases is there a foreign owner, and the auditor is one of the Big 4 in only 3%.

Table 6. Descriptive statistics (financial variables in real terms).

Variable	Obs.	Mean	Std. Dev.	Min	Max
Real Audit Fees	156	16,789.64	8898.36	3362.60	45,833.04
Real non Audit Fees	156	6397.88	9519.58	0.00	55,362.68
Lag. Real TA (thousands €)	119	134,000.00	146,000.00	8532.59	546,000.00
Reportlag (days)	159	124.01	79.00	26.00	758.00
Lag. ROA	119	0.01	0.23	−1.05	1.16
Lag. Leverage	119	1.08	0.60	0.25	4.50
Lag. Liquidity	119	0.67	0.40	0.08	2.49
Lag. Points	120	51.33	10.66	35.00	90.00
Lag. Average Attendance	120	23,796.19	10,724.38	4727.00	46,532.00
UCL + EL	161	0.28	0.45	0.00	1.00
Foreign owner	161	0.09	0.29	0.00	1.00
Lag. Losses	119	0.39	0.49	0.00	1.00
Lag. GCO	120	0.53	0.50	0.00	1.00
Big 4	160	0.03	0.17	0.00	1.00
Audit change	159	0.10	0.30	0.00	1.00
Gender	160	0.11	0.31	0.00	1.00

3.2.1. Regulation

As stated, Griffin et al. (2009), Vieru and Shadewitz (2010), De George et al. (2013), De Fuentes and Sierra-Grau (2015), Higgins et al. (2016), and Lin and Yen (2016) have analyzed the impact of changes in accountancy rules, or the impact of new ones on audit fees. Menon and Williams (2001), Ghosh and Lustgarten (2006), Raghunandan and Rama (2006), Griffin and Lont (2007), Ghosh and

Pawlewicz (2009), Huang et al. (2009), Salman and Salman and Carson (2009), Charles et al. (2010), and De Fuentes and Sierra-Grau (2015) have studied the impact of changes in auditing rules. Most of these studies distinguish between two or three periods: before the application of the regulation, during the first years of implementation, and after the implementation. This paper analyzes the time before the FFP (seasons 2007–2008, 2008–2009, and 2009–2010), a transitory period (2010–2011, 2011–2012, and 2012–2013), and the period when the FFP was fully implemented (2013–2014, 2014–2015, and 2015–2016). The first period is the basis. Audit fees are expected to be higher after the transitory or full implementation periods than they were before the new rules. The complexity of the audit work will increase with a subsequent increase in auditing effort. Moreover, the responsibility of auditors will be more highly exposed when they report their opinion.

3.2.2. Non Audit Fees

Studies trying to conjunctly determine the fees for audit and non-audit services have observed interdependency between both fees and they have identified the presence of efficiencies deriving from the exchange of knowledge between both activities (Monterrey and Sánchez 2007). Simunic (1984) discovered a positive association between both fees. He concluded that firms hiring non-audit services from the same auditor assume cost in the audit fees that are higher than those assumed by firms that do not do so. Palmrose (1986) and Bell et al. (2001) point out that the positive coefficients that are associated among audit and non-audit fees originate in scale economies that reduce the number of required auditing hours. Nevertheless, other authors, like Stein et al. (1994) and Whisenant et al. (2003), did not find a direct relationship between both variables.

3.2.3. Size of the Firm (the Club)

The size of the club is a widely tested explanatory variable and, according to Hay et al. (2006) it typically explains more than 70% of the variation in audit fees. This paper uses the lagged total assets in real terms of the company to avoid endogeneity. Casterella et al. (2004), and Basioudis et al. (2008) also use total assets to control for size. We expect a positive association with audit fees.

3.2.4. Foreign Ownership

Wilson et al. (2013) assert that foreign ownership may help clubs to improve their accounts, make them sustainable and improve their finances. At the same time, foreign investors have more difficulties in getting information than the local ones (Beneish and Yohn 2008; He et al. 2014). To compensate for this, foreign investors will look for more qualified auditors (Dimitropoulos 2016). We therefore expect a positive relationship regarding audit fees.

3.2.5. Delay in the Report

The existence of problems can imply longer periods of time to finish audit reports (Knechel and Payne 2001). Stanley (2011) found a positive relationship between audit fees and the time spent until the final audit report. More complex audit work may take longer to perform and it may imply a subsequent delay in the signing of the audit report. In such case, higher fees are expected. This is why the model includes the variable REPORTLAG.

3.2.6. Risk

Extensive literature reveals that the audit fees are positively related to risk, as evinced in the papers by Xu et al. (2013), Zhang and Huang (2013), Alexeyeva and Tobias (2015), and Groff et al. (2017). That is, higher client risk may expose the auditor. The auditor will then apply more tests and thereby increase the time employed. Thus, fees would be higher. Several variables measure risk direct or indirectly. ROA is included because a low return on assets may be symptomatic of mismanagement. We would therefore expect a negative relationship.

Leverage (LEV) and liquidity (LIQ) ratios, two of the proxies that are most commonly used to measure indebtedness (Hay et al. 2006; Hay 2013), reflect whether the club could have financial problems. A positive relationship between leverage and audit fees is expected (Callaghan et al. 2009; Casterella et al. 2004). On the contrary, a negative relationship is expected with the liquidity (Craswell et al. 1995; Simunic 1980).

Moreover, Casterella et al. (2004), Callaghan et al. (2009) find that firms with losses (LOSS) represent higher risk. This would imply higher audit fees as well.

3.2.7. Additional Risk

Football clubs have real financial difficulties in their operations (Ascari and Gagnepain 2006; Barajas and Rodríguez 2010; Beech et al. 2010; Boscá et al. 2008; Kuper and Szymanski 2009), which in some cases have led to bankruptcy. This creates an additional risk for the auditor. The auditor will have to pay special attention to these events, which can imply going concern. Audit fees are expected to be higher in the presence of a going concern opinion (Krishnan and Wang 2015; Stanley 2011; Wang and Chui 2015).

3.2.8. BIG 4

Previous studies indicate that the big international audit firms have a differential reputation that is derived from having a recognized brand name, and deliver audits of a higher quality than small and medium-sized audit firms (De Angelo 1981; DeFond 1992). The existence of a relationship between audit fees and an auditor's reputation has been studied by various authors with positive results. This is the case of Liu (2007), Monterrey and Sánchez (2007), and Whisenant et al. (2003). The variable BIG 4 has been included in the model as a dummy variable, making a distinction between the Big 4 (PwC, E&Y, KPMG, or Deloitte) and the other firms. A positive relation with the audit fees variable is expected.

3.2.9. Auditor Change

One of the most common reasons given by clients for deciding to change auditor is that the audit fee will decrease. Lower audit fees can have their origin in the intention of audit firms of attracting new customers (lowballing). Another reason would be that the new auditor can offer a more efficient service which could reduce their fees. Regardless of the reason for the decrease in the fees, previous research suggests that the continuity of the auditor must be considered in the audit fees models. The two most common proxies that are used to include the continuity of the auditor are a dummy variable that reflects a recent change in the auditor and the actual length of the current auditor in that role (Hay et al. 2006). Hay (2013), Wang and Chui (2015), and De Fuentes and Sierra-Grau (2015) use a dummy variable that reflects the auditor change. This paper also includes this variable and expects it to be negatively related to audit fees.

Auditor Features

Gul et al. (2013), Ittonen and Peni (2012), Ittonen et al. (2013), and Sundgren and Svanström (2014) have recently studied the effect of auditor features on auditing service quality. Hardies Kris and Branson (2015) affirm that audit fees may be higher for female auditors due to greater engagement effort (i.e., more hours) by female auditors. Female auditors may demand more audit effort because of systematic differences in knowledge, skills, abilities, preferences, and behavior. Ittonen and Peni (2012) found that audits performed by women in Denmark, Sweden, and Finland were more expensive that those performed by men. These authors justify their results due to the existence of factors, such as gender differences in risk tolerance, which may affect pricing decisions by increasing the audit investment and/or increasing the audit fee risk premium. In addition, they also refer to female auditors' diligence, lower overconfidence, and higher level of preparation could also lead to an increase in audit investment, and thereby result in higher audit fees.

Ittonen et al. (2013) refer to several papers considering cognitive psychology and behavioral economy that have found the existence of important gender differences related to information processing, diligence, conservatism, overconfidence, caution, and risk tolerance (Eckel and Grossman 2002; Nettle 2007; Schmitt et al. 2009). Other studies affirm that women are more conservative and risk adverse than men, and that their behavior is less risky when making economic and financial decisions (Barber and Odean 2001; Dwyer et al. 2002; Watson and McNaughton 2007). Our model includes a variable considering gender and we expect a positive association with audit fees.

Sporting Features

We expect those teams with better performance in the previous season to be capable of increasing their clubs' revenue and reducing financial risk. However, some clubs could overspend to achieve good sporting performance and this would make risk higher. Therefore, the sign of the coefficient could be positive or negative. After the FFP, with higher financial control, the chances of getting a negative sign could be greater.

On the other hand, we may expect reduced club risk if the average attendance to the stadium is high, because it reflects a wide fan base that would help to increase revenues. If the risk is low, the audit fees should also decrease. Therefore, the model includes variables that gather the information about points (performance measure) and average attendance in the previous season.

Finally, we have also included participation in the previous edition of UEFA competitions (Champions League and Europa League) to reflect the effect of sporting features. If a team took part in previous editions, it had to fulfill financial requirements in that season and this facilitates the fulfillment of the financial requirements of the current season. What is more, participation usually provides extra revenue to the club and it may reduce an eventual going concern situation under financial control.

4. Results

We have verified the Hypothesis (H1). The results are presented in Table 7. It has been demonstrated that on average auditors significantly increased their audit fees after implementing Fair Play regulation in comparison to pre-implementation fees. On average, the difference is slightly lower than €3500 in real terms.

On the other hand, some results regarding the determinants of audit fees in football clubs corroborate what was expected. However, most of the variables do not present a significant influence on audit fees. First, we find that the audit fees increased by nearly 1700 Euros (2000 in nominal terms) in the transition period as compared to the period in which FFP did not exist. That amount was practically two-fold in the period of full FFP regulation implementation. This was the expected result, even more so after the t-test.

Foreign ownership is another significant factor that explains the audit fees. In clubs with local owners, audit fees increased by nearly 4500 euros in the advent of foreign investment.

If the auditor is one of the Big 4, then audit fees are about 11,700 Euros higher than those of smaller audit firms, which falls in line with previous research. We should point out that apart from Real Madrid and Barcelona—both excluded from this analysis—only Sevilla CF and Valencia CF were audited by a Big 4 audit firm in seasons 2014–2015 and 2015–2016, in addition to Málaga CF in season 2015–2016, periods in which the FFP regulations were fully implemented. Moreover, Valencia CF and Málaga CF have foreign investors. On the other hand, only Ernst and Young and Deloitte, both of which belong to the Big 4, had audited football clubs throughout the whole period.

Another interesting result is that when the auditor is a woman, audit fees are about 3500 Euros higher than when the auditor is a man. It should be noted that only one of the female auditors works for a Big 4 (Ernst&Young). Recent studies find similar results when considering the gender of the auditor. Ittonen and Peni (2012) introduced gender differences in risk tolerance as potential reasons to explain this effect. These authors claim that this may increase audit investment and audit fee risk premium.

They also point out other factors, such as the diligence of female auditors, lower overconfidence, and a higher level of preparation could lead to an increased audit fees. Moreover, Ittonen et al. (2013) found that female auditors might have a constraining effect on earnings management, which may also contribute to higher audit fees. The results obtained by Hardies Kris and Branson (2015) show that firms pay higher audit fees (by about 7 percent) to female auditors. They suggest the existence of a female audit fee premium due to differences in knowledge, skills, abilities, preferences, and behavior or due to supply-side factors. Hu et al. (2014) found that female auditors charge significantly higher audit fees than their male counterparts. They explain that this is due to female auditors' preference for reducing audit risk. In the case of football clubs, the perception of risk by female auditors may also be a plausible reason.

Table 7. Outputs of the regression (real terms).

VARIABLES	Audit Fees
TRAN-FFP	1661 *
	(878.3)
FFP	3408 ***
	(1186)
NON_AUDITFEES	−0.00689
	(0.0518)
L.TA	2.49×10^{-7}
	(1.24×10^{-5})
FOWND	4436 **
	(2057)
REPORTLAG	−12.81
	(21.26)
L.ROA	−274.8
	(2,071)
L.LEV	−551.9
	(879.6)
L.LIQ	18.61
	(1680)
L.LOSS	−170.8
	(797.7)
L.GCO	1567
	(1238)
BIG 4	11,662 ***
	(2244)
AUDITCHANG	1289
	(1311)
GENDER	3516 *
	(1844)
L.POINTS	−8.329
	(56.53)
L.ATTENDANCE	0.00838
	(0.189)
L.UCL_EL	−1862
	(1179)
Constant	10,709 *
	(5400)
Clubs fix effect	YES
Observations	115
Number of id	25
R-squared	0.926

Standard errors in parentheses; *** $p < 0.01$, ** $p < 0.05$, * $p < 0.1$.

No evidence supports the possible influence of sporting factors on audit fees, which could possibly be explained by the absence of a relation between sports performance and economic results in Spanish football (Barajas et al. 2005). Variables that are related to risk have resulted in being non-significant as well. Increased risk for the auditor was expected to increase audit fees. In this sense, we expected that higher leverage, and the presence of losses and going concern opinion, to have an impact on higher audit fees. On the contrary, a higher return on assets and liquidity ratio resulted in lower risk and lower expected audit fees too. However, none of these variables were significant. This may be related to the real influence of the FFP regulations on club finances. In fact, as shown in Table 8, the financial situation of clubs improved on average. Throughout the period when the FFP regulations were fully implemented, the return on assets was much higher on average than it had been in the previous periods. The average of these three years was 11.5%, while the average of both previous periods was negative. A similar situation arose with the other indicators. The leverage was around 1 on average in the last period; this was lower than it had been in the previous years. Liquidity clearly improved with a 0.82 average over the last three years as compared to its prior 0.6 average. The number of clubs declaring losses declined to less than a third as compared to the peak of the whole period, in which over 60% of companies had reported losses. Finally, the percentage of clubs with problems of going concern dropped notably over the last years, especially in 2016. All of this may explain the contribution of FFP regulations to improving the financial situation of the clubs, thereby reducing risk and not influencing the fees that are charged by the auditors. This may represent a problem of endogeneity, but we must recall that we used lagged variables in the regression to avoid this.

Table 8. Evolution of risk indicators.

	2008	2009	2010	2011	2012	2013	2014	2015	2016
ROA	−12.4%	2.9%	5.6%	−7.9%	−8.9%	9.3%	10.1%	8.6%	15.9%
LEV	0.88	1.19	1.23	1.34	1.17	1.19	0.99	1.07	0.98
LIQ	0.62	0.65	0.54	0.63	0.58	0.76	0.80	0.90	0.75
LOSS	41.2%	27.8%	41.2%	47.1%	61.1%	33.3%	27.8%	33.3%	27.8%
GCO	52.9%	55.6%	64.7%	61.1%	55.6%	72.2%	44.4%	44.4%	29.4%

We have included clubs fixed effect as there are features of the clubs that remain constant throughout the period. It is interesting to observe which clubs pay more or less than the base team, which is Almeria CF in our case. The clubs that pay significantly higher audit fees are Atletico de Madrid (understandable due to its size), Athletic de Bilbao, Deportivo de la Coruña, Osasuna, Racing de Santander, Rayo Vallecano, Real Sociedad, and Zaragoza CF. Most of these clubs had faced serious financial problems. On the other hand, the clubs that pay significantly less are Eibar, Getafe, and Granada CF. All of them are 'small' clubs and Eibar had only been in First Division in the last 2 seasons, and for the first time in its history.

5. Summary and Discussion

As it has been proven, the audit fees have grown in real terms after the implementation of FFP regulations. Moreover, audit fees are explained by the presence of foreign investors, having one of the Big 4 as the auditing firm and having a female auditor. The fact that the Big 4 audit companies charge higher audit fees seems clear. The fact that the presence of a female auditor may increase the fees is surprising, but it is even more surprising to find that other studies have obtained results akin to ours. These studies explain the higher audit fees given female auditors' perception of risk. This may be relevant in the case of football clubs, which are 'risky businesses'.

This paper makes two main contributions. On the one hand, it analyzes the economic consequences of the implementation of FFP regulations by mainly considering their effect on audit fees. On the other hand, the behavior of audit fees is analyzed within a particular context, the football industry. It reveals no influence of sporting factors, even when they had been expected.

With respect to the implications of the paper, it seems that the change in regulations has had an impact on audit fees charged by auditors for their services. However, this increase may be compensated over future years because the clubs' financial situation is improving, and, subsequently, the risk taken by auditors is diminishing. This facilitates the reduction in audit fees. UEFA should monitor whether the audit fees are reasonable as well as the quality of the audit reports, which have become crucial for obtaining a license to participate in UEFA competitions.

Audit fees are symptomatic of the deeper effects of the changes brought about by FFP regulation. Furthermore, the role of auditors imposed by UEFA can contribute to avoiding the problem of earning management, as pointed out by Dimitropoulos et al. (2016).

This study presents some limitations. Some of them are derived from the nature of the study and it is almost impossible to address them. One of them is the problem of the size of the sample, but only 18 clubs each year (as Real Madrid and Barcelona are excluded) are affected by these regulations. Nevertheless, Hay et al. (2006) present a summary of 148 papers on audit fees describing the sample. The size of the samples varies, but 20.3% of the papers have a sample smaller than 100 and 46.6% smaller than 200. The size of the sample is relevant when the model includes many independent variables, as these diminish the degrees of freedom. This problem is common for most of the papers on this issue. However, the results are pretty much similar upon excluding some of the non-significant variables. For that reason, we consider it best to maintain them as they could theoretically determine audit fees.

On the other hand, some variables such as other personal features of the auditors or other types of ownership could be missed, as well as other changes in audit or accountancy regulations. At this point, it is worth remarking that during the period of study some changes in audit or accountancy regulations took place. In accounting matters, the reform of the Spanish General Accounting Plan (Spanish GAAP) was approved in 2007, with the aim of accommodating the new IRFS to Spanish accounting regulations. Subsequently, in 2010, a new modification of the Spanish GAAP standards was made and the rules for the formulation of the Consolidated Annual Accounts were approved. In 2016, new amendments were incorporated into Spanish legislation to comply with the provisions of the EU Directive 34/2013. Regarding auditing, there were two amendments of the Audit Act with the purpose of adapting Spanish domestic legislation to EU Directives 43/2006 EC and 56/2014 in 2010 and in 2015, respectively. These changes overlap the period that we have taken. These kinds of variables could be used for more specific studies on the topic. Moreover, studies with companies from other industries would help to understand if the changes in general regulations affect football clubs in different ways.

The results of this study provide several future research lines. First, it would be interesting to carry out this analysis on other European leagues. Second, it would also be worth studying other possible effects of FFP regulations such as the presence of significant changes in auditor opinion. Third, seeing whether the adoption of FFP regulation would lead to an increased likelihood of clubs choosing a Big 4 accounting firm is a further line of study to be pursued.

Author Contributions: Authors equally contributed to the research and writing of the paper

Acknowledgments: This paper is an output of a research project implemented as part of the Basic Research Program at the National Research University Higher School of Economics (HSE).

References

1. Abbott, Laurence J., Katherine Gunny, and Troy Pollard. 2017. The impact of litigation risk on auditor pricing behavior: Evidence from reserve mergers. *Contemporary Accounting Research* 34: 1103–27. [CrossRef]
2. Alexeyeva, Irina, and Svanström Tobias. 2015. The impact of the global financial crisis on audit and non-audit fee. *Managerial Auditing Journal* 30: 302–23. [CrossRef]

3. Archambeault, Deborah, and Tood DeZoort. 2001. Auditor opinion shopping and the audit committee: An analysis of suspicious auditor switches. *International Journal of Auditing* 5: 33–52. [CrossRef]
4. Ascari , Guido, and Philippe Gagnepain. 2006. Spanish football. *Journal of Sports Economics* 7: 76–89. [CrossRef]
5. Asthana, Shara, Steven Balsam, and Sungsoo Kim. 2009. The effect of Enron, Andersen, and Sarbanes-Oxley on the US market for audit services. *Accounting Research Journal* 22: 4–26. [CrossRef]
6. Badertscher, Brand, Bjorn Jorgensen, Sharon P. Katz, and William Kinney. 2014. Public equity and audit pricing in the United States. *Journal of Accounting Research* 52: 303–39. [CrossRef]
7. Barajas, Angel. 2004. *Modelo de Valoración de Clubes de Fútbol Basado en los Factores clave de su negocio [Valuation model for football clubs based on the key factors of their business]*. MPRA Paper 13158. Munich: University Library of Munich.
8. Barajas, Angel, Carlos Fernández-Jardón, and Liz Crolle. 2005. *Does Sports Performance Influence Revenues and Economic Results in Spanish Football?* MPRA Paper 3234. Munich: University Library of Munich, Available online: https://papers.ssrn.com/sol3/papers.cfm?abstract_id=986365 (accessed on 1 April 2018).
9. Barajas, Angel, and Plácido Rodríguez. 2010. Spanish football clubs' finances: Crisis and player salaries. *International Journal of Sport Finance* 1: 52–66.
10. Barajas, Angel, and Plácido Rodríguez. 2014. Spanish football in need of financial therapy: Cut Expenses and Inject Capital. *International Journal of Sport Finance* 9: 73–90.
11. Barber, Brad M., and Terrance Odean. 2001. Boys will be boys: Gender, overconfidence, and common stock investment. *Quarterly Journal of Economics* 116: 261–92. [CrossRef]
12. Basioudis, Ilias G., Evangelos Papakonstantinou, and Marshall A. Geiger. 2008. Audit fees, non-audit fees and auditor going-concern reporting decisions in the United Kingdom. *Abacus, A Journal of Accounting, Finance and Business Studies* 44: 284–307. [CrossRef]
13. Beech, John, Simon Horsman, and Jamie Magraw. 2010. Insolvency events among English football clubs. *International Journal of Sports Marketing & Sponsorship* 11: 53–6. [CrossRef]
14. Bedard, Jean C., Donald R. Deis, Mary B. Curtis, and J. Gregory Jenkins. 2008. Risk monitoring and control in audit firms: A research synthesis. *Auditing: A Journal of Practice and Theory* 27: 187–218. [CrossRef]
15. Bell, Timothy B., Rajib Doogar, and Ira Solomon. 2008. Audit labor usage and fees under business risk auditing. *Journal of Accounting Research* 46: 729–60. [CrossRef]
16. Bell, Timothy, Wayne R. Landsman, and Douglas A. Shackelford. 2001. Auditor´s perceived business risk and audit fees: Analysis and evidence. *Journal of Accounting Research* 39: 35–43. [CrossRef]
17. Beneish, Messod D., and Teri Lombardi Yohn. 2008. Information friction and investor home bias: A perspective on the effect of global IFRS adoption on the extent of equity home bias. *Journal Accounting Public Policy* 27: 433–43. [CrossRef]
18. Boscá, José E., Vicente Liern, Aurelio Martínez, and Ramón Sala. 2008. The Spanish football crisis. *European Sport Management Quarterly* 8: 165–77. [CrossRef]
19. Brumfield, Craig A., Robert K. Elliott, and Peter D. Jacobson. 1983. Business risk and the audit process. *Journal of Accountancy* 155: 60–68.
20. Callaghan, Joseph, Mohinder Parkash, and Rajeev Singhal. 2009. Going-concern audit opinions and the provision of non-audit services: Implications for auditor independence of bankrupt firms. *Auditing: A Journal of Practice & Theory* 28: 153–69. [CrossRef]
21. Casterella, Jeffrey R., Jere R. Francis, Barry L. Lewis, and Paul L. Walker. 2004. Auditor industry specialization, client bargaining power and audit pricing. *Auditing: A Journal of Practice and Theory* 23: 123–40. [CrossRef]
22. Charles, Shannon L., Steven M. Glover, and Nathan Y. Sharp. 2010. The association between financial reporting risk and audit fees before and after the historic events surrounding SOX. *Auditing: A Journal of Practice and Theory* 29: 15–39. [CrossRef]
23. Choi, Jong-Hang, Jeong Bon Kim, Xiaohong Liu, and Dan A. Simunic. 2008. Audit pricing, legal liability regimes, and Big 4 premiums: theory and cross-country evidence. *Contemporary Accounting Research* 25: 55–99. [CrossRef]
24. Choi, Jong-Hang, Jeong-Bon Kim, Xiaohong Liu, and Dan A. Simunic. 2009. Cross-listing audit fee premiums: Theory and evidence. *The Accounting Review* 84: 1429–63. [CrossRef]
25. Craswell, Allen T., Jere R. Francis, and Stephen L. Taylor. 1995. Auditor brand name reputation and industry specializations. *Journal of Accounting and Economics* 20: 297–322. [CrossRef]
26. Davis, Larry R., David N. Ricchiute, and Greg Trompeter. 1993. Audit effort, audit fees, and the provision of non-audit services to audit clients. *The Accounting Review* 68: 135–50.
27. De Angelo, Linda Elizabeth. 1981. Auditor size and audit quality. *Journal of Accounting and Economics* 3: 183–99. [CrossRef]
28. De Fuentes, Cristina, and Eva Sierra-Grau. 2015. IFRS adoption and audit and non-audit fees: Empirical evidence from

Spanish listed companies. *Spanish Journal of Finance and Accounting* 44: 387–426. [CrossRef]
29. De Fuentes, Cristina, and Eva Sierra-Grau. 2015. Industry specialization and audit fees: A meta-analytic approach. *Academia, Revista Latinoamericana de Administración* 28: 419–35. [CrossRef]
30. De George, Emmanuel T., Colin B. Ferguson, and Nasser A. Spear. 2013. How much does IFRS cost? IFRS adoption and audit fees. *Accounting Review* 88: 429–62. [CrossRef]
31. DeFond, Mark L. 1992. The association between changes in client company agency costs and auditor switching. *Auditing: A Journal of Practice & Theory* 11: 16–31.
32. Deloitte. 2014. Annual Review of Football Finance 2014 Highlights, Sports Business Group. Available online: https://www2.deloitte.com/content/dam/Deloitte/uk/Documents/sports-business- group/deloitte-uk-annual-review-football-finance.pdf (accessed on 20 March 2018).
33. Dimitropoulos, Panagiotis. 2016. Audit selection in the European football industry under Union of European Football Associations Financial Fair Play. *International Journal of Economics and Financial Issues* 6: 901–6.
34. Dimitropoulos, Panagiotis, Stergios Leventis, and Emmanouil Dedoulis. 2016. Managing the European football industry: UEFA's regulatory intervention and the impact on accounting quality. *European Sport Management Quarterly* 16: 459–86. [CrossRef]
35. Dwyer, Peggy, James Gilkeson, and John List. 2002. Gender differences in revealed risk taking: Evidence from mutual fund investors. *Economics Letters* 76: 151–58. [CrossRef]
36. Eckel, Catherine C., and Philip J. Grossman. 2002. Sex differences and statistical stereotyping in attitudes toward financial risk. *Evolution and Human Behavior* 23: 281–95. [CrossRef]
37. Francis, Jerre R., and Dechun Wang. 2008. The joint effect of investor protection and Big 4 audits on earnings quality around the world. *Contemporary Accounting Research* 25: 157–91. [CrossRef]
38. Gay, José M. 2009a. Fútbol finanzas: La economía de la liga de las estrellas (I). Radiografía económica del fútbol español (temporada 2006–07) [Football finance: The economy of the league of the stars (I). Economic in-depth analysis of Spanish football (season 2006–07)]. *Partida Doble* 208: 62–89.
39. Gay, José M. 2009b. Fútbol finanzas: La economía de la liga de las estrellas (II). Radiografía económica del fútbol español (temporada 2006–07) [Football finance: The economy of the league of the stars (II). Economic in-depth analysis of Spanish football (season 2006–07).]. *Partida Doble* 209: 62–87.
40. Gammelsæter, Hallgeir. 2010. Institutional pluralism and governance in 'Commercialized' sport clubs. *European Sport Management Quarterly* 10: 569–94. [CrossRef]
41. García, Jaume, and Plácido Rodríguez. 2003. From sports clubs to stock companies: The financial structure of football in Spain 1992–2001. *European Sport Management Quarterly* 3: 235–69. [CrossRef]
42. Ghosh, Aloke, and Steven Lustgarten. 2006. Pricing of initial audit engagements by large and small audit firms. *Contemporary Accounting Research* 23: 333–68. [CrossRef]
43. Ghosh, Aloke, and Robert Pawlewicz. 2009. The impact of regulation on auditor fees: evidence from the Sarbanes-Oxley Act. *Auditing: A Journal of Practice and Theory* 28: 171–97. [CrossRef]
44. Griffin, Paul A., and David H. Lont. 2007. An analysis of audit fees following the passage of Sarbanes-Oxley. *Asia-Pacific Journal of Accounting & Economics* 14: 161–92. [CrossRef]
45. Griffin, Paul A., David. H. Lont, and Estelle Y. Sun. 2009. Governance regulatory changes, international financial reporting standards adoption, and New Zealand audit and non-audit fees: Empirical evidence. *Accounting & Finance* 49: 697–724. [CrossRef]
46. Groff, Maja Z., Domen Trobec, and Aleksander Iglicˇar. 2017. Audit fees and the salience of financial crises: Evidence from Slovenia. *Economic Research Ekonomska Istraživanja* 30: 922–38. [CrossRef]
47. Gul, Ferdinand, Donghui Wu, and Zhifeng Yang. 2013. Do individual auditors affect audit quality: Evidence from archival data. *The Accounting Review* 88: 1993–2023. [CrossRef]
48. Hardies Kris, Diane Breesch, and Joël Branson. 2015. The female audit fee premium. *Auditing: A Journal of Practice & Theory* 34: 171–95. [CrossRef]
49. Hay, David. 2013. Further evidence from meta-analysis of audit fee research. *International Journal of Auditing* 17: 162–76. [CrossRef]
50. Hay, David, W. Robert Knechel, and Norman Wong. 2006. Audit fees: A meta-analysis of the effect of supply and demand attributes. *Contemporary Accounting Research* 23: 141–91. [CrossRef]
51. He, Xianjie, Oliver Rui, Liu Zheng, and Hongjun Zhu. 2014. Foreign ownership and auditor choice. *Journal of Accounting and Public Policy* 33: 401–18. [CrossRef]
52. Higgins, Stephen, David Lont, and Tom Scott. 2016. Longer term audit costs of IFRS and the differential impact of implied auditor cost structures. *Accounting and Finance* 56: 165–203. [CrossRef]
53. Hu, Naw-wei, Wen-si Ouyang, and Ning-jiao Deng. 2014. Research on auditors' gender and audit fees. Paper presented at 2014 International Conference on Management Science Engineering (ICMSE), Nirjuli, India, May 7–8; pp. 1307–12.

54. Huang, Hua-Wei, Kannan Raghunandan, and Dasaratha Rama. 2009. Audit fees for initial audit engagements before and after SOX. *Auditing: A Journal of Practice & Theory* 28: 171–90. [CrossRef]
55. Ittonen, Kim, and Emilia Peni. 2012. Auditor's gender and audit fees. *International Journal of Auditing* 16: 1–18. [CrossRef]
56. Ittonen, Kim, Emilia Vähämaa, and Sami Vähämaa. 2013. Female auditors and accruals quality. *Accounting Horizons* 27: 205–28. [CrossRef]
57. Kim, Jeong-Bong, Xiaohong Liu, and Liu Zheng. 2012. The impact of mandatory IFRS adoption on audit fees: Theory and evidence. *The Accounting Review* 87: 2061–94. [CrossRef]
58. Knechel, W. Robert, and Jeff L. Payne. 2001. Additional evidence on audit report lags. *Auditing: A Journal of Practice & Theory* 20: 137–46. [CrossRef]
59. Krishnan, Gopal V., and Changjiang Wang. 2015. The relation between managerial ability and audit fees and going concern opinions. *Auditing: A Journal of Practice & Theory* 34: 139–60. [CrossRef]
60. Kuper, Simon, and Stefan Szymanski. 2009. *Soccernomics: Why England Loses, Why Germany and Brazil Win, and Why the US, Japan, Australia, Turkey—and Even Iraq—Are Destined to Become the Kings of the World's Most Popular Sport*. New York: Nation Books.
61. Lin, Hsiao-Lun, and Ai-Ru Yen. 2016. The effects of IFRS experience on audit fees for listed companies in China. *Asian Review of Accounting* 24: 43–68. [CrossRef]
62. Liu, Ji-Hong. 2007. On determinants of audit fee: New evidence from China. *Journal of Modern Accounting and Auditing* 3: 60–64.
63. Mautz, Robert Kuhn, and Hussein Amer Sharaf. 1961. *The Philosophy of Auditing*. Sarasota: American Accounting Association Monograph, No. 6.
64. Menon, Krishnagopal, and David D. Williams. 2001. Long term trends in audit fees. *Auditing: A Journal of Practice and Theory* 20: 115–36. [CrossRef]
65. Monterrey, Juan, and Amparo Sánchez. 2007. Un estudio empírico de los honorarios del auditor [An Empirical Study of auditor's fees]. *Cuadernos de Economía y Empresa* 32: 81–210. [CrossRef]
66. Morrow, Stephen. 2014. Financial Fair Play-Implications for Football Club Financial Reporting. The Institute of Chartered Accountants of Scotland. Available online: http://www.storre.stir.ac.uk/bitstream/1893/ 21393/1/ICAS%20 Financial%20Fair%20Play%20Report%20-%20Stephen%20Morrow.pdf (accessed on 10 May 2018).
67. Nettle, Daniel. 2007. Empathizing and systemizing: What are they, and what do they contribute to our understanding of psychological sex differences? *British Journal of Psychology* 98: 237–55. [CrossRef] [PubMed]
68. Oxera Report. 2006. *Competition and Choice in the UK Audit Market*. Prepared for Department of Trade and Industry and Financial Reporting Council. Oxford: Oxera Consulting Ltd.
69. Palmrose, Zoe-Vonna. 1986. The effect of nonaudit services on the pricing of audit services: Further evidence. *Journal of Accounting Research* 24: 405–41. [CrossRef]
70. Raghunandan, Kannan, and Dasaratha Rama. 2006. Sox section 404 material weakness disclosures and audit fees. *Auditing: A Journal of Practice & Theory* 25: 99–114. [CrossRef]
71. Redmayne, Nives Botica, Michael E. Bradbury, and Steven F. Cahan. 2010. The effect of political visibility on audit effort and audit pricing. *Accounting and Finance* 50: 921–39. [CrossRef]
72. Rittenberg, Larry E., Karla Johnstone, and Audrey Gramling. 2012. *Auditing*, 8th ed. Cincinnati: South-Western College Publishing.
73. Robinson, Terry, and Robert Simmons. 2014. Gate-sharing and talent distribution in the English football league.\ *International Journal of the Economics of Business* 21: 413–29. [CrossRef]
74. Ruiz-Barbadillo, Emiliano. 2016. Regulación frente a reputación como medio de salvaguarda de la independencia del auditor [Regulation versus reputation as a means of safeguarding the independence of the audit]. *Revista de Contabilidad y Tributación* 401–402: 161–98.
75. Ruíz-Barbadillo, Emiliano, and Nieves Gómez-Aguilar. 2007. Análisis empírico de los factores que explican la mejora de opinión de auditoría: compra de opinión y mejora en las prácticas contables de la empresa [An empirical analysis of the factors explaining the change in audit opinion: opinion shopping and accounting practices improvements in firms]. *Spanish Journal of Finance and Accounting* 36: 317–50. [CrossRef]
76. Salman, Fazlina Mohd, and Elizabeth Carson. 2009. The impact of the Sarbanes-Oxley Act on the audit fees of Australian listed firms. *The International Journal of Auditing* 13: 127–40. [CrossRef]
77. Schmitt, David, Anu Realo, Martin Voracek, and Jüri Allik. 2009. Why can't a man be more like a woman? Sex differences in big five personality traits across 55 cultures. *Journal of Personality and Social Psychology* 94: 168–82. [CrossRef] [PubMed]
78. Seetharaman, Ananth, Ferdinand A. Gul, and Stephen G. Lynn. 2002. Litigation risk and audit fees: evidence from UK firms cross-listed on US markets. *Journal of Accounting and Economics* 33: 91–115. [CrossRef]

79. Silva, Rosana Cristina, Felipe Silva Moreira, José Emerson Firmino, Jaspe Padilha Miranda, and José Dionísio Gómez Silva. 2016. Julgamento dos Auditores Independentes sobre o Ativo Intangível: Um estudo sobre a qualidade da auditoria em clubes de futebol do Brasil [Judgment of independent auditors regarding intangible assets: A study on audit quality in Brazillian football clubs]. *Revista Contabilidade e Controladoria* 8: 65–88. Available online: http://revistas.ufpr.br/rcc/article/view/39449 (accessed on 2 May 2018).
80. Simunic, Dan A. 1980. The pricing of audit services: Theory and evidence. *Journal of Accounting Research* 18: 161–90. [CrossRef]
81. Simunic, Dan A. 1984. Auditing, Consulting, and Auditor Independence. *Journal of Accounting Research* 22: 679–702. [CrossRef]
82. Simunic, Dan A., and Michael T. Stein. 1996. Impact of litigation risk on audit pricing: A review of the economics and the evidence. *Auditing: A Journal of Practice and Theory* 15: 119–34.
83. Sarbanes Oxley-SOX. 2002. Committee on Financial Services, Sarbanes-Oxley Act. Available online: http://www.sarbanes-oxley.com (accessed on 23 February 2018).
84. Stanley, Jonathan D. 2011. Is the audit fee disclosure a leading indicator of clients' business risk? *Auditing: A Journal of Practice & Theory* 30: 157–79. [CrossRef]
85. Stein, Michael. T., Dan A. Simunic, and Terrence B. O'Keefe. 1994. Industry differences in the production of audit services. *Auditing: A Journal of Practice & Theory* 13: 128–42.
86. Storm, Rasmus K., and Klaus Nielsen. 2012. Soft budget constraints in professional football. *European Sport Management Quarterly* 12: 183–201. [CrossRef]
87. Sundgren, Stefan, and Tobias Svanström. 2014. Auditor-in-charge characteristics and going concern reporting. *Contemporary Accounting Research* 31: 531–550. [CrossRef]
88. UEFA. 2010. *UEFA Club Licensing and Financial Fair Play Regulations*, Edition 2010 ed. Nyon: UEFA.
89. Venkataraman, Ramgopal, Joseph P. Weber, and Michael Willenborg. 2008. Litigation risk, audit quality, and audit fees: Evidence from initial public offerings. *The Accounting Review* 83: 1315–45. [CrossRef]
90. Vieru, Markku, and Hannu Shadewitz. 2010. Impact of IFRS transition on audit and non-audit fees: Evidence from small and medium-sized listed companies in Finland. *The Finnish Journal of Business Economics* 1: 11–41. Wang, Yuequan, and Andy C.W. Chui. 2015. Product market competition and audit fees. *Auditing: A Journal of Practice & Theory* 34: 139–56. [CrossRef]
91. Watson, John, and Mark McNaughton. 2007. Gender differences in risk aversion and expected retirement benefits. *Financial Analysts Journal* 63: 52–62. [CrossRef]
92. Whisenant, Scott, Srinivasan Sankaraguruswamy, and Kannan Raghunandan. 2003. Evidence on the Joint Determination of Audit and Non-Audit Fees. *Journal of Accounting Research* 41: 721–44. [CrossRef]
93. Wilson, Robert, Daniel Plumley, and Girish Ramchandani. 2013. The relationship between ownership structure and club performance in the English Premier League. *Sport, Business and Management: An International Journal* 3: 19–36. [CrossRef]
94. Xu, Yang, Elizabeth Carson, Neil Fargher, and Liwei Jiang. 2013. Responses by Australian auditors to the global financial crisis. *Accounting and Finance* 53: 301–38. [CrossRef]
95. Zhang, Tianshu, and Jun Huang. 2013. The risk premium of audit fee: Evidence from the 2008 financial crisis. *China Journal of Accounting Studies* 1: 47–61. [CrossRef]

6

Organizational Mission and Revenue Diversification among Non-profit Sports Clubs

Pamela Wicker *, Svenja Feiler and Christoph Breuer

Department of Sport Economics and Sport Management, German Sport University Cologne, Am Sportpark Muengersdorf 6, Cologne 50933, Germany; s.feiler@dshs-koeln.de (S.F.); breuer@dshs-koeln.de (C.B.)

* Author to whom correspondence should be addressed; p.wicker@dshs-koeln.de

Abstract: The beneficial effects of diversified income portfolios are well documented in previous research on non-profit organizations. This study examines how different types of organizational missions affect the level of revenue diversification of organizations in one industry, a question that was neglected in previous research. Based on contingency theory, it is assumed that different missions are associated with different funding sources. Since missions can be complementary or conflicting, specific attention needs to be paid to the combination of missions. The sport sector is chosen as an empirical setting because non-profit sports clubs can have various missions while their overall purpose is promoting sport. Panel data from a nationwide survey of non-profit sports clubs in Germany are used for the analysis. The regression results show that revenue diversification is significantly determined by organizational mission. Historically, typical mission statements like promoting elite sport, tradition, conviviality, non-sport programs, and youth sport have a positive effect on revenue diversification, while clubs with a commercial orientation and a focus on leisure and health sport have more concentrated revenues. The findings have implications for club management in the sense that some missions are associated with higher financial risk and that the combination of missions should be chosen carefully.

Keywords: revenue diversification; income portfolio; organizational mission; contingency theory; non-profit organization; sports club

---

1. Introduction

The concept of revenue diversification and financial portfolio theory have received increased academic attention in the non-profit sector during the last two decades with Chabotar [1], Chang and Tuckman [2], and Kingma [3] making significant contributions amongst others. The main idea of this theory is that organizations try to diversify their income portfolios to be less susceptible to financial crisis [1] and to increase their financial viability [2]. Previous research has mainly supported the beneficial effects of revenue diversification on the financial situation of non-profit organizations (e.g., [4]), although a few studies refuted those benefits [5,6]. On the positive side, organizations with diversified revenues were less financially vulnerable (e.g., [7–10]), had a lower insolvency risk [11], and less volatile revenues [12].

While the beneficial effects of diversified revenues have been well investigated, only a few studies have examined what types of organizations have more diversified revenues than others. Chang and Tuckman [2] were the first to show that the level of revenue diversification (or concentration in their study) varies depending on the activity of the organization, a finding that was further supported by Kearns [13]. In their comprehensive study, Chang and Tuckman [2] compared organizations operating in 25 different industries and found that revenue concentration was lowest for non-profits concerned with environmental quality and for animal-related organizations, while it was highest in consumer protection and legal aid organizations. The type of activity [2] or mission [13] corresponds to the industry or the sector the organization is operating in. Thus, it is only a broad measure of activity or mission, which does not consider that organizations within one industry can have different missions while having the same overall purpose. Having this in mind, Chang and Tuckman [2] suggested that *"future researchers would do well to focus on the specific activities in which non-profits engage"*.

The purpose of this study is to examine the relationship between different organizational missions and the level of revenue diversification of non-profit organizations within one industry. Building on the Chang and Tuckman [2] study, this study advances the following main research question: How does the organizational mission affect an organization's level of revenue diversification? The sport industry serves as an empirical setting. Non-profit sports clubs are particularly suited to analyze this research question because they have different types of missions [14]. While every club has the overall mission of promoting sport, several *sub*-missions exist. One peculiarity is that those *sub*-missions are not only sport-related such as promoting competitive sport and/or mass sport, but also non-sport related like promoting sociability [14]. Previous research has supported the notion that sports clubs produce heterogeneous products for heterogeneous stakeholders [15–17]. For example, they do not only provide sport programs for their members, they also fulfill several social functions such as integrating youths and immigrants, and teaching youths applied democracy [18]. These functions, which contribute to public welfare and social cohesion, are appreciated by the community and by policy makers and represent one reason why sports clubs receive financial support from the government. Thus, clubs also produce other *products* in addition to sport programs.

The variety of stakeholders may be one reason why sports organizations were found to have more diversified revenues than non-profits in other industries [2,19]. Similar to the general non-profit sector, the beneficial effects of revenue diversification have also been shown in the sport industry. For example, previous research documented that non-profit sports organizations with a diversified income portfolio are in a better financial condition [19], are less financially vulnerable [20], and have less volatile revenues [21], although not all studies could support a positive relationship [22]. However, it has not yet been examined how different types of organizational missions affect the level of revenue diversification, *i.e.*, what types of clubs have more diversified revenues than others. To analyze this question, data from a nationwide panel survey of non-profit sports clubs in Germany are used (n = 45,074). The regression results show that the level of revenue diversification is affected by the organizational mission. The findings have implications for club management.

2. Theoretical Framework and Literature Review

Following Kearns [13], several theories can be advanced that explain an organization's revenue composition. The theoretical streams can be assigned to four main areas including organizational behavior, political science, economics, and strategic management. They provide different perspectives on the factors associated with income portfolios of non-profits. For the present research looking at the influence of organizational mission on revenue diversification only streams from organizational behavior, political sciences, and economics are considered relevant. Strategic management theories such as resource dependence approaches look at the relationship between organizations and the external entities that support those [2] and how those relationships result in external control and power. Their focus is more on the consequences of revenue composition and not on the influencing factors; therefore, strategic management theories are neglected. This study combines the organizational behavior perspective (contingency theory) with the political science and the financial perspective (financial portfolio theory) from economics.

Kearns [13] advances one theoretical approach that he calls the *contingency theory of income diversification* that can be assigned to the literature on organizational behavior. When looking at all the theoretical approaches, Kearns [13] notes that: *"the contingency theory seems to be the most promising and intuitively appealing"*. Yet, it has not been well developed in the context of revenue diversification so far. This is different for other organizational contexts such as organizational structure and leadership (e.g., [23,24]). The contingency theory was developed by Kearns [13] based on the findings of the Chang and Tuckman [2] study—the authors themselves have not developed such a theory in their paper. According to Kearns [13], the main idea of this theory is that an organization's mission determines the concentration (or diversification) of its income sources, an assumption that intuitively fits with the present study.

To provide some context, contingency theory is based on the seminal work of Woodward [25] who argued at the time that several contingencies such as technology and external stakeholders (e.g., government, consumers) influence organizational behavior. Generally speaking, contingency theories have the underlying assumption that there is no optimal way of managing organizations that can be applied to all organizations. In fact, the management of each organization is *contingent* on internal factors (e.g., organizational culture) and external factors (e.g., environment, regulations) that vary among organizations [23]. Consequently, those factors that are potentially variable are called *contingency factors*.

In this study, the focus is on internal contingency factors relating to organizational mission. The theory supports the notion that organizations within one industry cannot be treated equally because they are likely to have different missions that are contingent on various internal and external factors. Different missions may in turn attract different funding sources thus influencing an organization's income portfolio and its level of revenue diversification. The present study seeks to analyze the relationship between organizational mission (as one contingency factor) and revenue diversification. This study tries to enhance the understanding of contingency theory in the context of revenue diversification by applying it to the sports club context.

Following more established theories from political sciences [13]—also referred to as the institutional perspective [2]—an organization is mainly concerned with its legitimacy and acceptance in the community. Legitimacy is also created by the origin of its funding sources. Thus, not only the overall amount of money available to an organization is considered important, but also where the money comes from [13]. This means that organizations pursue funding from recognized sources that increase their social acceptance. Moreover, it is likely that organizations generating funds from recognized institutions will increase their revenues from other institutions because they are considered worth of being funded. This is what has been referred to as the crowd-in effect in previous research, while the opposite effect, *i.e.*, crowd-out effect, must also be considered [26]. Crowd-out and crowd-in effects have been examined both in general non-profit research [27,28] and in sport [29,30].

This theoretical stream has implications for portfolio management in the sense that both the origin of financial resources and the interactions among income sources have to be taken into account. This information is also critical to the present research. Given that an organization's revenue composition is a result of the services it provides [31], organizations should carefully choose their missions (and associated services) and pay attention to the relationships between different types of missions. Organizations' missions may have a complementary or conflicting character—content wise and consequently also financial wise. Missions can be complementary in the sense that funding institutions are likely to support both missions. In the sports club context, for example, missions relating to the promotion of competitive sport and the promotion of youth would be complementary because typically young people take part in competitive sport at the elite level. Thus, potential funding organizations would not see a discrepancy between the two missions. On the contrary, some mission statements could be regarded as conflicting. For example, the promotion of health sport and competitive sport at the same time may not be intuitively appealing to potential resource providers since both mission statements target different groups of people. While younger people are more likely to participate in competitive sport at the elite level, older people are more likely to demand health sport programs [32]. These examples show that the mix of mission statements may have an influence on the income portfolio of non-profit sports clubs.

The idea of managing income portfolios originally stems from financial portfolio theory (e.g., [33]), which is one of the economic theories [13]. This theory has already been applied to non-profit organizations in general [3] and in sport [21]. Originally, portfolio management relates to the composition of the income portfolio in the sense of financial risk and volatility. As stated earlier in this paper, the idea is that organizations diversify their revenues in order to be more financially viable and experience lower revenue volatility. Yet, this study focuses on organizational missions and not directly on financial risk (although it will be shown later in the paper that some missions may be indirectly associated with higher financial risk than others). Therefore, this study is more concerned with different types of missions than with income sources of different risk levels. Nevertheless, attention needs to be paid to the combination of different missions since they may have financial consequences.

3. Method

3.1. Data Source

This research is based on data from the Sport Development Report, a project looking at the situation of sports clubs in Germany. Germany is home to over 91,000 sports clubs that are well spread throughout the country and that provide sporting opportunities to the German population. Out of the approximately 80 million German citizens, 27.7 million are members of sports clubs [34,35]. Within this project, sports clubs are surveyed online every two years. Thus, the project has a panel character. The first wave was conducted in 2005 with another three waves following in 2007, 2009, and 2011. The email addresses for the online survey are provided by the 16 state sports confederations before the start of each wave. From the first to the fourth wave, the number of provided email addresses has increased considerably documenting that more and more clubs are *online*. In 2005, 18,085 valid email addresses were provided, 37,206 in 2007, 58,069 in 2009, and 67,708 in 2011 [15,16,18,36]. The sports clubs receive an invitation email including some information about the purpose of the project, anonymity and privacy of data, and a personalized link to the online questionnaire. This means that respondents can log in and out and that several people can complete the survey, which may be useful given its length and variety of questions. The survey usually starts in fall (with the exception of the first wave where the survey started in spring). The survey period is approximately three months and one or two reminders are sent to the clubs which have not yet responded. Similar to the number of provided email addresses, the response rates have increased during the years (2005: n = 3,731; 2007: n = 13,068; 2009: n = 19,345; and 2011: n = 21,998).

Each survey questionnaire consists of a standard set of questions that are similar in every wave (e.g., member statistics, sports offerings, volunteers, finances, organizational problems) and a set of questions addressing specific and current topics in sports club management (e.g., demographic change, doping, changes in the German school system, need of support). For the current study, only data from the first (2005), third (2009), and fourth wave (2011) can be used for the analysis since questions about the organizational mission of clubs were omitted in the second wave in 2007. Consequently, the final sample amounts to n = 45,074 sports clubs. Since the sub-samples of each wave are different in size and do not consist of the same clubs (although some clubs participated in more than one wave), the dataset is considered an unbalanced panel consisting of independently pooled cross sections [37]. Pooled samples drawn from the same population are considered favorable for the analysis since "*we can get more precise estimators and test statistics with more power*" [37]. Thus, this unbalanced panel is preferred over a normal cross-sectional dataset covering only one wave. Generally speaking, panel data are relatively rare in sports club research. To the knowledge of the authors, the data from the German Sport Development Report represent the largest panel data in quantitative sports club research.

3.2. Measures and Variables

An overview of the variables used in this study is presented in Table 1. In order to obtain revenue diversification, a concentration measure was calculated first. Revenue concentration is measured with an index (*Herf*) similar to the Herfindahl-Hirschmann Index, a measure which has already been used in previous research [2,7,10,12]. Importantly, the index covers two aspects of revenue concentration, *i.e.*, the number of different income sources and the extent to which revenues are distributed equally or unequally across sources [2]. The index is calculated with the following formula:

$$\text{Herf} = \sum_{i=1}^{n}(r_i/Rev)^2,\ i = 1, \ldots, 25, \quad (1)$$

where N represents the total number of income sources (25 in this study); r_i the revenue generated from source i; and *Rev* the total revenues a club generates in one year. To put it short, *Herf* is obtained by adding the squared proportions of all income sources.

Table 1. Overview of variables.

Variable	Description	Scale
Rev div	Revenue diversification = 1 − *Herf*; 0 = perfect concentration, *i.e.*, club has only one income source; 1 = perfect diversification; *Herf* = sum of the squared proportions of all 25 income sources of sports clubs	Metric
	Organizational mission (from 1 = do not agree at all to 5 = totally agree)	
Elite	Our club promotes competitive sport (elite sport)	Ordinal
Leisure	Our club promotes leisure and mass sport	Ordinal
Health	Our club provides health sport	Ordinal
Cheap	Our club offers a cheap opportunity to play sport	Ordinal
Quality	Our club cares about the quality of the sport programs	Ordinal
Commercial	Our club is geared towards the programs of commercial providers	Ordinal
Tradition	Our club sets value on tradition	Ordinal
Conviviality	Our club sets value on companionship and conviviality	Ordinal
Non-sport	Our club also provides non-sport programs	Ordinal
Youth	Our club is engaged in the promotion of youth	Ordinal
LN Rev/m	Total logged revenues/number of club members	Metric
Members	Total number of members in the club	Metric
Members^2	Members squared	Metric
Sports	Number of sports provided by the club	Metric
Sports^2	Sports squared	Metric
Sport	Type of sport provided by the club (ten most frequent sports: badminton, football, track and field, shooting, swimming, dancing, tennis, table tennis, gymnastics, volleyball; 1 = yes)	Dummy
Year	Year of survey (2005, 2009, or 2011; 1 = yes)	Dummy
State	Federal state (Germany has 16 states; from 1 = Bavaria to 16 = Schleswig-Holstein	Dummy

In the survey, sports clubs were asked to state their revenues in the following 25 different categories: revenues from (1) membership fees; (2) admission fees; (3) donations; (4) subsidies from sport organizations; (5) subsidies from the state; (6) subsidies from the district/community; (7) subsidies from the European Union; (8) subsidies from the friends' association; (9) subsidies from other programs (e.g., employment office); (10) fund management (e.g., interests); (11) self-operated restaurant; (12) sport events (e.g., gate revenues); (13) service fees from members (e.g., facility fees); (14) convivial gatherings (e.g., club parties and festivities); (15) sponsorship: jerseys, equipment; (16) sponsorship: boards; (17) sponsorship: broadcasting rights; (18) sponsorship: advertisements; (19) own business company; (20) course fees; (21) service fees from non-members (e.g., facility fees); (22) service fees from collaborating institutions; (23) rent/lease of own facilities; (24) credits; and (25) other (*i.e.*, sum of all other miscellaneous revenues that could not be assigned to one of the 24 categories). All 25 income sources are used to calculate *Herf*. Since the index (*Herf*) represents a measure for revenue concentration, the final value was subtracted from 1 to capture revenue diversification (*Rev div*):

$$\text{Rev div} = 1 - \text{Herf} \quad (2)$$

Organizational mission was assessed with a closed question. Respondents were asked to state the extent to which the club's board agreed to a list of mission statements using five-point Likert scales (from 1 = do not agree at all to 5 = totally agree). As noted previously, organizational mission was assessed in wave 1, 3, and 4. Out of the list of 19 statements that were assessed in all three waves, 10 statements are selected for the current analysis. Using more items was not considered useful given the redundancy of some items (e.g., several items capture competitive sport or a commercial orientation).

The 10 statements cover the main areas of sports clubs' missions. Their concrete wording in the questionnaire can be seen in Table 1.

The 10 mission statements under investigation can be divided into six sport-related and four non-sport statements. With regard to sport-related statements, promoting competitive sport at the elite level (*Elite*) is one of the core missions of sports clubs historically. Sports clubs have the monopoly for competitive sport in Germany. This means that people who want to take part in league competitions or championships at the district, state, or national level have to be a member of a sports club. Thus, promoting competitive sport is one of the clubs' original missions. Also, clubs promote sport for the masses and ensure the provision of sport programs all over the country. Yet, leisure and mass sport programs (*Leisure*) have less of a competitive character. More recently, some clubs also provide health sport programs (*Health*) as a result of changes in individual demand. Many people are less interested in sport competitions; they want to play sport in order to become or remain fit and healthy. Thus, providing health sport programs can be considered a relatively new mission of clubs. Following Heinemann [38], providing relatively cheap programs (*Cheap*) compared with other providers is one of the core strengths of clubs. One of the reasons for the low membership fees lies in the fact that many clubs receive public subsidies [38]. Given the increasing number of fitness centers with some chains also offering relatively cheap prices, more and more sports clubs are faced with increasing competition from commercial sport providers. One of the strength of commercial providers is the focus on quality, both in terms of facilities and in terms of the qualification of coaches. As a result of increasing competition, some clubs have started *copying* the programs of commercial providers (*Commercial*) and pay more attention to the quality of their sport programs (*Quality*).

Regarding non-sport missions, sports clubs are organizations with a fine tradition and thus set value on tradition (*Tradition*). Since many sports clubs were founded in the late 1890s or at the beginning of the 20th century, they are known for being traditional organizations. Notwithstanding tradition is not only associated with positive aspects since it may also lead to resistance to change [39]. Tradition can be fostered through non-sport programs (*Non-sport*) such as all sorts of social events and festivities where values and social cohesion are fostered. Social events are an integral part of many clubs, particularly of those setting value on companionship and conviviality (*Conviviality*). Previous research has documented the beneficial effects of social events for the functioning of sports clubs [22]. Finally, the promotion of youth (*Youth*) is one of the core areas of sports clubs. Historically, sports clubs are particularly concerned with getting youths off the street and provide them with a location to play sport and to learn values.

Since revenue diversification is not only influenced by organizational mission, this study also controls for other potential influencing factors. Since previous research has shown that organizational size has an impact on the functioning of sports clubs (specifically on production costs and organizational problems) [40], organizational size should be controlled for in the present research. The size measures are *LN Rev/m* which is obtained by dividing total logged revenues by club members, *Members* representing the total number of club members and its squared term ($Members^2$), and *Sports* representing the total number of different sports provided by the club and its squared term ($Sports^2$). The squared terms are included to capture quadratic effects of size in terms of members and sports. These size measures have already been used in previous research on non-profit sports clubs [40].

In addition to organizational size, this study also controls for type of sport, year of the data, and state. Sports clubs in Germany provide more than 60 different sports [35]. For this research, the 10 most frequently stated sports in the survey are selected to see whether there are sports that lead to more concentrated or diversified revenues. Since approximately 40% of the sports clubs in Germany are multi-sports clubs (*i.e.*, they provide more than one type of sport), one dummy is calculated for each sport. The types of sport variables are dummy variables, where 1 indicates that the sport is provided by the club, and 0 otherwise. Since the dataset contains observations from three waves, the year dummies control for the year of the survey. It could be that changes in the revenue composition result from events that happened in the year of the survey. For example, financial crisis or other external events could influence a club's revenues. The study also controls for the state the club is located since there are differences among German states in terms of e.g., financial realities of state government, funding, and regulations that may influence a club's revenue composition.

Since this English article is based on German survey data, possible translation issues need to be considered [41]. While the questionnaire was designed by native German speakers in the German language and the survey was also conducted in the German language, the questions and resulting variables were translated into English for the purpose of this article. Thus, translation issues were not present for the design and conduction of the survey, but may be present for the writing of the article. Following Temple and Young [41], the researcher can serve as the translator or the translation can be performed by an external (professional) translator. While the term revenue diversification is a common term that has already been used in previous research [2], the translation of the organizational mission statements is more challenging because the translator needs to pay attention that the statements maintain their original meaning [42]. Therefore, the translation by the researcher was preferred in this article since the researcher is more experienced regarding the meaning of (mission) statements. The translation of the statement *Our club is geared towards the programs of commercial providers* was the most challenging because it could not be translated directly from the German language. The statement should express that clubs are aware of the types of programs commercial providers offer and tend to imitate or copy the programs of those providers. The challenge was to find one verb for the long explanation provided in the earlier sentence. If a word by word translation had been performed, part of the meaning would have been lost. The translation of the control variables was not considered problematic since these terms are used throughout the literature (e.g., [14,20]).

3.3. Statistical Analysis

Following Kearns [13], an organization's income portfolio is adapted *"to its changing mission and activities"*. Therefore, the use of panel data seems appropriate because they capture changes in organizational missions over time. To obtain panel data, the three datasets from each wave are matched and integrated into one vertical panel dataset. Specific attention was paid to ensuring that all variables used for the analysis were assessed similarly in all waves, and are thus comparable. A similar data cleaning procedure had been undertaken in each wave to ensure the comparability of data. During this procedure, specifically the answers to any open-ended questions were checked for plausibility and content validity. Implausible values were set to missing values. Descriptive statistics are provided to give an overview of the sample structure.

In a second step, regression analyses are performed to answer the main research question of this study (*i.e.*, how does organizational mission affect an organization's level of revenue diversification?). The regression models are of the following general form:

$$\text{Rev div} = \beta_0 + \beta_1\,\text{Elite} + \beta_2\,\text{Leisure} + \beta_3\,\text{Health} + \beta_4\,\text{Cheap} + \beta_5\,\text{Quality} + \beta_6\,\text{Commercial} + \beta_7\,\text{Tradition} + \beta_8\,\text{Conviviality} + \beta_9\,\text{Non-sport} + \beta_{10}\,\text{Youth} + \beta_{11}\,\text{LN Rev/m} + \beta_{12}\,\text{Members} + \beta_{13}\,\text{Members}^2 + \beta_{14}\,\text{Sports} + \beta_{15}\,\text{Sports}^2 + \Sigma_{i=1}^{3}\,\beta_i\,\text{Year} + \Sigma_{i=1}^{16}\,\beta_i\,\text{State} + \varepsilon \tag{3}$$

Altogether, two regression models are estimated. In model 2 the variables *Sports* and *Sports*^{2} are replaced by the type of sport variables to avoid collinearity issues. Importantly, there is no reference category for type of sport since it is not a nominal variable—the 10 dummy variables are included the analysis. When T is small relative to N (which is the case for this study where $T = 3$ and $N = 45{,}074$), time dummies should be included in the models [37]. Therefore, two year dummies (2009, 2011) are included; the reference category for *Year* is 2005. The study also controls for state influences with Bavaria being the reference category for *State*. There should be no collinearity problems in the models since all variance inflation factors (including those of *Members*^{2} and *Sports*^{2}) are below the suggested threshold of 10 [43].

The two models are Ordinary Least Squares (OLS) regressions like in the Chang and Tuckman [2] study. In addition to the OLS estimator, several specifications were tried. Yet, typical panel regression models like random-effects or fixed-effects models could not be estimated because of the unbalanced nature of the panel. There are too many clubs which have only participated in one or two of the three waves. Thus, fixed-effects models cannot be estimated without losing observations. It was also not possible to use clustered standard errors to control for unobserved club heterogeneity. Regression models with robust standard errors are estimated to control for heteroskedasticity [44].

4. Results and Discussion

4.1. Descriptive Statistics

The descriptive statistics are summarized in Table 2. They show that the average level of revenue diversification among German sports clubs is .473. This value is similar to previous research on sports clubs where revenue concentration based on the Herfindahl Index was .518 leading to a diversification value of .482 [22]. A slightly higher value of .525 was obtained in another study on sports clubs using the same measure [21]. Revenue diversification has also been examined for sports governing bodies which represent the sports organizations at the middle layers (e.g., at the community level, district level, state level, and national level) of the pyramid of the German sports system. A similar value of .46 was obtained for sports governing bodies in Germany [19]. The average revenue diversification values from this study and from previous research indicate that non-profit sports organizations in Germany have a medium level of revenue diversification.

Table 2. Descriptive statistics.

	Mean	SD
Rev div	0.473	0.241
Elite	2.80	1.27
Leisure	4.12	1.05
Health	3.07	1.29
Cheap	4.45	0.88
Quality	4.12	0.87
Commercial	2.06	1.01
Tradition	3.60	1.08
Conviviality	4.29	0.83
Non-sport	3.04	1.11
Youth	4.06	1.15
LN Rev/m	0.121	0.155
Members	373.9	1113.9
Members^2	1,380,493.6	85,754,551.0
Sports	3.32	3.95
Sports^2	26.61	73.27
Badminton	0.102	/
Football (soccer)	0.283	/
Track and field	0.136	/
Shooting	0.104	/
Swimming	0.078	/
Dancing	0.094	/
Tennis	0.137	/
Table tennis	0.165	/
Gymnastics	0.307	/
Volleyball	0.167	/

The German values are higher than the value obtained in the Chang and Tuckman [2] study for non-profits in the area of recreation, leisure, or sports in the United States. In their study, they had an average level of revenue concentration of .64 (which is equivalent to a diversification level of .36). Yet, the values are hardly comparable since there are no organizations in the United States that are equivalent to the European sport club concept.

When comparing the average level of revenue diversification of sports clubs with non-profit organizations in other industries (e.g., [2,12]), it stands out that non-profits in sport tend to have more diversified revenues. One reason could be the measurement of revenues which is relatively detailed in this study using 25 different income sources. This relatively high number of income sources could ultimately lead to higher levels of diversification since *Herf* considers the number of income sources. Yet, this explanation is speculative since details about the number of income sources assessed in the Chang and Tuckman [2] study are not provided. Another explanation could relate to the variety of income sources of sports clubs being a result of heterogeneous stakeholders. As mentioned earlier in this article, sports clubs produce a variety of *products*, not only sport programs, but also non-sport programs like social events. Moreover, they produce other *products* such as applied democracy and integration of multiple population groups that may attract funding from different stakeholders. Following Fischer *et al.* [31], an organization's revenue composition is a result of the products it provides and therefore, the variety of products may lead to a variety of income sources among sports clubs which may in turn lead to more diversified revenues.

Looking at the organizational mission of sports clubs, Table 2 shows that the provision of a cheap opportunity to play sport is most important to clubs on average ($M = 4.46$), followed by setting value on companionship and conviviality ($M = 4.29$), promoting leisure and mass sport, and caring about the quality of sport programs (both $M = 4.12$). The mean values show that both historical and more recent missions are important which may not be compatible with each other. For example, the mission of providing high quality programs is cost-intensive and may be conflicting with providing cheap programs. At the bottom of the mission ranking are promoting competitive sport at the elite level ($M = 2.80$) and being geared towards the programs of commercial providers ($M = 2.06$; Table 2).

The clubs in this sample have on average 374 members and provide 3.3 different sports. German clubs are thus larger in terms of members and sports than clubs in other countries such as the UK [45], Scotland [46], Belgium [47], and Switzerland [17]. The high standard deviation of 1113.9 indicates that German clubs are heterogeneous in size, a finding that is similar to previous research [48]. The most frequently stated sport (30.7%) is gymnastics, which includes all disciplines that are covered by the German Gymnastics Association, the national governing body for gymnastics. These are, for example, apparatus gymnastics, floor exercise, trampoline, and gym wheel. The second most frequently stated sport is football (soccer; 28.3%), followed by volleyball (16.7%), table tennis (16.5%), and tennis (13.7%; Table 2).

4.2. Regression Models

The regression models are presented in Table 3. The results in model 1 show that all organizational missions (with the exception of *Cheap*) have a significant influence on the dependent variable. While the variables *Elite, Tradition, Conviviality, Non-sport*, and *Youth* have a positive effect, *Leisure, Health, Quality*, and *Commercial* have a negative impact on *Rev div*. Thus, sports clubs pursuing those missions they historically stand for have more diversified revenues than clubs having more recent and commercial missions.

Table 3. Summary of regression models for the dependent variable *Rev div* (OLS).

	Model 1		Model 2	
	Coeff.	*t*	*Coeff.*	*t*
Constant	0.384	19.30 ***	0.384	19.76 ***
Elite	0.009	4.94 ***	0.011	5.52 ***
Leisure	−0.014	−6.93 ***	−0.013	−6.41 ***
Health	−0.012	−6.56 ***	−0.008	−4.50 ***
Cheap	0.003	1.26	0.000	0.20
Quality	−0.014	−5.03 ***	−0.008	−2.87 **
Commercial	−0.005	−2.22*	−0.007	−3.26 ***
Tradition	0.004	1.98 *	0.001	0.33
Conviviality	0.007	2.51 *	0.004	1.45
Non-sport	0.009	4.66 ***	0.009	4.75 ***
Youth	0.039	16.83 ***	0.036	15.86 ***
LN Rev/m	−0.330	−10.67 ***	−0.311	−10.41 ***
Members	0.000	3.16 **	0.000	3.73 ***
Members^2	−0.000	−2.48 *	−0.000	−2.93 **
Sports	0.011	6.64 ***	/	/
Sports^2	0.000	−4.89 ***	/	/
Badminton	/	/	−0.023	−3.58 **
Football (soccer)	/	/	0.091	18.73 ***
Track and field	/	/	0.017	2.75 **
Shooting	/	/	0.017	2.60 **
Swimming	/	/	0.009	1.26
Dancing	/	/	−0.030	−4.46 ***
Tennis	/	/	−0.004	−0.67
Table tennis	/	/	0.004	0.85
Gymnastics	/	/	0.018	3.17 **
Volleyball	/	/	−0.036	−6.28 ***
Year Dummies (Ref: 2005)	included		included	
State Dummies (Ref: Bavaria)	included		included	
R^2	0.205		0.229	
F	100.753		92.297	
p	<0.001 ***		<0.001 ***	

Note: Displayed are the unstandardized coefficients; robust standard errors reported [44]; * $p < 0.05$; ** $p < 0.01$; *** $p < 0.001$.

The question is why this is the case. Typically, non-profit organizations having financial difficulties try to increase their commercial activities in order to generate revenues from service fees *etc.* These revenues from commercial activities are used to finance core areas of the organization through cross-subsidization [49]. This phenomenon is also referred to as the *social enterprise movement* [26], a phenomenon which also applies to the non-profit sports club sector [30]. Looking at non-profit sports clubs in this research, some clubs also *imitate* commercial providers in terms of programs (specifically health sport programs) and quality. While such a commercial orientation may increase revenues in some areas (otherwise clubs would not pursue it), it also comes at a price. The results of this study show that those clubs generate a high share of revenues from one source or a few sources, but are not able to attract revenues from a variety of funders. Consequently, clubs pursing a commercial orientation increase their financial risk since organizations with a high level of revenue concentration were found to be more financially vulnerable [4,9,10] and had more volatile revenues [12,21].

The nature of the coefficients of the organizational mission variables in model 1 also indicate that some missions are complementary, while others may be conflicting. Mission statements with the same sign can be considered complementary, *i.e.*, combining those missions seems appropriate since the combination does not *irritate* possible funders. For example, promoting competitive sport at the elite level and promoting youth are complementary missions which both lead to more diversified revenues. Similarly, the missions of setting value on tradition, setting value on companionship and conviviality, and providing non-sport programs go hand in hand in terms of their effect on the clubs' revenue portfolio. As introduced earlier, all three missions belong to what clubs historically stand for. The missions of being geared towards the programs of commercial providers and caring about the quality of sport programs are also complementary, but lead to more concentrated revenues.

Some mission statements are conflicting meaning that their influence on the level of revenue diversification is not of the same nature. For instance, the mission of promoting competitive sport at the elite level seems to be conflicting with promoting leisure and mass sport respectively health sport. While the first mission attracts a variety of revenues from different sources, the latter two lead to more concentrated revenues. Thus, clubs promoting leisure and mass sport as well as health sport increase their financial risk more than do clubs promoting competitive sport. The missions of promoting health sport programs and providing cheap opportunities to play sport represent another conflicting combination of missions. While the first leads to more concentrated revenues, the latter increases revenue diversification (although the effect of *Cheap* is not significant). The nature of effects indicates that those missions are hardly combinable. The same applies to caring about the quality of sport programs and providing a cheap opportunity to play sport. Intuitively, such a combination seems inappropriate since quality programs are typically more cost intensive. Those costs have to be covered somehow. Typically clubs charge service fees for those programs to both members and non-members using the programs. Thus, they increase their commercial revenues, but at the cost of giving up a variety of revenues from other funders. Not surprisingly, the missions of setting value on tradition and being geared towards the programs of commercial providers are conflicting in terms of their influence on the composition of the income portfolio. While the first affects revenue diversification positively, the latter has a negative impact. The findings support that clubs should carefully choose their organizational missions and pay specific attention to the combination of missions.

The results of model 1 also show that the level of revenue diversification is determined by club size. Total logged revenues per member (*LN Rev/m*) have a significant negative impact on the dependent variable. This means that clubs with higher per-capita revenues have more concentrated revenues. Thus, the more financial power clubs have, the more concentrated are their revenues, *i.e.*, clubs rely on only a few, but strong income sources. The size variables *Members* and *Sports* have a significant positive effect on revenue diversification, while their squared terms ($Members^2$, $Sports^2$) negatively impact the dependent variable. The larger clubs get in terms of members and sports, the more diversified are their revenues. Yet, the negative effects of the squared terms show that this relationship is not linear, but quadratic. At some stage, increases in members and sports do not contribute to more diversified revenues anymore—there is a saturation effect.

In model 2 (Table 3), the variables *Sports* and $Sports^2$ are replaced by the 10 sport dummies. The effects of the 10 organizational mission statements under investigation and the size variables are similar supporting the robustness of findings. The coefficients on *Tradition* and *Conviviality* still have the same sign, but the effect is not significant anymore. It seems that the sport dummies have overlapped these two effects. Out of the 10 sport dummies in model 2, seven have a significant impact on the dependent variable. Yet, the nature of effects is mixed. While *Football, Track and field, Shooting*, and *Gymnastics* have a positive effect, *Badminton, Dancing*, and *Volleyball* have a negative impact.

The question is why some sports lead to more diversified revenues than other sports. One explanation could be the potential attractiveness of the sport to funders who support the sport. Evidently, clubs providing football, track and field, shooting, or gymnastics attract revenues from more sources than clubs providing badminton, dancing, or volleyball. Intuitively, the positive coefficient on *Football* is not surprising since football clubs are able to generate sponsorship income, even when their best team plays in a relatively low division. Another hint comes from the model itself. It appears that the sport dummies have overlapped the positive *Tradition* and *Conviviality* effects which are not significant anymore. Thus, there must be some sports, such as football, track and field, shooting, and gymnastics that stand for tradition and conviviality, and some sports, like badminton, dancing, and volleyball that stand less for these missions. For this reason, clubs providing programs in specific sports (*i.e.*, football, track and field, shooting, and gymnastics) may be able to generate more diversified revenues than other clubs. The advanced explanation with tradition seems plausible particularly for gymnastic clubs because they were among the first clubs that were founded in Germany (the German *Turnverein*).

5. Conclusions

This study looked at the influence of different organizational missions on the level of revenue diversification among non-profit sports clubs in Germany. Panel data from a survey of German sports clubs are used for the empirical analysis. The results show that the level of revenue diversification differs among sports clubs depending on the type of organizational mission. Clubs with mission statements such as promoting competitive sport at the elite level, setting value on tradition, companionship and conviviality, providing non-sport programs, and promoting youth have more diversified revenues than those pursuing missions like promoting leisure and health sport, caring about the quality of sports programs, and being geared towards commercial providers. Thus, clubs pursuing missions in areas clubs historically stand for are able to generate revenues from more sources than clubs with more recent commercial-like missions. Given that previous research has documented a positive relationship between an organization's level of revenue diversification and financial health (e.g., [12]), pursuing commercial-like missions increases the financial risk of clubs since they make themselves dependent on a few income sources. Consequently, clubs should be aware of the financial consequences of pursuing specific missions.

The findings also indicate that sports clubs should carefully choose their mission portfolio. The nature of effect of mission statements differs supporting the presence of complementary and conflicting missions. While the missions of tradition and non-sport programs go hand in hand in terms of their financial consequences (*i.e.*, they are considered complementary), promoting competitive sport and health sport represent conflicting missions. Thus, similar to the choice of an income portfolio as suggested by financial portfolio theory, sports clubs should carefully select their combination of organizational missions.

This research also showed that sports clubs are a useful research setting for examining the assumptions of contingency theory. In this study, the focus was on internal contingency factors respectively different types of organizational missions. Like in previous research [2,13], the level of revenue diversification was determined by organizational mission. Yet, this study compared organizations within one industry, while mission was equivalent to industry in previous research [2,13]. Thus, this study increases the application area of contingency theory.

This study has some limitations that represent directions for future research. First, this research is limited to three years of panel data. While the sample size is relatively large, the panel is too unbalanced to estimate panel regression models. This may be an avenue that could be pursued in future sports clubs projects. Second, this research is limited to the sports industry and the findings of the current study can only be generalized to the sports sector. They may be applicable to sports clubs in other Western European countries since they were found to have similar financial circumstances despite different policy systems [50]. The generalizability of findings may be extended to comprehensive community sports clubs in Japan that also offer sport and non-sport programs [51] indicating similarities to the Western European sport club system. The results may also inform sport and recreation organizations in Canada that serve a variety of population groups [52]. It would be interesting to examine whether non-profit organizations in other industries also pursue such a variety of missions and how those missions affect revenue diversification.

Acknowledgments: The authors would like to thank the Federal Institute of Sport Sciences (BISp), the German Olympic Sports Confederation (DOSB), and the 16 state sports confederations for supporting the research into sports clubs in Germany (Sport Development Report).

References

1. Chabotar, K.J. Financial ratio analysis comes to nonprofits. *J. High. Educ.* **1989**, *60*, 188–208. [CrossRef]
2. Chang, C.; Tuckman, H. Revenue diversification among non-profits. *Voluntas* **1994**, *5*, 273–290. [CrossRef]
3. Kingma, B. Portfolio theory and nonprofit financial stability. *Nonprof. Volunt. Sect. Q.* **1993**, *22*, 105–120. [CrossRef]
4. Trussel, J.; Greenlee, J. A financial rating system for nonprofit organizations. *Res. Gov. Nonprof. Account.* **2004**, *11*, 105–128.
5. Chikoto, G.L.; Neely, D.G. Building nonprofit financial capacity: The impact of revenue concentration and overhead costs. *Nonprof. Volunt. Sect. Q.* **2013**. [CrossRef]
6. Mayer, J.W.; Wang, H.; Egginton, J.F.; Flint, H.S. The impact of revenue diversification on expected revenue and volatility for nonprofit organizations. *Nonprof. Volunt. Sect. Q.* **2012**. [CrossRef]
7. Chang, C.F.; Tuckman, H.P. Financial vulnerability and attrition as measures of nonprofit performance. *Ann. Public Coop. Econ.* **1991**, *62*, 655–672. [CrossRef]
8. Greenlee, J.S.; Trussel, J.M. Predicting the financial vulnerability of charitable organizations. *Nonprofit Manag. Lead.* **2000**, *11*, 199–210. [CrossRef]
9. Trussel, J.M. Revisiting the prediction of financial vulnerability. *Nonprof. Manag. Lead.* **2002**, *13*, 17–31. [CrossRef]
10. Tuckman, H.P.; Chang, C.F. A methodology for measuring the financial vulnerability of charitable nonprofit organizations. *Nonprofit Volunt. Sect. Quart.* **1991**, *20*, 445–460. [CrossRef]
11. Keating, E.K.; Fischer, M.; Gordon, T.P.; Greenlee, J. Assessing financial vulnerability in the nonprofit sector; working paper No. 27. The Hauser Center for Nonprofit Organizations, Harvard University: Cambridge, MA, USA, 2005; Available online: http://ksgnotes1.harvard.edu/research/wpaper.nsf/rwp/RWP05-05-002/ (accessed on 14 September 2013).
12. Carroll, D.A.; Stater, K.J. Revenue diversification in nonprofit organizations: Does it lead to financial stability? *J. Publ. Adm. Res. Theor.* **2009**, *19*, 947–966. [CrossRef]
13. Kearns, K. Income Portfolios. In *Financing Nonprofits: Putting Theory into Practice*; Young, D.R., Ed.; AltaMira Press: Lanham, MD, USA, 2007; pp. 291–314.
14. Nagel, S. Goals of sports clubs. *Eur. J. Sport Soc.* **2008**, *5*, 121–141.
15. Breuer, C.; Wicker, P. *Sports Development Report 2009/2010. Analysis of the Situation of Sports Clubs in Germany*; Abbreviated Version; Sportverlag Strauß: Cologne, Germany, 2011.
16. Breuer, C.; Feiler, S. *Sports Development Report 2011/2012: Analysis of the Situation of Sports Clubs in Germany*; Abbreviated Version; Sportverlag Strauß: Cologne, Germany, 2013.
17. Lamprecht, M.; Fischer, A.; Stamm, H. *Die Schweizer Sportvereine: Strukturen, Leistungen, Herausforderungen [Sports clubs in Switzerland: Structures, performances, and challenges]*; (in German). Seismo: Zürich, Swizerland, 2012.
18. Breuer, C.; Wicker, P. Sports Clubs in Germany. In *Sport Development Report 2007/2008. Analysis of the Sports Clubs' Situation in Germany*; Abbreviated Version; Breuer, C., Ed.; Sportverlag Strauß: Cologne, Germany, 2009; pp. 5–50.
19. Wicker, P.; Breuer, C. Examining the financial condition of sport governing bodies: The effects of revenue diversification and organizational success factors. *Voluntas* **2013**, in press. [CrossRef]
20. Cordery, C.J.; Sim, D.; Baskerville, R.F. Three models, one goal: Assessing financial vulnerability in New Zealand amateur sports clubs. *Sport Manag. Rev.* **2013**, *16*, 186–199. [CrossRef]
21. Wicker, P.; Longley, N.; Breuer, C. Revenue volatility in German nonprofit sports clubs. *Nonprof. Volunt. Sect. Q.* **2013**. [CrossRef]
22. Wicker, P.; Breuer, C. Understanding the importance of organizational resources to explain organizational problems: Evidence from nonprofit sport clubs in Germany. *Voluntas* **2013**, *24*, 461–484. [CrossRef]
23. Morgan, G. *Images of organization*; Sage Publications: Thousand Oaks, CA, USA, 2007.
24. Thompson, J.D. *Organizations in action*; McGraw Hill: New York, NY, USA, 1967.
25. Woodward, J. *Management and Technology*; Her Majesty's Stationary Office: London, UK, 1958.
26. Young, D. Why Study Nonprofit Finance? In *Financing Nonprofits: Putting Theory into Practice*; Young, D.R., Ed.; AltaMira Press: Lanham, MD, USA, 2007; pp. 3–20.
27. Okten, C.; Weisbrod, B.A. Determinants of donations in private nonprofit markets. *J. Public Econ.* **2000**, *75*, 255–272. [CrossRef]

28. Steinberg, R. Does government spending crowd out donations? *Ann. Public Coop. Econ.* **1991**, *62*, 591–612. [CrossRef]
29. Enjolras, B. The commercialization of voluntary sport organizations in Norway. *Nonprof. Volunt. Sect. Q.* **2002**, *31*, 352–376. [CrossRef]
30. Wicker, P.; Breuer, C.; Hennigs, B. Understanding the interactions among revenue categories using elasticity measures—evidence from a longitudinal sample of non-profit sport clubs in Germany. *Sport Manag. Rev.* **2012**, *15*, 318–329. [CrossRef]
31. Fischer, R.L.; Wilsker, A.; Young, D.R. Exploring the revenue mix of nonprofit organizations: Does it relate to publicness? *Nonprof. Volunt. Sect. Q.* **2011**, *40*, 662–681. [CrossRef]
32. Breuer, C.; Hallmann, K.; Wicker, P. Determinants of sport participation in different sports. *Manag. Leis.* **2011**, *16*, 269–286. [CrossRef]
33. Markowitz, H. Portfolio selection. *J. Financ.* **1952**, *7*, 77–91.
34. It must be considered that people who are members of several sports clubs are counted several times in the member statistics. Thus, the overall number of club members in Germany is likely to be smaller than 27.7 million.
35. DOSB. *Bestandserhebung 2012 [Member statistics 2012].* (in German). 2013. Available online: http://www.dosb.de/fileadmin/sharepoint/Materialien%20%7B82A97D74--24-2687--47-4A29--99-9C16--46-4232BAC7DC73%7D/Bestandserhebung_2012.pdf (accessed on 10 September 2013).
36. Breuer, C.; Haase, A. Methode. In *Sportentwicklungsbericht 2005/2006. Analyse zur Situation der Sportvereine in Deutschland [Sport Development Report 2005/2006. Analysis of the sport clubs' situation in Germany]*; (in German). Breuer, C., Ed.; Sport und Buch Strauß: Cologne, Germany, 2009; pp. 641–663.
37. Wooldridge, J.M. *Introductory Econometrics: A Modern Approach*, 5th ed.; South-Western: Mason, OH, USA, 2013.
38. Heinemann, K. *Einführung in die Ökonomie des Sports: Ein Handbuch [Introduction into the economics of sports: a handbook]*; (in German). Hofmann: Schorndorf, Germany, 1995.
39. Thiel, A.; Mayer, J. Characteristics of voluntary sports clubs management: A sociological perspective. *Eur. Sport Manag. Quart.* **2009**, *9*, 81–98. [CrossRef]
40. Wicker, P.; Breuer, C.; Lamprecht, M.; Fischer, A. Does club size matter? An examination economies of scale, economies of scope, and organizational problems. *J. Sport Manag.* **2013**, in press.
41. Temple, B.; Young, A. Qualitative research and translation dilemmas. *Qual. Res.* **2004**, *4*, 161–178. [CrossRef]
42. Esposito, N. From meaning to meaning: The influence of translation techniques on Non-English focus group research. *Qual. Health Res.* **2001**, *11*, 568–579. [CrossRef]
43. Hair, J.F.; Black, W.; Babin, B. *Multivariate Data Analysis*; Pearson Prentice Hall: Upper Saddle River, NJ, USA, 2006.
44. White, H. A heteroskedasticity-consistent covariance matrix estimator and a direct test for heteroskedasticity. *Econometrica* **1980**, *48*, 817–838. [CrossRef]
45. Taylor, P.; Barrett, D.; Nichols, G. *Survey of Sports Clubs 2009*; CCPR: London, UK, 2009.
46. Allison, M. *Sports Clubs in Scotland*; Sportscotland: Edinburgh, UK, 2001.
47. Scheerder, J.; Vos, S. *Sportclubs in beeld: Basisrapportering over het Vlaamse Sportclub Panel 2009 (VSP09) [Sport clubs at a glance: Basic report of the Flemish sport club panel 2009] (in Flemish) (Sport Policy & Management Report No. 4)*; K.U. Leuven/Research unit of Social Kinesiology and Sport Management: Leuven, Belgium, 2010.
48. Emrich, E.; Pitsch, W.; Papathanassiou, V. *Die Sportvereine: Ein Versuch auf empirischer Grundlage [The sports clubs: An attempt on an empirical basis]*; (in German). Hofmann: Schorndorf, Germany, 2001.
49. James, E.; Young, D.R. Fee Income and Commercial Ventures. In *Financing Nonprofits: Putting Theory into Practice*; Young, D.R., Ed.; AltaMira Press: Lanham, MD, USA, 2007; pp. 93–119.
50. Vos, S.; Wicker, P.; Breuer, C.; Scheerder, J. Sports policy systems in regulated Rhineland welfare states: Similarities and differences in financial structures of sports clubs. *Int. J. Sport Pol. Polit.* **2013**, *5*, 55–71. [CrossRef]
51. Okayasu, I.; Kawahara, Y.; Nogawa, H. The relationship between community sport clubs and social capital in Japan: A comparative study between the comprehensive community sport clubs and the traditional community sport clubs. *Int. Rev. Sociol. Sport* **2010**, *45*, 163–186. [CrossRef]
52. Gumulka, G.; Barr, C.; Lasby, D.; Brownlee, B. *Understanding the Capacity of Sports and Recreation Organizations*; Imagine Canada: Toronto, ON, Canada, 2005.

7

Financial and Sporting Performance in French Football Ligue 1: Influence on the Players' Market

Wladimir Andreff †

Scientific Council at the Observatory of the Sports Economy, French Ministry for Sports, 75013 Paris, France; andreff@club-internet.fr

† Emeritus Professor at the University Paris 1 Panthéon Sorbonne.

Abstract: Despite the globalisation of European soccer, each professional league exhibits specificities. French Ligue 1 sometimes contends with the trading-off of financial performance against sporting performance of its teams in European soccer competitions, and its inner auditing body, the Direction Nationale du Contrôle de Gestion (DNCG), is in charge of controlling clubs' financial accounts. Moreover, Ligue 1 operates with one of the best competitive balances in the Big Five, which is detrimental to its clubs' success at the European level. However, the league and a number of clubs have not been able to curb payroll inflation and have not avoided being recurrently run in a deficit and accumulating debts, in particular payment arrears and player transfer overdue. Lax management occurs, since very few clubs have been sanctioned by a payment failure, even fewer by liquidation, and there has been no bankruptcy. The concept of a soft budget constraint theoretically encapsulates such empirical evidence. The novelty of the paper is to establish a link between the soft budget constraint and the players' labour market where it crucially triggers market disequilibria: an excess of demand for superstars' talents and an excess of supply for journeymen players are modelled. Data paucity about player individual wages hinders econometric testing of the aforementioned link and the model. However, a look at transfer fees that concentrates on a few of the top European soccer clubs provides a first insight into the arms race for talent that fuels an excess of demand for superstars and dips a number of clubs' finance into the red.

Keywords: sports finance; soft budget constraint; payment failure; disequilibrium modelling; segmented labour market; French soccer

JEL Classification: Z10; G30; J42

---

1. Introduction

The globalisation of European football (soccer) started up in the 1990s. The labour market for football players was fully liberalised as a result of the Bosman case (1995), a liberalisation that was extended to most developing countries by an international agreement called the Lomé Convention (2001). In 1999, following a failed attempt by Media Partners to launch a European football super league, a dramatic change in the format and financial endowment of UEFA (Union of European Football Associations) competitions completed the transformation of the economic model in a number of professional football clubs and leagues, in particular those benefiting from the new money godsend.

However, all national football leagues have kept some specificity when compared to the new global model. French professional football Ligue 1 is a case in point, namely as regards its trade-off between financial and sporting performance (Section 1), evolving financial structure, and management of deficits and debts (Section 2), payment arrears, and payment failures (Section 3). Such a recurrent situation can be conceptualised with the notion of a soft budget constraint that rules the economic model of clubs in an open league system; the soft budget constraint paves the way to a disequilibrium labour market for talent: players. This is in no way specific to French professional football, and can be encapsulated into more general disequilibrium modelling (Section 4) that opens up an avenue for further research and empirical testing of the relationship between lax financial disciplines on the one hand and, on the other hand, skyrocketing payroll and transfer fee inflation in the case of superstar players.

2. Trading-Off Financial versus Sporting Performance in Ligue 1

The economic model of top professional football in France is marked by various specificities. First, television (TV) rights revenues account for the lion's share of the league's finance (Andreff and Staudohar 2000) and, through a redistribution scheme, in club finance. Second, French football clubs attempt to cover their operating deficits by a players' transfer excess balance, sometimes without success, and a rather effective marketing strategy (Andreff and Scelles 2017). Some French football analysts are used to considering a third characteristic, according to which the French Ligue 1 (FL1) is the best-managed football league in Europe or, at least, they admit that it is one of the two best-managed leagues together with the German Bundesliga (GBL). Indeed, the experiences of auditing clubs' financial accounts before delivering them a license to participate in the Bundesliga, as well as the Direction Nationale du Contrôle de Gestion (DNCG)'s role of inner audit for the sake of the French football league (the Ligue du Football Professionnel, LFP), had been scrutinised at the UEFA level before launching the Financial Fair Play (FFP) rules in 2012, and might have had some influence on the design of this new financial regulation in European football.

However, the French model of management and financing for professional football is not actually admired, especially in those countries with the richest and highest-performing football leagues. It is sometimes an argument pushed forward by the LFP and other French football stakeholders that the price to pay for maintaining a sound financial management à la française is a relatively weak sporting performance of the French clubs in UEFA competitions (Champions League and Europa League) compared to other Big Five leagues. In a nutshell, the level of sporting achievement is lower in FL1 than in other major European football leagues, while the financial performance does not appear to be worse than in other Big Five soccer leagues on average (Andreff 2014a). As a consequence, in the UEFA rankings, France's rank dropped from fourth in 2008 to eighth in 2015, though it recovered to fifth in 2017.

A glimpse at Table 1 confirms the FL1's low sporting performance and shows that the argument applies also to some extent to the German Bundesliga; indeed, these two leagues exhibit small numbers of winners and quarter-finalists in European football competitions over 2000–2018. From such an observation it may be derived that there is a kind of trade-off between financial and sporting performance that is somewhat detrimental to the sporting performance. The opposite strategy is conducted by the English Premier League (EPL) and the Spanish La Liga (SLL), where sporting performance seems to be privileged, with some efficiency, over financial disciplines, while the Italian Serie A (ISA) is in dire financial straits and has not had many significant sporting successes over the past decade.

Table 1. The performance of major European leagues in UEFA competitions, 2000–2018.

Champions League	**EPL**	**FL1**	**GBL**	**ISA**	**SLL**
Number of winners from	2	0	1	3	11
Number of quarter finalists	38	13	21	21	43
Europa League	**English EPL**	**French FL1**	**German BL**	**Italian LC**	**Spanish LF**
Number of winners from	2	0	0	0	10
Number of quarter finalists	14	9	19	12	31
Total	**English EPL**	**French FL1**	**German BL**	**Italian LC**	**Spanish LF**
Number of winners from	4	0	1	3	21
Number of quarter finalists	52	22	40	33	74

EPL, English Premier League; FL1, French Ligue 1; GBL, German Bundesliga; ISA, Italian Serie A; SLL, Spanish La Liga. Source: UEFA (2000 is for the 1999–2000 season, and so on).

The FL1's most favourable sporting dimension is often presented as being also its level of competitive balance. The most widely used measure of competitive balance over one season, the Noll–Scully index, which refers to the observed win percentage distribution to the distribution that would be theoretically expected if the league were perfectly balanced, in which all teams would have exactly a 50% win percentage, is written as:

$$NS = \sigma/(0.5/\sqrt{N}) \quad (1)$$

where $\sigma = \sqrt{1/N\, \Sigma_i\, (v_i - 0.5)^2}$ is the actually observed standard deviation of a real league, $0.5/\sqrt{N}$ is the standard deviation of the theoretical perfectly balanced league, N is the number of matches played by each team in the league, and v_i is the win percentage of team i. The closer is NS to 1, the more a championship is balanced in a season; the further it is from 1, the less the league is balanced.

With such a metric at hand, FL1 appears to have been the most balanced major European league over the 1996–2012 period on average (Table 2), followed by La Liga and Bundesliga in 1996–2008, and by Bundesliga and Serie A in 2008–2012. The general trend is that all of the Big Five leagues are becoming more imbalanced, except for Serie A in 2008–2012. Since 2012, the introduction of the UEFA FFP has not stopped imbalances from increasing in the five leagues; quite the contrary. The three leagues that benefit from the most important player transfers from abroad, i.e., the EPL, SLL, and ISA, were much more imbalanced than the two other leagues on average in 2012–2018. FL1 is no longer the most balanced league among the Big Five, since the Bundesliga exhibited a slightly lower Noll–Scully index in 2012–2018. This switch not only coincides with the UEFA FFP's enforcement, but also probably more with the aggressive talent recruitment strategy of Paris Saint-Germain, which is fuelled by Qatari funding, and, to a lesser extent, Monaco's recruitment strategy, which is benefiting from Mr. Rybolovlev's finance and recently Marseille's one after its takeover by Frank McCourt, an American billionaire and former owner of a major league baseball (MLB) franchise, the Los Angeles Dodgers.

Table 2. The competitive balance in five major European football leagues.

		1997–2018			
A/Noll–Scully Index					
Season	**French L1**	**English PL**	**Italian SA**	**Spanish LF**	**German BL**
1996/1997	1.47	1.23	1.33	1.61	1.43
1997/1998	1.31	1.28	1.76	1.39	1.14
1998/1999	1.42	1.52	1.35	1.41	1.52
1999/2000	0.88	1.69	1.65	1.03	1.43
2000/2001	1.15	1.43	1.60	1.29	1.14
2001/2002	1.18	1.72	1.71	1.14	1.54
2002/2003	1.28	1.62	1.56	1.32	1.23
2003/2004	1.46	1.57	1.86	1.28	1.61
2004/2005	1.10	1.73	1.45	1.51	1.50
2005/2006	1.44	1.94	1.97	1.49	1.53
2006/2007	1.06	1.64	1.78	1.39	1.30
2007/2008	1.36	2.09	1.60	1.46	1.47
Mean 1996/2008	1.26	1.62	1.64	1.36	1.40
2008/2009	1.58	1.91	1.59	1.50	1.59
2009/2010	1.60	1.87	1.56	1.84	1.53
2010/2011	1.25	1.33	1.52	1.71	1.38
2011/2012	1.48	1.78	1.56	1.70	1.60
Mean 2008/2012	1.48	1.72	1.56	1.69	1.53
2012/2013	1.42	1.82	1.71	1.82	1.73
2013/2014	1.69	1.99	2.02	1.89	1.85
2014/2015	1.62	1.69	1.59	2.11	1.45
2015/2016	1.56	1.67	1.78	1.82	1.68
2016/2017	1.82	2.09	2.13	2.13	1.59
2017/2018	1.84	1.92	2.14	1.94	1.49
Mean 2012/2018	1.66	1.86	1.90	1.95	1.63

Table 2. *Cont.*

B/Spearman Rank Correlation between Season t and Season t − 1 Rankings					
Season t	**French L1**	**English EPL**	**Italian LC**	**Spanish LF**	**German BL**
1996/1997	0.50	0.63	n.d.	0.55	**0.34**
1997/1998	0.46	0.43	0.65	0.61	**0.39**
1998/1999	0.49	0.71	0.53	0.71	**0.37**
1999/2000	**0.24**	0.83	0.81	0.59	0.70
2000/2001	**0.00**	0.88	0.85	0.65	0.25
2001/2002	**0.08**	0.61	0.75	0.61	0.69
2002/2003	**0.28**	0.63	0.62	0.55	0.53
2003/2004	0.60	**0.43**	0.81	0.45	0.44
2004/2005	0.68	**0.45**	0.64	0.59	0.61
2005/2006	0.67	0.66	**0.43**	0.48	0.75
2006/2007	**0.48**	0.66	0.52	0.58	0.72
2007/2008	**0.20**	0.66	0.65	0.59	0.49
2008/2009	**0.23**	0.70	0.80	0.87	0.65
2009/2010	0.71	0.75	0.59	0.63	**0.34**
2010/2011	0.33	0.87	0.46	0.60	**0.09**
2011/2012	0.48	0.86	0.75	0.40	**0.09**
2012/2013	**0.40**	0.77	0.75	0.52	0.58
2013/2014	0.59	0.56	0.49	0.49	**0.34**
2014/2015	0.57	0.83	**0.47**	0.86	0.80
2015/2016	0.66	0.57	0.59	0.71	**0.43**
2016/2017	0.43	0.53	0.61	0.78	**0.21**
2017/2018	0.75	0.53	0.92	0.48	**0.40**
Mean 1996/2017	**0.45**	**0.66**	**0.65**	**0.58**	**0.51**

In bold (except the mean value): the lowest value of the rank correlation coefficient in a year; Source: calculated from the leagues' rankings.

The long-term competitive balance can be measured by a Spearman rank correlation between one year's final ranking and the previous year's ranking in the championship, which is written as:

$$r_s = 1 - \frac{6 \sum_i d_i^2}{n\,(n^2 - 1)}. \quad (2)$$

The closer is this index to zero, the less two consecutive championships in the same league exhibit a correlated ranking, and the more the competition is balanced. The other way round, $r_s = 1$ would mean that the same ranking is observed in a season t and the past season $t - 1$, i.e., the competition is absolutely imbalanced. Therefore, one can exactly predict the t ranking when one knows the $t - 1$ ranking; the championship result is entirely predictable, and there is no outcome uncertainty.

As Table 2 shows, FL1 performs even better in terms of long-term competitive balance, in particular from 1999 to 2002 and from 2006 to 2008, but also on average over all the observed period. Until 2008, on average, FL1 definitely was the least imbalanced among the Big Five leagues. In the following seasons, in particular after 2013, the competitive imbalance was fuelled by Paris Saint-Germain's and Monaco's recruitment strategy, which was geared toward attracting superstars. Since then, the German Bundesliga has become the most balanced league every year in the long run, except for 2012 and 2014. This confirms again that those clubs that belong to a more balanced league do not perform the best in European competitions, even if German clubs are ahead of French ones in this regard (Table 1).

The most imbalanced among the Big Five are, on average, the English Premier League and the Italian Serie A, followed by the Spanish La Liga (which is the only league among the five that has never been the most balanced in a year), i.e., the best three performing leagues in terms of winning European competitions. Since 2009, and despite the enforcement of the UEFA FFP after 2012, two trends have emerged: (a) the competitive balance in the Big Five leagues has deteriorated on average except for the Bundesliga; and (b) the English and Spanish leagues are becoming increasingly imbalanced, with a 2009–2017 Spearman correlation mean (0.70 and 0.61, respectively) that is higher than their overall long-term average over 1996–2017.

One can conclude that the more a league is balanced, the less strong are its top clubs compared to lower-ranked clubs, and the weaker they are in European competitions. As put by Sloane (2006, p. 221) "The most successful national teams gain entry into European club competitions and it may be necessary to be 'too strong' in terms of domestic competitions to compete successfully in Europe". It was found (Andreff and Bourg 2006) that FL1's most balanced championship eventually was a handicap for the top French clubs, whereas a worse domestic competitive balance seemed to be a good precondition or even a required launch pad in the English, Italian, and Spanish leagues for achieving the best sport performances in European competitions. The FL1 is still a typical case in point, all the more so because it is the poorest of the Big Five leagues in terms of average stadium attendance—that eventually translates also into the lowest TV rights revenues—and annual league revenue (Table 3). Even in 2017, the FL1 was still lagging behind the Italian Serie A in terms of attendance and revenue, and far behind the three other Big Five European soccer leagues. Conclusion: a more balanced domestic competition in a lower revenue league is not a springboard for its clubs toward high performance in European football contests.

Table 3. The average attendance per match and annual revenue, Big Five 1997–2017.

Big Five Leagues	Average Attendance (in Thousands)					Annual Revenue (in Million Euros)				
Season	**GBL**	**EPL**	**SLL**	**ISA**	**FL1**	**GBL**	**EPL**	**SLL**	**ISA**	**FL1**
1996–1997	30.9	28.4	24.2	29.5	14.2	444	689	524	551	293
1998–1999	30.9	30.6	22.4	30.7	19.8	577	995	612	714	393
1999–2000	28.9	30.7	23.1	29.7	21.6	681	1147	722	1059	607
2000–2001	28.4	32.8	21.4	29.1	22.6	880	1392	676	1151	644
2001–2002	31.1	34.3	23.2	25.9	21.4	1043	1682	776	1127	643
2002–2003	31.9	35.4	25.0	25.5	19.6	1108	1851	847	1162	689
2003–2004	35.0	35.0	25.2	25.7	20.1	1058	1970	953	1153	655
2004–2005	35.2	33.9	24.6	25.0	21.3	1236	1975	1029	1219	696
2005–2006	38.2	33.9	25.7	21.4	21.5	1195	1995	1158	1277	910
2006–2007	37.6	34.4	25.7	18.9	21.8	1379	2273	1326	1064	972
2007–2008	39.0	36.1	25.3	23.1	21.8	1438	2441	1438	1421	989
2008–2009	41.9	35.7	24.6	24.7	21.1	1575	2326	1501	1494	1048
2009–2010	41.8	34.2	25.3	24.1	20.1	1664	2479	1644	1532	1072
2010–2011	42.1	35.4	25.9	23.5	19.7	1746	2517	1719	1553	1040
2011–2012	44.3	34.6	26.1	22.0	18.9	1872	2917	1782	1585	1136
2012–2013	41.9	35.9	25.5	22.6	19.2	2018	2946	1868	1677	1297
2013–2014	42.6	36.7	25.3	23.0	21.1	2275	3897	1933	1699	1498
2014–2015	42.7	36.2	25.7	21.6	22.3	2392	4400	2053	1792	1418
2015–2016	42.4	36.5	27.6	21.7	20.9	2712	4865	2437	1917	1485
2016–2017	40.7	35.8	27.6	21.3	21.1	2793	5297	2854	2075	1643

EPL, English Premier League; FL1, French Ligue 1; GBL, German Bundesliga; ISA, Italian Serie A; SLL, Spanish La Liga. Source: Deloitte (1998–2018).

Finally, compared to the other Big Five leagues, although the FL1 was the most-balanced league, it did not perform exceptionally well in European competitions, and did not attract large crowds to the stadia and large revenues to the clubs' budgets. Two questions emerge in the background: in current European football, are uncertainty of outcome (Rottenberg 1956) and competitive balance (Groot 2008) still strong factors of fan attractiveness, as has been assumed for decades about team sports leagues in standard sports economics? Is the described FL1 situation an acceptable price that is worthwhile paying to impose stringent club management and potential sanctions when a club does not stick to the DNCG rules and recommendations?

3. Financial Deficits and Debts

Lower sporting performance and lower revenue unfortunately did not translate into significantly lower wages and payrolls in top French football. Defining the gross payroll or gross wage cost of a football club as the sum of salaries and associated social contributions, the ratio between these expenditures and total revenue signals the pressure of labour (players' talent) costs on a club's management. In 1997, 1998, 2007, and 2008, this ratio was the highest in the FL1 among the Big Five leagues; in the other years, the FL1 often showed the second highest payroll to revenue ratio—usually over 60%—behind the Italian Serie A, which is anything but an exemplary benchmark of good financial league management (Table 4).

Table 4. The ratio between gross payroll * (wage cost) and total revenue, Big Five 1997–2007.

Season	GBL	EPL	SLL	ISA	FL1
1996–1997	50	48	44	58	61
1997–1998	54	52	53	64	69
1998–1999	55	58	56	72	69
1999–2000	56	62	54	62	53
2000–2001	54	60	73	75	64
2001–2002	53	62	72	90	69
2002–2003	50	61	72	76	68
2003–2004	55	61	64	73	69
2004–2005	47	59	64	62	63
2005–2006	51	62	64	58	59
2006–2007	45	63	62	62	64
2007–2008	50	62	63	68	71
2008–2009	51	67	63	73	69
2009–2010	54	69	59	77	73
2010–2011	53	70	60	75	75
2011–2012	51	70	59	74	74
2012–2013	51	71	57	71	66
2013–2014	49	58	63	71	64
2014–2015	52	61	62	72	67
2015–2016	49	63	61	70	69
2016–2017	53	55	59	67	66

Source: Deloitte (1998–2018).

The common explanation for such a high weight of wages in the clubs' and league's budgets is, in an open league system, an arms race between clubs to acquire the best talents (Andreff 2012), which ends up in an excess of investment into players (Dietl et al. 2008). Clubs overbid each other for the best players and pay both high wages and skyrocketing transfer fees so that the arms race continuously fuels wage and fee inflation. More specifically, in the FL1 case, it was found that, in order to cover the cost of the arms race and the subsequent overinvestment in the payroll, the French league was able to ex post negotiate increasing TV rights revenues with TV channels in a kind of vicious circle between payroll inflation and TV rights inflation (Andreff 2007a). What is the consequence of such a strategy on the FL1's operating profit or loss?

First, it must be considered that, in the long run, the FL1 is a net exporting league as regards trade in players' talent. A priori, a trade surplus in player transfers could compensate, or more, for a league operating deficit. In some periods since 1997 (2000–2002, 2009, 2012–2013, 2016), the French league was a net importer of players for an overall amount of €502.7 million; all other years, it was a net exporter with a cumulative €692.4 million trade surplus (Table 5). At the end of the day, player transfer activity helped the FL1 come closer to balancing its current accounts thanks to a €189.7 million surplus over 20 seasons. However, this was not enough to guarantee that, every year, the league would break even or make an operating profit.

Table 5. The French league's operating profit/loss and transfer fee balance, 1997–2007.

	(Million €)	
Season	Operating	Transfer
	Profit/Loss	Fee Balance
1996–1997	−7.0	25.1
1997–1998	−46.0	51.1
1998–1999	−70.0	65.9
1999–2000	36.0	8.1
2000–2001	−41.0	−19.3
2001–2002	−98.0	−68.1
2002–2003	−61.0	−100.2
2003–2004	−102.0	17.9
2004–2005	−15.0	3.0
2005–2006	37.0	14.7
2006–2007	23.0	31.7
2007–2008	−84.0	58.8
2008–2009	−64.0	41.9
2009–2010	−102.0	−91.7
2010–2011	−97.0	73.4
2011–2012	−67.0	38.9
2012–2013	−3.0	−26.8
2013–2014	−208.1	−184.5
2014–2015	−57.3	114.7
2015–2016	42.6	147.2
2016–2017	−31.8	−12.1

Source: Direction Nationale du Contrôle de Gestion (DNCG 1998–2018).

For 17 years out of 20, the entire league was in the red, which means that the losses of those clubs in deficit were higher than the profits of those in the black despite the recurrent DNCG control and watchword for balancing expenditures with actual revenues. Recurrent deficits are quite common in open European football leagues. For instance, in 2012, right before the enforcement of the UEFA FFP, 63% of the 733 top division clubs in European football were in the red with an aggregate loss of €1675 million. French clubs, whatever their good or bad management and the role of the DNCG, were not able to escape this consequence of the arms race for talent on their current accounts.

Moreover, even though it has been assessed that the UEFA FFP regulation started to have an effect after 2012–2013, namely as presented in the UEFA benchmarking reports, this conclusion is not crystal clear in the case of the FL1. Indeed, its 2012–2013 deficits (€3 million) were the lowest since the two profitable years 2006 and 2007. As early as 2013–2014, the FL1 exhibited its highest deficit ever reached. Over the next three years, the 2015–2016 operating profit did not compensate for the operating losses that were cumulated in 2014–2015 and 2016–2017. Thus, the UEFA FFP has not yet mopped up the recurrent deficits in the top French football league.

One problem with player transfers in European football is that often they are not entirely paid right at the moment when the player moves from club A to club B. Therefore, such a delayed payment creates in club A's balance sheet a specific debt that is coined the 'player transfer overdue' or a payment arrear. The payment arrear does not appear per se in Table 6, but the player transfer overdue represented 14% of all payment arrears in 2005–2006, 10% in 2006–2007, 18% in 2007–2008, and, though they have been subject to more control since the enforcement of the UEFA FFP, these specific arrears were still up to 13% of the overall payment arrears in 2013–2014, 9% in 2014–2015, and 11% in 2015–2016 and 2016–2017.

Table 6. The Ligue 1 balance sheet: liabilities, 2000–2017 (million €).

Season	Net Equity	Shareholders Accounts	Provisions Risks	Financial Debts	Payment Arrears *	Total Liabilities	Arrears/Total Debts (%)
1999–2000	89.3	163.5	123.0	64.5	362.9	803.2	84.9
2000–2001	84.0	223.1	101.0	96.3	424.9	929.3	81.5
2001–2002	142.8	141.7	59.6	86.1	416.9	847.2	82.9
2002–2003	93.2	119.9	49.9	112.7	344.8	720.5	75.4
2003–2004	139.4	60.1	37.3	66.1	298.1	601.0	81.9
2004–2005	111.7	53.1	37.5	63.0	403.4	668.7	86.5
2005–2006	159.6	75.2	52.5	70.4	461.6	819.3	86.8
2006–2007	208.6	51.2	54.0	71.3	507.7	892.8	87.7
2007–2008	213.4	61.8	34.6	62.4	627.6	999.7	91.0
2008–2009	265.6	56.6	32.7	60.2	532.6	947.7	89.8
2009–2010	189.0	104.9	25.4	94.2	515.7	929.3	84.6
2010–2011	183.7	100.9	29.0	87.2	524.3	925.1	85.7
2011–2012	143.2	214.6	24.6	105.2	392.8	1007.8	78.9
2012–2013	167.5	83.5	32.1	105.0	597.6	1112.6	85.1
2013–2014	225.3	243.8	39.9	194.3	806.4	1509.8	80.6
2014–2015	286.4	412.3	42.5	297.4	814.5	1853.2	73.3
2015–2016	291.2	449.8	51.9	460.2	718.0	1971.1	60.9
2016–2017	346.0	573.0	62.1	386.5	735.8	2103.4	65.6

* Payment arrears, tax arrears, and social contribution arrears. Source: DNCG (1998–2018).

Notice that other payment arrears aggregate in the league's balance sheet different commercial payment arrears, tax arrears, and social contribution arrears. Until 2011, they were about half of the total liabilities of FL1 clubs and the most important share, compared to financial debts (owed to banks and other credit institutions), of the clubs' debt: usually over 80% of total debts (Table 6). Whatever the assessment about the stringency or the latitudinarianism of DNCG auditing over French professional football clubs, recurrent, and rather large, payment arrears are not a signal that clubs are as well-managed as is often advertised by some French football supporters and decision-makers. Such evidence calls for a more theoretical approach (Section 5 below) of the so-called soft budget constraint in French and European football leagues and clubs.

4. Payment Arrears and Payment Failure: A French Football Club Would Never Die!

As early as 1974, the supervision of French professional football clubs' management had been entrusted to a body that became the DNCG in 1990. Since then, the DNCG has acted as a real auditing body, capable of implementing disciplinary sanctions against poorly managed clubs. Every season, the DNCG inspects the financial accounts of all clubs, and, since 2002, clubs' financial data are openly published. The DNCG's main official tasks are to audit clubs' financial accounts, supervise their bookkeeping, detect instances of misreporting, and assess the clubs' financial situation.

When a club is continually in the red, the DNCG can use carrot-and-stick tactics to encourage changes in management practice, so that the club's accounts return to the black. The process begins with warnings, advice, and recommendations with regard to urgent policy measures to be taken by the club's management. If the financial deficit does not disappear, sanctions can be applied: the DNCG is allowed to audit the payroll in detail, to prohibit the recruitment of new players for a certain period, to impose fines, and, as a last resort, to relegate the club to a lower division. Several clubs have been relegated since 1990 under this provision. The objective is to ensure the financial viability of the French championship in the sense that any club that starts the competition must be able to complete its fixture list over the entire season. The DNCG guarantees that each club will have sufficient financial resources throughout the season. However, the FL1 has experimented with more years in the red than in the black, although the deficits and debts were smaller than in the English, Italian, and Spanish leagues. The auditing body has prevented French clubs from sinking as deeply into indebtedness as some Italian, Spanish, and English clubs.

It may seem strange that, on the one hand, French football has a strong auditing body, while on the other hand the FL1 repeatedly reports financial deficits. This paradox can be explained by a so-called soft budget constraint (Section 5 below). Questions have also been raised as to whether the DNCG is an independent auditor. All of its members are appointed from football backgrounds, such as the French Football Federation (FFF), the Ligue du Football Professionnel (LFP), and football players', coaches', and managers' unions.

As regards club debts, since 1999 the enforcement of the European competition policy has restricted the possibility of providing direct municipal subsidies to professional football clubs, in particular for bailing them out. Nevertheless, in contrast to most other industries, in European football a company (club) that is in the red will always find a way to be rescued, for instance through exceptional public subsidisation as during the Italian Calcio crisis in the mid-2000s, or with Catalan banks granting credits to FC Barcelona and Castillan banks to Real Madrid (Ascari and Gagnepain 2007), or by some sugar daddy, such as Abramovich in Chelsea, sheikh Mansur in Manchester City, Qatar Sports Investment in Paris-Saint-Germain, and Rybolovlev in Monaco. Leaving payment arrears to accumulate is another option for indirectly rescuing professional football clubs, if not bailing them out, a solution that was for many years privileged in the FL1.

Consequently, heavily indebted clubs—that would have been going bankrupt in another industry—are used to survive in French as well as European football. Storm and Nielsen (2012) underlined that a number of European professional football clubs chronically operated on the brink of insolvency for over a decade or so without going out of the business. For example, most Spanish clubs were operating at loss without ending in bankruptcies (Barajas and Rodriguez 2010). Despite recurrent losses, deficits, and debts, the clubs' survival rate is very high in English football (Kuper and Szymanski 2009). Even from 1893 to 1935, 22 English football clubs were liquidated, including well-known teams, such as Manchester United, Arsenal, and Aston Villa; most of them reappeared with the same or a different name, and only three definitely disappeared for ever, i.e., were actually liquidated.

In French football, and under French law, any debtor unable to meet its obligations is liable to enter a collective insolvency proceeding (Bayle 2009). More precisely, payment failure situations that trigger a legal response, which are defined as situations where current liabilities are greater than disposable assets,[1] have been studied for the top two professional divisions (Ligue 1 and Ligue 2) from the 1970–71 to the 2013–14 seasons, and for the third basically amateur division (National 1) from 1993–94 to 2013–14 (Scelles et al. 2018). Seventy-nine cases of payment failure were found, of which only seven were from clubs in Ligue 1 despite many FL1 clubs having been in the red over the observed period. This again calls for an analysis of lax management fuelled by the soft budget constraint of FL1 clubs that are capable of attracting bailing out funds from banks, sugar daddies, other financiers, or, more simply, football regulation authorities that allow payment arrears to grow instead of calling for payment failure, liquidation, or bankruptcy.

The biggest share of payment failures is concentrated in Ligue 2, where smaller clubs (with lower revenue) are less able to attract bail-outs or new benefactors (Table 7). In fact, among the 25 professional and amateur clubs (in the top seven divisions) that have actually been liquidated[2] between 1978 and 2017, only one really vanished: Calais, which was liquidated in 2017, has not (yet?) re-created an amateur team of adult football (Arrondel and Duhautois 2018). Arrondel and Duhautois paradoxically contend that professional football clubs are 'too small to fail' companies; even more so as regards amateur clubs.

---

1 Thus, a payment failure situation is different from what is usually defined as insolvency, i.e., when total liabilities are greater than total assets.

2 Only three of them are professional clubs that were, respectively, liquidated in 1991 (Reims, Ligue 2), 1993 (Tours, Ligue 2), and 2011 (Strasbourg, Ligue 1). In 2018–2019, they, respectively, played in Ligue 1 (Reims and Strasbourg) and Ligue 2 (Tours).

Table 7. The number of payment failures in French football, 1970–2014.

Period	Ligue 1	Ligue 2	National 1	Total
1970–1981	2	8	0	10
1981–1992	2	27	0	29
1992–2003	2	6	16	24
2003–2014	1	3	12	16
Entire period	7	44	28	79

Source: Scelles et al. (2018).

Scelles et al. (2018) were not able to find a clear-cut relationship between pre-failure average stadium attendances that were assumed to be declining—thus match day revenues were decreasing as well—and the occurrence of payment failures. Such a result is consistent with the view that failures are probably more linked to lax club management—a soft budget constraint in more theoretical terms—than to a demand shock, as was contended by Szymanski (2012) in the case of English soccer.

5. The Soft Budget Constraint's Influence on the Players' Labour Market

The standard equilibrium model of North American closed team sports leagues (Fort and Quirk 1995) has been adapted to open leagues by Késenne (1996) under the following assumptions: (a) teams are win-maximisers; (b) therefore, they recruit as much talent as possible within their budget constraints and break-even; (c) talent is measured in units such that an additional unit of talent increases the win percent by one unit; under this convention, $\frac{\partial w_i}{\partial t_i} = 1$, which allows for the substitution of the win percent w_i of team i by the quantity of recruited talent t_i in its revenue function R_i; and (d) in a now globalised labour market that is triggered by the Bosman jurisprudence that rules open leagues, the free entry of players makes irrelevant the assumption of a fixed supply of talent (Késenne 2017). Teams are wage-takers in this market so that team i:

$$Max\ t_i \tag{3}$$

$$R_i\ (m_i,\ t_i) - s.\ t_i - c_i{}^0 = 0 \tag{4}$$

where m_i stands for team i's market size, s for the market equilibrium wage, and $c_i{}^0$ for team i's fixed cost.

Obviously, constraint Equation (4) is not satisfied in the European and French football leagues, since, recurrently, a number of clubs are in the red. It must be replaced by:

$$R_i\ (m_i,\ t_i) - s.\ t_i - c_i{}^0 \leq 0. \tag{5}$$

However, such a constraint substitution has both theoretical and modelling implications. First, Equation (5) means that some teams recurrently or permanently are not able to break even; thus, they are in the red without going bankrupt or being liquidated. This was a regular characteristic of state-owned enterprises in former communist centrally planned economies. Firms or other entities that were recurrently losing money without their activity being phased out were enjoying a so-called soft budget constraint in communist shortage economies (Kornaï 1980); a similar situation may theoretically and empirically prevail in some sectors of a market economy as well (Kornaï et al. 2003). When firms are run with a soft budget constraint, they form an excess demand for inputs that is coined a "Kornaï effect"; the Kornaï effect has been tested successfully (Goldfeld and Quandt 1988, 1993). When all or most enterprises do not break even, the whole economy is all the time in a typical disequilibrium of global excess demand of inputs, which is coined a 'shortage economy'.

When applied to a football league (Andreff 2007b, 2014b), the same theoretical story says: clubs that are run with a soft budget constraint recurrently develop an excess demand for their major input, i.e., players' talent. In practical terms, they overbid for talent on the players' labour market and engage in an arms race for inputs that are in short supply, in particular superstar players. Consequently, the players' market is in a permanent state of excess demand.

If several or most football clubs are managed with a soft budget constraint, the modelling consequences are as follows. Clubs Max t_i under constraint Equation (5). Without a hard or balanced budget constraint (break-even point), there is no brake on an ever-growing demand for talent, while the number of players that are talented enough to play in professional football leagues is limited, say to T_0. The labour market for talents is in disequilibrium due to a team's aggregated excess demand in the face of a limited supply of player talents to the league T_0:

$$\sum_{i=1}^{n} t_i = T; T \geq T_0 \tag{6}$$

where the number of teams in the league is n ($i = 1, \ldots, n$).

With an excess demand for talents, the marginal revenue productivity of labour $RM_i = \frac{\partial R_i(m_i, t_i)}{\partial t_i}$ cannot equalise the marginal unit cost of labour when the last unit of the T_0 talents is recruited, and the disequilibrium in the labour market for talents implies:

$$RM_i = \frac{\partial R_i(m_i, t_i)}{\partial t_i} \leq s. \tag{7}$$

All of the labour units, up to the last one recruited, are overpaid when excess demand prevails in the players' market. Due to their aggregate overall excess demand, teams are rationed by a short supply of talents and are eager to pay a salary that is much higher than the marginal labour productivity of talent, that is, to overpay players in order to attract them in a context of relative player shortage and harsh competition across the teams on the demand side of the labour market.[3] Then, recruited players provide a lower labour productivity than the equilibrium salary they are paid for, which sounds like the exact opposite of Scully's sense of player exploitation (Scully 1974).

In European football leagues with win-maximising teams that operate under a soft budget constraint, players are paid more than they would have been at an equilibrium wage. Since all teams have embarked on an arms race to recruit players, namely, the few available superstars, they accept paying a wage that is quite higher than the marginal revenue productivity of labour[4] in order to outbid competing teams: a fact that is evidenced in all European leagues after the Bosman case. At the end of the day, teams are cursed into paying too many wages for the marginal labour productivity they obtain from players (Andreff 2014b). Paying more than the equilibrium wage and recruiting less than the quantity of talents they demand, rationed teams are involved in an endless skyrocketing race of payroll and transfer fee increases, which is observed in European football as regards superstars' recruitment.

Another implication of excess demand in the labour market for player talents is that football teams with soft budget constraints attempt to recruit too many players, although they cannot afford as many as they would have wished due to the short supply of superstars. Teams spend their money without counting and accept making losses—and sometimes they cook the books to hide this reality—due to soft budget constraints. Moreover, when operating on the demand side of an excess demand input market, teams are always scared of being short of inputs without being certain that they will find one more superstar in the market due to inequality Equation (6). Thus, in reaction,

3 When a market is in disequilibrium, one side (for instance, supply) of the market is shorter than the other one (demand); therefore, excess demand. In an excess demand market, aggregating all the microeconomic demands (of all teams) results in a bigger quantity of talents than the aggregated quantity that is supplied by suppliers (all players). Usually, those economic agents on the shorter side of a market have stronger bargaining power than those on the longer side; they successfully negotiate and bargain on their own terms—for prices and transaction conditions—and obtain a better payoff for what they deliver to the market. Those agents on the longer side of the market have to adjust, reduce their demand (when there is excess demand), and accept forced substitutions.

4 And skyrocketing transfer fees as well.

teams hoard labour (in large rosters) to circumvent the consequences of operating on a short supply input market. In European football, the very existence of a reservation and transfer system, until the Bosman ruling in 1995, enabled teams to keep their players. After the Bosman case, teams recruited on their rosters more players than they really needed.[5] Thus, there is some slack in each team; teams are overmanned. This slack is beneficial to players in terms of the relationship between wages and both working time (very few players play all 90 min of each game in a season)—that is, work intensity—and labour productivity.

If one gives up the unrealistic and simplifying assumption of a homogeneous unit of talent that is adopted in the above standard model of team sports leagues, one has to introduce a qualitative differentiation between the most talented superstars and less talented journeymen players. It was assumed above that the supply of player talents is limited. Is this as likely to be true for journeymen players as for superstars? Obviously not, since one can witness in all top European football leagues a number of journeymen players who are unemployed at the start of every season.[6] Unemployment is a crucial index of excess supply. Such an observation apparently contradicts inequality Equation (6). Therefore, for the journeymen player segment of the labour market, excess supply is to be modelled instead of excess demand on a superstar segment.

The next point to consider is whether teams' excess demand for superstars in one market segment is compensated by an excess supply of journeymen players in the other market segment. It is assumed here that there is not full compensation: excess demand for superstars exceeds excess supply of journeymen players, and inequality Equation (6) still remains relevant for the players' market overall.

Let T_s stand for the overall number of available superstars and T_a the overall number of available journeymen players. It follows that:

$$T_s + T_a = T_0. \tag{8}$$

Now, a team has to maximise an assortment of superstar and journeymen player talents in order to maximise its wins Equation (9), and its soft budget constraint is to be rewritten in such a way as to take this assortment into account Equation (10). Below, t_{si} is defined as the demand for superstars by team i, t_{ai} the demand for journeymen players by team i, s_s the market wage for superstars, and s_a the market wage for journeymen players. Thus, for team i:

$$\text{Max } (t_{si} + t_{ai}). \tag{9}$$

Under a soft budget constraint, such as:

$$R_i\ (m_i, t_{si} + t_{ai}) - s_s.\ t_{si} - s_a.\ t_{ai} \leq 0 \tag{10}$$

And

$$\sum_{i=1}^{n} (t_{si} + t_{ai}) \geq T_0 \tag{11}$$

If, as is assumed, the excess demand for superstars more than compensates for the excess supply for journeymen players, the labour market disequilibrium in the superstar segment becomes:

$$\sum_{i=1}^{n} t_{si} \geq T_s. \tag{12}$$

5 Since a soft budget constraint leads to labour hoarding within the enterprise (team)—thus hedging against the expected future labour market shortage—all European football teams are eager to recruit as many players as possible, including disposing of a great number of potential substitutes to seat on the touch-bench. This is also a means to deprive competing teams of talents.

6 Some of them, often not accounted for as unemployed, simply revise downwards the terms of their supply of talent and spill over their labour supply to a lower division team or a weaker foreign league. Supply (and demand) revision by spilling over from one market to another is a basic effect that results from rationing schemes and quantitative adjustment processes in disequilibrium models.

In the superstar segment of the market, excess demand coincides with a wage that is higher than the marginal revenue productivity of labour:

$$RM_{si} = \frac{\partial R_i(m_i, t_{si})}{\partial t_i} \le s_s. \tag{13}$$

Superstars are not directly competing against each other, with every superstar being in a monopoly position over his/her practically non-substitutable specific talent. In the journeymen player segment of the market, the excess supply of talents Equation (14) drives the market wage down until it is lower than the marginal revenue productivity of labour Equation (15) for these lower quality and higher-competing talents:

$$\sum_{i=1}^{n} t_{ai} \le T_a \tag{14}$$

$$RM_{ai} = \frac{\partial R_i(m_i, t_{ai})}{\partial t_i} \ge s_a. \tag{15}$$

Inequality Equation (15) shows that journeymen players are subject to exploitation in Scully's sense; they are paid less than their marginal productivity. They suffer from being in excess supply as well as from the monopsonistic situation of the league, which encompasses team owners that are more or less coordinated in the labour market; thus, journeymen players bear a rent that is levied by owners on their salaries. An opposite asymmetry prevails in the superstar segment, where the league's monopsony is countervailed by a strong monopoly situation of each superstar due to the uniqueness of his/her talents, skills, reputation, performances, record of achievements, and so on, and his/her absolute exclusivity over them. Thus, team owners have to overbid in terms of wage and transfer fee for recruiting Lionel Messi, Cristiano Ronaldo, and other superstars.

A disequilibrium model of a league with win-maximising teams operating under soft budget constraints in a segmented labour market describes an arms race for superstar talents that is fuelled by excess demand, superstars' skyrocketing wages that trigger teams' payroll overruns—and superstars' skyrocketing transfer fees—that deteriorate teams' financial balance, the unemployment of journeymen players that are in excess supply and are used as a safety valve or an adjustment variable by team owners, and their lower wages, which are paid at a rate below their marginal labour productivity. Consequently, both superstar wages and transfer fee inflation jeopardise clubs' financial stability, increase the risk of repeated deficits, and, in a kind of vicious circle, trigger lax management, which is possible due to a soft budget constraint that is fuelled by payment arrears (including overdue transfer fees), bail-outs, or another kind of subsidisation; in such a context, payment failure, and even more so bankruptcy, are more the exception than the rule.

The above model remains to be empirically tested. The paucity of data regarding clubs' payrolls and individual wages in all Big Five leagues cannot afford a straightforward testing of inequalities Equations (13) and (15). However, Bryson et al. (2014) have found a wage premium for migrant professional football players that partly reflects the superstar status of such players. Thus, observing the biggest transfers in European football can provide a first insight into the very existence of a superstar segment on the player transfer market with skyrocketing fees, which are probably accompanied by high wages.

Table 8 shows the aggregated value of transfer fees over 2014–2018 in the seven highest-spending clubs of the Big Five leagues. Most of them operate on the superstar segment of the market, and some of them have been implicated in transfers with fees in excess of €50 million (Neymar, M'Bappé, Pogba, etc.). Notice the large disparities across the leagues whose clubs drag the superstars: the English Premier League's top seven spending clubs have spent 70% more on transfer fees than the top seven spending clubs in La Liga and Serie A, and even 2.4 times and 3.2 times, respectively, the amount spent by the top seven clubs in the Bundesliga and Ligue 1. Expenditure disparities in the superstar transfer market, which generate financial gaps, are even deeper across the clubs than the leagues, with only FC

Barcelona, Atletico Madrid, Real Madrid, Juventus, Inter Milan, AS Roma, and Paris Saint-Germain operating at a nearly comparable level of transfer expenditures as the top seven spending English clubs.

Table 8. The transfer fees for each of the Big Five's top seven spending clubs, 2014 to 2018.

English PL	Fees	Spanish LL	Fees	German BL	Fees
Manchester City	951.4	FC Barcelona	778.0	Bayern Munich	390.9
Manchester United	777.9	Atletico Madrid	479.6	Borussia Dortmund	368.7
Chelsea	749.2	Real Madrid	457.5	Wolfsburg	308.1
Liverpool	582.9	Valencia	308.5	Bayer Leverkusen	230.5
Tottenham Hotspur	446.5	Sevilla	253.0	Leipzig	191.0
Arsenal	420.6	Villareal	183.9	Schalke 04	155.8
Everton	410.2	Real Sociedad	83.1	Borussia Monchenglad	134.2
Total	4338.6	Total	2543.6	Total	1779.1
Italian SA	**Fees**	**French L1**	**Fees**		
Juventus	592.7	Paris Saint-Germain	678.0		
Inter Milan	432.7	Olympique Marseille	191.1		
AS Roma	428.7	Olympique Lyon	139.2		
AC Milan	368.5	Lille OSC	108.4		
Napoli	344.3	Rennes	92.00		
Fiorentina	186.5	Saint-Etienne	67.2		
Sampdoria	167.8	Bordeaux	63.8		
Total	2521.2	Total	1339.6		

Source: Transfermarkt (2018).

A further empirical test would be to check whether the positive difference between the wage and the marginal revenue productivity of labour for superstar players is bigger in the English Premier League than in the Spanish La Liga and the Italian Serie A, and whether the difference in the Italian Serie A is bigger than in the German Bundesliga and the French Ligue 1. Analysing whether such differences are correlated with more or less stringent financial management in each league would open a new avenue for further research.

6. Conclusions

The empirical evidence that was gathered in this paper shows, in the case of French football Ligue 1, that financial performance has usually been presented by the league as a trade-off between sporting performance in European competitions and the league's finance, often detrimental to the first option, even though the actual financial performance of some French clubs is far from outstanding. The poor performance of French clubs in European competitions is worsened by the league having the best competitive balance among the Big Five European soccer leagues in the long run. This trend may be changing, though slightly, since the acquisition of Paris-Saint-Germain by Qatar Sports Investment, whose strategy of providing an abundance of money enables the club to recruit intensively with the explicit aim of winning a European competition. However, the UEFA's Financial Fair Play rules, in addition to the DNCG's financial audits, contain such a strategy within some definite limits. Clubs' accounting, deficits, payment arrears, player transfer overdue, and debts are now audited twice more in the French Ligue 1, once by the DNCG and then by the UEFA financial rules; however, some clubs are not yet able to curb payroll inflation and skyrocketing transfer fees. Nevertheless, clubs' budget constraints will remain soft as long as the threat of bankruptcy or definitive liquidation continues to be more a potential rather than a real practical perspective.

The novelty of the paper is to establish a link between the soft budget constraint and the players' labour market for talent where it crucially triggers an excess demand for players, in particular superstar players. Disequilibrium modelling of the labour market for talent has shown that the link with a club's finance is more complex than is usually analysed in theoretical mainstream (equilibrium) models of a team sports league. Overbidding to attract superstars, such as Neymar, Ronaldo, Messi, and M'Bappé, clubs consequently save on the other side of their payroll; that is, lower-paid journeymen players that are in excess supply on the labour market. Data paucity about players' individual wages hinders econometric testing of the aforementioned link and model so far, but a look at transfer fees, concentrating on a few of the top European soccer clubs, has provided a first insight into the arms race for talent that fuels excess demand for superstars and drives a number of clubs' finances into the red. Excess demand on the players' labour market will continue to be the price to pay for a persistent soft budget constraint with its fellow travelers payroll inflation and skyrocketing transfer fees.

There are two sides of the coin as regards policy implications. The first one is strictly financial, while the second one is about the belief that recruiting superstars is the only avenue to sporting success, recouping recruitment costs, and the subsequent club demand policy on the labour market for talent. The financial prerequisites of the UEFA's Financial Fair Play rules must be satisfied; otherwise, a club will be exposed to the threat of financial and sporting sanctions, including disqualification from participating to European competitions. With the French soccer league, a club will always be well advised to preliminary comply with the DNCG rules before passing the test of the UEFA rules, in particular if the DNCG rules will be stringently enforced. Subsequently, the number of French soccer clubs that do not break even should reduce and tend toward zero. However, this will neither make the payroll management easier nor the overbidding strategy on the labour market for talent viable.

The second set of implications is that those clubs that are overbidding for superstars must be aware that only a few of them (those winning the national championships or qualifying for European competitions) will be able to recoup their recruitment expenditures—transfer fees—and their subsequent superstar-inflated payrolls. Most of them are regularly doomed to be driven into a deficit after a poorer sporting performance than expected that does not accrue enough revenue to recoup recruitment expenditures. A number of French clubs have been cases in point, even Paris-Saint-Germain, in the past few years. Advising a less ambitious—often meaning less expensive—strategy on the labour market for talent in any case is sensible whatever the means. For example, the French rugby league has experimented with a salary cap since 2012, whereas soccer superstars playing in the French league are committed to paying an extra tax over €1 million revenue per month threshold (but, in fact, their clubs pay this tax instead). Overbidding, overbidding again, and repeatedly overbidding for superstar players is the easiest way for a club to attract the winner's curse in the labour market with its payment arrears, deficit, and debt.

References

1. Andreff, Wladimir. 2007a. Governance issues in French professional football. In *Governance and Competition in Professional Sports Leagues*. Edited by Jaume Garcia, Stefan Késenne and Placido Rodriguez. Oviedo: Ediciones de la Univeridad de Oviedo, pp. 55–86. ISBN 978-84-8317-667-2.
2. Andreff, Wladimir. 2007b. French football: A financial crisis rooted in weak governance. *Journal of Sports Economics* 8: 652–61. [CrossRef]
3. Andreff, Wladimir. 2012. *Mondialisation économique du Sport. Manuel de référence en Economie du Sport*. Bruxelles: De Boeck.
4. Andreff, Wladimir. 2014a. French professional football: how much different? In *Handbook on the Economics of Professional Football*. Edited by John Goddard and Peter Sloane. Cheltenham: Edward Elgar, pp. 298–321. ISBN 978 1 78100 316 9.
5. Andreff, Wladimir. 2014b. Building blocks for a disequilibrium model of a European team sports league. *International Journal of Sport Finance* 9: 20–38.
6. Andreff, Wladimir, and Jean-François Bourg. 2006. Broadcasting rights and competition in European football. In *The Economics of Sport and the Media*. Edited by Claude Jeanrenaud and Stefan Késenne. Cheltenham: Edward Elgar, pp. 37–70. ISBN 978 1 84542 743 6.
7. Andreff, Wladimir, and Nicolas Scelles. 2017. Economic model of a professional football club in France. In *Routledge Handbook of Football Marketing*. Edited by Nicolas Chanavat, Michel Desbordes and Nicolas Lorgnier. London:

Routledge, pp. 60–72. ISBN 978 1 13828 932 1.

8. Andreff, Wladimir, and Paul Staudohar. 2000. The evolving European model of professional sports finance. *Journal of Sports Economics* 1: 257–76. [CrossRef]
9. Arrondel, Luc, and Richard Duhautois. 2018. *L'argent du Football*. Paris: Editions du CEPREMAP.
10. Ascari, Guido, and Philippe Gagnepain. 2007. Evaluating rent dissipation in the Spanish football industry. *Journal of Sports Economics* 8: 468–90. [CrossRef]
11. Barajas, Angel, and Placido Rodriguez. 2010. Spanish football clubs' finances: Crisis and player salaries. *International Journal of Sport Finance* 5: 52–66.
12. Bayle, Marcel. 2009. Description of French collective insolvency proceedings. In *World Insolvency Systems: A Comparative Study*. Edited by Otto Eduardo Fonseca Lobo. Toronto: Carswell, pp. 224–79. ISBN 978 0 77982 228 7.
13. Bryson, Alex, Giambattista G. Rossi, and Robert Simmons. 2014. The migrant wage premium in professional football: A superstar effect. *Kyklos* 67: 12–28. [CrossRef]
14. Deloitte. 1998–2018. *Annual Review of Football Finance*. Manchester: Sports Business Group.
15. Dietl, Helmut, Egon Franck, and Markus Lang. 2008. Overinvestment in team sports leagues: A contest theory model. *Scottish Journal of Political Economy* 55: 353–68. [CrossRef]
16. DNCG. 1998–2018. *Rapport Financier du Football Professionnel Français*. Paris: Direction Nationale du Contrôle de Gestion, Ligue de Football Professionnel.
17. Fort, Rodney D., and James Quirk. 1995. Cross-subsidization, incentives, and outcomes in professional team leagues. *Journal of Economic Literature* 33: 1265–99.
18. Goldfeld, Stephen M., and Richard E. Quandt. 1988. Budget constraints, bailouts and the firm under central planning. *Journal of Comparative Economics* 12: 502–20. [CrossRef]
19. Goldfeld, Stephen M., and Richard E. Quandt. 1993. Uncertainty, bailouts, and the Kornaï effect. *Economics Letters* 41: 113–19. [CrossRef]
20. Groot, Loek. 2008. *Economics, Uncertainty and European Football: Trends in Competitive Balance*. Cheltenham: Edward Elgar, ISBN 978 1 84720 591 9.
21. Késenne, Stefan. 1996. League management in professional team sports with win maximising clubs. *European Journal of Sport Management* 2: 14–22.
22. Késenne, Stefan. 2017. The Economic Theory of Professional Team Sports: An Analytical Treatment, 2nd ed.Cheltenham: Edward Elgar, ISBN 978 1 78195 538 3.
23. Kornaï, Janos. 1980. *Economics of Shortage*. Amsterdam: North Holland, ISBN 978 0 44486 059 0.
24. Kornaï, Janos, Eric Maskin, and Gérard Roland. 2003. Understanding the soft budget constraint. *Journal of Economic Literature* 41: 1095–136. [CrossRef]
25. Kuper, Simon, and Stefan Szymanski. 2009. *Why England Loses, Why Spain, Germany, and Brazil Win, and Why the U.S., Japan, Australia and Even, Iraq Are Destined to Become the Kings of the World's Most Popular Sport*. London: Harper Collins. ISBN 978 0 00 730111 9.
26. Rottenberg, Simon. 1956. The baseball players' labor market. *Journal of Political Economy* 54: 242–58. [CrossRef]
27. Scelles, Nicolas, Stefan Szymanski, and Nadine Dermit-Richard. 2018. Insolvency in French soccer: The case of payment failure. *Journal of Sports Economics* 19: 603–24. [CrossRef]
28. Scully, Gerald. 1974. Pay and performance in Major League Baseball. *American Economic Review* 64: 915–30.
Sloane, Peter J. 2006. Rottenberg and the economics of sport after 50 years. In *Sports Economics after Fifty Years:*
29. *Essays in Honour of Simon Rottenberg*. Edited by Placido Rodriguez, Stefan Késenne and Jaume Garcia. Oviedo: Ediciones de la Universidad de Oviedo, pp. 211–26. ISBN 978 84 8317 605 4.
30. Storm, Rasmus K, and Klaus Nielsen. 2012. Soft budget constraints in professional football. *European Sport Management Quarterly* 12: 183–201. [CrossRef]
31. Szymanski, Stefan. 2012. Insolvency in English Professional Football: Irrational Exuberance or Negative Shocks? IASE & NAASE Working Paper Series. Paper No. 12-02. Available online: college.holycross.edu/RePEc/ spe/Szymanski_Insolvency.pdf (accessed on 1 November 2012).
32. Transfermarkt: Football Transfers, Rumours, Market Values, News and Statistics. Available online: https://www.transfermarkt.fr (accessed on 8 June 2018).W

8

The NBA's Maximum Player Salary and the Distribution of Player Rents

Kelly M. Hastings and Frank Stephenson *

Department of Economics, Berry College, Box 5024, Mount Berry, GA 30149, USA; kelly.hastings@vikings.berry.edu

* Author to whom correspondence should be addressed; efstephenson@berry.edu

Academic Editor: Brian Soebbing

Abstract: The NBA's 1999 Collective Bargaining Agreement (CBA) included provisions capping individual player pay in addition to team payrolls. This study examines the effect the NBA's maximum player salary on player rents by comparing player pay from the 1997–1998 and 2003–2004 seasons while controlling for player productivity and other factors related to player pay. The results indicate a large increase in the pay received by teams' second highest and, to a lesser extent, third highest paid players. We interpret this result as evidence that the adoption of the maximum player salary shifted rents from stars to complementary players. We also show that the 1999 CBA's rookie contract provisions reduced salaries of early career players.

Keywords: NBA; maximum player salary; 1999 collective bargaining agreement; rookie contract

JEL Classification: Z22

> They arrived at this specific point after salaries ballooned over the past 15 years—not for superstars, but for complementary players who don't sell tickets, can't carry a franchise, and, in a worst-case scenario, operate as a sunk cost . . .
>
> It's about Andre Iguodala, Emeka Okafor, Elton Brand, Andrei Kirilenko, Tyson Chandler, Larry Hughes, Michael Redd, Corey Maggette and Luol Deng making eight figures a year but being unable to sell tickets, create local buzz or lead a team to anything better than 35 wins.—Bill Simmons (2010) [1]

1. Introduction

A prominent feature of the 1999 Collective Bargaining Agreement (CBA) between National Basketball Association's (NBA) owners and players was the imposition of a maximum player salary. Previously teams re-signing their own free agents had been allowed to pay those any amount that was mutually agreeable to the teams and players regardless of the NBA's salary cap. Likewise, the 1999 CBA reduced the pay going to early-career players subject to so-called rookie contracts. With superstar players no longer able to negotiate unlimited salaries with their teams and rookie contract players receiving less pay, some of the revenues generated by those players were available to be captured by team owners, other players, or other providers of NBA inputs. This paper investigates the possibility that the rents were (at least partially) captured by other players, particularly those referred to by basketball commentator Bill Simmons as "complementary players" in the quotation above [1]. [1] We begin with an overview of the 1999 CBA before turning to our empirical model and results.

2. The 1999 Collective Bargaining Agreement [2]

In their 1983 CBA, the NBA and its players agreed to impose a salary cap on teams with no limit on individual player salaries. However, the cap contained many exceptions, most notably a team's right to re-sign its players even if doing so put it over the salary cap. [3] The combination of unlimited player salaries and teams' ability to re-sign their players led team wage bills to frequently exceed the cap.

Because of escalating player expenses, the NBA won a provision in the 1995 CBA allowing the league to re-open the labor agreement if total player compensation exceeded 51.8% revenue (referred to as "basketball-related income"). After player pay exceeded the 51.8% threshold in the 1997–1998 season, the league exercised its right to re-open the CBA and locked the players out effective 1 July 1998. The lockout lasted longer than six months and caused the 1998–1999 season to be shortened from 82 to 50 games before the league and its players agreed to a new CBA in early 1999.

The 1999 CBA contained many significant changes to the NBA's labor-management environment. The most important features for the purposes of this paper were the CBA's imposition of maximum individual player salaries, reduced pay for players in their first contracts after entering the league (so-called "rookie contracts"), and a new "midlevel" team salary cap exception that would be equal to 108% of the mean salary after a phase-in period during the first years of the CBA. [4] The maximum player salary depends on experience, topping out at the maximum of 35% of the team cap, 105% of the player's previous salary, or $14 million for players with at least 10 years of experience. Although existing player contracts would be "grandfathered" from the maximum player salary provisions, the new caps meant that superstar pay such as Michael Jordan's salary in excess of $30 million would be a thing of the past as these players left the league. Likewise, the new CBA's rookie contract provisions reduced the slot amounts going to rookie players, [5] stopped allowing players to negotiate lucrative contract extensions after only two seasons in the league, and extended team control from three to five years by granting teams an option year for fourth year players and the right of first refusal for fifth-year players. By limiting player pay for stars and for early-career players, the 1999 CBA redistributed rents that would have gone to these players. This paper tests the conjecture that rents were captured, at least in part, by complementary players, such as those listed in Bill Simmons quote [1].

3. Empirical Framework

To assess the possibility that imposing maximum player salaries led to rents for complementary players, this paper compares player salaries from the 1997–1998 and 2003–2004 seasons. The 1997–1998 season was the last full season played under the CBA permitting unlimited payment by teams re-signing their free agents. The 1999 CBA allowed existing contracts to be honored, hence, our choice of a comparison season that comes five years after the new collective bargaining agreement went into

1 That the NBA's 1999 collective bargaining agreement was expected to redistribute rents away from superstars toward other players was explained by Hill and Groothuis [2]. They argue that, consistent with previous research in labor economics, the redistribution of rents can be explained by a median voter model of union membership.

2 This section is based on [2–4].

3 Teams' ability to offer their free agent players unlimited pay regardless of salary cap implications was sometimes referred to as the Larry Bird Exception. However, the 1999 Collective Bargaining Agreement still contained provisions, sometimes referred to as "Bird Rules," permitting teams to pay their free agents more than the players could earn by moving to other teams but no longer allowing unlimited player pay. Because of the potential for confusion between the so-called Bird Exception and Bird Rules, this paper does not use those terms.

4 Other notable provisions included minimum player salaries that escalated with player experience, a luxury tax imposed on teams exceeding the team salary cap, and a salary recovery provision allowing team owners to "clawback" some player pay if aggregate salaries exceed certain basketball-related income thresholds.

5 Drafted player pay is determined by their "slot" or position taken in the draft.

effect. Most, though perhaps not all, 2003–2004 player salaries should have been negotiated under the new rules promulgated by the 1999 CBA. [6] The analysis focuses on the salary earned by the 250 highest paid players (and ties) in each year, yielding a pooled sample size of 507. Using the 250 highest paid players corresponds roughly to the eight highest paid players per team in each year.

The dependent variable for the analysis, RSAL, is each player's inflation-adjusted salary. The nominal salary data for both years are obtained from Rod Fort's sports data website [8]. [7] The 1997–1998 salaries are then converted to their inflation-adjusted 2003–2004 equivalents using the CPI. Descriptive statistics for RSAL and all explanatory variables are reported in Table 1.

Table 1. Descriptive Statistics.

Variables	Mean	Std. Dev.	Minimum	Maximum
Dependent				
RSAL	4,758,353	4,001,079	37,938,672	37,938,672
Independent				
WS/48	0.099	0.059	−0.186	0.316
PPG	11.11	6.02	0.80	32.10
MIN	1855	879	6	3485
EXPERIENCE	6805	3.660	0	19
HEIGHT	79.301	3.787	63	90
1st	0.114	0.319	0	1
2nd	0.114	0.319	0	1
3rd	0.114	0.319	0	1
4th	0.114	0.319	0	1
ROOKIECONTRACT	0.205	0.404	0	1
DV2003	0.504	0.500	0	1
CTR	0.223	0.417	0	1
PF	0.217	0.413	0	1
SG	0.185	0.389	0	1
PG	0.181	0.386	0	1

To control for player quality, the model includes win shares per forty-eight minutes played (WS/48) which is a measure of the number of wins contributed by a player based on his offensive and defensive performance. These data are obtained from basketball-reference.com where additional details about the calculation of win shares can be found. Since better players should have larger salaries than less talented players, WS/48 should be positively correlated with RSAL. The model also includes minutes played (MIN) during the season; ceteris paribus, players who play more should be more valuable to their teams, resulting in a positive coefficient on MIN. These data are also obtained from basketball-reference.com [9]. In an alternate specification, we use points per game (PPG) instead of win shares because Berri *et al.* [10] find scoring is more strongly related to player salaries than are other measures of performance such as rebounds, steals, and assists.

6 In examining contemporaneous salaries, our approach follows that of papers such as [5,6] in ignoring whether players had multi-year contracts and the year in which those contracts were signed. Jenkins [7] points out that using contemporaneous salary and contemporaneous productivity is potentially problematic because actual productivity may not match the anticipated productivity at the time a multi-year contract was signed. In any event, we know of no comprehensive source for data on the length or signing dates of NBA player contracts.

7 Fort indicates that the salary data were originally published by *USA Today*.

HEIGHT (in inches) is included in the model because Berri *et al.* [11] implies that taller players should receive a pay premium because of their relative scarcity. Likewise, the model includes EXPERIENCE (in years) and its square (EXPERIENCESQ) to capture the relationship between experience and pay. Including both experience and its square is common in studies of athlete pay because it is expected that players will improve as they gain experience during the early years of their careers before eventually having performance decline because of age or competitive wear-and-tear. Beyond this usual rationale for including experience and experience squared in the model, it is important to do so because, as noted above, the 1999 CBA adopted both minimum and maximum salaries that increased with experience. [8]

The variables 1st, 2nd, 3rd, and 4th are dummies for the first, second, third, and fourth highest paid players on a given team, respectively. Since the model already includes a measure of player productivity (WS/48), the coefficients on these dummy variables can be thought of as measures of rents captured by the highest paid players on each team. [9] DV2003 is a dummy variable that takes a value of one for all 2003–2004 season observations and a value of zero for all 1997–1998 season observations. A positive correlation between DV2003 and RSAL would indicate that NBA player salaries have increased over time (even after adjusting for inflation). The model also includes four interaction terms (1st * DV2003 *etc.*) between the rank dummies and the 2003–2004 dummy variable. The estimated coefficients on these interaction terms would be interpreted as the change in the rents accruing to the highest, second highest, third highest, and fourth highest paid players, respectively, in 2003–2004 relative to 1997–1998. Our conjecture, as discussed above, is that the 1999 CBA increased the rents accruing to a team's complementary players rather than the highest paid player on each team.

The model also includes a dummy variable ROOKIECONTRACT for players in their first contract after being drafted. Since the 1999 CBA reduced slot amounts for early-career players and extended the duration of team control, the model also includes an interaction term ROOKIECONTRACT * DV2003 to capture any change in rookie pay following the new CBA. Lastly, in some specifications, the model also includes dummy variables for player positions in case there are systematic pay differences across positions. [10] The included variables are dummies for centers (CTR), power forwards (PF), shooting guards (SG), and point guards (PG), with small forwards as the reference category. The player position data were also obtained from basketball-reference.com [9].

4. Estimation Results

Table 2 contains OLS regression results; the parentheses contain t-statistics derived from White-corrected standard errors. The results in columns 1 and 3 use win shares as the measure of player performance while the estimations reported in columns 2 and 4 use points per game. Columns 1 and 2 are estimated without position dummies (center, power forward, *etc.*) while columns 3 and 4 include the position dummies.

---

8 That mandating pay increase with experience could incentivize teams to substitute less experienced players for more experienced players is supported by Ducking *et al.* [12].

9 Kendall [13] takes this approach to examining player misbehavior and finds that a player's pay rank on his team has a strong relationship with the number of technical fouls received.

10 A possible reason for systematic pay differences is the finding by Berri *et al.* [11] that the scarcity of talented tall players (centers or perhaps power forwards) is a source of competitive imbalance in the NBA.

Table 2. Regression Results.

Variable	(1)	(2)	(3)	(4)
WS/48	11,448,470 * (3.53)		11,570,400 * (3.48)	
PPG		205,665 * (4.01)		214,282 * (4.20)
MIN	137.10 (1.10)	−513.83 * (−2.22)	111.92 (0.85)	−522.89 * (−2.31)
EXPERIENCE	448,316 * (4.05)	485,442 * (4.06)	452,496 * (4.09)	482,232 * (4.01)
EXPERIENCESQ	−19,835 * (−2.93)	−19,960 * (−2.65)	−19,818 * (−2.92)	−19,771 * (−2.61)
HEIGHT	45,934 * (1.69)	73,983 * (2.88)	99,898 * (2.17)	74,870 * (1.66)
1st	6,801,080 * (5.95)	5,954,402 * (5.68)	6,795,856 * (5.95)	5,849,532 * (5.54)
2nd	2,663,831 * (8.35)	2,202,278 * (5.71)	2,671,115 * (8.43)	2,169,702 * (5.51)
3rd	1,802,492 * (6.98)	1,662,274 * (6.12)	1,806,055 * (7.21)	1,674,239 * (5.96)
4th	783,174 * (3.37)	931,056 * (3.75)	766,748 * (3.26)	926,015 * (3.65)
ROOKIECONTRACT	572,744 * (1.68)	247,285 (0.74)	613,638 * (1.81)	243,901 (0.73)
DV2003	1,128,398 * (5.73)	1,363,341 * (7.14)	1,127,071 * (5.59)	1,341,995 * (6.92)
1st * DV2003	1,903,845 (1.34)	1,627,122 (1.15)	1,914,272 (1.32)	1,716,194 (1.19)
2nd * DV2003	2,772,432 * (4.40)	2,492,349 * (3.78)	2,771,133 * (4.38)	2,559,076 * (3.88)
3rd * DV2003	1,053,477 * (1.95)	909,989 * (1.69)	1,026,794 * (1.90)	843,480 (1.56)
4th * DV2003	761,291 * (1.77)	405,425 (0.95)	790,390 * (1.85)	416,236 (0.98)
ROOKIECONTRACT * DV2003	−638,726 * (−2.11)	−676,659 * (−2.25)	−690,485 * (−2.26)	−649,338 * (−2.13)
CTR			−299,661 (−0.94)	294,576 (0.92)
%hline PF			−236,912 (−0.81)	52,520 (0.19)
SG			−3131 (−0.01)	−146,332 (−0.38)
PG			398,326 (1.11)	325,586 (0.89)
Constant	−4,502,654 * (−2.05)	−6,755,296 * (−3.18)	−8,731,644 * (−2.33)	−6,985,388 * (−1.91)
R^2	0.672	0.681	0.673	0.683

Notes: Parentheses contain *t*-statistics derived from White-corrected standard errors. * Indicates $p < 0.10$.

As expected, player pay is strongly related to performance whether measured by win shares or points per game. Likewise, the positive coefficient on EXPERIENCE and negative coefficient on EXPERIENCESQ indicates that there are diminishing marginal returns to experience; the maximum effect of experience occurs at about 12 years of experience. An additional inch of height is associated with a salary increase of $45,000–$100,000.

ROOKIECONTRACT has a positive coefficient, though it is statistically significant only in the win share specifications. That early-career players prior to the 1999 CBA were reaping pay of up to $600,000 in excess of their productivity might explain why that labor agreement reduced the pay for players playing under their first contracts. The negative coefficient on ROOKIECONTRACT * DV2003 indicates that the 1999 CBA reduced highly paid early-career players' salaries by about $650,000. There is little evidence of systematic salary differences based on position as found in Berri *et al.* [10], but this result may be caused by including HEIGHT as an explanatory variable.

The coefficient on 1st indicates that the top paid players were earning large salaries even after controlling for their productivity. The coefficient on 1st is more than twice as large as the coefficient on 2nd and more than triple the coefficient on 3rd in the specification. As for the effects of the 1999 CBA, the coefficient on DV2003 indicates that salaries rose by more than $1 million on average (even after adjusting for inflation). However, the rank-year interaction terms (1st * DV2003, *etc.*), especially in the win share specifications, indicate large gains for complementary players. Comparing 2nd * DV2003 to 2nd indicates that the gains to the second ranked players more than doubled. Similar comparisons indicate that pay for third ranked and, in some specifications, fourth ranked players increased by more than 50%. The gains to star players are much smaller (about one-fourth) and are imprecisely estimated. Hence, the estimation results are consistent with the conjecture that the 1999 CBA shifted the distribution of player pay toward complementary players, particularly the second highest paid players on each team. The results, therefore, may help explain Bill Simmons's observation [1] about the high pay of complementary players, such as Elton Brand and Luol Deng.

5. Conclusions

A formal model for why the rents should accrue to complementary players instead of going to other input suppliers (e.g., coaches) or to team owners is beyond the scope of this short paper, but tournament theory [14] is the implicit basis underlying our conjecture that the individual salary cap redistributed rents to complementary players. In tournament theory, compensation rests not only on productivity but on rank order. In our context, the maximum player salary could be viewed as a mechanism that attenuates the return to being the top ranked player on a team thereby allowing for the redistribution of those rents.

In college sports, economists hypothesize that rents derived from not paying college athletes lead to increased compensation for coaches or to more lavish athletic facilities [15,16]. For example, Andrew Zimbalist (quoted in Nocera 2007 [17]) states, "Since the players don't get paid, you can't just go out and hire the Tom Bradys of college sports, so instead (colleges) throw money at everything else." Although the notion that coaches or others capture the rents generated by unpaid college athletes may be widely accepted, we know of no empirical tests of this hypothesis. The lack of empirical testing is probably the result of there not being any rule changes regarding payment of athletes or other empirical frameworks appropriate for such tests.

In the NBA, however, evidence suggests that coaches have little effect on player performance [18]. Thus it would make little sense to expect rents created from capping individual player salaries to flow to NBA coaches. Under the 1999 CBA, therefore, the most productive NBA resource for which pay could be bid up might have been role players, such as Brand and Deng, who were not earning the league's maximum allowable salary. This paper's findings that imposing maximum player salaries led to a large increase in pay for the second and third highest paid players on NBA teams is consistent with the conjecture that the 1999 CBA led to a shift in rents from star players to complementary players.

Author Contributions: Both authors contributed to the data collection, empirical analysis, and writing of this paper.

References

1. Simmons, B. A Fan-Friendly Solution to Fix the NBA. ESPN.com, 24 February 2010. Available online: http://sports.espn.go.com/espn/page2/story?page=simmons/100224 (accessed on 18 March 2015).
2. Hill, J.R.; Groothuis, P.A. The new NBA collective bargaining agreement, the median voter model, and a Robin Hood rent redistribution. *J. Sports Econ.* **2001**, *2*, 131–144. [CrossRef]
3. Beck, H. For N.B.A. owners, 1999 labor deal was win with regrets. *New York Times*, 3 July 2011; SP6.
4. Kaplan, R.A. The NBA luxury tax model: A misguided regulatory regime. *Columbia Law Rev.* **2004**, *104*, 1615–1650. [CrossRef]
5. Hakes, J.K.; Sauer, R.D. An economic evaluation of the moneyball hypothesis. *J. Econ. Perspect.* **2006**, *20*, 173–186. [CrossRef]
6. Bradbury, J.C. Does the baseball labor market properly value pitchers? *J. Sports Econ.* **2007**, *8*, 616–632. [CrossRef]
7. Jenkins, J.A. A reexamination of salary discrimination in professional basketball. *Soc. Sci. Q.* **1996**, *77*, 594–608.
8. Rod Fort's Sports Data Website. Available online: https://sites.google.com/site/rodswebpages/codes (accessed on 18 March 2015).
9. Basketball-Reference.com. Available online: http://www.basketball-reference.com/ (accessed on 18 March 2015).
10. Berri, D.J.; Brook, S.L.; Schmidt, M.B. Does one simply need to score to score? *Int. J. Sport Finance* **2007**, *2*, 190–205.
11. Berri, D.J.; Brook, S.L.; Frick, B.; Fenn, A.J.; Vicente-Mayoral, R. The short supply of tall people: Competitive imbalance and the National Basketball Association. *J. Econ. Issues* **2005**, *39*, 1029–1041.

12. Ducking, J.; Groothuis, P.A.; Hill, J.R. Minimum pay scale and career length in the NBA. *Ind. Relat. J. Econ. Soc.* **2014**, *53*, 617–635. [CrossRef]
13. Kendall, T.D. Celebrity misbehavior in the NBA. *J. Sports Econ.* **2008**, *9*, 231–249. [CrossRef]
14. Lazear, E.P.; Rosen, S. Rank-order tournaments as optimum labor contracts. *J. Polit. Econ.* **1981**, *89*, 841–864. [CrossRef]
15. Kahn, L.M. Cartel behavior and amateurism in college sports. *J. Econ. Perspect.* **2007**, *21*, 209–226. [CrossRef]
16. Farmer, A.; Pecorino, P. Is the coach paid too much? Coaching salaries and the NCAA cartel. *J. Econ. Manag. Strategy* **2010**, *19*, 841–862. [CrossRef]
17. Nocera, J.; Skybox, U. *New York Times*, 28 October 2007; 38.
18. Berri, D.J.; Leeds, M.A.; Leeds, E.M.; Mondello, M. The role of managers in team performance. *Int. J. Sport Finance* **2009**, *4*, 75–93.

9

Attendance in the Canadian Hockey League: The Impact of Winning, Fighting, Uncertainty of Outcome and Weather on Junior Hockey Attendance

Rodney Paul [1,*], Andrew Weinbach [2] and Nick Riccardi [1]

1 Department of Sport Management, Syracuse University, Syracuse, NY 13244, USA; nrricar@syr.edu
2 Department of Finance and Economics, E. Craig Wall Sr. College of Business Administration, Coastal Carolina University, Conway, SC 29528, USA; aweinbac@coastal.edu
* Correspondence: rpaul01@syr.edu

Abstract: An attendance model is specified for the Canadian Hockey League (CHL), the top level of junior hockey in Canada with some teams located in the United States. The natural log of attendance is used as the dependent variable, with explanatory variables consisting of the timing of the game, team performance characteristics, uncertainty of outcome measures, and weather-related variables. Weekends and Mondays were the most popular days for games. Winning and fighting were shown to be popular team characteristics that drive attendance. Uncertainty of outcome plays little role, if any, in fan interest at this level, while precipitation significantly reduces attendance.

Keywords: attendance; hockey; fighting; uncertainty of outcome

JEL Classification: Z20; D12

---

1. Introduction

In sports, an important component of financial performance of a franchise is attendance. Attendance as a key factor of financial performance has been shown in sports such as soccer in France (Andreff 2018; Scelles et al. 2018) and in England (Szymanski 2017). Even in leagues with major television deals, attendance has a significant positive impact on the financial value of sports firms (i.e., Scelles et al. 2013c, 2016a, 2017).

This article focuses on the determinants of attendance in the Canadian Hockey League (CHL), which is the top-tier of junior hockey in Canada (with some franchises located in the United States as well). In recent years, two variables have been explored and debated as it relates to their role in hockey attendance. These two variables are fighting and uncertainty of outcome. Fighting has seemingly always been a hot topic as it relates to its implications on the sport. Recent examples of the study of the role of fighting in hockey include Burdekin and Morton (2015) and Rockerbie (2016). One argument on the business-side of hockey, as it relates to fighting, is that fisticuffs[1] between the players is an aspect of the game that is enjoyed by fans. Various studies have linked the frequency of fighting to attendance, but these studies have mostly focused on older players as professionals. About uncertainty of outcome in relation to game competitive balance[2], measured directly from game odds in the betting market, the

---

1 Fisticuffs refers to fighting with the fists, which occurs in hockey fights when players discard their gloves and fight with each other.

2 This study focuses on uncertainty of outcome related to the individual game. Other elements of uncertainty of outcome relate to seasonal factors such as a team being in contention for the playoffs or for a qualification in continental competitions. Studies related to this aspect of outcome uncertainty include Fort and Maxcy (2003), Garcia and Rodriguez (2002), Andreff and Scelles (2015), Scelles (2017), and Scelles et al. (2013a, 2013b, 2016b).

traditional theory that fans enjoy games between evenly matched-teams (resulting in a high level of uncertainty of outcome) has been challenged by an alternative theory based upon reference-dependent preferences, loss aversion, and a desire to witness upsets (Coates et al. 2014). While these issues have been studied at the professional level for adults playing the sport, it is informative to ascertain how these factors, and others, affect fan decisions at the junior hockey level, where players are much younger than those participating in the professional ranks.

The CHL consists of three leagues, the Ontario Hockey League (OHL), the Quebec Major Junior Hockey League (QMJHL), and the Western Hockey League (WHL). Each league has their own regional restrictions in Canada and the United States from which they draw players and there are limited allowances for players from Europe and other places in the world through the CHL Import Draft. The CHL Import Draft allows CHL teams to draft players whose parents are not residents of Canada or the United States. These imports can only be obtained through the draft and each team may only have a maximum of two imports on their roster. The three leagues play their own individual seasons, followed by playoffs. In the two seasons (2016–17 and 2017–18) studied, the Ontario Hockey League had twenty teams, the Quebec Major Junior Hockey League had eighteen teams, and the Western Hockey League had twenty-two teams. In each league, sixteen teams qualified for the playoffs each season. The winner of each league's playoff, combined with the team from the host city (chosen in advance), played for the championship of the CHL in the MasterCard Memorial Cup at the conclusion of the hockey season.

To compete in the CHL, players must be at least sixteen years of age, with exemptions granted for players of "exceptional status", who may begin playing at the age of fifteen. Some players who were granted "exceptional status" include current National Hockey League (NHL) (the top hockey league in North America and the world) stars John Tavares, Aaron Ekblad, and Connor McDavid. Players in the CHL may play until they reach the age of twenty. Teams can have three "overage" (20-year old) players and up to four sixteen-year-old players (or fifteen with "exceptional status") on their rosters. The rules of the game mimic those of the NHL, including the allowance of fighting in the sport, which earns each player a five-minute penalty for this infraction. As a side note, from the perspective of the National Collegiate Athletic Association (NCAA) (a non-profit organization that regulates collegiate athletics), players who play in the CHL are considered professionals and lose their eligibility to play college hockey in the United States.

As mentioned at the start of the introduction, this study investigates the determinants of attendance for teams in the CHL. Using an ordinary least squares regression model, factors related to game timing, weather conditions, team performance, and outcome uncertainty are tested to determine their significance and influence on individual game attendance for each of the teams in the three leagues that comprise the Canadian Hockey League. Specifically, the main null hypotheses tested include the implications of the uncertainty of outcome hypothesis, the role of winning (measured as a points-per-game running average), and the role of fighting as it relates to fan interest. The uncertainty of outcome hypothesis has been shown to have mixed results across sports and it is informative to ascertain if this factor plays any role (and if so, what role) in fan decisions for junior hockey. Logically, winning would be expected to influence fan decisions and fighting has been shown in the past to be a significant factor in fan decisions. However, this league is for young players (twenty years of age and under) and is a key developmental level in the training of many young players. These factors may lead to fans having different preferences for junior hockey compared to professional hockey. Therefore, this research explicitly models and tests these null hypotheses for a sample of two complete regular seasons (playoff games were not included) in the CHL (2016–17 and 2017–18 seasons).

The paper is structured as follows. Section 2 provides a brief literature review on attendance studies as it relates to the sport of hockey. Section 3 describes the empirical model and presents the regression model results. The final section discusses the findings and concludes the paper.

2. Literature Review

Recent literature on hockey attendance has focused on the role of structural breaks in time-series data over many seasons. Using data on teams in existence for over forty seasons (29 in Major League Baseball, 13 in the National Basketball Association, and 11 in the National Hockey League), Mills and Fort (2018) extended the study of structural break points to the team level. They found mixed evidence of the role of outcome uncertainty on attendance through empirical testing of game uncertainty, playoff uncertainty, and consecutive season uncertainty. They also found considerable differences in their team-level analysis compared to league-level analysis as it relates to break points in the data.

Treber et al. (2018) examined the NHL lockouts in 1994–95, 2004–05, and 2012–13. They found evidence of a decrease in attendance following the lockout of 1994–95 and a decrease in revenue for the league following the lockouts of 2004–05 and 2012–13. Although the lockouts had a negative influence on fan demand for NHL games, the authors suggest that the cost savings generated by the lockouts could be enough to offset the reduction in attendance and revenue, leading to the lockouts still being an optimal strategy for the league.

One of the key components of the economic research surrounding game-to-game hockey attendance is an investigation into fighting. The role of fighting in the NHL has been studied previously in Jones (1984), Jones et al. (1993), Jones et al. (1996) and Paul (2003). Fighting was shown to have a positive and significant effect on attendance in each study. Although there were differences in magnitude as it relates to the country where NHL games were played, the impact of fighting on attendance was seen in both Canadian and American cities. Rockerbie (2012) found that NHL fans respond positively to greater violence, with hitting having a greater effect on attendance than fighting.

In most European leagues, fighting is met with immediate rejection from the match, not a 5-min penalty as it is in the NHL and other leagues in North America. Although fighting is not allowed in the DEL league in Germany, evidence was found that penalty minutes, a proxy for physical play, increased attendance in this league (Coates et al. 2012). Physical play (using penalty minutes as a proxy) was not found to significantly impact attendance in the SM-Liiga in Finland (Coates et al. 2012). Fighting was not shown to have a statistically significant impact on attendance in junior hockey in the Quebec Major Junior Hockey League (Paul and Weinbach 2011).

Fighting and physicality may play a role in attendance in some leagues, but studies have also investigated if fighting tends to contribute to game outcome success. Leard and Doyle (2011) studied fighting, determining winners and losers of individual fights in the NHL, and did not find a statistically significant relationship between winning fights and winning games. Coates et al. (2012) found a negative relationship between fighting and team success in the NHL.

In terms of the North American minor hockey leagues, fighting has been shown to increase attendance in both the American Hockey League (Paul et al. 2013) and in the ECHL[3] (Paul et al. 2015). At both levels, fighting had a positive and statistically significant effect on attendance. Further details, developed in research by Rockerbie (2017), describe fighting as a profit-maximizing strategy for American Hockey League teams. Fighting was also shown to have a positive and statistically significant impact on attendance in a lower-level minor league, the Southern Professional Hockey League (SPHL) (Paul 2018). Other factors that were found to influence attendance in these studies of minor league hockey were days and months of the season, city-specific demographics, and promotions.

Attendance at minor league games has also been studied in various capacities by Rascher et al. (2009) and Hong (2009). Rascher et al. (2009) discovered increases in attendance for minor league hockey during the NHL lockout of 2004–05. Hong (2009) performed research on the

---

[3] ECHL used to stand for the East Coast Hockey League. As the league expanded, the abbreviation was no longer geographically accurate and the league name was shortened to just "ECHL" in 2003. ECHL still exists as the name, but each letter no longer stands for anything.

marketing of minor league hockey games and found that teams that successfully drew fans to the arena had higher win percentages, star players, good fan relations, affordable prices, and substantial community involvement.

Another method of research surrounding interest in hockey is with surveys of fans at games. Zhang et al. (1996) found that familiarity with the sport, i.e., hockey knowledge, was important in forecasting game attendance and the level of ticket purchases for International Hockey League games. Zhang et al. (2001) studied social factors influencing minor league hockey attendance and found that health-promoting, achievement seeking, and stress and entertainment factors should be part of the marketing strategies of minor league teams. In a survey of Southern Professional Hockey League (SPHL) fans, violence was found to be important in explaining why fans attended games, although results differed by both gender and the level of ticket purchase (Andrew et al. 2009).

A separate key angle of this study relates to outcome uncertainty. A game expected to be uncertain could be an important consideration in the minds of fans when considering attending a game. The uncertainty of outcome hypothesis (UOH) was first stipulated by Rottenberg (1956) and stated that fans would prefer to attend games where teams were evenly matched. Coates and Humphreys (2012) rejected the uncertainty of outcome hypothesis for the NHL. An alternative hypothesis has been suggested in the literature by Coates et al. (2014) that incorporates reference-dependent preferences and loss aversion. Although this research focuses on individual game level uncertainty of outcome, other uncertainty of outcome measures have been developed as it relates to season-long outcome uncertainty. Studies such as Fort and Maxcy (2003), Garcia and Rodriguez (2002), Andreff and Scelles (2015), Scelles (2017), and Scelles et al. (2013a, 2013b, 2016b) refer and/or examine the role of playoff or qualification for continental competition contention for seasonal outcome uncertainty.

Although outcome uncertainty and similar related theories are important for game-to-game attendance studies, such as the research in this paper, it is closely related to season-to-season studies of attendance that include estimates for competitive balance. Competitive balance is the concept of how evenly balanced a particular sports league is within a season and across seasons. Different measures include the use of the idealized standard deviation of win percentage (i.e., Scully 1989; Quirk and Fort 1997), the CB Ratio statistic (Humphreys 2002), and the use of Herfindahl Indices related to championships (i.e., Kringstad and Gerrard 2004). Another recent innovation as it relates to studies of competitive balance is the Hope Statistic (Kaplan et al. 2011; O'Reilly et al. 2008), which uses statistics related to how far out of a playoff spot a team finished (and has finished over a span of different seasons) to estimate "hope" for a franchise to turn into competitors for a playoff spot and championships in the coming season.

Although this research focuses on the determinants of game-to-game attendance for CHL teams, attendance is only part of the equation as it relates to team profitability. Nadeau and O'Reilly (2006) gathered data from NHL franchises for three NHL seasons and estimated a model to establish the determinants of NHL franchise profitability. They found that team success is important, but influences profits indirectly through the overall level of market support in the city. Other key components to franchise profitability they identified include historical performance, team playing style, team composition, arena location, local market characteristics and competition, and television, among others.

3. Attendance Model and Results

The dependent variable in the regression model is the log of attendance. Attendance figures were taken from the box scores of CHL games on the league websites. As box score figures, they suffer from the well-known fact that teams may not report the actual turnstile attendance for each game, perhaps including sold tickets for season ticket holders who were "no-shows" or other similar activities. Given that we did not have access to the true attendance figures from the team/leagues, we used the publicly available figures on team attendance. That said, there is considerable variation from game-to-game on attendance figures for each team that logically makes sense (i.e., higher attendance on weekends, with considerable variation across those weekend games throughout the season) which is revealed in the study. Until teams are forced to report actual attendance figures, this will always be a limitation of studies by researchers using publicly available figures.

The independent variables consist of controls for the timing of the game, on-ice performance variables, home win probability measures, and weather variables. The controls for the timing of the game include a dummy for the home opener in the sample where all games are included (specifications I and II). Home openers are typically popular with fans due to the festivities surrounding the start of the hockey season. We would expect the home opener dummy to have a positive and statistically significant effect on the log of attendance. The days between games variable (days between) is the number of days between the current home game and the last home game played. This measure is capped at 14 days (any period of longer than 14 days is listed as 14 days) across the sample. Home games played in rapid succession may suffer from a decline in fan interest due to the availability of attending another game in a short timeframe. If this variable impacts the decisions of fans, it should have a positive and significant effect on the log of attendance.

Dummy variables for the days of the week (with the excluded reference category of Wednesday), the months of the season (with the excluded reference category of January), and season (with the reference category of 2016–17) are included in the model to control for the differences in likely fan interest due to the chronological timing of the game. In terms of the days of the week, weekends are likely to be much more popular for fans due to the opportunity cost of their time on weekends compared to weekdays. Therefore, Fridays, Saturdays, and Sundays are likely to have positive and significant effects on attendance in the model. In terms of the months of the season, early season games (other than opening night) typically are tougher draws for fans, while late season games represent a push toward the playoffs. Therefore, we would expect the early months to have a negative effect on attendance and the late season months to have a positive impact. The season dummy is included to account for any structural difference between the two seasons in the sample.

The on-ice team performance variables include team success and fighting as it relates to game attendance. Team success is measured by points earned (on a per-game basis) during the season, which is a function of how often teams won games. In the CHL, teams receive two points for a win, one point for an overtime or shootout loss, and zero points for a regulation loss. These points are computed as a running average of points earned per game throughout the season. Fans have been shown to prefer successful teams to poorly performing teams across many sports and we would expect this variable to have a positive and significant effect on attendance.

Fighting is a controversial topic in hockey, but previous research has shown that fighting tends to attract fans in different North American hockey leagues. If fans of junior hockey in Canada prefer to see teams that fight more often, this variable should have a positive and significant effect on attendance. If, on the other hand, these players are deemed to be too young to be involved in fighting or fans do not want to see this as part of the game, the coefficient could be negative. Both points per game (PPG) and fights per game (FPG) are quite noisy at the start of the season as they are computed as running averages. Therefore, an alternative specification was run that did not include early-season games (September and early October) with the sample starting after October 15 (around a month into the season). These are shown as specifications III and IV in the table of results.

Home team win probabilities are computed to test the uncertainty of outcome hypothesis at the game level. Rottenberg (1956) first suggested that fans prefer to see games between evenly matched teams, which would result in an uncertain outcome. Various studies have shown conflicting results as it relates to outcome uncertainty across a wide range of sports. For the NHL, Coates and Humphreys (2012) rejected outcome uncertainty as games expected to be close showed lower in-person attendance figures. Recently, Coates et al. (2014) theoretically modelled outcome uncertainty and showed the possibility of a convex relationship (as opposed to a traditional concave relationship under the traditional uncertainty of outcome hypothesis) due to factors such as reference-dependent preferences and loss aversion on the part of fans. To measure home team win probability, we used betting market data for the CHL available from www.oddsportal.com and computed the implied home team win probability from the odds adjusting for the over round. To test for outcome uncertainty, we include two specifications. The first is a linear model that only includes the home team win probability. The other model is quadratic in nature and includes the home team win probability and home team win probability squared. If fans prefer outcome uncertainty, the home team win probability term should be positive and its square should be negative. If fans have loss aversion, preferences to see upsets, or other types of reference-dependent preferences, the signs on the coefficients could be reversed. If fans do not care about any of these factors when attending games, the results will be statistically insignificant.

The odds from www.oddsportal.com used in constructing the home team win probability include wagering market data for a home win, draw, or road win. There are not draws in hockey, but the draw bet represents a wager on the game being tied at the end of regulation. An alternative measure of home win probability which sums the home win probability and one-half of the draw probability of the game was also tried using the betting data. The results did not deviate much from the main results shown in the body of the paper, nor did it impact the statistical significance of the hypothesis tests. Results of this measure are available upon request from the authors.

The last category of independent variables included in the model relates to game day weather. Weather data for each city in the CHL was gathered from www.weatherunderground.com. Temperature, measured as degrees Fahrenheit, and precipitation level (in inches) were included in the model. These weather-related variables do not relate to conditions while fans are sitting at a game, as games are held indoors in arenas in the CHL, but to the transaction costs to fans of actually getting to and from the game from home or work. Cold weather, rain, and especially ice and snow could discourage fans from leaving the house to brave the elements to attend a game in person. If cold temperatures and rain or snow keep fans from attending junior hockey games, these variables should have negative and significant effects on the log of attendance.

Summary statistics of the non-binary variables in the model are shown in Table 1 below for the full sample of games.

Table 1. Summary statistics.

Variable	Mean	Median	Standard Deviation
Attendance	3950.02	3454.00	2049.89
PPG	1.13	1.14	0.313
FPG	0.38	0.36	0.22
Temperature	29.82	32	18.06
Precipitation	0.05	0	0.15
Home Win Probability	0.45	0.44	0.13
Days Between	5.11	4	4.15

The regression model results are shown in Table 2. Models I and II use the full season, while models III and IV omit the first month of the season (data starts on October 15) to allow for the points-per-game and fights-per-game running averages to stabilize. The coefficients and their respective *t*-values are shown for each specification. Due to heteroskedasticity and autocorrelation issues with the original results, HAC (heteroskedasticity- and autocorrelation-consistent)-consistent standard errors and covariances were used and reported in Table 2 with the Newey–West estimator.

Table 2. Regression results for Canadian Hockey League (CHL) attendance model 2016–17 to 2017–18 seasons.

Dependent Variable:	**Full Season Results**		**Results without Early Season Games**	
Log(Attendance)	**(n = 4163)**		**(n = 3707)**	
Independent Variable	(I) Linear	(II) Quadratic	(III) Linear	(IV) Quadratic
Intercept	7.3140 *** (155.0427)	7.2733 *** (131.7108)	7.2563 *** (180.4596)	7.2123 *** (149.8318)
Home Open	0.2721 *** (11.1604)	0.2724 *** (11.1742)		
Days Between	0.0049 *** (6.6067)	0.0049 *** (6.6002)	0.0058 *** (5.9985)	0.0058 *** (5.9897)
Sunday	0.1262 *** (8.8796)	0.1265 *** (8.8884)	0.1351 *** (8.1790)	0.1352 *** (8.1683)
Monday	0.2024 *** (6.1314)	0.2023 *** (6.1281)	0.2185 *** (5.1458)	0.2185 *** (5.1433)
Tuesday	−0.0289 * (−1.8330)	−0.0289 * (−1.8281)	−0.0242 (−1.2239)	−0.0242 (−1.2214)
Thursday	0.0584 *** (3.4758)	0.0583 *** (3.4770)	0.0622 *** (2.7770)	0.0622 *** (2.7726)
Friday	0.1402 *** (11.9616)	0.1400 *** (11.9489)	0.1450 *** (10.1132)	0.1446 *** (10.0548)
Saturday	0.2117 *** (14.5227)	0.2117 *** (14.5172)	0.2254 *** (14.9650)	0.2253 *** (14.9418)
September	−0.1350 *** (−6.5388)	−0.1375 *** (−6.6472)		
October	−0.1211 *** (−9.0090)	−0.1235 *** (−9.1110)	−0.1097 *** (−7.5897)	−0.1120 *** (−7.7294)
November	−0.0378 *** (−3.4465)	−0.0394 *** (−3.5651)	−0.0390 *** (−3.0714)	−0.0406 *** (−3.1905)
December	−0.0049 (−0.5069)	−0.0064 (−0.6494)	−0.0056 (−0.3789)	−0.0071 (−0.4823)
February	0.0531 *** (5.2573)	0.0538 *** (5.3455)	0.0528 *** (4.6666)	0.0537 *** (4.7437)
March	0.1483 *** (12.6849)	0.1499 *** (12.7717)	0.1477 *** (10.8667)	0.1495 *** (10.8252)
17–18 Season	0.0021 (0.2726)	0.0007 (0.0954)	0.0016 (0.1887)	−0.0001 (−0.0144)
Points Per Game Average	0.0326 *** (3.1352)	0.0406 *** (3.1009)	0.0665 *** (3.9883)	0.0656 *** (3.9435)
Fights Per Game Average	0.0327 (1.4727)	0.0321 (1.4517)	0.0690 *** (2.5987)	0.0677 ** (2.5630)
Home Win Probability	−0.0087 (−0.0088)	0.1834 (1.2858)	−0.0248 (−0.8837)	0.1872 (1.4447)
Home Win Probability^2		−0.2019 (−1.3976)		−0.2225 * (−1.6840)
Precipitation (in)	−0.0445 *** (−2.2474)	−0.0451 ** (−2.2734)	−0.0580 ** (−2.3236)	−0.0589 ** (−2.3496)
Temperature (F°)	−0.0003 (−1.0381)	−0.0003 (−0.9913)	−4.30e−05 (−0.1420)	−2.60e−05 (−0.0857)
Home Team Dummies	Yes	Yes	Yes	Yes
R-squared	0.8436	0.8437	0.8341	0.8342
Adj. *R*-squared	0.8404	0.8405	0.8304	0.8305

Statistical significance is noted by *-notation. Rejection of the null hypothesis that the coefficient is equal to zero is noted at the 10% (*), 5% (**), and 1% (***) levels.

In summarizing the results, we will discuss the findings, in order, by category of independent variables. In terms of the control variables for the day, calendar date, and related variables, positive and statistically significant results at the 1% level were shown for teams' home openers in both specifications for the full sample of data (not included in the restricted sample due to the early season being eliminated from the data set). The number of days between home games (days between) was shown to have a positive and statistically significant effect on attendance across the four model specifications shown. Saturation of home games across a short period of time appear to be a detriment to attendance when it comes to the decision of fans to attend major Canadian junior hockey games.

The dummy variables for the days of the week revealed anticipated results as it related to weekend games. Friday, Saturday, and Sunday variables each had positive and statistically significant results at the 1% level, compared to the reference category day of Wednesday. Saturday had the highest attended weekend games in the CHL, followed by Friday and Sunday. A surprising result showed that the dummy variable for Monday had one of the largest effects on attendance. It was positive and statistically significant at the 1% level. Monday games are relatively infrequent in the CHL, but these games attracted larger crowds than other days. This could be due to scarcity of hockey on Mondays, due to a typically lighter NHL schedule on this day of the week as well. A word of caution on the Monday results is warranted, however, as the Monday result could be a direct effect of its relative infrequency on the schedule. The other days of the week were not shown to have statistically significant results across each of the model specifications shown.

Month of the season dummy variables (compared to January as the reference category) revealed distinct results about the importance of the timing of the season to CHL attendance. Dummy variables for September and October were shown to be negative and statistically significant at the 1% level across the relevant model specifications. November was also shown to have negative and significant effects on the log of attendance, but at the 5% or 10% level. On the other hand, games played late in the season in February and March were shown to have a positive and significant effect at the 1% level on attendance. During the late season push for the playoffs, more fans were shown to attend CHL games. A dummy for the 2017–18 Season, to distinguish the two seasons of attendance in our sample, was not shown to be statistically significant. Structurally, very little appeared to differ between the two seasons when it came to fan preferences for attending games across the three leagues of the CHL.

In terms of the on-ice performance variables of interest, the results revealed that fans preferred teams that both win and fight more often. The points-per-game variable was shown to have a positive and significant effect on the log of attendance at the 5% level and at the 1% level for all four models. Fans are sensitive to the win percentage of their local team. In addition, the other on-ice performance variable, fights-per-game, was also shown to have a positive and significant effect on attendance. As with the points-per-game variable, fights-per-game was not significant in the whole sample, but significant at the 5% and at the 1% levels in the restricted sample. Despite negative publicity about fighting in hockey, hockey fans attended games of teams that have players who fight more often. Even with the majority of the players in the CHL being under twenty years of age, with some as young as fifteen, the prospect of seeing fighting on the ice was shown to have a positive effect on attendance.

The regression results as it relates to outcome uncertainty revealed fans did not appear to care much about uncertainty of outcome. In both samples, the linear model showed that the home team win probability was statistically insignificant. In the quadratic specification, the probability of a home team win (and its square) were not found to be statistically significant in the overall sample and only the squared term was statistically significant (negative coefficient) in the sample, not including the beginning of the season. An f-test of the joint significance of both the home team win probability and its square could not reject the null that both coefficients simultaneously are equal to zero (f-stat of 1.8563 with a probability value of 0.1564). Fans of the CHL did not appear to be concerned with outcome uncertainty, nor did they appear to exhibit any of the preferences described by the model of Coates et al. (2014) as it relates to reference-dependent preferences or loss aversion.

Precipitation, measured on game day in inches, was shown to have a negative impact on the log of attendance and was statistically significant at the 5% level. Temperature was not found to be statistically significant. CHL fans preferred to attend games on days with less (or no) precipitation. Even though the games occur indoors, precipitation appears to play a role in terms of the transaction costs in attending games in the rain or snow.

4. Discussion and Conclusions

This study investigated attendance in the CHL through an ordinary least squares regression model with the natural log of the attendance as the dependent variable. The CHL is the top tier of junior hockey in Canada, with some teams located in the United States. The three leagues in the CHL, the Ontario Hockey League (OHL), the Quebec Major Junior Hockey League (QMJHL), and the Western Hockey League (WHL) are proving grounds for many players who aspire to play in the NHL and are relatively popular leagues in Canada and the United States. The independent variables in the model consisted of variables representing the timing of the game, on-ice performance measures, uncertainty of outcome, and weather-related variables.

Overall, fans of the CHL appear to mimic other fans of hockey in North America. They prefer successful home teams that tend to fight more often. This is despite the negative press associated with fighting in the game and the fact that most of these players are under twenty years of age. Fans prefer to go to games on weekends, rather than weekdays, are more interested in attending games late in the season during the playoff push, and the more recent the last home game, the lower the attendance. Uncertainty of outcome is not a major concern for the fans, while rain and snow tends to decrease attendance figures. The only real surprising finding for the league, outside of perhaps the influence of fighting, was the popularity of the few Monday games on the schedule. Due to a general scarcity of hockey in North America on Mondays, perhaps a more regular schedule of Monday contests could benefit the league if these games could replace less popular mid-week contests. In general, fans of junior hockey appear to value the same characteristics as professional hockey fans, just with younger players and smaller arenas.

Author Contributions: R.P. contributed background research, empirical modeling and analysis, and writing of the paper. A.W. contributed background research and writing of the paper. N.R. contributed data gathering and background research for the paper.

References

1. Andrew, Damon P. S., Gi-Yong Koo, Rob Hardin, and T. Christopher Greenwell. 2009. Analyzing Motives of Minor League Hockey Fans: The Introduction of Violence as a Spectator Motive. *International Journal of Sport Management and Marketing* 5: 73–89. [CrossRef]
2. Andreff, Wladamir. 2018. Financial and sporting performance in French football Ligue 1: Influence on the players' market. *International Journal of Financial Studies* 6: 91. [CrossRef]
3. Andreff, Wladimir, and Nicholas Scelles. 2015. Walter C. Neale fifty years after: Beyond competitive balance, the league standing effect tested with French football data. *Journal of Sports Economics* 16: 819–34. [CrossRef]
4. Burdekin, Richard C. K., and Matthew G. Morton. 2015. Blood money: Violence for hire in the National Hockey League. *International Journal of Sport Finance* 10: 328–56.
5. Coates, Dennis, and Brad Humphreys. 2012. Game Attendance and Competitive Balance in the National Hockey League. *Journal of Sports Economics* 13: 364–77. [CrossRef]
6. Coates, Dennis, Marcel Battre, and Christian Deutscher. 2012. Does Violence in Professional Ice Hockey Pay?
7. Cross Country Evidence from Three Leagues. *Sports Economics: Management and Policy* 4: 47–63.
8. Coates, Dennis, Brad Humphreys, and Li Zhou. 2014. Reference-Dependent Preferences, Loss Aversion, and Live Game Attendance. *Economic Inquiry* 52: 959–73. [CrossRef]
9. Fort, Rodney, and Joel Maxcy. 2003. Comment: Competitive balance in sports leagues: An introduction. *Journal of Sports Economics* 4: 154–60. [CrossRef]

10. Garcia, Jaume, and Placido Rodriguez. 2002. The determinants of football match attendance revisited: Empirical evidence from the Spanish football league. *Journal of Sports Economics* 3: 18–38. [CrossRef]
11. Hong, Jinbae. 2009. A comparison of Motivational Factors Affecting Attendance between Avid and Casual Fans at Minor League Hockey Games. *International Journal of Sport Management and Marketing* 5: 115–31. [CrossRef] Humphreys, Brad R. 2002. Alternative Measures of Competitive Balance in Sports Leagues. *Journal of Sports Economics* 3: 133–48. [CrossRef]
12. Jones, J. Colin H. 1984. Winners, Losers, and Hosers: Demand and Survival in the National Hockey League. *Atlantic Economic Journal* 12: 54–63. [CrossRef]
13. Jones, J. Colin H., Donald G. Ferguson, and Kenneth G. Stewart. 1993. Blood Sports and Cherry Pie: Some Economics of Violence in the National Hockey League. *American Journal of Economics and Sociology* 52: 87–101. [CrossRef]
14. Jones, J. Colin H., Kenneth G. Stewart, and R. Sunderman. 1996. From the Arena into the Streets: Hockey Violence, Economic Incentives, and Public Policy. *American Journal of Economics and Sociology* 55: 231–49. [CrossRef]
15. Kaplan, Alan, John Nadeau, and Norm O'Reilly. 2011. The Hope Statistic as an Alternative Measure of Competitive Balance. *International Journal of Sport Finance* 6: 170–84.
16. Kringstad, Morten, and Bill Gerrard. 2004. The Concepts of Competitive Balance and Uncertainty of Outcome. *IASE Conference Papers*, 0412. International Association of Sports Economists.
17. Leard, Benjamin, and Joanne Doyle. 2011. The Effect of Home Advantage, Momentum, and Fighting on Winning in the National Hockey League. *Journal of Sports Economics* 12: 538–60. [CrossRef]
18. Mills, Brian M., and Rodney Fort. 2018. Team-level time series analysis in MLB, the NBA, and the NHL: Attendance and outcome uncertainty. *Journal of Sports Economics* 19: 911–33. [CrossRef]
19. Nadeau, John, and Norm O'Reilly. 2006. Developing a Profitability Model for Professional Sport Leagues: The Case of the National Hockey League. *International Journal of Sport Finance* 1: 46–62.
20. O'Reilly, Norm, Alan Kaplan, Ryan Rahinel, and John Nadeau. 2008. If You Can't Win, Why Should I Buy a Ticket? Hope, Fan Welfare, and Competitive Balance. *International Journal of Sport Finance* 3: 106–18.
21. Paul, Rodney J. 2003. Variations in NHL Attendance: The Impact of Violence, Scoring, and Regional Rivalries. *American Journal of Economics and Sociology* 62: 345–64. [CrossRef]
22. Paul, Rodney J. 2018. The Role of Team Success, Fighting, and Other Factors in Southern Professional Hockey League Attendance. *Southern Business and Economic Journal*.
23. Paul, Rodney J., and Andrew P. Weinbach. 2011. Determinants of Attendance in the Quebec Major Junior Hockey League. *Atlantic Economic Journal* 39: 303–11. [CrossRef]
24. Paul, Rodney J., Andrew P. Weinbach, and Daniel Robbins. 2013. American Hockey League Attendance: A Study of Fan Preferences for Fighting, Team Performance, and Promotions. *International Journal of Sport Finance* 7: 21–38.
25. Paul, Rodney J., Andrew P. Weinbach, and Daniel Robbins. 2015. Fighting, Winning, Promotions, and Attendance in the ECHL. *Sport, Business, and Management: An International Journal* 5: 139–56. [CrossRef]
26. Quirk, James, and Rodney D. Fort. 1997. *Pay Dirt: The Business of Professional Team Sports*. Princeton: Princeton University Press.
27. Rascher, Daniel, Matthew Brown, Mark Nagel, and Chad McEvoy. 2009. Where did National Hockey League fans go during the 2004–05 Lockout? An Analysis of Economic Competition between Leagues. *International Journal of Sport Management and Marketing* 5: 183–95. [CrossRef]
28. Rockerbie, Duane W. 2012. The Demand for Violence in Hockey. In *The Oxford Handbook of Sports Economics*. Edited by L. Kahane and S. Shmanske. New York: Oxford University Press, vol. 1, pp. 159–76.
29. Rockerbie, Duane W. 2016. Fighting as a profit maximizing strategy in the National Hockey League: More evidence. *Applied Economics* 48: 292–99. [CrossRef]
30. Rockerbie, Duane W. 2017. Fighting as a Profit-Maximizing Strategy: The American Hockey League. In *Breaking the Ice*. Edited by B. Frick. New York: Springer, pp. 17–40.
31. Rottenberg, Simon. 1956. The Baseball Players' Labor Market. *Journal of Political Economy* 64: 242–58. [CrossRef] Scelles, Nicholas. 2017. Star quality and competitive balance? Television audience demand for English Premier League football reconsidered. *Applied Economics Letters* 24: 1399–402. [CrossRef]
32. Scelles, Nicholas, Christophe Durand, Lillane Bonnal, Daniel Goyeau, and Wladimir Andreff. 2013a. Competitive balance versus competitive intensity before a match: Is one of these two concepts more relevant in explaining attendance? The case of the French football Ligue 1 over the period 2008–2011. *Applied Economics* 45: 4184–92. [CrossRef]
33. Scelles, Nicholas, Christophe Durand, Lillane Bonnal, Daniel Goyeau, and Wladimr Andreff. 2013b. My team is in contention? Nice, I go to the stadium! Competitive intensity in the French football Ligue 1. *Economics Bulletin* 33: 2365–78.
34. Scelles, Nicholas, Boris Helleu, Christophe Durand, and Lillanne Bonnal. 2013c. Determinants of professional sports firm values in the United States and Europe: A comparison between sports over the period 2004–2011. *International Journal of Sport Finance* 8: 280–93.
35. Scelles, Nicholas, Boris Helleu, Christophe Durand, and Lillane Bonnal. 2016a. Professional sports firm values: Bringing new determinants to the foreground? A study of European soccer, 2005–2013. *Journal of Sports Economics* 17: 688–715. [CrossRef]
36. Scelles, Nicholas, Christophe Durand, Lillane Bonnal, Daniel Goyeau, and Wladimir Andreff. 2016b. Do All Sporting Prizes Have

a Significant Positive Impact on Attendance in a European National Football League? Competitive Intensity in the French Ligue 1. *Ekonomicheskaya Politika/Economic Policy* 11: 82–107, English Version. Available online: https://mpra.ub.uni-muenchen.de/73844/ (accessed on 1 February 2019). (In Russian)

37. Scelles, Nicholas, Boris Helleu, Christophe Durand, Lillane Bonnal, and Stephen Morrow. 2017. Explaining the number of social media fans for North American and European professional clubs with determinants of their financial value. *International Journal of Financial Studies* 5: 25. [CrossRef]
38. Scelles, Nicholas, Stefan Szymanski, and Nadine Dermit-Richard. 2018. Insolvency in French soccer: The case of payment failure. *Journal of Sports Economics* 19: 603–24. [CrossRef]
39. Scully, Gerald W. 1989. *The Business of Major League Baseball*. Chicago: University of Chicago Press.
40. Szymanski, Stefan. 2017. Entry into exit: Insolvency in English professional football. *Scottish Journal of Political Economy* 64: 419–44. [CrossRef]
41. Treber, Jaret, Lawrence Mulcahy, and Manjul B. Sharma. 2018. Empty seats or empty threats? Examining the effects of the 1994–1995 and 2004–2005 lockouts on attendance and revenue in the National Hockey League. *Journal of Sports Economics* 19: 677–95. [CrossRef]
42. Zhang, James J., Dennis W. Smith, Dale G. Pease, and Matthew. T. Mahar. 1996. Spectator Knowledge of Hockey as a Significant Predictor of Game Attendance. *Sport Marketing Quarterly* 5: 41–48.
43. Zhang, James J., Dale G. Pease, Eddie T. Lam, U. L. Pham, L. M. Bellerive, J. T. Lee, D. P. Williamson, and K. A. Wall. 2001. Sociomotivational Factors Affecting Spectator Attendance at Minor League Hockey Games. *Sport Marketing Quarterly* 10: 43–56.

10

Earnings Persistence of European Football Clubs under UEFA's FFP

Panagiotis E. Dimitropoulos * and Konstantinos Koronios

Department of Sport Organization and Management, University of Peloponnese, Sparta 23100, Greece; konskoron@hotmail.com

* Correspondence: dimitrop@uop.gr

Abstract: The goal of this study was to examine the predictability and persistence of earnings of the European football clubs and whether the new Union of European Football Associations (UEFA) Financial Fair Play (FFP) licensing regulation has forced clubs to produce a more predictable earnings stream. We utilized a sample of 109 European top-tier clubs over the period 2008–2016, summing up to 844 firm-year observations. Empirical evidence indicated that the cash flow component of earnings is more relevant in predicting one-year ahead earnings than accruals. This positive impact of cash flows for predicting earnings is more significant after the FFP regulation since earnings predictability has increased during that period. Moreover, the abovementioned finding is more significant for the smaller league clubs rather than the Big-5 league clubs. This finding is attributed to the fact that smaller league clubs are more in need of UEFA prize money relative to Big-5 league clubs, thus they are more incentivized to produce a more predictable earnings stream.

Keywords: earnings persistence; accruals; earnings predictability; European football clubs; financial fair play

JEL Classification: M41; G32; G34

1. Introduction and Theoretical Background

The professionalization of European football has been considered by academics, practitioners and regulators for several years now, especially since clubs have been transformed to well establish corporations with separate ownership and control (Andreff 2007) and some of them have been floated on the stock exchange. Clubs have managed to attract significant amounts of revenues from several sources, not only the classic match day receipts, but also from sponsoring, advertising, merchandising, broadcasting contracts, league prizes, etc. Nevertheless, the financial viability of the majority of European clubs has been deteriorating significantly for several years leading to accumulated debt and losses, despite the increased revenue streams and amounts invested on behalf of the shareholders (Dermit-Richard et al. 2017).

These are the symptoms of clubs' financial instability yet the actual culprit lies within the operational framework of the clubs and their relation to their fans and other stakeholders. Dimitropoulos et al. (2016) argud that clubs establish close relationship with their fans and in several instances fans affect managers' decisions. Fans cannot be considered as customers since they are emotionally attached to the club and even intervene to assist clubs when financial troubles knock at their door. Moreover, fans exert significant pressure on managers to enhance athletic success, and, therefore, to achieve higher on-field performance, managers are willing to pay exorbitant salaries and transfer fees for improving club's roster competitiveness. Thus, a club's relation with fans is one source of financial irrationality but is not the only one faced by clubs. Furthermore, Mourao (2012) verified the abovementioned arguments suggesting that clubs in Europe face a triangle of behavioral forces that does not let them escape from indebtedness. The triangle is formed by the pressure of athletic success, football players' increased wages (attributed to the pressure for on-field success) and media coverage which exerts the biggest portion of revenues. Football player wages have increased over the years such that more than 50–60 percent of clubs' revenues are channeled to cover player wages (Nicoliello and Zampatti 2016). This wage inflation trend is exacerbated by the majority of leagues in the European continent. According to Rohde and Breuer (2016), the pursuit of higher on-field performance is achieved via paying increasing player transfer fees and wage contracts and on-field success contributes to higher revenues from league prizes and media coverage. However, the goal of athletic success is not always achieved, bestowing on the investment in player transfers high risk, leading to a deterioration of soccer quality and an increase in costs and debt levels.

The issue of financial vulnerability and indebtedness has been on the agenda of the UEFA and the issuance of the financial fair play regulation (FFP) aimed at the rationalization of club finances. The financial principles of the FFP are not distant from the common logic of financial sustainability: (a) debt must be kept within manageable levels and paid on time; and (b) expenditure must be kept within the parameters of each club's ability to pay based on their revenues (Cordery et al. 2013). Practically, UEFA introduced profitability as the most important financial characteristic of the new licensing regulation since clubs have to prove that they will honor their debt obligations (no overdue payables). According to Nicoliello and Zampatti (2016), clubs need to reduce the cost side of the equation (player and staff wages) or increase revenues to achieve profitability. Moreover, several clubs in both major and minor European Leagues are operating in the "red" since descriptive evidence from the sample of the current study indicate that the average shareholder's funds are negative and up to −5.9 percent of total assets, over the period 2008–2016. Practically, 30 percent of our observations have negative equity and this fact corroborates previous arguments in the above-mentioned literature regarding the insolvency of European football clubs.

Within this framework, the current study aimed to examine whether the new FFP regulation has impacted on clubs' motives to produce a more reliable and sustainable earnings stream to achieve future profitability and adhere to the new regulatory guidelines. Earnings persistence is a crucial characteristic of earnings quality since, according to Kang et al. (2012), the role of financial reporting is to provide useful information to investors for assessing future cash flows and earnings, thus is a very useful attribute for financial decision making. Practically, earnings persistence expresses the extent that present profits may be maintained in the future. This was estimated by a regression of future earnings on current earnings. The closer the regression coefficient was to unity (1), the higher was the earnings persistence. Studies by Sloan (1996), Richardson et al. (2005), and Oei et al. (2008) in samples of American and Australian firms estimated an earnings persistence coefficient ranging from 0.609 in Australia to 0.84 in the US. This is interpreted as, if a company earns $1 of earnings during year t, then $0.84 would be expected to persist in the following year t + 1. In other words, earnings figures of firms with higher earnings persistence are more predictable (thus those firms are associated with lower information uncertainty) and is consequently easier for investors and regulators to assess the future status of the firm.

The consensus among financial economists is that the improved quality of financial numbers produces advantages such as better allocation of resources, higher liquidity to the markets and firms, a reduction of cost of capital, and lower information asymmetry (Kothari et al. 2009). Those findings suggest that earnings that map closely into cash are more favorable, are more persistent and can help investors to predict future earnings. Since investors are relying on earnings to make investment decisions to a higher extent than cash flows and dividends, if earnings are of poor quality, they will reduce the coordination between firms and their stakeholders, creating information risk. This in turn will lead investors to demand a higher risk premium for their investments, contributing to increased cost of capital (Francis et al. 2004). This fact was corroborated by Rascher et al. (2012) in the NFL. They argued that clubs with volatile or unpredictable revenues face increased cost of debt, since the desired uncertainty in sport outcomes has the consequence of reducing the predictability of revenue streams, leading to more information asymmetry and thus to increased cost of capital. Nevertheless, investment in new stadia reduces this information asymmetry and leads to more predictable revenue streams. Even though the study of Rascher et al. (2012) focused on revenues and not profits, it provided a useful example of the positive impact of persistence on corporate attributes such as financial risk.

Earnings persistence is even more important for economic sectors that face significant regulatory changes (Kang et al. 2012). Altamuro and Beatty (2010) and LaFond and You (2010) provided analyses of regulatory change in the US banking industry (the FDICIA internal control regulation) arguing that, when regulation is formatted out of a crisis and this regulation reforms and enhances corporate supervision and imposes stricter financial reporting requirements, it impacts on the predictability and persistence of firm earnings. Especially in the US banking industry, this new regulatory intervention increased the predictability of banks' cash flows and earnings persistence, and reduced income smoothing for those banks that were obliged to comply with the new regulation. The football industry and the new FFP regulation share several common characteristics with the abovementioned study. UEFA introduced more strict criteria (not only financial but also strong merit is attributed to financial criteria) for granting licenses to prestigious leagues (Champions League and Europa League). Moreover, the Club Financial Control Body (CFCB) was established as an additional mechanism for examining the reliability of clubs' financial reports and assessing the effectiveness of clubs achieving the FFP criteria and whether they comply with the designated regulation. Overall, the new FFP regulation increased scrutiny placed on football clubs and undoubtedly increased club monitoring and oversight.

To examine whether the FFP regulation has improved clubs' earnings persistence, we utilized a sample of 109 European top-tier clubs over the period 2008–2016. Empirical evidence indicated that the cash flow component of earnings is more relevant in predicting future earnings than accruals. This positive impact of cash flows for predicting earnings is more significant after the FFP regulation since earnings predictability increased during that period. Moreover, the abovementioned finding is more significant for the smaller league clubs rather than the Big-5 league clubs. This finding is attributed to the fact that smaller league clubs are more in need of UEFA prize money relative to Big-5 league clubs (Menary 2016) because UEFA prize money constitutes a larger part of their annual revenues. Thus, they are more incentivized to produce a more predictable earnings stream.

This study adds to a growing literature on earnings persistence within an industry facing severe financial problems. A recent study by Dermit-Richard et al. (2017) showed that, in France, clubs' budget is targeting towards funding losses (by 74 percent) instead of investments. This fact accords with the issue that shareholders' contributions do not suffice to cover losses (for the majority of top-tier clubs), leading clubs to disinvest or downsize business activities, creating a volatile economic environment. FFP regulation aims to mitigate these problems by forcing clubs to live on their own resources and sustain their viability. Thus, this study provided ample evidence of the impact of the new regulation on the tendency of football clubs to focus on a medium to long term policy towards profitability, thus enhancing their financial reporting quality as a way to sustain their participation in UEFA's lucrative championships.

The rest of the paper is organized as follows: Section 2 is devoted to the literature review and the formation of the research hypotheses. Section 3 presents the data selection procedure and the research design. Section 4 discusses the empirical results of the study and related sensitivity analysis. Section 5 concludes the paper, offering useful policy implications for clubs and regulators and potential avenues for future research.

2. Related Literature and Research Hypotheses

As previously mentioned, a crucial role of the financial accounting reporting system is to serve as a mechanism to signal firms' future performance to the public and also to discipline managerial behavior (Kang et al. 2012). Nevertheless, financial accounting follows the accrual principle for recognizing revenues and expenses[1], a fact that helps portray more effectively firms' actual financial condition, yet it has the disadvantage of greater subjectivity on the estimation of several accounting figures (provisions, depreciation, inventories, etc.). As Richardson et al. (2005) mentioned, if accrual accounting were not in effect, the only asset or liability that would appear on a firm's balance sheet would be the cash asset amount. Put differently, all other assets and liabilities on the balance sheet are the outcome of the accrual accounting process (Oei et al. 2008).

Under this framework, previous studies on the issue of accruals persistence indicated that accruals are less persistent than cash flows due to the increased subjectivity of accruals relative to cash flows and also because accruals can easily be manipulated with less material impact on the firms' fundamentals, relative to cash flows (Sloan 1996). The reduced persistence of accruals is also attributed to their lower reliability because accruals require judgments for the estimation of the relative figures, and even in the case of no manipulation of those figures, they definitely contain errors that will be corrected in accruals recorded in future periods. Earnings persistence (as a measure of earnings informativeness) does not suffer from the potential measurement errors inherent in accrual models and is characterized as an important feature of financial reporting integrity and firm value (Kormendi and Lipe 1987; Kang et al. 2012).

These types of errors could be the estimating outcome of future economic effects of current or past transactions which are measured with error (Oei et al. 2008). For example, the provision or allowance for doubtful debt will never be completely accurate. In addition, in the European football industry, UEFA's (2015) FFP regulation declares that, for the estimation of the clubs' relevant revenues (for those clubs which follow the capitalization and amortization method), the profit from disposal of player registration rights is calculated by deducting the net book value at the time of the transfer from the net disposal proceeds received or receivable. This means that clubs generate large accrual accounting from player registration rights which are not always received in total due to other arrangements[2], creating errors in the estimation.

Furthermore, Dermit-Richard et al. (2017) argued that several determinant figures of the relevant revenues and expenses which come from related parties must be adjusted to reflect the fair value of such transactions. For instance, sponsorship deals must be evaluated at fair values yet those might not be comparable to other respective deals for other clubs, so they are inherent to enhanced subjectivity by managers. The main issue here is the input information that clubs use to estimate those fair values. If the information come from verifiable sources, then subjectivity is diminished (not eliminated), but, if information is derived from non-verifiable sources and includes more judgment on behalf of the club management, then accruals are definitely estimated with error. Consequently, following the previous discussion, due to the measurement error in accruals, the persistence coefficient on the accrual component should be smaller than the persistent coefficient on the cash flow component of earnings due to less or no error in tis measurement. Thus, the first research hypothesis is stated as follows:

H1: *Accruals will be less persistent than cash flows.*

Previous studies on the impact of regulatory intervention on earnings persistence provided ample but contradictory evidence. For instance, Kang et al. (2012) indicated that the abolition of the 20-F reconciliation requirement for firms cross-listing in the US was not improved for all firms but only for those that were originating from weak investor protection countries. This fact was explained as 20-F reconciliation playing a signaling role for the financial statement users and its elimination led to an increase in firms' incentives to improve the reporting quality voluntarily. Additionally, LaFond and You (2010) argued that the introduction of the Federal Deposit Insurance Corporation Improvement Act (FDICIA) as a response of the US government to the 2007–2008 financial crisis, imposed stricter

1 Revenues and expenses are recognized when they are materialized, irrespectively of the time of payment.

2 For example, several clubs re-arrange those deals by lending players to each other for a short-period, a fact which does not affect cash assets.

reporting requirements such as the disclosure of the fair market values of bank assets. This legislation increased the supervision of banks imposing annual on-site inspections on banks and the formation of an independent audit committee. Relative interventions were imposed on those banks that failed to meet the respective requirements of the law. Practically, the new regulation forced management to report their responsibilities for preparing financial statements, sustaining an adequate internal control structure and conform to laws and regulations. According to Altamuro and Beatty (2010), this regulation increased banks earnings persistence and earnings predictability due to increased monitoring and oversight, which contributed to less reporting discretion. This reduced managerial discretion increased the association between current reported accruals and future cash flows.

The financial fair play (FFP) regulation in European football shares several common features relative to the above-mentioned cases. The new UEFA regulation increased the amount of financial information that clubs have to publish, introduced greater scrutiny on clubs' finances via the financial oversight board, and dictated that national football federations must exercise additional control on clubs' operations. Failure of clubs to adhere to the new regulations would lead to sanctions, in the form of transfer restrictions, refusing to grant licenses, cash fines, withholding prizes and several other measures. This new environment impacts clubs' financial reporting decisions since the failure to conform to the new regulation definitely impacts clubs' future athletic success and financial performance. Thus, clubs are more incentivized to report earnings that are more stable and predictable in the future. Therefore, the second hypothesis is stated as follows:

H2: *Earnings persistence has increased after the FFP regulation implementation.*

Moreover, regulatory changes are expected to have a different impact on earnings persistence between smaller and larger firms, belonging to different size markets. LaFond and You (2010) indicated that, after the FDICIA regulation in the US banking industry, smaller banks experienced larger increases in earnings persistence and predictability, a result attributed to the increased motivation by managers of smaller banks to signal their financial statement quality in the market and mainly because any negative outcome regarding non-compliance with the new regulation would result in severe or unaffordable implications relative to larger banks. In addition, Kang et al. (2012) documented that the level of investor protection mechanisms in a market directly impacts the reporting incentives. For example, in a market where there is more regulation on the reporting system and decisions are more transparent (thus protecting the interests of shareholders and various stakeholders), there is less incentive for those firms to enhance their earnings predictability due to the smaller marginal benefit that they receive from this behavior. On the contrary, firms in countries with smaller firms and markets (and less investor protection mechanisms) are more incentivized to voluntarily improve their reporting quality to gain access to financing.

Following the above-mentioned reasonin,g the size of the leagues and hence the teams is expected to have an effect on the persistence of earnings. Specifically, smaller clubs gain a significant percentage of their annual budget (and revenues) from UEFA prizes. According to Solberg and Haugen (2010), Swedish clubs increased their revenues by almost 80 percent in the case that they were qualified to the first round of Europa League or Champions League. The same situation stands for other small European Leagues (Cyprus, Bulgaria, Greece, etc.) where, according to Menary (2016), the adherence of small clubs to the FFP can yield significant revenues able to finance the club's budget and even achieve club's sustainability. On the contrary, clubs from larger leagues (such as the Top-5 championships) are not so dependent on UEFA prizes since they present a balance between revenues from their national league and UEFA tournaments (Menary 2016). Consequently, based on the above discussion, clubs from smaller leagues are expected to report more persistent earnings figures to enhance their reliability towards the financial control body and also their chances to adhere to the new regulatory requirements, relative to clubs from larger leagues. However, the opposite reasoning can also be true since larger clubs might lose more if they fail to conform to FFP regulation, since they are more likly to advance their presence in the prestigious UEFA tournaments and gain more revenues. Thus, due to the conflicting arguments mentioned above, the third and final hypothesis is formed in the null form as follows:

H3: *There will be a difference on the earnings persistence between smaller and larger league clubs.*

3. Data Selection and Research Design

The sample selection procedure included the selection of financial accounting data, namely net profit, operating cash flows and total assets from the annual financial statement from clubs in European countries (Belgium, Finland, France, Greece, Italy, Netherlands, Norway, Spain, and United Kingdom) that had at least two football clubs with available financial data for more than two fiscal years over the period 2008–2016. The sample selection started by collecting data from 117 football clubs which fit the legal form of a corporation, however we had to delete six clubs due to data unavailability. Moreover, to reduce the impact of outliers and thus eliminate potential biases in the estimation of the variables, we removed the upper and lower 1 percent of the data distribution of earnings and cash flows. Consequently, the final unbalanced sample includes 109 football clubs and 869 firm year observations. Table 1 presents the distribution of our sample clubs per country. The majority of the sample observations originated from the Big-4 championships, namely United Kingdom, Italy, France, and Spain. Greece presented a significant portion of the sample observations followed by Belgium. The fact that Big-4 leagues constituted the majority of our sample observations warranted the examination of earnings persistence between Big-4 and Non-Big-4 leagues, as discussed in Section 4.

Table 1. Observations distribution per country and year.

Countries	2008	2009	2010	2011	2012	2013	2014	2015	2016	Total
Belgium	7	7	6	7	6	6	5	7	7	58
Finland	2	1	1	2	2	1	2	2	2	15
France	11	11	11	11	11	11	10	11	11	98
Greece	10	10	9	10	10	10	10	10	10	89
Italy	20	19	18	20	20	20	20	20	20	177
Netherlands	3	3	3	3	3	3	3	3	3	27
Norway	2	2	2	2	2	2	1	1	1	15
Spain	6	7	7	7	7	7	7	7	7	62
United Kingdom	37	37	37	37	37	37	29	43	43	328
Total	98	97	92	97	96	94	87	104	104	869

The final sample exclusively included football clubs that participate in the top division of their country's official league (as in Dimitropoulos et al. 2016) for two main reasons: those clubs competing in the top division of the national league are more likely to participate in UEFA championships and therefore are more inclined to conform to the criteria set by the FFP regulation. Thus, we expect that they are more motivated to report more persistent earnings figure to improve their chances to adhere to the new regulation's financial criteria.

Our research design required dividing the sample into two sub-periods: the pre-FFP implementation period (including fiscal years ending in June 2008–2011) and the post-FFP period (fiscal years ending in June 2012–2016). The reason for selecting 2012 as the beginning of the FFP-period (even though the regulation was first published in 2010) is because the 2011–2012 football season (and fiscal year) is the first during which the FFP regulation was in full force. Practically, the implementation of the FFP regulation was not in full effect during (and before) the fiscal year ending June 2011, since several exemptions and acceptable levels of deviation were imposed from the regulation's financial criteria to assist clubs to steadily adjust to the new regulatory environment. Therefore, we considered the 2011 fiscal year belonging to the pre-FFP regulation period to draw more precise inferences regarding the impact of the new regulation on earnings persistence.

We measured earnings persistence by regressing the future return on assets on the current return on assets following previous studies by Richardson et al. (2005) and Oei et al. (2008) according to the following model:

$$ROA_{it+1} = a_0 + a_1 ROA_{it} + e_{it} \tag{1}$$

where *ROA* is the return on assets estimated as net income after tax to lagged total assets and *e* is the regression error term. Subscripts *i* and *t* denote the club and the year, respectively. Model (1) was estimated including club fixed effects to capture any impact on the regression model attributed to specific club characteristics. Model (1) was estimated using the panel fixed effect estimation since panel analysis contains more information with more variability and less collinearity among the variables, leading to more efficient estimates and precise parameters of model estimation, allowing us to detect many effects that are not detectable in plain cross-sectional data analysis. In addition, we performed the Breusch–Pagan Lagrangian multiplier test for random effect, which tests the null hypothesis that the error variance is equal to zero. The test produced an insignificant value leading us not to reject the null and thus the fixed effect estimation is considered as the most appropriate estimation method. Coefficient a_1 measures earnings persistence, and the closer to unity (1), the higher the earnings persistence, indicating a more stable and predictable earnings stream.

The first hypothesis states that the accrual component of earnings will be less persistent than cash flow component of earnings in the determination of future earnings. To test this hypothesis, we estimated the following equation to capture the differential persistence of the accrual components of earnings:

$$ROA_{it+1} = \beta_0 + \beta_1 ROA_{it} + \beta_2 TACC_{it} + e_{it} \tag{2}$$

where *TACC* denotes the club's total accruals estimated as the different between net income and operating cash flows divided by lagged total assets. The rest of the variables are defined as above.

According to Richardson et al. (2005), the accrual component of earnings is expected to be less persistent than the cash flow component of earnings, which is the difference between earnings performance and the accrual component of earnings performance. Thus, the initial functional form of Model (2) was as follows:

$$ROA_{it+1} = \gamma_0 + \gamma_1 (ROA_{it} - TACC_{it}) + \gamma_2 TACC_{it} + u_{it+1} \tag{2a}$$

where γ_1 capture the persistence of cash flows and γ_2 captures the persistence of accruals. Thus, the modified version Model (2a) is Model (2) with earnings performance itself instead of cash flow performance. Rewriting Equation (2a) in terms of the persistence parameters produced the following:

$$ROA_{it+1} = \gamma_0 + \gamma_1 ROA_{it} + (\gamma_2 - \gamma_1) TACC_{it} + u_{it+1} \tag{2b}$$

Thus, $\beta_1 = \gamma_1$ and $\beta_2 = (\gamma_2 - \gamma_1)$[3]. According to Richardson et al. (2005), the advantage of estimating Model (2) instead of Model (2b) is that β_2 provides a direct estimate of $(\gamma_2 - \gamma_1)$[4].

Model (2) was estimated including club fixed effects to capture any impact on the regression model attributed to specific club characteristics. For example, there could be small differences in the revenues sharing process between leagues. A recent report by KPMG (2017) indicated that the Big-5 European leagues present a somehow uniform process of broadcasting revenue distribution with the majority of revenues being shared equally between clubs, and an equal percentage is distributed based on sport performance and popularity. This form of distribution is evidenced in other minor leagues as well such as Greece. The relative distribution percentages of each factor may differ from league

3 Please refer to the study by Richardson et al. (2005), Section 4.2 for the derivation of this formula.

4 We estimated Model (2β) as well, but untabulated results provide qualitatively similar findings compared with those on the main tables, so we discuss the results from the estimation of Model (2).

to league so the club fixed effect aims to capture this impact. In Equation (2), coefficient β_1 captures the persistence of the cash flow component of earnings, while coefficient β_2 captures the differential persistence of the accrual component of earnings. If H1 is valid, we expect coefficient β_2 to be smaller in magnitude and significance relative to coefficient β_1.

To examine the second research hypothesis, Models (1) and (2) were reestimated during the pre (2008–2011) and post (2012–2016) FFP regulation sub-periods. If H2 is valid, we expect a highly significant and positive coefficient with larger magnitude during the post-FFP period relative to the pre-FFP period. Finally, to examine the third research hypothesis, both models were reestimated after partitioning the sample between sample clubs belonging to the top European leagues (Italy, France, Spain and UK) and clubs belonging to the other European leagues. H3 is verified if coefficient β_1 is larger in magnitude and significant for Non-Top-4 leagues relative to Top-4 leagues.

4. Empirical Results

Table 2 presents the descriptive statistics of the main variables for the whole research period, as well as during the pre- and post-FFP periods. The average total accruals are negative and cover 17 percent of total assets, indicating that net income is less than cash flows for the sample clubs, thus clubs operate with more accruals on their profit and loss account. In addition, average return on assets is negative and covers 10 percent of total assets. This result is relevant to previous studies on European football regarding the clubs' financial performance (Dimitropoulos et al. 2016). Average ROA does not present any significant change before and after the implementation of FFP regulation, while, on the contrary, TACC have been reduced after FFP initiation from −0.18 to −0.16, indicating the tendency of clubs to report accounting earnings that are more associated with operating cash flows.

Table 2. Descriptive statistics of sample variables.

Variables	TACC	ROA
FULL SAMPLE		
Mean	−0.169	−0.101
St.Dev.	0.241	0.417
Min	−1.355	−2.859
Max	3.641	4.854
PRE-FFP		
Mean	−0.180	−0.102
St.Dev.	0.205	0.475
Min	−1.355	−2.859
Max	0.281	4.854
POST-FFP		
Mean	−0.160	−0.100
St.Dev.	0.267	0.365
Min	−1.339	−2.784
Max	3.641	2.090

The sample period includes fiscal years from 2008 to 2016. The pre-FFP period is 2008–2011 and the post-FFP period is 2012–2016. TACC is total accruals estimated as the different between net income and operating cash flows divided by lagged total assets, and ROA is the return on assets estimated as net income after tax to lagged total assets.

Table 3 presents the estimation of regression Model (1) for the whole period under investigation as well as during the pre- and post-FFP periods. Overall, earnings persistence is 0.183, suggesting that on average from a €1 profit during the current year 0.18 cents are expected to persist in the following year. This coefficient is far below the persistence coefficient of previous studies in the US, Australia and Korea (Richardson et al. 2005; Oei et al. 2008; Jeon et al. 2006). This result can be attributed to the increased volatility of football clubs' profits and revenues, as evidenced by Rascher et al. (2012), and the fact that several clubs in Europe do not focus on sustaining their profitability but just breaking even (Dermit-Richard et al. 2017). Nevertheless, the coefficient on earnings persistence is higher in magnitude and statistically significant only in the post-FFP period (0.296) indicating that almost €0.30 of current earnings will persist in the following year. The coefficient of ROA during the pre-FFP period is positive, yet not statistically significant within conventional levels. Taken together, findings in Table 2 verify H2 and indicate that the new UEFA regulation increased the amount of financial information that clubs have to publish, and introduced greater scrutiny on clubs finances via the financial oversight board, and this impacted clubs' financial reporting decisions, leading them to report earnings that are more persistent and predictable in the future.

Table 3. Earnings persistence results.

Variables	Coef.	*T*-Test (*p*-Value)
	FULL SAMPLE	
Constant	−0.083 ***	−6.44 (0.001)
ROA	0.183 **	2.22 (0.026)
R^2-Adj.	0.334	
F-stat	4.95 **	(0.024)
	PRE-FFP	
Constant	−0.107 ***	−5.16 (0.001)
ROA	0.098	0.93 (0.520)
R^2-Adj.	0.115	
F-stat	2.87 **	(0.05)
	POST-FFP	
Constant	−0.059 ***	−3.99 (0.001)
ROA	0.296 ***	2.46 (0.014)
R^2-Adj.	0.723	
F-stat	6.04 **	(0.014)

*** and ** indicate statistical significance at the 1% and 5% significance level, respectively. The sample period includes fiscal years 2008–2016. The pre-FFP period is 2008–2011 and the post-FFP period is 2012–2016. ROA is the return on assets estimated as net income after tax to lagged total assets. Club fixed effects are included in the estimation.

To verify this argument and provide an additional robustness check on the findings in Table 3, we examined whether earnings predictability enhanced after the FFP regulation came into act. For this reason, we followed previous studies by Kousenidis et al. (2013) and Gaio (2010) and estimated earnings predictability (*EarnPredict*) as the standard deviation of residuals of Model (1). *EarnPredict* measures the ability of earnings to be predicted in the future and thus be more persistent and have higher quality. Larger values of the standard deviation of residuals indicate less predictable earnings and vice versa. Therefore, we estimated a simple regression model including earnings predictability as the dependent variable and a dummy variable FFP_D (which designates the initiation of the FP regulation) acts as the independent variable. The results are presented in Table 4:

Table 4. Earnings predictability during FFP regulation.

Variables	Coef.	*T*-Test (*p*-Value)
	Dependent variable: *EarnPredict*	
Constant	0.081 ***	51.41 (0.001)
FFP_D	−0.016 ***	−9.32 (0.001)
R^2-Adj.	0.106	
F-stat	86.85 ***	(0.001)

*** indicate statistical significance at the 1% significance level. The sample period includes fiscal years from 2008 to 2016. FFP_D is a dummy variable receiving unity (1) for the post-FFP period (2012–2016) and zero (0) otherwise. The dependent variable (*EarnPredict*) is the standard deviation of the residuals of Model (1).

The coefficient on the FFP_D variable is negative and highly significant, indicating that earnings predictability increased (the standard deviation of residuals is smaller, suggesting more predictable earnings) after the FFP implementation. The economic meaning of this coefficient is that, after the initiation of FFP regulation, the standard deviation of earnings residuals decreased by 1.6 percent suggesting enhanced earnings predictability. This finding complements the evidence in Table 3 and provides another justification for accepting H2.

Table 5 presents the results from the estimation of Model (2). The coefficient on the cash flow component of earnings (captured by the ROA variable) is positive and significant, while the relative coefficient of the TACC variable is insignificant, thus the cash flow component of earnings is more persistent than that of accruals, verifying H1. This finding corroborates previous evidence by Kormendi and Lipe (1987) and Kang et al. (2012) that the lower persistence of accruals is attributed to their lower reliability since accruals require judgments for the estimation of the relative figures. Moreover, the analysis during the pre- and post-FFP periods corroborates the evidence in Table 3. Specifically, the accrual component of earnings (TACC) was a significant determinant of future earnings before the FFP regulation came into act but becomes insignificant after FFP. On the contrary, the cash flow component of earnings has a positive and significant coefficient during the FFP period while the coefficient on TACC is insignificant. This evidence verifies our previously mentioned arguments about the impact of the new UEFA regulation on clubs' incentives to report more predictable earnings figures (based on cash flows) thus enhancing earnings persistence.

Table 5. Results on the persistence of accruals and cash flows.

Variables	Coef.	*T*-Test (*p*-Value)
FULL SAMPLE		
Constant	−0.056 ***	−2.52 (0.012)
ROA	0.162 **	1.93 (0.054)
TACC	0.150	1.26 (0.210)
R^2-Adj.	0.416	
F-stat	3.86 **	(0.021)

Table 5. *Cont.*

Variables	Coef.		*T*-Test (*p*-Value)
PRE-FFP			
Constant	−0.1061 ***		−2.48 (0.013)
ROA	0.067		0.66 (0.512)
TACC	0.270 **		2.25 (0.025)
R^2-Adj.		0.266	
F-stat	2.73 **		(0.06)
POST-FFP			
Constant	−0.042		−1.57 (0.117)
ROA	0.288 **		2.20 (0.028)
TACC	0.066		0.45 (0.655)
R^2-Adj.		0.791	
F-stat	3.68 **		(0.026)

*** and ** indicate statistical significance at the 1% and 5% significance level, respectively. The sample period includes fiscal years 2008–2016. The pre-FFP period is 2008–2011 and the post-FFP period is 2012–2016. ROA is the return on assets estimated as net income after tax to lagged total assets, and TACC is total accruals estimated as the difference between net income and operating cash flows divided by lagged total assets. Club fixed effects are included in the estimation.

Furthermore, to examine the validity of the third research hypothesis, we reestimated Models (1) and (2) between clubs belonging to the top European leagues and the rest, as well as also during the pre- and post-FFP periods. Results are presented in Table 6A. For both models, the persistence of the cash flow component of earnings (the coefficient on the ROA variable) is higher for clubs belonging to the minor leagues relative to clubs from major European leagues. Practically, results of Model (2) indicate that smaller clubs have €0.34 of current earnings persisting in the following year, relative to €0.11 for larger clubs. This evidence combined with the fact that accruals are more significant determinants of future earnings only for larger clubs verifies the third research hypothesis and indicates that clubs from smaller leagues are expected to report more persistent earnings figures to enhance their reliability towards the financial control body and also their chances to adhere to the new regulatory requirements. Put differently, since clubs from larger leagues gain a significant percentage of their annual budget (and revenues) from UEFA prizes, they are not so dependent on this type of financing, since they already present a balance between revenues from the league and UEFA prizes (Menary 2016).

Table 6B presents the results regarding the impact of FFP regulation on earnings persistence between major and minor leagues. The results seem to corroborate the findings in Table 6A and the main conclusions. Specifically, earnings persistence has decreased for the major leagues after the FFP initiation since the relative coefficient on ROA is statistically insignificant. On the one hand, the relative coefficient for clubs on the minor leagues has increased for the post-FFP period to 0.439 from 0.372 during the pre-FFP period. The same conclusion can be drawn by the estimation of Model (2) where TACC is only significant for the major league clubs but insignificant for minor leagues clubs. Overall, evidence in Table 6B verifies the third research hypothesis and indicates that clubs from smaller leagues are expected to report more persistent earnings figures to enhance their reliability towards the financial control body to conform to the new regulatory requirements.

Table 6. Results of the persistence of accruals and cash flows between major and minor European leagues and during the pre and post FFP periods. (A) Panel A: Overall estimation between major and minor leagues; (B) Panel B: Results between major and minor leagues during the pre and post FFP periods.

Panel A: Overall estimation between major and minor leagues.

Variables	Coef.	*T*-Test (*p*-Value)	Coef.	*T*-Test (*p*-Value)
	Model 1		Model 2	
Major European Leagues				
Constant	−0.090 ***	−6.07 (0.001)	−0.045 **	−2.37 (0.018)
ROA	0.147 ***	4.29 (0.001)	0.113 ***	3.21 (0.001)
TACC			0.259 ***	3.52 (0.001)
R^2-Adj.	0.253		0.462	
F-stat	18.43 ***	(0.001)	15.87 ***	(0.001)
Minor European Leagues				
Constant	−0.046	−1.20 (0.231)	−0.046	−1.06 (0.291)
ROA	0.336 ***	3.61 (0.001)	0.341 ***	3.42 (0.001)
TACC			−0.010	−0.09 (0.926)
R^2-Adj.	0.630		0.633	
F-stat	13.14 ***	(0.001)	6.18 ***	(0.002)

Panel B: Results between major and minor leagues during the pre and post FFP periods.

Variables	Coef.	*T*-Test (*p*-Value)	Coef.	*T*-Test (*p*-Value)	Coef.	*T*-Test (*p*-Value)	Coef.	*T*-Test (*p*-Value)
	Model 1				Model 2			
Major European Leagues								
	PRE-FFP		POST_FFP		PRE-FFP		POST-FFP	
Constant	−0.139 ***	−6.59 (0.001)	−0.101 ***	−5.91 (0.001)	−0.224 ***	−5.63 (0.001)	−0.055 **	−2.13 (0.033)
ROA	0.279 ***	5.14 (0.001)	0.078	1.13 (0.261)	0.253 ***	4.62 (0.001)	0.210 ***	3.00 (0.003)
TACC					0.493 **	2.50 (0.013)	0.300 **	2.27 (0.024)
R^2-Adj.	0.348		0.417		0.379		0.128	
F-stat	26.39 ***	(0.001)	21.27 ***	(0.001)	16.61 ***	(0.001)	5.34 ***	(0.005)
Minor European Leagues								
	PRE-FFP		POST-FFP		PRE_FFP		POST-FFP	
Constant	−0.219	−2.00 (0.139)	−0.139 ***	−3.48 (0.001)	0.115	0.54 (0.641)	−0.147 ***	−3.00 (0.001)
ROA	0.372 **	2.50 (0.012)	0.439 **	2.29 (0.029)	0.128 **	2.22 (0.028)	0.418 **	1.99 (0.049)
TACC					0.393	1.73 (0.227)	0.043	0.40(0.687)
R^2-Adj.	0.348		0.227		0.629		0.168	
F-stat	15.25 ***	(0.001)	4.98 **	(0.028)	7.70 ***	(0.001)	12.39 ***	(0.001)

*** and ** indicate statistical significance at the 1% and 5% significance level, respectively. ROA is the return on assets estimated as net income after tax to lagged total assets, and TACC is total accruals estimated as the difference between net income and operating cash flows divided by lagged total assets. Major European leagues include clubs from Italy, France, Spain and UK, while the rest of the clubs belong to the minor European leagues. Club fixed effects are included in the estimation.

Finally, to check for the sensitivity of the main findings, we performed some robustness tests regarding the definition of the variables and the period under study. First, we re-estimated all models by estimating TACC based on two different definitions. The first is the difference between net income and overall cash flow (instead of operating cash flow) and the second is the balance sheet approach proposed by Ball and Shivakumar (2006) where TACC is estimated as the change in current assets minus change in current liabilities minus depreciation. Both alternative estimations yielded qualitatively similar results as those presented on Tables 3–6. In addition, all models were re-estimated by calculating ROA using net income before tax, but we observed no change in the main findings. In addition, we considered the case that, even though FFP regulation started in full effect from the 2012 fiscal year, several clubs could have been adjusting their financial reporting practices prior to that year. Thus, all models were re-estimated by defining the post-FFP period from 2011 to 2016. Empirical evidence indicated that the cash flow component of earnings was more significant than the accrual component of earnings after the FFP inauguration, thus verifying H2 and corroborating the robustness of our main results presented in Tables 3 and 5. Finally, we controlled for the potential impact of club's on-field success on their earnings persistence, since success on the field can be a driver of profitability. For this reason, we re-estimated both models by including their percentages of wins for every season as an additional control variable. Empirical evidence remained qualitatively unchanged from this test.

5. Conclusions

The present study investigated the issue of earnings persistence and predictability within a sample of European football clubs and whether the UEFA's new FFP regulation had any impact on the persistence of accruals and cash flow components of earnings. The analysis over the period 2008–2016 indicated that the cash flow component of earnings is more useful in predicting future earnings compared to accruals. This positive impact of cash flows for earnings prediction is more significant after the FFP regulation implementation because earnings predictability increased during that period. Moreover, the abovementioned finding is more significant for the smaller league clubs rather than the Top-5 league clubs. This finding is attributed to the fact that smaller league clubs are more in need of UEFA prize money relative to Big-5 league clubs (Menary 2016) because UEFA prize money constitutes a larger part of their annual revenues, thus they are more incentivized to produce a more predictable earnings stream.

In total, the empirical evidence from this study (within a services industry, i.e. football) seems to corroborate previous studies on the impact of financial regulation on the motivation of firms to improve or not the quality of their financial reporting. The examples of FDICIA, the Sarbanes–Oxley Act (SOX), and the compulsory implementation of IFRS in the European Union are characteristic cases where new regulation lead to an improvement of financial reporting (LaFond and You 2010; Barth et al. 2008; Doyle et al. 2007). The UEFA FFP regulation serves as a natural experiment on this study, since it shares several common characteristics with some of the abovementioned regulations: it forced clubs to report a larger amount of financial information, it introduced stricter control and monitoring on clubs' fundamentals and posed significant sanctions on clubs failing to fully conform to this regulation. Therefore, this paper provides an additional perspective on the debate regarding regulation and earnings persistence.

The findings of this study can provide useful implications for regulators since they indicate that, on average, football clubs report more predictable earnings streams after the new regulation initiation. Whether this is a secondary goal of the FFP (or a byproduct of the main goals of FFP regulation) is an issue for potential future exploration. As LaFond and You (2010) argued, regulation and control mechanisms in corporations cannot prevent bad decisions. Although is more difficult to make bad decisions under stricter financial regulation (due to enhanced control and strict sanctions), stricter regulation cannot prevent fraud or manipulation. Most times, regulation may lead human behavior in the opposite direction and efforts to circumvent regulation (Dimitropoulos et al. 2016). Thus, future research can extend current evidence by examining clubs' ownership and corporate governance structure as additional determinants of earnings persistence and how FFP regulation impacted that relation. Moreover, it would be interesting to examine the potential impact of different revenues sources (broadcasting, match day, UEFA prizes, etc.) on earnings persistence and the impact of sponsorship deals on the predictability of clubs' revenues and earnings streams. In addition, another avenue for future research is the examination of the impact of earnings persistence on clubs' cost of debt (or financing) and whether clubs with higher quality financial statements are compensated by investors.

Acknowledgments: We would like to thank the editor and two anonymous reviewers for helpful comments and suggestions that improved the paper significantly. Remaining errors and omissions are authors' responsibility. No research funding was provided to the authors by any source.

Author Contributions: Authors equally contributed to the research and writing of the paper.

References

1. Altamuro, Jennifer, and Anne Beatty. 2010. How does internal control regulation affect financial reporting? *Journal of Accounting and Economics* 49: 58–74. [CrossRef]
2. Andreff, Wladimir. 2007. French football: A financial crisis rooted in weak governance. *Journal of Sports Economics* 8: 652–61. [CrossRef]
3. Ball, Ray, and Lakshmanan Shivakumar. 2006. The Role of Accruals in Asymmetrically Timely Gain and Loss Recognition. *Journal of Accounting Research* 44: 207–42. [CrossRef]
4. Barth, Mary, Wayne. R. Landsman, and Mark H. Lang. 2008. International accounting standards and accounting quality. *Journal of Accounting Research* 46: 467–98. [CrossRef]
5. Cordery, Carolyn J., Dalice Sim, and Rachel F. Baskerville. 2013. Three models, one goal: Assessing financial vulnerability in New Zealand amateur sports clubs. *Sport Management Review* 16: 186–99. [CrossRef]
6. Dermit-Richard, Nadine, Nicolas Scelles, and Stephen Morrow. 2017. French DNCG management control versus UEFA Financial Fair Play: a divergent conception of financial regulation objectives. *Soccer and Society*. [CrossRef]
7. Dimitropoulos, Panagiotis, Stergios Leventis, and Emmanouil Dedoulis. 2016. Managing the European football industry: UEFA's regulatory intervention and the impact on accounting quality. *European Sport Management Quarterly* 16: 459–86. [CrossRef]
8. Doyle, Jeffrey, Weili Ge, and Sarah McVay. 2007. Determinants of weaknesses in internal control over financial reporting and the implications for earnings quality. *Journal of Accounting and Economics* 44: 193–223. [CrossRef]
9. Francis, Jennifer, Ryan LaFond, Per M. Olsson, and Katherine Schipper. 2004. Costs of equity and earnings attributes. *The Accounting Review* 79: 967–1010. [CrossRef]
10. Gaio, Cristina. 2010. The relative importance of firm and country characteristics for earnings quality around the world. *European Accounting Review* 19: 693–738. [CrossRef]
11. Jeon, Sungil, Joungman Kim, and Sangjae Lee. 2006. The persistence of abnormal earnings and systematic risk. *Tourism Management* 27: 867–73. [CrossRef]
12. Kang, Tony, Gopal V. Krishnan, Michael C. Wolfe, and Han S. Yi. 2012. The impact of eliminating the 20-F reconciliation requirement for IFRS filers on earnings persistence and information uncertainty. *Accounting Horizons* 26: 741–65. [CrossRef]
13. Kormendi, Rogen, and Robert Lipe. 1987. Earnings innovations, earnings persistence and stock returns. *Journal of Business* 60: 323–45. [CrossRef]
14. Kothari, S.P., Li Xu, and James E. Short. 2009. The effect of disclosures by management, analysts, and business press on cost of capital, return volatility, and analysts forecasts: a study using content analysis. *The Accounting Review* 84: 1639–70. [CrossRef]
15. Kousenidis, Dimitrios V., Anestic C. Ladas, and Christos I. Negakis. 2013. The effects of the European debt crisis on earnings quality. *International Review of Financial Analysis* 30: 351–62. [CrossRef]
16. KPMG. 2017. *Broadcasting Revenue Distribution: Fine-Tuning the Balance*. Available online: www.footballbenchmark. com/ broadcasting_revenue_distribution (accessed on 27 March 2018).
17. LaFond, Ryan, and Haifeng You. 2010. The federal deposit insurance corporation improvement act, bank internal controls and financial reporting quality. *Journal of Accounting and Economics* 49: 75–83. [CrossRef]
18. Menary, Steve. 2016. One rule for one: the impact of Champions League prize money and Financial Fair Play at the bottom of the European club game. *Soccer and Society* 17: 666–79. [CrossRef]
19. Mourao, Paulo. 2012. The indebtedness of Portuguese soccer teams – looking for determinants. *Journal of Sports Sciences* 30: 1025–35. [CrossRef] [PubMed]
20. Nicoliello, Mario, and Davide Zampatti. 2016. Football clubs' profitability after the Financial Fair Play regulation: Evidence from Italy.

Sport, Business and Management: An International Journal 6: 460–75. [CrossRef]
21. Oei, Rosalyn, Alan Ramsay, and Paul Mather. 2008. Earnings persistence, accruals and managerial share ownership. *Accounting and Finance* 48: 475–502. [CrossRef]
22. Rascher, Daniel A., Matthew T. Brown, Mark S. Nagel, and Chad D. McEvoy. 2012. Financial risk management: The role of a new stadium in minimizing the variation in franchise revenues. *Journal of Sports Economics* 13: 431–50. [CrossRef]
23. Richardson, Scott A., Richard G. Sloan, Mark T. Soliman, and Irem Tuna. 2005. Accrual reliability, earnings persistence and stock returns. *Journal of Accounting and Economics* 39: 437–85. [CrossRef]
24. Rohde, Marc, and Christoph Breuer. 2016. Europe's elite football: Financial growth, sporting success, transfer investment and private majority investors. *International Journal of Financial Studies* 4: 12. [CrossRef]
25. Sloan, Richard G. 1996. Do stock prices fully reflect information in accruals and cash flows about future earnings? *The Accounting Review* 71: 289–315.
26. Solberg, Harry Arne, and Kjetil K. Haugen. 2010. European club football: Why enormous revenues are not enough? *Sport in Society* 13: 329–43. [CrossRef]

11

"Hot Hand" in the National Basketball Association Point Spread Betting Market: A 34-Year Analysis

Benjamin Waggoner, Daniel Wines, Brian P. Soebbing *, Chad S. Seifried and Jean Michael Martinez

School of Kinesiology, Louisiana State University, Baton Rouge, LA 70803, USA; bwaggo2@lsu.edu (B.W.); dwines2@lsu.edu (D.W.); cseifried@lsu.edu (C.S.S.); jmmartinez@lsu.edu (J.M.M.)

* Author to whom correspondence should be addressed; bsoebb1@lsu.edu

External Editor: Nicholas Apergis

Abstract: Several articles have looked at factors that affect the adjustments of point spreads, based on hot hands or streaks, for smaller durations of time. This study examines these effects for 34 regular seasons in the National Basketball Association (NBA). Estimating a Seemingly Unrelated Regression model using all 34 seasons, all streaks significantly impacted point spreads and difference in actual points. When estimating each season individually, differences emerged particularly examining winning and losing streaks of six games or more. The results indicate both the presence of momentum effects and the gambler's fallacy.

Keywords: basketball; hot hand; streak; point spread; NBA (National Basketball Association)

1. Introduction

Traditionally, sports betting markets have been compared to simple financial markets, which allowed researchers to examine financial phenomena difficult to observe in other markets [1]. For example, early research regarding sports betting markets focused on the efficiency of these markets (see Sauer [2]) through the rationality between the opening and closing betting lines [3]. Specifically, Sauer's [4] review of the sports betting markets outlined three different types of market efficiency: weak, semi-strong, and strong. Within these forms of market efficiency, numerous other studies looked at biases such as the favorite/longshot bias [5–8], reverse favorite/longshot bias [5,9,10], racial bias [11], and sentiment bias [12–16].

The present research focuses on the team momentum (sometimes called the "hot hand" effect), which received considerable attention in the literature both from psychological [17] and financial [18] perspectives. Paton and Vaughan Williams [19] defined the hot hand as "[...] a tendency by bettors to overestimate the extent to which a team or individual's performance is positively autocorrelated" (p. 140). Generally, the literature examining the hot hand effect in betting markets focused on team's winning and losing streaks that occur throughout the regular season. When it comes to betting on the National Basketball Association (NBA), research suggests bettors tend to favor and over bet teams on winning streaks [7,20–23]. In addition, known as betting on the "hot hand", Arkes [18] found evidence showing gamblers overstate the importance of streaks and how it affects the next game's outcome. This belief of streaks is also more commonly known as the gambler's fallacy [24] (p. 1370). Within, it should be noted the over betting on winning streaks can adjust lines and eliminate possible opportunities for truly informed bettors to make a profit [7,22].

One problem with the existing research on the hot hand is the small sample period; thus it may lack generalizability and the data necessary to convince bettors and bookmakers it is indeed a fallacy. As an example, Camerer [20] collected data only from the 1983–1986 seasons, Paul and Weinbach [7] from 1995–2001, Paul and Weinbach [23] from 2004–2006, and Paul and Weinbach [25] from the 2008–2009 season. As Osborne [26] implied, previous research has not considered a long enough time frame to determine if inefficiencies exist in betting markets. In other words, while short-term effects are seen, it is unclear whether these effects persist in the long-term.

Another problem found in the current literature is that there was not much research examining losing streaks. Paul and Weinbach [7] noted, this lack of research could be due to the fact gamblers were more apt to follow teams on winning streaks *versus versus* losing streaks. However, a closer examination of losing streaks could reveal potential profitable betting strategies for bookmakers and bettors over time. While it is important to further current research in betting on favorites, it is just as interesting to analyze teams on losing streaks.

The purpose of the present research is to look at the impact that winning and losing streaks have in NBA point spread betting markets. The time period under examination is the 1979–1980 season through the 2012–2013 season. Covering more than 37,000 games during the sample period, results from a Seemingly Unrelated Regression model to examine point spreads and the actual difference in points scored during the contest indicate momentum effects do exist. However, significant variation is seen from season to season in terms of these momentum effects.

2. Literature Review

While the hot hand effect and potential bias has been a popular area of research in sports betting markets, it has been examined in other contexts as well. Seminal work by Gilovich, Vallone, and Tversky [27] illustrated individuals believed a basketball player would be more likely to make a free throw after making two or three free throws in a row prior to the attempt. Since their study, many other studies have similarly looked at the hot hand belief. [1] Additional research by MacMahon, Köppen, and Raab [29] provided some context as to the reason why people may believe in hot hand effects. They outlined two reasons for the hot hand. The first reason is evolutionary where individuals can identify hot and cold streaks over time and rationalize them. The second reason is exposure based upon Tversky and Kahneman's [30] representativeness heuristic where people misinterpret the actions in front of them as generalized truths. Nickerson [31] stated individuals do not fully comprehend the role of randomness in sports outcomes.

In sports betting markets, previous research examining the hot hand based on winning and losing can also be classified as momentum effects [18]. Camerer [20] sought to understand whether NBA betting markets take into account streaks by measuring the profitability of placing a bet on teams on winning and losing streaks. Examining three seasons of NBA betting odds, he found evidence of momentum effects existing in betting markets but not in actual game outcomes. This finding, he observed, was evidence of the hot hand. However, individuals betting on teams on winning or losing streaks could not make a profit. Interestingly, Brown and Sauer [21], questioned Camerer's [20] original premise of the hot hand being a misrepresentation of randomness when they examined winning and losing streaks of two or three games and four and more games. Within, Brown and Sauer [21] argued Camerer's [20] results reflected a mythical hot hand and did not examine whether observable changes in both point spreads and actual game outcomes were a function of a hot hand. Brown and Sauer [21] found support for Camerer's [20] hypothesis but did not find any support for an actual hot hand. Gray and Gray [32] similarly analyzed the role that NFL team's winning and losing streaks have in betting outcomes (*i.e.*, covering the spread) from 1976 through 1994. Their results found the point spread market during this time period reacted more quickly to recent performance of the NFL teams, but was slow in reacting to the winning and losing streaks of teams over the course of the season.

Paul and Weinbach [7] discovered in their analysis of point spreads 1995–1996 through 2001–2002 the existence of the hot hand effect where bettors over bet teams on winning streaks. However, they

---

1 See Bar-eli, Avugos, and Raab [28] and Avugos *et al.* [17] for a recent review of this literature regarding the hot hand effect.

did not find that bettors tended to over bet teams on losing streaks. Paul and Weinbach [7] attributed this difference to a gambler's lower utility with betting on losing teams. Examining the NBA totals market, which is a bet on the combined final point total for the two teams playing in the game, during the same time period, Paul and Weinbach [7] found the hot hand belief did not affect betting behavior.

Paul, Weinbach, and Wilson [22] also found that using streaks to create betting strategies of either betting with the streak or against the streak is not profitable. The only case where the fair bet was violated involved betting the under in games where both teams are coming into play on two or more game under streaks. In addition, they tested strategies of betting with or against streaks under the hot hand hypothesis and no profitability was found. These findings were similar to the results found for totals in professional football, baseball, and hockey. In all cases, the null of a fair bet could be rejected for the largest favorites or largest totals as underdogs won significantly more than 50% of the time. The authors suggested the size of the basketball market is not large enough for uninformed bettors to dominate informed bettors. Therefore, the totals market for the NBA was found to violate a fair bet, but not profitability.

Paul, Weinbach, and Humphreys [33] further looked at the role the hot hand effect plays in betting volume of NBA games over a period from 2003–2004 season through the 2008–2009 season. Their hypothesis was bettors influenced by the hot hand effect would bet more for teams that are winning streaks compared to losing streaks. Results from their research supported this hypothesis. Specifically, they found away teams on winning streaks of two games generated a higher percentage of bets compared to home teams on winning streaks. Home teams on winning streaks of four games or more generated a higher proportion of bets (2.2%) compared to away teams on similar streaks (1.9%).

Other recent research by Arkes [18] examined team momentum in NBA betting markets, which was defined by winning and losing streaks but also the strength of game outcomes. Examining a longer sample of NBA regular season games, Arkes [18] concluded hot hand effects were real. Despite gamblers being correct that a hot hand effect exists, there was evidence showing gamblers overstated the importance of streaks and their effect on the streaking team's next game's outcome [18].

In summary, a rich literature has been developed toward examining team momentum in all different contexts. Within sport betting markets, momentum effects present evidence that bettors believe in a mythical hot hand effect. However, there are conflicting findings showing whether or not the hot hand is real. One limitation of the previous research is the short sample periods to look at this effect. As Osborne [26] remarked, previous studies looking at inefficiencies in the sports betting markets do not examine a long enough time horizon. Thus, momentum effects such as the winning and losing streak of teams may persist in the short-term but not necessarily in the long-term. The present research investigates this effect over a longer time period.

3. Methods

To examine the hot hand in the NBA, the sample period looks at regular season point spreads and game outcomes from the 1979–1980 season through the end of the 2012–2013 season. NBA regular season game data from multiple websites including Basketball Reference and NBA.com were retrieved. Information regarding the point spread data for these games was collected from both online websites as well as newspapers. In total, there were 37,179 individual games over this period of time. Over the time period, there were 17 games in which point spreads were not located when using various sources such as websites and newspaper articles. Thus, the final data set includes 37,162 NBA games during the sample period.

In the present research, the following model is estimated:

$$DV_{hags} = \alpha_{DV} + A_{hgs} + A_{ags} + STRK_{hgs} + STRK_{ags} + \varepsilon_{hags} \quad (1)$$

where h indexes home teams, a indexes away teams, g indexes games and s indexes seasons, and ε is the equation error term. There are two dependent variables in the present research. The first is the point spread for the game in relation to the home team (*PS*). The second dependent variable is the difference in the final score between the home team and the away team (*DP*). A_{hgs} is a parameter examining the home ability index for team h in game g in season s. A_{ags} is the visiting ability index for team a in game g in season s.[2] ε is the equation error term. The main variables of interest are the streaks for the home ($STRK_{hgs}$)) and away ($STRK_{ags}$)) teams prior to the observed game. In the present research, these streak variables look at winning and losing streaks of two, four, and six or more games. For example, the variable *VL2* takes the value of 1 if the away team is on a losing streak of two or three games going into the observed game. As a result, there are 12 indicator variables.

Table 1 presents the summary statistics for the variables in the present research. It shows the average point spread is −3.77 meaning the home team is favored by 3.77 points which reflects the home court advantage in the NBA. The average difference in points is −3.71 meaning the home team won by an average of 3.71 points during the sample period. *Error* is the difference between the point spread and the actual difference in points showing that the spread favors the home team by about 0.06 of a point compared to the actual final difference in points. This reflects the accuracy of the bookmakers in predicting the final outcome of the match.

Table 1. Summary Statistics (n = 37,162).

Variable	Description	Mean	Std. Dev.	Min	Max
PS	Closing point spread in observed game	−3.775	6.208	−25	49
DP	Actual difference in points in observed game (visiting team–home team)	−3.714	12.885	−68	56
Error	Difference between the closing point spread and difference in points	0.061	11.398	−61.5	62.5
VL2	Visiting team has a losing streak of 2 or 3 games	0.215	0.411	0	1
VL4	Visiting team has a losing streak of 3 or 4 games	0.065	0.246	0	1
VL6	Visiting team has a losing streak of 6 or more games	0.045	0.208	0	1
VW2	Visiting team has a winning streak of 2 or 3 games	0.136	0.343	0	1
VW4	Visiting team has a winning streak of 3 or 4 games	0.046	0.208	0	1
VW6	Visiting team has a winning streak of 6 or more games	0.031	0.174	0	1
HL2	Home team has a losing streak of 2 or 3 games	0.131	0.338	0	1
HL4	Home team has a losing streak of 3 or 4 games	0.045	0.208	0	1
HL6	Home team has a losing streak of 6 or more games	0.036	0.186	0	1
HW2	Visiting team has a winning streak of 2 or 3 games	0.221	0.415	0	1
HW4	Home team has a winning streak of 3 or 4 games	0.066	0.248	0	1
HW6	Home team has a winning streak of 6 or more games	0.044	0.205	0	1

The main variables of interest are the 12 streak variables. A visiting team with a losing streak of two or three games occurred in more than 21 percent of the sample. Similar percentages were found for a two or three game home winning streak. The smallest streak that occurred in the sample was a home team on a losing streak of six or more games (3.6% of the sample observations).

Consistent with Brown and Sauer's [21] research, the present research estimates a Seemingly Unrelated Regression (SUR) to analyze the relationship between the point spreads and the actual game outcomes. We use generalized least squares in the SUR technique to control for the heteroscedasticity of both error terms [34]. As Arkes [18] explained, "[t]he justification [for using SUR] is that the error terms for both models would includ*e factor*s known to the odds makers and gamblers, but not observable or quantifiable to the Researcher" (p. 36). These factors could include the game's referee assignments and knowledge of injuries to players. Similar to Brown and Sauer [21], all the seasons are pooled into one model. Thus, there are home and away abilities for each team for each season to control for the changing abilities of teams from year to year.

2 The ability indexes for the home and visiting team are measured using home and visiting team fixed effects.

4. Results and Discussion

Table 2 presents the SUR results. The "R^2" reported in both models is consistent with previous research where Equation 1 explains more of the observed variation in the point spreads than in the actual difference in points. Looking at Table 2, significant results are found for all but one of the streak variables' coefficients. Only the coefficient for the variable indicating the visiting team is on a winning streak of two or three games is insignificant. This result could be that bettors do not perceive visiting teams on a small winning streak to be "hot".

Table 2. Seemingly Unrelated Regression (SUR) Regression Results: Pooled Model.

Dep. Var.	Point Spread			Difference in Points		
Variable	**Coef.**	**Stnd.Error**	***p*-value**	**Coef.**	**Stnd.Error**	***p*-value**
VL2	−0.176	0.035	<0.001	−4.320	0.129	<0.001
VL4	−0.646	0.056	<0.001	−4.408	0.206	<0.001
VL6	−1.182	0.069	<0.001	−4.583	0.252	<0.001
VW2	0.032	0.043	0.458	7.574	0.157	<0.001
VW4	0.435	0.066	<0.001	7.288	0.241	<0.001
VW6	0.727	0.080	<0.001	7.203	0.292	<0.001
HL2	0.121	0.043	0.005	7.608	0.159	<0.001
HL4	0.683	0.066	<0.001	7.601	0.243	<0.001
HL6	1.463	0.076	<0.001	7.651	0.280	<0.001
HW2	−0.130	0.035	<0.001	−4.401	0.128	<0.001
HW4	−0.398	0.055	<0.001	−4.148	0.202	<0.001
HW6	−0.745	0.068	<0.001	−4.402	0.250	<0.001
"R2"	0.8472			0.5236		

Looking specifically at the other eleven significant coefficients, the signs on the coefficients are expected based upon previous research. For example, the coefficient on the variable where the visiting team is on a losing streak of two or three games decreases the point spread by 0.176 points meaning the home team is more favored in the match. Overall, the results presented in Table 2 are consistent with Arkes' [18] findings and the belief in momentum effects showing up in point spreads. The results provided within this paper also confirm belief in the hot hand within betting markets as shown in earlier research such as Camerer [20], Brown and Sauer [21] and Paul and Weinbach [7]. Thus, when a home team is on a losing streak, the point spread will react by increasing, meaning that the home team is becoming more of an underdog.

It is also observed that streaks of six or more games whether on winning or losing or home or away, showed a greater influence on the point spread than teams on streaks of four or more. This observation may be attributed to the gambler's fallacy [24]. Streaks of two or three games occur frequently throughout the season of the NBA. When a team is on a losing streak of four or five games, bettors may believe that the team will win (lose) soon because they are "due" for a win (loss) since they have lost (won) several games in a row, thus committing the gambler's fallacy. However, when these streaks continue on and become streaks of six or more games, bettors may be more likely to contribute this scenario to the team being legitimately good if they are on a winning streak or legitimately bad if they are on a losing streak.

Examining the results with the dependent variable being the difference in actual points scored, all of the streak variables' coefficients are significant with the expected signs. Recall a negative difference in points means that the home team scores more points than the away team. In Table 2, a visiting team on a losing streak of two or three games decreases the difference in points by 4.3. Looking at the magnitude of the coefficients, visiting team winning streaks and home team losing streaks have a higher impact in terms of the difference in points compared to visiting team losing streak and home team winning streaks. These results are inconsistent with Brown and Sauer's [21] findings. In their research, they found streaks did not have any effect on actual game outcomes.

Alternative Estimation

While the pooled model looks at the impact of the hot hand effect over the course of the 34-year period, significant variation could exist between seasons in examining the hot hand effects. Thus, we estimated Equation 1 for each individual season, consistent with Soebbing and Humphreys' [34] approach for examining the perception of tanking in NBA betting markets. Table 3 presents the findings for the point spread portion of the SUR model while Table 4 provides the difference in points. The coefficients in bold on both tables are significant at the 1 percent level while the last column and last row on both tables reflect the totals for the row/column. In looking at Table 3, there are approximately three significant streak parameters per year. The largest streaks (*HL6, HW6, VL6, VW6*) are the highest frequency in terms of the significance at the 1 percent level. This finding is evidence of the mythical hot hand or team momentum effects since point spreads adjust the most for winning and losing streaks of six or more games. Examining Table 4, there are almost 11 significant streak parameters per season when looking at the difference in points. In contrast to Table 3 where the largest streaks had the highest frequency in terms of significance, they tend to have the lowest frequency in terms of significance for the actual difference in points. While there cannot be any definitive conclusions, it would seem to indicate the presence of an occurrence where bettors tend to perceive that long streaks will continue and bookmakers account for this perception. In actuality, however, there is no indication that large streaks affect the actual difference in points.

Overall, the results presented in Table 4 shows team momentum do consistently impact actual game outcomes throughout the same period. There is no indication that gambling behavior changes systematically from one year to the next year. When examining changes in the NBA, however, there are several reasons why this result may occur. The first reason is changes in the NBA's amateur draft, the mechanism in which amateur players are allocated to professional clubs, to deter teams to intentionally lose late in the regular season to earn a higher probability of selecting first overall in the amateur draft [34]. Thus, the significant coefficients on the winning and losing streak variables may reflect this behavior that has been found in previous research to occur throughout this time period (see Soebbing and Humphreys for a review of this literature [34]). The second reason is due to additional fundamental factors that may impact the point spread and actual game outcomes. Research by Brown and Sauer [35] found evidence that point spreads are impacted by fundamental factors rather than just irrelevant noise. The significant coefficients in both Tables 3 and 4 may also reflect some of these fundamental factors.

Table 3. Season SUR Results: Point Spread.

Season/Streak	VL2	VL4	VL6	VW2	VW4	VW6	HL2	HL4	HL6	HW2	HW4	HW6	Total
1979	0.16	−0.26	−0.45	0.16	−0.59	0.38	−0.06	−0.46	**1.23**	0.01	0.28	−0.33	1
1980	0.12	0.02	−0.21	0.04	0.44	**−0.67**	0.02	0.17	0.79	0.25	0.31	−0.07	1
1981	−0.16	**−1.18**	**−1.84**	0.10	0.07	0.53	0.11	−0.01	**2.53**	0.07	−0.30	−0.62	3
1982	−0.26	−0.54	**−1.49**	0.46	**1.45**	0.97	−0.37	−0.35	0.64	−0.12	−0.01	−0.81	2
1983	−0.29	−0.82	−1.36	−0.10	0.29	0.13	−0.21	−0.29	−0.03	−0.21	**−1.14**	−1.03	1
1984	−0.28	−0.27	**−2.16**	0.00	**1.20**	**1.43**	−0.03	**1.46**	**2.30**	0.01	−0.11	**−1.04**	6
1985	−0.09	−0.27	−0.95	−0.41	0.25	0.38	0.08	**1.13**	1.12	−0.24	−0.35	−0.43	1
1986	0.16	−0.54	−0.86	−0.15	−0.04	0.25	0.27	−0.40	0.82	−0.15	−0.61	−0.58	0
1987	−0.05	0.10	0.36	−0.18	−0.10	0.79	0.28	0.59	0.65	−0.40	−0.05	**−1.16**	1
1988	0.06	−0.40	**−1.76**	0.07	0.02	0.62	0.03	−0.18	1.06	−0.25	−0.75	−0.97	1
1989	−0.09	−0.67	**−0.92**	−0.13	**1.16**	0.98	0.41	0.71	**1.25**	**−0.51**	−0.34	**−0.90**	5
1990	−0.11	−0.62	**−1.08**	0.09	0.24	0.63	−0.06	0.93	0.76	−0.18	−0.30	−0.28	1
1991	−0.10	**−1.38**	**−1.80**	−0.12	0.76	1.14	0.21	**1.19**	**1.77**	−0.10	−0.29	−1.15	4
1992	−0.34	−0.82	−0.97	−0.34	−0.08	**1.33**	0.28	0.78	**1.28**	−0.09	**−1.08**	**−1.45**	4
1993	−0.42	−0.55	**−1.36**	0.22	**1.24**	0.07	0.07	0.33	**1.08**	−0.28	−0.39	**−0.78**	4
1994	0.04	−0.18	−0.75	0.16	0.51	**1.24**	−0.08	0.21	0.43	−0.07	−0.38	−0.99	1
1995	−0.11	−0.59	−0.64	−0.18	0.65	**1.46**	−0.05	0.60	0.99	−0.32	−0.65	**−1.24**	2
1996	−0.11	−0.40	−0.60	−0.06	0.48	0.91	0.45	0.51	**1.79**	−0.53	−0.50	−0.44	1
1997	−0.27	−0.39	−0.79	−0.28	0.41	**1.38**	0.15	0.59	**1.20**	−0.25	**−0.80**	−0.48	3
1998	−0.26	−0.10	−0.44	−0.67	−0.32	0.93	0.27	**1.43**	0.80	−0.15	−0.66	−0.16	1
1999	−0.04	−0.41	**−1.42**	0.08	0.47	**1.41**	−0.27	0.60	**2.00**	−0.05	−0.50	−0.02	3
2000	−0.21	−0.39	−0.83	0.23	0.42	0.50	0.12	0.31	**1.35**	−0.19	−0.44	−1.00	1
2001	−0.17	**−1.45**	−0.97	0.04	0.32	0.51	0.23	1.06	**1.64**	−0.42	−0.02	−0.61	2
2002	−0.14	−0.77	**−1.34**	0.25	0.67	0.58	0.00	0.59	0.60	0.10	−0.15	−0.54	1
2003	−0.21	−0.71	**−1.12**	0.20	**1.39**	**1.89**	0.05	0.31	**2.58**	0.12	−0.42	**−1.67**	5
2004	−0.37	**−0.99**	**−1.28**	0.14	**1.86**	**1.54**	0.43	**1.36**	**2.32**	−0.22	−0.75	**−1.52**	7
2005	−0.47	**−1.00**	**−2.40**	0.30	0.86	0.64	0.03	**1.11**	**1.31**	0.09	**−0.92**	−1.05	5
2006	**−0.61**	**−1.75**	**−1.76**	0.12	0.51	0.73	0.27	0.99	**2.71**	−0.07	**−0.88**	−0.85	5
2007	**−0.75**	−0.86	−1.17	−0.11	0.30	0.47	0.12	**1.51**	1.16	−0.19	−0.38	−0.89	2
2008	0.35	−0.16	−1.09	0.08	0.25	1.06	−0.11	0.89	1.05	−0.33	−0.70	**−1.56**	1
2009	0.22	−0.17	**−1.29**	0.04	0.73	**1.56**	**0.71**	0.85	**1.79**	−0.08	−0.51	−0.93	4
2010	−0.22	−0.53	**−1.12**	0.42	−0.14	1.01	0.12	**1.39**	**1.76**	0.22	−0.24	−0.71	3
2011	−0.38	−0.95	**−1.94**	−0.01	0.28	0.61	0.02	1.03	**2.51**	0.02	−0.01	**−3.10**	3
2012	−0.21	−0.56	**−1.15**	0.14	−0.03	0.57	0.14	0.53	**2.33**	−0.11	−0.34	−0.47	2
Total	2	6	19	0	6	10	1	8	20	1	5	10	

Table 4. Season SUR Results: Difference in Points.

Season/Streak	VL2	VL4	VL6	VW2	VW4	VW6	HL2	HL4	HL6	HW2	HW4	HW6	Total
1979	−4.18	**−3.37**	**−5.46**	**7.68**	1.26	4.77	**8.15**	**7.33**	**7.66**	**−4.02**	−3.00	−4.07	7
1980	**−2.67**	−2.34	−3.17	**8.84**	−0.71	**8.98**	**7.36**	**4.53**	**8.01**	**−4.31**	−1.04	−1.87	7
1981	**−2.68**	−3.14	−3.08	**8.02**	**6.74**	**7.77**	**7.69**	**6.92**	**6.16**	**−3.46**	**−3.85**	−2.84	9
1982	**−4.34**	**−5.10**	**−4.11**	**7.52**	**4.96**	**7.92**	**6.34**	**7.98**	**8.13**	**−5.33**	**−3.87**	**−7.36**	12
1983	**−2.10**	−2.59	−3.06	**8.09**	**8.45**	**5.99**	**9.10**	**7.86**	**8.96**	**−4.22**	**−3.77**	−0.71	9
1984	**−4.74**	**−5.52**	−4.50	**7.49**	**8.63**	**6.59**	**8.11**	**5.87**	**8.48**	**−4.64**	**−3.51**	**−4.15**	11
1985	**−4.83**	**−4.88**	−3.55	**8.28**	**5.90**	**7.71**	**7.69**	**9.29**	**6.05**	**−4.12**	**−3.55**	−3.16	10
1986	−3.18	−2.41	−3.04	**9.33**	**7.15**	5.88	**8.91**	**10.58**	**10.13**	**−3.53**	−2.22	−4.32	6
1987	**−3.29**	**−4.17**	**−3.60**	**7.51**	**7.04**	**9.73**	**8.75**	**7.69**	**10.33**	**−3.26**	**−3.48**	−3.70	11
1988	**−3.72**	**−3.84**	**−3.83**	**8.68**	**9.03**	**8.69**	**7.87**	**6.20**	**8.33**	**−3.34**	**−4.29**	−3.58	11
1989	**−4.15**	**−5.29**	**−5.07**	**7.80**	**7.47**	**7.66**	**8.87**	**8.34**	**6.61**	**−3.35**	**−4.24**	**−7.64**	12
1990	**−4.02**	**−4.76**	−2.75	**9.42**	**7.21**	**10.42**	**8.09**	**7.12**	**11.60**	**−2.95**	−2.82	**−4.04**	10
1991	**−5.04**	**−3.71**	**−4.11**	**7.27**	**7.62**	**5.24**	**6.82**	**6.55**	**8.84**	**−4.24**	**−5.24**	**−5.46**	12
1992	**−4.44**	**−4.17**	**−5.98**	**6.42**	**6.86**	**9.42**	**9.33**	**9.12**	**8.95**	**−5.00**	**−6.39**	**−5.13**	12
1993	**−3.91**	**−5.68**	**−4.07**	**7.80**	**5.38**	**6.72**	**7.49**	**8.25**	**7.55**	**−4.49**	**−3.96**	**−3.68**	12
1994	**−5.18**	**−4.08**	−2.19	**7.92**	**8.30**	**7.23**	**7.38**	**7.13**	**7.17**	**−4.68**	**−5.65**	**−5.37**	11
1995	**−4.68**	**−3.66**	**−5.54**	**7.34**	**8.45**	**7.69**	**8.59**	**5.25**	**7.41**	**−3.08**	**−4.76**	−3.65	11
1996	**−5.97**	**−6.52**	**−5.74**	**7.21**	**9.98**	**9.82**	**5.44**	**6.32**	**5.45**	**−4.60**	−2.85	**−4.51**	11
1997	**−4.47**	**−5.13**	**−3.22**	**7.33**	**7.02**	**8.55**	**7.15**	**8.47**	**6.60**	**−4.22**	**−3.59**	**−4.16**	12
1998	**−4.87**	**−4.63**	−4.04	**7.71**	**6.95**	**9.17**	**7.02**	**8.26**	3.49	**−3.56**	−2.50	**−6.32**	9
1999	**−3.92**	−2.09	**−5.10**	**7.82**	**7.61**	**8.40**	**6.86**	**8.02**	**7.29**	**−4.44**	**−4.51**	−2.09	10
2000	**−4.91**	**−6.36**	**−6.56**	**7.25**	**8.68**	**5.91**	**6.61**	**4.72**	**8.31**	**−4.69**	**−5.42**	**−4.60**	12
2001	**−4.21**	**−5.52**	**−6.34**	**7.58**	**9.21**	**7.48**	**5.58**	**7.02**	**7.27**	**−5.23**	**−4.88**	**−6.97**	12
2002	**−4.74**	**−3.36**	**−5.30**	**7.73**	**7.57**	**6.93**	**7.74**	**6.43**	**4.77**	**−4.94**	**−5.12**	**−6.87**	12
2003	**−3.50**	**−4.45**	**−4.93**	**6.40**	**6.87**	**8.91**	**8.15**	**10.00**	**8.04**	**−4.42**	**−5.25**	**−5.79**	12
2004	**−5.12**	**−4.14**	**−4.39**	**6.72**	**9.34**	**6.26**	**6.67**	**7.38**	**5.72**	**−4.76**	**−4.46**	**−7.01**	12
2005	**−4.01**	**−3.24**	**−5.16**	**8.07**	**8.81**	**8.39**	**7.55**	**7.26**	**8.87**	**−4.09**	**−5.87**	**−4.56**	12
2006	**−5.41**	**−5.65**	−2.33	**6.68**	**8.49**	**7.16**	**7.70**	**8.48**	**8.61**	**−5.20**	**−4.21**	**−3.95**	11
2007	**−3.62**	−2.79	**−4.26**	**7.96**	**8.35**	**9.43**	**6.29**	**10.40**	**7.34**	**−5.66**	**−6.19**	**−5.45**	11
2008	**−3.68**	**−5.28**	**−5.55**	**7.67**	**6.34**	**7.69**	**8.06**	**7.17**	**8.71**	**−4.47**	**−5.83**	**−5.98**	12
2009	**−5.06**	**−5.62**	**−6.88**	**8.87**	**8.12**	**7.52**	**7.30**	**7.00**	**7.02**	**−5.49**	**−3.13**	**−5.19**	12
2010	**−4.68**	**−3.51**	**−5.75**	**6.65**	**6.96**	**8.55**	**7.93**	**7.69**	**6.23**	**−5.05**	**−4.84**	−3.12	11
2011	**−5.54**	**−5.11**	**−5.79**	**6.60**	**8.29**	**6.78**	**8.60**	**8.40**	**8.90**	**−4.57**	**−4.47**	**−9.99**	12
2012	**−4.78**	**−6.20**	**−4.61**	**7.64**	**7.60**	**8.41**	**8.21**	**8.18**	**7.11**	**−5.10**	**−3.01**	−2.56	11
Total	32	26	24	34	32	32	34	34	33	34	28	22	

5. Conclusions

The theory of the "hot hand" has been a topic studied by several researchers in different fields. Within sports betting markets, team momentum effects are a popular area of analysis with particular emphasis looking at NBA games. While previous research indicates that point spreads are adjusted based upon winning and losing streaks indicating the myth of the hot hand occurs, the research is mixed in terms of how winning and losing streaks affect actual games outcomes, which would signify an actual hot hand. However, previous research examined only short sample periods. The present research looked at a 34-year period of NBA regular season point spreads and actual games outcomes. A pooled sample found streaks impacted both point spreads and actual games outcomes. Furthermore, estimating each year individually found significant variation in how streaks impact point spreads and actual games outcomes. In particular, it was found that large winning and losing streaks imposed the most effect on point spreads but not on actual game outcomes.

Overall the findings looking at the hot hand effect measured by streaks in the present research are consistent with Arkes' [18] findings in a larger study of NBA regular season games. Furthermore, Arkes [18] concluded that momentum effects do exist and are not mythical. The results in Table 2 would suggest that momentum effects are indeed real and they affect both the point spreads set by bookmakers and the actual difference in points scored by the two teams.

Finally, although this research is not examining a strategy of betting on the streaks, it does provide information that future research could use to look at long-term betting strategies. As recent research provides increasing information that bookmakers are profit maximizers instead of balancing the dollar values between the favorites and underdogs of a particular match (e.g., [23,36,37]), future research could look at how book makers use betting beliefs regarding the hot hand to maximize profits. Recent research by Paul *et al.* [33] began to analyze this phenomenon using five years of betting volume data. An additional area of future research would be the analysis of how the point spread changes from the opening line to closing line to see how accurately the original point spread was set. The movement of the point spread would also reflect the placement of bets that would occur on a game.

Acknowledgments: We would like to thank Andy Weinbach and Richard Gandar for their assistance in obtaining many of the earlier point spreads used in this manuscript and Josh Pratt for his helpful research assistance.

Author Contributions: Benjamin Waggoner and Daniel Wines constructed the streak variables, collected 5 seasons of NBA point spreads and provided the initial statistical analysis. Brian P. Soebbing merged the data together and conducted the final statistical analysis. Soebbing along with Chad S. Seifried and Jean Michael Martinez wrote the final manuscript.

References

1. Gandar, J.M.; Dare, W.H.; Brown, C.R.; Zuber, R.A. Informed traders and price variations in the betting market for professional basketball games. *J. Financ.* **1998**, *53*, 385–401. [CrossRef]
2. Sauer, R.D. The state of research on markets for sports betting and suggested future directions. *J. Econ. Financ.* **2005**, *29*, 416–426. [CrossRef]
3. Gandar, J.M.; Zuber, R.A.; O'Brien, T.; Russo, B. Testing rationality in the point spread betting market. *J. Financ.* **1998**, *43*, 995–1008. [CrossRef]
4. Sauer, R.D. The economics of wagering markets. *J. Econ. Lit.* **1998**, *36*, 2021–2064.
5. Gandar, J.M.; Zuber, R.A.; Johnson, R.S.; Dare, W. Re-examining the betting market on Major League Baseball games: Is there a reverse favourite-longshot bias? *Appl. Econ.* **2002**, *34*, 1307–1317. [CrossRef]
6. Golic, J.; Tamarkin, M. The degree of inefficiency in the football betting market. *J. Financ. Econ.* **1991**, *30*, 311–323. [CrossRef]
7. Paul, R.J.; Weinbach, A.P. Bettor misconceptions in the NBA: The overbetting of large favorites and the "hot hand". *J. Sport. Econ.* **2005**, *6*, 390–400. [CrossRef]
8. Williams, L.V.; Paton, D. Why are some favourite-longshot biases positive and others negative? *Appl. Econ.* **1998**, *30*, 1505–1510. [CrossRef]
9. Woodland, L.M.; Woodland, B.M. The reverse favourite-longshot bias and market efficiency in Major League Baseball: An update. *Bull. Econ. Res.* **2003**, *55*, 113–123. [CrossRef]
10. Woodland, L.M.; Woodland, B.M. Market efficiency and the favourite-longshot bias: The baseball betting market. *J. Financ.* **1994**, *49*, 269–279. [CrossRef]
11. Larsen, T.; Price, J.; Wolfers, J. Racial bias in the NBA: Implications for betting markets. *J. Quant. Anal. Sport.* **2008**, *4*. Article 7.
12. Avery, C.; Chevalier, J. Identifying investor sentiment from price paths: The case of football betting. *J. Bus.* **1999**, *72*, 493–521. [CrossRef]
13. Bernile, G.; Lyandres, E. Understanding investor sentiment: The case of soccer. *Financ. Manag.* **2011**, *40*, 357–380. [CrossRef]
14. Braun, S.; Kvansnicka, M. National sentiment and economic behavior: Evidence from online betting on European football. *J. Sport. Econ.* **2013**, *14*, 45–64. [CrossRef]
15. Feddersen, A.; Humphreys, B.R.; Soebbing, B.P. Sentiment bias in National Basketball Association Betting. Available online: http://www.be.wvu.edu/phd_economics/pdf/13-03.pdf (accessed on 14 April 2014).
16. Forrest, D.; Simmons, R. Sentiment in the betting market of Spanish football. *Appl. Econ.* **2008**, *40*, 119–126. [CrossRef]
17. Avugos, S.; Köppen, J.; Czienskowski, U.; Raab, M.; Bar-Eli, M. The "hot hand" reconsidered: A meta-analytic approach. *Psychol. Sport. Exerc.* **2013**, *14*, 21–27. [CrossRef]
18. Arkes, J. Do gamblers correctly price momentum in NBA betting markets? *J. Predict. Mark* **2011**, *5*, 30–52.
19. Paton, D.; Vaughan Williams, L. Forecasting outcomes in spread betting markets: Can bettors use 'Quarbs' to beat the book? *J. Forecast.* **2005**, *24*, 139–154. [CrossRef]

20. Camerer, C.F. Does the basketball market believe in the "hot hand"? *Am. Econ. Rev.* **1989**, *79*, 1257–1261.
21. Brown, W.O.; Sauer, R.D. Does the basketball market believe in the 'hot hand'? *Am. Econ. Rev.* **1993**, *83*, 1377–1386.
22. Paul, R.J.; Weinbach, A.P.; Wilson, M. Efficient markets, fair bets, and profitability in NBA totals 1995–96 to 2001–02. *Q. Rev. Econ. Financ.* **2004**, *44*, 624–632. [CrossRef]
23. Paul, R.J.; Weinbach, A.P. Price setting in the NBA gambling market: Tests of the Levitt model of Sportsbook behavior. *Int. J. Sport Financ.* **2008**, *3*, 137–145.
24. Ayton, P.; Fischer, I. The hot hand fallacy and the gambler's fallacy: Two faces of subjective randomness? *Mem. Cogn.* **2004**, *32*, 1369–1378. [CrossRef]
25. Paul, R.J.; Weinbach, A.P. The determinants of betting volume for sports in North America: Evidence of sports betting as consumption in the NBA and NHL. *Int. J. Sport Financ.* **2010**, *5*, 128–140.
26. Osborne, E. Efficient markets? Don't bet on it. *J. Sport. Econ.* **2001**, *2*, 50–61. [CrossRef]
27. Gilovich, T.; Vallone, R.; Tversky, A. The hot hand in basketball: On the misperception of random sequences. *Cogn. Psychol.* **1985**, *17*, 295–314. [CrossRef]
28. Bar-Eli, M.; Avugos, S.; Raab, M. Twenty years of "hot hand" research: Review and critique. *Psychol. Sport Exerc.* **2006**, *7*, 525–553. [CrossRef]
29. MacMahon, C.; Köppen, J.; Raab, M. The hot hand belief and framing effects. *Res. Quart. Exerc. Sport.* **2014**, *85*, 341–350. [CrossRef]
30. Tversky, A.; Kahneman, D. Belief in the law of small numbers. *Psychol. Bull.* **1971**, *76*, 105–110. [CrossRef]
31. Nickerson, R.S. The production and perception of randomness. *Psychol. Rev.* **2002**, *109*, 330–357. [CrossRef] [PubMed]
32. Gray, P.K.; Gray, S.F. Testing market efficiency: Evidence from the NFL sports betting market. *J. Financ.* **1997**, *52*, 1725–1737. [CrossRef]
33. Paul, R.J.; Weinbach, A.P.; Humphreys, B. Revisiting the "hot hand" hypothesis in the NBA betting market using actual sportsbook betting percentages on favorites and underdogs. *J. Gambl. Bus. Econ.* **2011**, *5*, 42–56.
34. Soebbing, B.P.; Humphreys, B.R. Do gamblers think that teams tank? Evidence from the NBA. *Contemp. Econ. Policy* **2013**, *31*, 301–313. [CrossRef]
35. Brown, W.O.; Sauer, R.D. Fundamentals or Noise? Evidence from the professional basketball betting market. *J. Financ.* **1993**, *48*, 1193–1209. [CrossRef]
36. Humphreys, B.R. Point spread shading and behavioral biases in NBA betting markets. *Rivista Di Diritto Ed Economia Dello Sport* **2010**, *VI*, 13–26.
37. Levitt, S.D. Why are gambling markets organized so differently from financial markets? *Econ. J.* **2004**, *114*, 223–245. [CrossRef]

12

Revenue Sharing in Major League Baseball: The Moments that Meant so much

Duane Rockerbie [1,*] and Stephen Easton [2]

[1] Department of Economics, University of Lethbridge, Lethbridge, AB T1K3M4, Canada
[2] Department of Economics, Simon Fraser University, Burnaby, BC V5A1S6, Canada; easton@sfu.ca
* Correspondence: rockerbie@uleth.ca

Abstract: Revenue sharing is a common league policy in professional sports leagues. Several motivations for revenue sharing have been explored in the literature, including supporting small market teams, affecting league parity, suppressing player salaries, and improving team profitability. We investigate a different motivation. Risk-averse team owners, through their commissioner, are able to increase their utility by using revenue sharing to affect higher order moments of the revenue distribution. In particular, it may reduce the variance and kurtosis, as well as affecting the skewness of the league distribution of team local revenues. We first determine the extent to which revenue sharing affects these moments in theory, then we quantify the effects on utility for Major League Baseball over the period 2002–2013. Our results suggest that revenue sharing produced significant utility gains at little cost, which enhanced the positive effects noted by other studies.

Keywords: revenue sharing; welfare; moments; risk aversion

JEL Classification: Z28

1. Introduction

Many papers in the sports economics literature have studied the effects of different types of revenue sharing systems on league outcomes. The majority have focused on its effects on league parity using both theoretical models (Kesenne (2000, 2015); Miller (2007); Rockerbie (2009); Szymanski (2004) and Vrooman (2009) are examples), and empirical evidence (Maxcy 2009; Rockerbie 2017). Others have focused on the effects on player salaries (Hill and Jolly 2015), while others have focused on team profitability (Easton and Rockerbie 2005; Kesenne 2007). These papers assume that the motivation for a league to adopt revenue sharing is to encourage financial stability and to minimize the credible threats of rival leagues. Financial stability is an often-used term that is addressed only indirectly by creating links between parity and profitability to financial stability. Our purpose in this paper is to investigate the effects of revenue sharing on financial stability more directly by considering its effects on the league distribution of local revenues, and the potential benefits (and costs) that they generate for team owners. Specifically, we show that a straight pool revenue sharing system affects the variance, skewness, and kurtosis of the league revenue distribution in a systematic but non-linear fashion. We then quantify the gains to a representative team owner by assuming a risk-averse league commissioner whose objective is to reduce financial uncertainty for team owners. Our results using data for Major League Baseball (MLB) suggest that the benefits to team owners can be significant, and that they provide a motivation for revenue sharing that we have not seen explored in the literature.

A growing literature has considered how trade-induced economic growth has resulted in greater income inequality (Dixit and Norman 1986; Goldberg and Pavcnik 2007), and how an income tax system can redistribute income to enhance the potential gains from free trade and integration. Revenue sharing is essentially a tax system to redistribute revenues from rich to poor teams in professional sports leagues. We focus on the sharing of local revenues in this paper. However, sharing of marketing, media, and television revenues has become a standard practice as well. The National League of MLB adopted gate revenue sharing in 1876 and the American League in 1903 (fixed dollar amounts per home ticket sold).[1] The National Hockey League (NHL) adopted a limited gate revenue sharing plan in 1925 (3.5% of home gate receipts)[2] and the National Football League (NFL) a much more extensive gate sharing plan in 1960 (40% of home gate receipts).[3] Early in their histories, leagues often adopted revenue sharing during periods of rapid expansion that created a large imbalance in league revenues. Maintaining the financial stability of the league was important to ensure that teams had opponents to play games against and to stave off the threat of rival leagues.[4] Today's revenue sharing plans are complex and extensive and are agreed to with players in their collective bargaining agreements. Virtually all local revenues are shared to some extent, including the local television network and cable revenues.

The long-standing gate sharing plan was used in both the National League and the American League up to the 1995 season. The 1996–2001 seasons saw MLB experimenting with different hybrid plans in each season. It was not until the 2002 season that MLB adopted the simple straight-pool revenue sharing plan that required each team to contribute 34% of its local revenue to the pool, with the pool then split up evenly among all 30 teams.[5] A supplemental revenue sharing plan was established to divide up monies from the Major League Central Fund (national television rights, apparel and other rights held by Major League Baseball Properties) that were formally distributed evenly to all clubs. Each club's equal share was adjusted based on their revenue circumstance for the previous three seasons. The amount of the Central Fund to perform the adjustment was calculated to be 41.066% of the net transfer value of the straight-pool revenue sharing plan. For instance, in the last year of the agreement (2006) the net transfer value (the amount transferred from payer teams to payee teams) was approximately $1.62 billion, giving the size of the Central Fund to be shared at $665.3 million. To qualify to receive monies from this shared portion of the Central Fund, a club had to be a net payee in the straight-pool plan for the same season and had to have a mean local revenue for the preceding three seasons that was less than the mean local revenue for the league. The equal share for a payee was then topped up by multiplying size of the fund ($665.3 million in 2006) by a ratio, comprised of the difference in the league mean local revenue for the previous three seasons, and the recipient's mean local revenue for the previous three seasons, divided by the sum of these differences of all recipient teams in the last three seasons. All MLB teams received monies from the Central Fund; however, high revenue teams received less than low revenue teams.

The 2007 Collective Bargaining Agreement (CBA) saw the contribution rate drop to 31% in the straight-pool revenue sharing plan of local revenues, and a new supplemental pool plan.[6] The supplemental pool contained enough revenue, taken from the Major League Central Fund, to top up the total revenue sharing pool to 48% of local revenues (or roughly 17% of total local revenues amounting to $967.3 million in the last year of the agreement (2011)) and this was distributed to teams based on performance factors that reflected the size of local television and media markets.

---

1 See Surdham (2007).
2 See Ross (2015).
3 See Surdham (2007).
4 The NHL welcomed the Boston Bruins, New York Americans, and the Pittsburgh Pirates in 1925, and approved new franchises in Chicago and Detroit in 1926. The addition of these large American cities to the much smaller four Canadian cities already in the NHL created a bidding war for professional players that put the smaller franchises at a considerable financial disadvantage. The NFL had just survived the threat of the now defunct All-American Football Conference (AAFC) by absorbing three AAFC teams in 1950. The new American Football League (AFL) began operations in 1960 as a direct competitor to the long-established NFL.
5 http://roadsidephotos.sabr.org/baseball/BasicAgreement.pdf.
6 http://www.steroidsinbaseball.net/cba/cba_07_11.pdf.

Large market teams carried negative performance factors, while small market teams carried positive performance factors (the sum of the performance factors being zero). These monies were then added to the equal shares received from the Central Fund to calculate a net among the amount received. Again, all teams received monies from the Central Fund, but large market teams received less than small market teams.

The contribution rate was increased to 34% in the 2012 CBA, while the basic form of the supplemental pool from the Central Fund was maintained from the 2007 CBA.

We did not model the supplemental revenue sharing pool in the rest of the paper due to its asymmetric effects on team revenues, and the fact that the plan changed significantly from the 2002–2006 to the 2007–2011 CBA's. Incorporating the plan into an algebraic model to predict the effects on the *league total revenue* distribution proved difficult, despite our efforts. Instead we chose to focus only on the straight-pool revenue sharing plan and its effects on the moments of the league local revenue distribution. This was a shortcoming of our approach; however, we leave the problem of the distribution of the Central Fund revenues to further research.

Theoretical models have focused mainly on the effects on parity and team profitability in levels. However, it is uncertain as to how a movement towards or away from parity in winning percentages affects the stability of league revenues. We considered the effects of revenue sharing on the league distribution of team revenues in terms of its second (variance), third (skewness), and fourth moments (kurtosis). Figures 1 and 2 plot the histograms and reports the relevant moments of local revenue for the 2002 and 2011 MLB seasons. The variance of local team revenue (excluding national media, apparel, and other rights revenues shared by all teams) after revenue sharing (σ_A^2) was less than half (43.5% and 46.7%) of the variance of local team revenue before revenue sharing (σ^2) in each respective season, and the third (29%) and fourth (19%) moments were also reduced. The biggest contributor to the revenue sharing plan in both seasons was the New York Yankees, contributing a net sum of approximately $52 million in 2002 and $100 million in 2011. The Yankees owners (G. and H. Steinbrenner) could not have been happy with making a net contribution of $754 million over the 2002 to 2011 seasons; however, the Yankees carry only one vote when it comes to changing league policy. Although it is a net zero gain to the league in terms of total and average local revenue, the reduction in risk alone that revenue sharing provided must have been greatly valued by a majority of other owners.

Reducing its variance has obvious benefits with risk-averse team owners, but reducing its third and fourth moments[7] has a more complex effect on benefits.[8] Reducing skewness implies a more equal distribution of team revenues—a desirable result for a league composed of socialist owners, but team owners are capitalists who prefer more rather than less, and their commissioner is chosen to represent their financial interests. As we shall show, a league with a higher positive skewness has a lower likelihood of downside risk, and is preferred by the representative team owner. While it is not the worst outcome, equality of team revenues is preferred to a higher downside risk ($\sigma^3 < 0$).

---

7 We refer to the average cubed deviation around the mean as σ^3 as it is clearly related to the idea of skewness. It is not the coefficient of skewness. The Pearson definition of skewness is $n^{-1} \sum ((R_i^A - \overline{R})/\sigma)^3$; however, we refer to σ^3 as a characterization of skewness in the rest of the paper.

8 The third moment is characterized as being associated with "prudence" (Kimball 1990), and the fourth moment as being associated with "temperance" (Eeckhoudt et al. 1995). See Chiu (2005), or Eeckhoudt and Schlesinger (2013) for additional interpretation of these and higher order moments.

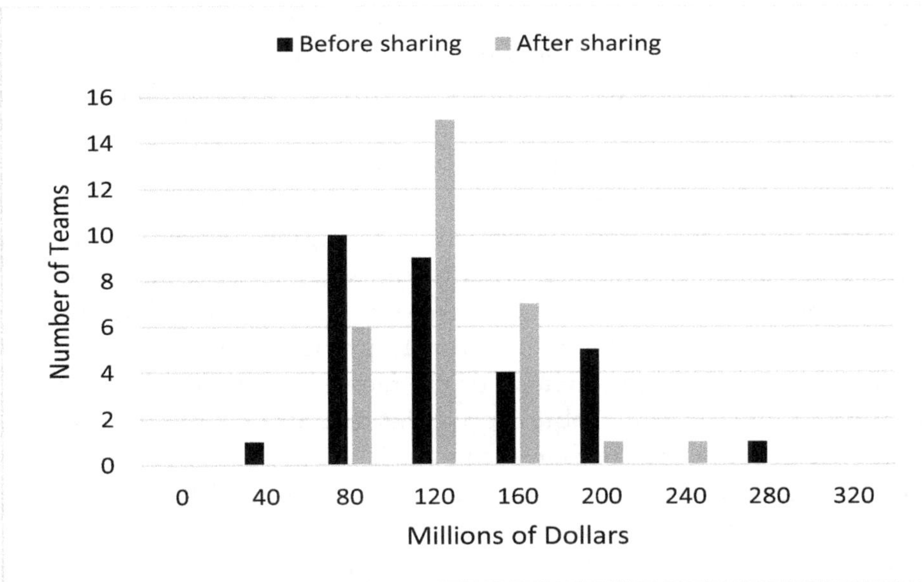

Figure 1. Local revenues pre- and post-revenue sharing in Major Baseball League (MLB), 2002 season. ($\overline{R} = \$109.4$ million, $\sigma^2 = 2607.2$, $\sigma^2{}_A = 1135.7$, $\sigma^3 = 3,720,200$, $\sigma^3{}_A = 1,069,542$, $\sigma^4 = 24,251,058$, $\sigma^4{}_A = 4,601,574$). Pre-revenue sharing data based on author's calculations.

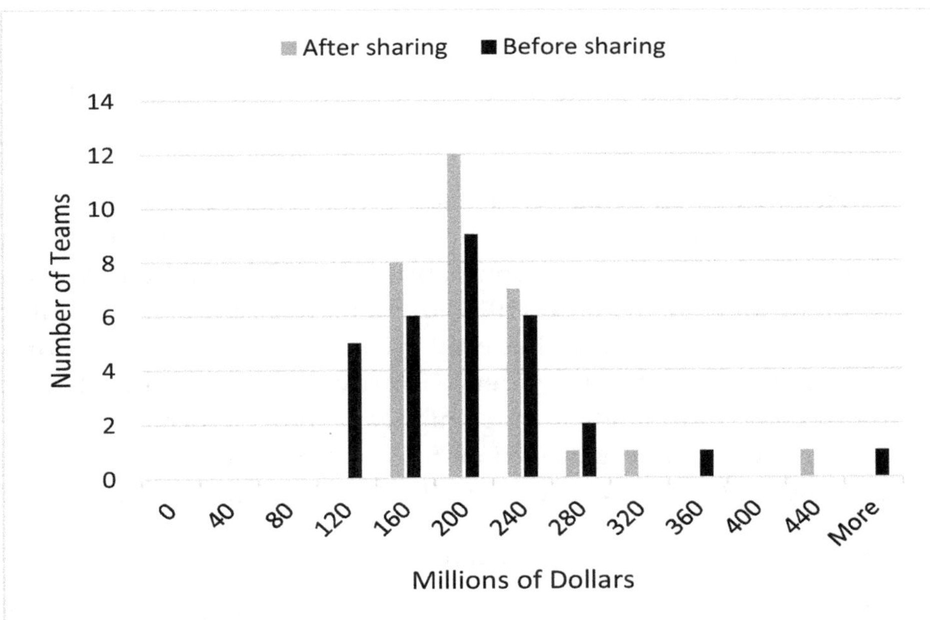

Figure 2. Local revenues pre and post-revenue sharing in MLB, 2011 season. ($\overline{R} = \$189.7$ million, $\sigma^2 = 6234.2$, $\sigma^2{}_A = 2968.1$, $\sigma^3 = 36,153,429$, $\sigma^3{}_A = 5,053,763$, $\sigma^4 = 166,465,178$, $\sigma^4{}_A = 93,707,469$). Pre-revenue sharing data based on author's calculations.

2. Risk Aversion and Revenues

To motivate the effects of revenue sharing, we will assume that team owners are risk-averse and maximize their utility from profit. This differs from the standard sports league model that assumes risk-neutral team owners who maximize profit (or winning or a combination of the two).

Consumers are often thought of as being risk-averse when facing a gamble that will affect their income or wealth. In the simplest case of a sports league, a representative team owner faces an uncertain portion of team revenue (excluding fixed revenues that arise from the Major League Central Fund) from season to season, that takes on only two outcomes, high or low. These uncertain revenues arise from the inherent uncertainty of team performance due to injuries or changes in the performance of competing teams, or changing local market conditions. While team owners do not have the choice of accepting a certainty equivalent amount of revenue, as explained below, they may prefer league policies that reduce the variation (or higher moments) of team revenues and raise their utility.

When speaking of risk aversion in firms, the economics literature defines the owner of a firm as an "entrepreneur". The connotation is that being an entrepreneur means starting a new business that has risky/uncertain financial outcomes, instead of the faceless widget producer who faces a certain demand that is assumed in textbooks.[9] Table 1 provides a summary of ownership structures in the four major North American professional sports leagues. The vast majority are partnerships (with the exception of MLB at 16 out of 30 teams) that identify as limited liability corporations (LLCs) for tax purposes[10] and identify one individual as the majority owner. In fact, the NFL prohibits standard corporate ownership of its teams, with the historical exception of the Green Bay Packers, which is community-owned. Consequently, thinking about professional sports teams as having one or two investor/owners who are responsible for most business decisions is completely appropriate, given their actual ownership structures.

Table 1. Ownership structures in North American professional sports leagues, 2018.[11]

	Normal Corporation	Partnerships/LLC	Identify Majority Owner
MLB	14	16	28
NBA	10	20	30
NHL	6	25	30
NFL	1	31	31

In the simplest case, if the firm delegates decisions to a manager whose pay is linked to firm performance, the firm may display risk-averse behavior. However, firms may display risk-aversion for several other reasons. Firms in a perfectly competitive industry may reduce output when facing demand uncertainty (Sandmo 1971); Leland (1972) demonstrates the same result for a risk-averse monopoly, while Asplund (2002) suggests that only greater cost uncertainty reduces output for a risk-averse oligopoly firm. Some empirical evidence is provided by Herranz et al. (2015) who show that risk-averse entrepreneurs run smaller, more highly leveraged firms with lower default risk. This behavior is consistent with U.S. business data for approximately 5 million small firms whose owners invest a large amount of their own wealth in the business, and typically work at the business.

A League: When Monopoly Does Not Maximize Individual Profit

Team owners are entrepreneurs who invest in costly talent that produces an uncertain outcome (wins). As Neale (1964) first noted, a professional sports firm requires other firms (teams) to produce an output (games) and earn revenue. At the local level, team owners are competitive on the field,

9 Frank Knight (1921) in Risk, Uncertainty and Profit, called attention to this reality as early as 1921.

10 The assets of owners of limited liability corporations (LLCs) are protected from creditors in the event of default of the LLC. Their corporate structure does not include a Board of Directors or Officers; instead, decisions rest with the owner(s). Any profit from the LLC is reported as taxable personal income for the owner(s) to avoid the double taxation of corporate profit and personal income received from dividends.

11 Source: https://www.baseball-reference.com/bullpen/List_of_Major_League_Baseball_principal_owners, https://en.wikipedia.org/wiki/List_of_NBA_team_owners, http://icehockey.wikia.com/wiki/List_of_NHL_Owners, https://en.wikipedia.org/wiki/List_of_NFL_franchise_owners.

but engage in a joint venture at the league level.[12] League policies that might appear to be collusive (a common set of rules, a playing schedule, a player draft, free agency, and so on) must be adopted to insure the survival of the league and, thus, each team. The fact that team owners often argue that revenue sharing is necessary for the stability of the league (Bontemps 2017) is some evidence that they are sensitive to profit risk. Revenue sharing requires the approval of a majority of team owners. For those owners who earn consistent profits, giving up some profit to insure that smaller market teams survive is a form of insurance premium for future revenue stability. Outside of a professional sports league, any movement towards a monopoly benefits the profit position for a firm, but not so for a professional sports team owner.

Risk aversion has a long tradition in the labor economics literature. Generally, risk-averse firms suffer much lower utility in the low demand state than in the high demand state; thus, they reduce their output and hire fewer workers to reduce costs and maintain profitability. Choudhary and Levine (2010) review this literature. Professional sports teams do not hire and fire homogeneous workers, but instead face fixed roster sizes. Hence, they must adjust payroll costs by increasing or reducing the stock of team talent. Krautmann (2017) found evidence to suggest that team owners demonstrate risk aversion by paying a premium to MLB players who demonstrate consistent performance. Maxcy (2004) suggested that team owners reward consistent players with longer term contracts. Consistent player performance translates into consistent team revenues, suggesting that team owners value consistent revenues that can be made even less variable with revenue sharing.[13]

Risk aversion has also been used to explain why workers prefer stable employment contracts that pay a lower wage in the face of uncertain productivity. Wages and employment will then appear to be somewhat inflexible during swings in productivity (business) cycles. Employers who are risk-neutral will be indifferent between such a contract and a bonus-based contract. A good reference is Thomas and Worrall (1988). This might explain why professional athletes may prefer long-term contracts with stable salaries to short-term performance-based contracts. Although this is an interesting research area, we consider the effects of revenue sharing only on team owners, admitting that risk aversion might play a role in contract negotiations and subsequent team owner utility.

Prudence, or in our case the reduction of downside risk, is a characteristic of the individual who buys insurance, and is described by the skewness of revenues. Risk aversion and prudence are not identical, but they are related (Kimball 1990; Chiu 2005). As we show below, a risk-averse team owner benefits from prudence and consequently reduces the likelihood of a bad revenue state.

To fix ideas, Eeckhoudt and Schlesinger (2013) imagine a lottery with two outcomes. In state 1, we receive $X - k$ in which k is a fixed amount, and in state 2, we receive $X + e$ where e is a mean zero random payout with finite variance. Now consider a second lottery in which the good state receives X and the bad state receives $X - k + e$. Since the second lottery increases the downside risk but leaves the mean and the variance unchanged, a prudent individual is defined as one who prefers the first lottery to the second. The first lottery attaches the sure loss to the state with no risk, while in the second lottery, the sure loss is attached to the state with risk, e. This behavior means that for a given mean and variance, negative skewness in revenues is undesirable for the league.

Temperance describes a representative team owner who wishes to avoid a large probability density in both tails of the revenue distribution—avoiding extreme outcomes. This translates to a small value for the fourth moment (kurtosis) of the league revenue distribution.

12 See for example https://www.lexology.com/library/detail.aspx?g=31d92fbf-9e64-4aaa-a5e4-a1f56bc23c8a.

13 We are grateful to a referee for pointing out that there is a derived demand for minor league performance leading to major league outcomes. Although we do not explore this relationship, it has been considered with dramatically different conclusions in two sources. https://www.baseballamerica.com/stories/quantifying-the-effects-of-winning-in-the-minor-leagues-on-player-development/, http://washusportsanalytics.weebly.com/our-research/the-value-of-minor-league-seasoning.

3. The Model

Our sports league is composed of n teams. Each team owner contributes a share $(1 - \alpha)$ of its local revenue into a straight pool, which is then divided evenly among the team owners at the end of each playing season. Local revenues are obtained primarily from ticket sales, but they may also contain other local revenues that increase with the performance of the team. We ignore other types of revenue that are not typically dependent upon team performance. To focus on the static consequences of revenue sharing, we do not explicitly model the determination of the profit-maximizing revenue for each team. We acknowledge that revenue sharing can affect the optimal choice of talent and thus team revenue. It is an undisputed result in the theoretical literature that revenue sharing reduces the demand for talented players and subsequently lowers salaries (Fort and Quirk 1995). This is a positive benefit for team profits that we cannot model without resorting to a simultaneous equation system composed of a marginal revenue function for each team. If one could model such a complex system, the increase in team profitability due to revenue sharing could only enhance the positive effects that we demonstrate here.

The bulk of the theoretical literature on revenue sharing has come into agreement that increased revenue sharing reduces league parity (Kesenne (2000, 2015), Miller (2007), Szymanski (2004), and Vrooman (2009) that could have negative consequences for consumer welfare if fans value close contests (the uncertainty of outcome hypothesis or UOH). Fort and Quirk (2010a, 2010b) use the sum of consumer and producer surpluses to compare welfare at different levels of league parity. Dietl, Lang and Werner (Dietl et al. 2009) show that revenue sharing increases welfare measured as the sum of consumer surplus and team profits. To capture this effect in our model would require an estimation of the effects of the 2002, 2007, and 2012 changes to the straight-pool revenue sharing plan on league parity, and an assumption of some sort of consumer welfare function that values the UOH. Instead we have chosen to focus on the isolated effect of revenue sharing on the moments of the league distribution of revenues. We acknowledge this as a shortcoming of our approach and leave it to further research to investigate the salary and parity effects of revenue sharing on total league and consumer welfare.

Revenue for team i after revenue sharing (where an "A" distinguishes revenue after sharing) is given by:

$$R_i^A = \alpha R_i + (1-\alpha)\sum R_j/n = \alpha R_i + (1-\alpha)\overline{R} \tag{1}$$

In (1), $\overline{R} = \sum_{j=1}^{n} R_j/n$, the average team local revenue for the league before revenue sharing.[14] We need not consider the theoretical result that revenue sharing reduces the incentive of team owners to acquire talent and earn revenue, since we are not solving a team owner maximization problem. Instead we accept that each R_j has been determined ex-post by the profit maximizing decision of the owner of team j, accounting for the revenue sharing payments that each will contribute or receive.

Utility is representative of any one of the owners (a representative agent model) and is calculated as a constant relative risk aversion utility function of the form[15]:

$$U = R^{1-\theta}/1-\theta \tag{2}$$

The θ term is the coefficient of relative risk aversion and R is the local revenue of a representative team owner. Revenue sharing affects the league distribution of revenues, and we focus our analysis on the utility effects for the resulting representative owner.

---

14 It is easy to show that the average local revenue is unchanged by revenue sharing. Using (1), $\overline{R}^A = \sum R_j^A/n = (\sum \alpha R_j + \sum(1-\alpha)\overline{R})/n = \alpha\overline{R} + (1-\alpha)\overline{R} = \overline{R}$.

15 The CRRA utility function is a popular choice in models of consumption and real business cycles for two reasons: risk aversion is invariant to the level of consumption, income and wealth; utility is stationary, that is, moving the same consumption path forward one or more periods does not change the preference ordering of goods to consume. See Lucas (1987).

We utilize a Taylor series expansion of a representative owner's CRRA utility function as an approximation to the utility obtained from an expected utility maximization problem. This is the approach pioneered by Markowitz (1952) to develop his mean-variance portfolio model, although he only considered the first two moments of the return distribution. Kraus and Litzenberger (1976) extend the CAPM analysis to the third moment. This approach is not without controversy. Loistl (1976) demonstrated that a Taylor series expansion does not approximate the portfolio results of expected utility maximization very well, except for the case of a quadratic utility function. However, a number of papers have suggested that the degree of error is very slight, by the use of simulations of different choice models (Levy and Markowitz (1979), Pulley (1981), Kroll et al. (1984), Tew et al. (1991), and Tompkins (2000) are a few), typically on the order of \$0.00025 per dollar invested. In addition, their results suggest that the error decreases with the number of assets in the portfolio; in our case, teams sharing the revenue in the league. In our case, the Taylor series approximation adds the ease of measurement of utility, as well as bringing in the first four moments of the league revenue distribution into the discussion in a coherent way.

To approximate utility for the representative owner and to introduce the first four moments of the league revenue distribution, we take a Taylor series expansion of (2) around the average team local revenue, limited to the first four terms.[16]

$$U \approx \frac{\overline{R}^{1-\theta}}{1-\theta} + \overline{R}^{-\theta}(R-\overline{R}) - \frac{\theta}{2}\overline{R}^{-\theta-1}(R-\overline{R})^2 + \frac{\theta(\theta-1)}{3!}\overline{R}^{-\theta-2}(R-\overline{R})^3 - \frac{\theta(\theta-1)(\theta-2)}{4!}\overline{R}^{-\theta-3}(R-\overline{R})^4 \tag{3}$$

Before revenue sharing in any season, local revenue for the representative owner can deviate from its mean due to shocks that we specify as $R = \overline{R} + e$ without specifying the nature of these shocks, and assuming $E(e) = 0$ and $Var(e) = \sigma^2$. The average local revenue is unchanged after revenue sharing, hence the second term in (3) vanishes after taking its expected value, while the variance and skewness and kurtosis of local revenue after revenue sharing are denoted as:

$$\begin{aligned} E(R_i^A - \overline{R})^2 &= \sigma_A^2 = \tfrac{1}{n}\Sigma(R_i^A - \overline{R})^2 \\ E(R_i^A - \overline{R})^3 &= \sigma_A^3 = \tfrac{1}{n}\Sigma(R_i^A - \overline{R})^3 \\ E(R_i^A - \overline{R})^4 &= \sigma_A^4 = \tfrac{1}{n}\Sigma(R_i^A - \overline{R})^4 \end{aligned}$$

Thus:

$$E(U) = [R^{1-\theta}/1-\theta] - \frac{\theta}{2}\overline{R}^{-(1+\theta)}\sigma_A^2 + \frac{\theta(\theta-1)}{6}\overline{R}^{-(2+\theta)}\sigma_A^3 - \frac{\theta(\theta-1)(\theta-2)}{4!}\overline{R}^{-(3+\theta)}\sigma_A^4 \tag{4}$$

3.1. Risk Aversion

Risk aversion suggests that greater variability in team revenue (σ_A^2) reduces utility. Risk-averse team owners seek to reduce the variability in revenues by diversifying their revenue "portfolios", and revenue sharing provides a mechanism to do this, although we do not pursue this team-specific

[16] Lucas (1987) used the same expansion method to evaluate the welfare gain from consumption smoothing. He did not expand to the fourth term in (3), since he did not have the data necessary to compute the moments of the distribution of U.S. aggregate consumption.

portfolio effect.[17] Rather, we assume that the representative team owner is concerned with the variance and higher orders of the distribution of team local revenues around the team average.

3.2. Skewness Reflects Prudence

The effect of skewness on utility depends upon the degree of relative risk aversion. If the representative owner is risk-averse and we assume $\theta > 1$, positive skewness in revenues ($\sigma_A^3 > 0$) will increase expected utility.[18] Positive skewness will reduce the likelihood that poor revenue for one or more teams will threaten the stability of the league. Revenue sharing is a policy that will also contribute to stability. Prudent owners will benefit from skewness. It is important not to confuse skewness in revenues with a lack of revenue equity that some might associate with lower welfare. In our model, the league wishes to see the majority of teams doing well on the revenue side. How revenue sharing affects skewness is specifically addressed in a later section; however, any improvement in revenue equity, as measured by a movement to a more symmetric league revenue distribution from positive skewness, will lower league utility.

To see each of the effects of the variance, skewness and kurtosis on utility, we consider each individually before amalgamating.

3.3. Revenue Sharing and the Variance of Team Revenues

To calculate the variance of team revenues after revenue sharing, one might be tempted to use the simple rule of variances that $Var\ aX = a^2 Var\ X$, since part of the local revenue after sharing is just αR_i, but this would ignore the payment received from the revenue-sharing pool. The variance of team revenues around the league average after revenue sharing is not as obvious as the simple rule, but it is not hard to derive:

$$\sigma_A^2 = E(R_j^A - \overline{R})^2 = \frac{1}{n}\sum_{j=1}^{n}(R_j^A - \overline{R})^2 \quad (5)$$

Consider the bracketed term only for team i and insert (1):

$$(R_i^A - \overline{R})^2 = (\alpha R_i + (1-\alpha)\overline{R} - \overline{R})^2 = (\alpha(R_i - \overline{R}))^2 = \alpha^2 (R_i - \overline{R})^2 \quad (6)$$

Each of the n teams will have the same expression as (6), with the terms inside the brackets using values for the individual team. Summing over the n teams gives:

$$\sigma_A^2 = \frac{1}{n}\sum_{j=1}^{n}(R_j^A - \overline{R})^2 = \alpha^2 \frac{1}{n}\sum_{j=1}^{n}(R_j - \overline{R})^2 = \alpha^2\sigma^2 \quad (7)$$

The reduction in the variance of league revenues after revenue sharing is proportional to α^2. If we think of the variance of local revenues as a measure of risk, revenue sharing reduces this risk by a factor of $0.69^2 = 0.4761$ in MLB ($\alpha = 0.69$ as per the 2016 CBA), which is a 31 percent reduction from no revenue sharing.

---

17 Revenue sharing in the form assumed in this paper allows team owners to diversify their revenue portfolios by essentially investing in the economic health of other teams. Two requirements are necessary for team owners to benefit from a portfolio effect. First, team revenues should display some sort of cyclical behavior; second, and related to the first requirement, a majority of teams should display a negative covariance with the revenues of other teams or the league average revenue. Most professional sports teams have periods of strong revenue growth, followed by periods of revenue stagnation or decline. The cyclical nature of winning percentages and a possible cause of this has been explored by Easton and Rockerbie (2010), and Rockerbie and Easton (2014). Revenues are at least partially determined by success on the field, however the cyclical nature of team revenues has not been deeply explored in the literature. The majority of team owners that vote in favor of revenue sharing might do so if they perceive a benefit from the portfolio effect, implying that their local revenue displays a negative covariance with the local revenues of other teams.

18 Below, we will argue for $\theta > 3$. In the special case of $\theta = 1$, we have a log utility function, and skewness does not affect the utility, from inspection of (4).

Risk-averse team owners will value the reduction in risk that revenue sharing delivers. But by how much? The relevant part of (4) is $-\frac{\theta}{2}\overline{R}^{-(1+\theta)}\sigma_A^2$. Consider the one-shot adoption of revenue sharing that reduces $\alpha = 1$ to $\alpha = 0.69$. Expressing the increase in utility relative to marginal utility ($\overline{R}^{-\theta}$ when evaluated at the mean) gives the increase in dollars per unit of utility. Next, dividing by the average local revenue for the league ($\overline{R}$) expresses the welfare change as a percentage of average league revenue[19]:

$$\frac{\Delta U/U'}{\overline{R}} = -\frac{(\theta/2)\overline{R}^{-(1+\theta)}(\sigma_A^2 - \sigma^2)}{\overline{R}^{-\theta}\overline{R}} = -\frac{\theta(\alpha^2-1)\sigma^2}{2\overline{R}^2} = \left(\frac{\theta}{2\overline{R}^2}\right)0.5239\sigma^2 > 0 \tag{8}$$

The larger the variance in league local revenues before revenue sharing, the larger the welfare gains are from revenue sharing, and the larger is the average local revenue of the league, the smaller are the utility gains from revenue sharing. Leagues composed of very wealthy teams playing in large markets may stand little to gain in utility by instituting revenue sharing.

3.4. Revenue Sharing and the Skewness of League Revenues

Skewness is also important to the utility of the representative. Positive skewness provides higher utility because it indicates a low probability of a poor revenue outcome for one or more of the teams. Skewness after revenue sharing is defined as:

$$\sigma_A^3 = E(R_j^A - \overline{R})^3 = \frac{1}{n}\sum_{j=1}^{n}(R_j^A - \overline{R})^3 \tag{9}$$

Using the same method used to derive the variance, the skewness in local revenues is given by:

$$\sigma_A^3 = \alpha^3\sigma^3 \tag{10}$$

The reduction in skewness of the league revenue distribution that revenue sharing delivers is proportional to α^3. For MLB, this is $0.69^3 = 0.3285$, again a significant reduction, but in this case, a reduction in utility for the league if the league revenue distribution is positively skewed. How much will the league (representative owner) value the reduction in skewness with greater revenue sharing? The relevant part of (4) is $\frac{\theta(\theta-1)}{6}\overline{R}^{-(2+\theta)}\sigma_A^3$. Again, expressing the increase in utility relative to marginal utility, and then expressing it as a percentage of average league revenue gives the results of a decrease in welfare for the league by increasing revenue sharing:

$$\frac{\Delta U/U'}{\overline{R}} = \frac{\theta(\theta-1)}{6\overline{R}^3}\sigma^3(0.69^3-1) = -\frac{\theta(\theta-1)}{6\overline{R}^3}0.6715\sigma^3 < 0 \tag{11}$$

3.5. Revenue Sharing and the Kurtosis of League Revenues

Positive kurtosis indicates that the league revenue distribution has "heavy tails", or that there is a significant probability of extreme revenue results. This reduces the utility for the representative owner from the last term in (4). Kurtosis after revenue sharing is defined as:

$$\sigma_A^4 = E(R_j^A - \overline{R})^4 = \frac{1}{n}\sum_{j=1}^{n}(R_j^A - \overline{R})^4 \tag{12}$$

19 The average revenue for the representative owner is the same as the average league revenue across all teams.

Using the same method used to derive the variance, the kurtosis in local revenues is given by:

$$\sigma_A^4 = \alpha^4\sigma^4 \tag{13}$$

The reduction in kurtosis of the league revenue distribution that revenue sharing delivers is proportional to α^4. A representative owner that displays temperance, values the reduction in kurtosis as provided by revenue sharing, by the amount $-\frac{\theta(\theta-1)(\theta-2)}{4!}\overline{R}^{-(3+\theta)}\sigma_A^4$ from (4). Here, we are also assuming that $\theta > 2$. Expressing the utility gain as a percentage of the average team revenue gives:

$$\frac{\Delta U/U'}{\overline{R}} = \frac{\theta(\theta-1)(\theta-2)}{24\overline{R}^4}\sigma^4(0.69^4 - 1) = \frac{\theta(\theta-1)(\theta-2)}{24\sigma^4}0.7733\sigma^4 > 0 \tag{14}$$

4. Overall Utility Gains from Revenue Sharing

Revenue sharing increases the utility for the representative owner by reducing the variance of local revenues around the league average and reducing kurtosis, but lowers the utility by reducing positive skewness. However, if skewness were to be negative, then revenue sharing would raise utility. The net change in utility is the sum of (8), (11), and (14).

$$Net\ \frac{\Delta U/U'}{\overline{R}} = -\frac{\theta(\alpha^2-1)\sigma^2}{2\overline{R}^2} + \frac{\theta(\theta-1)(\alpha^3-1)\sigma^3}{6\overline{R}^3} - \frac{\theta(\theta-1)(\theta-2)(\alpha^4-1)\sigma^4}{24\overline{R}^4} \tag{15}$$

The measurement of the utility gain in (15) requires the accurate data concerning the distribution of team revenues to be meaningful. Professional sports leagues do not make these data publicly available. We require local revenues before revenue sharing for every team in a professional sports league. MLB released accurate data for the 1995 through 2001 seasons in a supplement to its Blue Ribbon report (Major League Baseball 2001). Team local revenues before revenue sharing are reported in Table 2 of the report.[20] Unfortunately MLB did not use the straight-pool revenue sharing plan that we assumed, in deriving Equations (7), (10), and (13) in any of these seasons. The Blue Ribbon report provided a unique glimpse into the financial numbers for MLB.[21] As much as we would like to use data from the report, we cannot for two reasons. First, as already noted, the derivations of Equations (7), (10), and (13) that determine the properties of straight-pool revenue sharing on the variance and skewness of the league revenue distribution do not hold for the forms of revenue sharing used in the 1995–2001 seasons. Second, team owners form expectations of the amount of revenue to be contributed to the revenue sharing pool when making their talent acquisitions, setting ticket prices, and other financial decisions. These decisions incorporate the pre-revenue sharing local revenue figures. Using local revenue data for different revenue sharing plans is not consistent with team owner expectations.

Forbes magazine publishes estimates of gate revenue before revenue sharing for MLB, beginning in 1990. We have chosen the 2002–2013 MLB seasons, since the straight-pool revenue sharing plan was used in each season. Forbes reports the estimates of gate revenue, other revenue, and total revenue.[22] Other revenue includes all other sources of local revenue (parking, concessions, marketing, local media,

---

20 Local revenue consists of gate receipts, local television, radio and cable rights fees, ballpark concessions, local advertising, sponsorship and publications, parking, suite rentals, and postseason and spring training revenues. Local revenues are the largest single component of most clubs' total annual revenues. The only other significant source of revenue is the Major League Central Fund revenue that is not distributed from the supplemental revenue sharing plan. See footnote 21.

21 Financial statements for MLB clubs are sometimes leaked by the press or presented voluntarily by MLB clubs, but only sporadically. See Rod Fort's website for limited data for the Seattle Mariners, Milwaukee Brewers, and Cleveland Indians (https://sites.google.com/site/rodswebpages/codes). More recent data for the Los Angeles Angels, Florida Marlins, and Pittsburgh Pirates can be found at http://deadspin.com/5615096/mlb-confidential-the-financial-documents-baseball-doesnt-want-you-to-see-part-1.

22 The data are conveniently located at Rod Fort's website, https://sites.google.com/site/rodswebpages/codes.

and so on), as well as the net revenue sharing payment received and the share of the national broadcast revenue. To evaluate Equation (15), we require total local revenue before revenue sharing. We first subtract the share of the national television broadcast revenue from the reported total local revenue[23] that is not shared through the supplemental revenue sharing plan. All the remaining local revenue is shared and is reported net of any revenue sharing payment. We calculate local revenue before sharing using the formula $R_1 = (R_1^A - (1-a)\overline{R})/\alpha$ using the values $\alpha = 0.66$, $\alpha = 0.69$, and $\alpha = 0.66$, $\alpha = 0.69$, and $\alpha = 0.66$ for the 2002–2006, 2007–2011, and 2012–2013 periods respectively. Finally, we divided by the national consumer price index (2002 = 100) to convert to real local revenues.[24]

In our Table 2, we estimated the utility gains to MLB in the 2002–2013. We use the parameter values $\alpha = 0.66$ (2002–2006), $\alpha = 0.69$ (2007–2011), $\alpha = 0.66$ (2012–2013) and $\theta = 3$. Our choice of value for θ is based on survey evidence found in Mehra and Prescott (1985); however, using $\theta = 2$ eliminates any utility gains from temperance, and using $\theta = 1$ eliminates any gains from skewness, so we chose $\theta = 3$ to include all of the utility gains. The utility gain due to the decrease in the variance of team revenues ranged from 9.5% to 18.4%, averaging 14.1% of the average team revenue, over and above what the change would have been without revenue sharing. The losses due to reducing positive skewness were modest, ranging from −3.8% to −22.5%, averaging −9.4%. This utility-reducing effect of revenue sharing was evident in all of the 2002–2013 seasons.

Table 2. Average utility gains per team in MLB, 2002–2013 seasons. ($\alpha = 0.66$ (2002–2006), $\alpha = 0.69$ (2007–2011), $\alpha = 0.66$ (2012–2013), $\theta = 3$).

Season	$\overline{R}$ ($millions)	σ^2	σ^3	σ^4	Utility Gain from Variance [1]	Utility Gain from Skewness [1]	Utility Gain from Kurtosis [1]	Total Utility Gain [1]	Total Utility Gain in $ Millions
2002	109.4	2607.2	124,007	24,251,058	0.184	−0.067	0.034	0.151	16.55
2003	114.33	2031.3	149,561	25,301,566	0.132	−0.071	0.030	0.090	10.32
2004	123.77	2445.9	162,612	35,292,374	0.135	−0.061	0.030	0.105	12.94
2005	133.86	2023.4	129,960	27,444,089	0.095	−0.038	0.017	0.074	9.91
2006	142.06	2409	173,012	36,258,488	0.101	−0.043	0.018	0.076	10.81
2007	131.32	2524.1	187,469	40,161,132	0.114	−0.055	0.026	0.085	11.19
2008	134.92	3214	366,268	85,376,237	0.135	−0.096	0.047	0.086	11.78
2009	137.62	4696.4	849,723	255,211,618	0.191	−0.212	0.131	0.110	15.36
2010	150.78	3858.9	603,760	169,196,801	0.132	−0.117	0.062	0.078	11.78
2011	152.19	3995.4	603,327	166,465,178	0.134	−0.113	0.059	0.080	12.21
2012	159.3	4370.5	722,975	203,827,486	0.143	−0.124	0.062	0.081	13.03
2013	161.1	4717.7	559,595	147,568,889	0.145	−0.087	0.039	0.097	16.12

[1] As a percentage (×100) of the average team local revenue.

Our model suggests that revenue sharing should reduce any leptokurtic characteristic (kurtosis) of the league revenue distribution. From Table 2, the utility gain ranged from 1.7% to 6.2% of the average annual team revenue, with an average of 4.64%. The last row of Table 2 presents the utility gain or loss from revenue sharing in dollars. For an individual team owner, revenue sharing delivered an average annual utility gain of $12.7 million. The present value of these gains or losses for the average team is $138.5 million, discounted back to the 2002 season using a 3% discount rate, or $146.5 million using a 2% discount rate.[25] Much of this net utility gain arises from the decrease in variance of team revenues that revenue sharing delivers, while decreasing the leptokurtic league revenue distribution (kurtosis) provided smaller net benefits. The net utility gain could have been even larger if the league local revenue distribution (before revenue sharing) did not become increasingly positively skewed over the seven seasons: from a Pearson skewness coefficient value of 0.935 in 2002 to 2.64 in 2009, falling back to 1.73 in the 2013 season.

23 Each team received approximately $18.6 million in each of the 2002 through 2006 seasons, and $23.7 million in each of the 2007 through 2013 seasons. https://sites.google.com/site/rodswebpages/codes. These amount to an average share of local revenue of 18.5% in 2002, gradually declining to 11.8% in 2013.

24 http://www.usinflationcalculator.com/.

25 The average real interest rate (reported by the World Bank) was 3% for the U.S. over the 2002–2011 period.

Figure 3 reports the effect of changes in θ on the present value of the utility increase over the period. The curve reflects the increasing importance of skewness to the final utility gain. From (15) it is apparent that the impact on utility is a positive function of θ. Higher values of θ reflect higher values of risk aversion, but as is clear it does not mean that utility changes must be uniform. Our choice of $\theta = 3$ is quite conservative in light of the shape of Figure 3, and suggests that the utility gains from revenue sharing could be much larger than we compute.

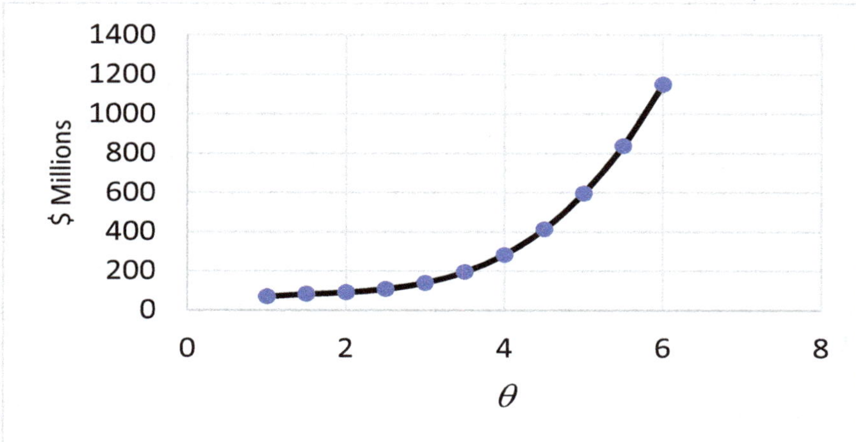

Figure 3. The prevent value in Dollars of the net utility gain with changes in θ. (Discount rate r = 0.03 and $\alpha = 0.69$ and $\alpha = 0.66$ as per text).

5. Conclusions

We have demonstrated significant utility gains to MLB from the straight pool revenue sharing system first adopted in the 2002 CBA. However, our measures of utility gain could be understated for several reasons. It may be that team owners are more risk-averse than we have assumed, implying that our values for θ are too small, but this seems unlikely. At the league level, stability of revenues could enhance the ability of a league commissioner to negotiate lucrative rights packages for television, internet, merchandising and so on. In the past, revenue sharing has also been a useful policy to prevent the formation of rival leagues by making the existing league attractive to cities that wish to join. At the team level, revenue sharing reduces the variance of local revenues after revenue sharing and hence reduces risk. This could have two beneficial effects for team owners. Lower risk can reduce the capital costs of new facilities for teams that wish to finance a portion or all of their new facilities. Local governments might be more willing to pick up a portion of the construction costs when they know that the team is on a stable financial footing and unlikely to leave for greener pastures once construction is finished. More importantly for team owners, low financial risk enhances the market value of the team when potential buyers are risk-averse. For many team owners, the financial rewards are the greatest when the team is sold.

Since revenue sharing costs little to implement, it would seem to be advantageous for a professional sports league to adopt it. In fact, further utility gains could be had by utilizing a progressive revenue tax. However, the wealthiest teams could oppose revenue sharing since the system penalizes on-field success and financial smarts. MLB has used a progressive competitive balance tax since the 1996 CBA. If their payrolls exceed the payroll threshold set in the most current CBA ($195 million for the 2017 season) and if they are first-time offenders, teams pay a tax rate of 22.5% of the payroll overage. The tax rate increases to 30% for second-time offenders, 40% for third-time offenders and 50% for four or more offenses. It is estimated that the New York Yankees paid

\$304 million in tax over the 2002–2016 seasons.[26] Even though the tax system is progressive in some sense, the tax revenue is not redistributed to any of the MLB teams; hence the tax system lacks the redistributive effects of revenue sharing. Neither revenue sharing nor the competitive balance tax is an ideal system in a league utility sense.

Mirlees (1971) demonstrated that an optimal income tax system still features a progressive income tax rate, even after accounting for the negative work-incentive effects of the tax, although his criteria of welfare differed from ours in that he focused on utility from consumption for individual workers. It would be useful to explore whether the same result holds for the use of revenue sharing in a professional sports league using our measure of league welfare. However, it would necessitate specifying how the progressive revenue sharing tax affects the talent decisions of team owners; that is, stating what the function $R_i = R_i(\alpha, w_i)$ looks like.[27] We leave that problem for future research.

Our paper is not without its shortcomings. Straight-pool revenue sharing has fairly predictable effects on team behavior that we chose to ignore in our static analysis. These include a decrease in player salaries, a redistribution of talent to large market teams, and a worsening of league parity. The ultimate effect on team profit is uncertain. Our concern is with the moments of the league local revenue distribution. Endogenizing these dynamic effects into a league model of local revenue with revenue sharing is a challenging task. We also abstract from the welfare effects of revenue sharing, and choose to only focus on the utility gains for the representative team owner. A more encompassing model of welfare would include the effects on team profits, and the effects on utility for consumers of MLB games arising from changes in consumer surplus and parity effects. This would require a general equilibrium model of league outcomes and consumer utility that we chose not to attempt. Finally, we consider only the effects of the straight-pool revenue sharing plan on the league local revenue distribution, ignoring the potential utility gains from the sharing of Central Fund revenues. Central Fund revenues do not arise from a tax on local revenues that arise from the profit-maximizing decisions of team owners. Instead they are typically treated in the literature as a fixed revenue that does not affect profit-maximizing decisions, although they obviously increase team profit. Nevertheless, we believe that the overlooking the distribution of Central Fund revenues is misplaced and worthy of future study.

Author Contributions: Authors equally contributed to the research and writing of the paper.

References

1. Asplund, Marcus. 2002. Risk-averse firms in oligopoly. *International Journal of Industrial Organization* 20: 995–1012. [CrossRef]
2. Bontemps, Tim. 2017. Why revenue sharing, one of the NBA's thorniest issues, demands a solution. *The Washington Post*, September 28, (Extracted on 6 February 2018).
3. Chiu, W. Henry. 2005. Skewness preference, risk aversion and the precedence changes on stochastic relations. *Management Science* 51: 1816–28. [CrossRef]
4. Choudhary, M. Ali, and Paul Levine. 2010. Risk-averse firms and employment dynamics. *Oxford Economic Papers* 3: 578–602. [CrossRef]
5. Dietl, Helmut, Markus Lang, and Stephan Werner. 2009. Social welfare in sports leagues with profit-maximizing and/or win-maximizing clubs. *Southern Economic Journal* 76: 375–96. [CrossRef]
6. Dixit, Avinash, and Victor Norman. 1986. Gains from trade without lump-sum compensation. *Journal of International Economics* 21: 111–22. [CrossRef]

[26] Orinick (2017).
[27] Marburger (1997) considers the effect of a progressive competitive balance tax on owner incentives and equilibrium outcomes, but does not consider a progressive revenue sharing tax.

7. Easton, Stephen, and Duane Rockerbie. 2005. Revenue sharing, conjectures and scarce talent in a sports league model. *Journal of Sports Economics* 6: 359–78. [CrossRef]
8. Easton, Stephen, and Duane Rockerbie. 2010. The ebbs and flows of the game: Multiple equilibria in a sports league model. *Journal of Sports Economics* 11: 172–85.
9. Eeckhoudt, Louis, and Harris Schlesinger. 2013. Higher order risk attitudes. In *Handbook of Insurance*. Edited by Georges Dionne. New York: Springer, pp. 41–57.
10. Eeckhoudt, Louis, Christian Gollier, and Thierry Schneider. 1995. Risk-aversion, prudence and temperance: A unified approach. *Economic Letters* 48: 331–36. [CrossRef]
11. Fort, Rodney, and James Quirk. 1995. Cross-subsidization, incentives and team outcomes in professional team sports leagues. *Journal of Economic Literature* 33: 1265–99.
12. Fort, Rodney, and James Quirk. 2010a. Optimal competitive balance in single-game ticket sports leagues. *Journal of Sports Economics* 11: 587–601. [CrossRef]
13. Fort, Rodney, and James Quirk. 2010b. Optimal competitive balance in a season ticket league. *Economic Inquiry* 49: 464–73. [CrossRef]
14. Goldberg, Pinelopi Koujianou, and Nina Pavcnik. 2007. Distributional effects of globalization in developing countries. *Journal of Economic Literature* 45: 39–82. [CrossRef]
15. Herranz, Neus, Stefan Krasa, and Anne P. Villamil. 2015. Entrepreneurs, risk aversion and dynamic firms. *Journal of Political Economy* 123: 1133–76. [CrossRef]
16. Hill, James Richard, and Nicholas A. Jolly. 2015. Revenue sharing and player salaries in Major League Baseball. *Journal of Sports Economics* 18: 831–49. [CrossRef]
17. Kesenne, Stefan. 2000. Revenue sharing and competitive balance in professional team sports. *Journal of Sports Economics* 1: 56–65. [CrossRef]
18. Kesenne, Stefan. 2007. Revenue sharing and owner profits in professional sports models. *Journal of Sports Economics* 8: 519–29. [CrossRef]
19. Kesenne, Stefan. 2015. Revenue sharing and absolute league quality, talent investment and talent allocation. *Scottish Journal of Political Economy* 62: 51–58. [CrossRef]
20. Kimball, Miles. 1990. Precautionary saving in the small and in the large. *Econometrica* 58: 53–73. [CrossRef] Knight, Frank. 1921. *Risk Uncertainty and Profit*. Boston: Houghton Mifflin Company, Reprinted in New York: Augustus M. Kelley, 1964.
21. Kraus, Alan, and Robert Litzenberger. 1976. Skewness preference and the valuation of risky assets. *Journal of Finance* 31: 1085–100.
22. Krautmann, Anthony. 2017. Risk-averse team owners and player's salaries in Major League Baseball. *Journal of Sports Economics* 18: 19–33. [CrossRef]
23. Kroll, Yoram, Haim Levy, and Harry Markowitz. 1984. Mean-variance versus direct utility maximization. *Journal of Finance* 39: 47–61. [CrossRef]
24. Leland, Hayne. 1972. Theory of the firm facing random demand. *American Economic Review* 62: 278–91.
25. Levy, Haim, and Harry Markowitz. 1979. Approximating expected utility by a function of mean and variance. *American Economic Review* 69: 308–17.
26. Loistl, Otto. 1976. The erroneous approximation of expected utility by means of a Taylor series expansion. *American Economic Review* 66: 904–10.
27. Lucas, Robert. 1987. *Models of Business Cycles*. Oxford: Blackwell Publishers.
28. Major League Baseball. 2001. Updated Supplement to the Report of the Independent Members of the Commissioner's Blue Ribbon Panel on Baseball Economics. December. Available online: http:// roadsidephotos.sabr.org/baseball/BRpanelupd.doc (accessed on 2 August 2017).
29. Marburger, Daniel. 1997. Gate revenue sharing and luxury taxes in professional sports. *Contemporary Economic Policy* 15: 114–23. [CrossRef]
30. Markowitz, Harry. 1952. Portfolio selection. *Journal of Finance* 7: 77–91.
31. Maxcy, Joel. 2004. Motivating long-term employment contracts: Risk management in Major League Baseball. *Managerial and Decision Economics* 25: 109–20. [CrossRef]
32. Maxcy, Joel. 2009. Progressive revenue sharing in Major League Baseball: The effect on player transfers and talent distribution. *Review of Industrial Organization* 35: 275–97. [CrossRef]
33. Mehra, Rajnish, and Edward Prescott. 1985. The equity premium: A puzzle. *Journal of Monetary Economics* 15: 145–61. [CrossRef]
34. Miller, Phillip. 2007. Revenue sharing in sports leagues: The effects on talent distribution and competitive balance. *Journal of Sports Economics* 8: 62–82. [CrossRef]
35. Mirlees, James. 1971. An exploration in the theory of optimal income taxation. *Review of Economic Studies* 38: 175–208. [CrossRef]
36. Neale, Walter. 1964. The peculiar economics of professional sports. *Quarterly Journal of Economics* 78: 1–14. [CrossRef]
37. Orinick, Steve. 2017. Competitive Balance Tax. Available online: http://www.stevetheump.com/luxury_tax.htm (accessed on 2 August 2017).

38. Pulley, Lawrence. 1981. A general mean-variance approximation to expected utility for short holding periods. *Journal of Financial and Quantitative Analysis* 16: 361–73. [CrossRef]
39. Rockerbie, Duane. 2009. Free agent auctions and revenue sharing: A simple exposition. *Journal of Sport Management* 23: 87–98. [CrossRef]
40. Rockerbie, Duane. 2017. The invariance principle in baseball: New evidence. *Applied Economics* 50: 2613–21. [CrossRef]
41. Rockerbie, Duane, and Stephen Easton. 2014. *The Run to the Pennant: A Multiple Equilibria Approach to Professional Sports Leagues*. New York: Springer.
42. Ross, J. Andrew. 2015. *Joining the Clubs: The Business of the National Hockey League to 1945*. Syracuse: Syracuse University Press.
43. Sandmo, Agnar. 1971. On the theory of the competitive firm under price uncertainty. *American Economic Review* 61: 65–73.
44. Surdham, David. 2007. A tale of two gate-sharing plans: The National Football League and the National League, 1952–56. *Southern Economic Journal* 73: 931–46.
45. Szymanski, Stefan. 2004. Professional team sports are only a game: The Walrasian fixed-supply conjecture model, contest-Nash equilibrium, and the invariance principle. *Journal of Sports Economics* 5: 111–26. [CrossRef]
46. Tew, Bernard, Donald Reid, and Craig Witt. 1991. Opportunity cost of a mean-variance efficient choice. *Financial Review* 26: 31–44. [CrossRef]
47. Thomas, Jonathan, and Tim Worrall. 1988. Self-enforcing wage contracts. *Review of Economic Studies* 55: 541–53. [CrossRef]
48. Tompkins, D. 2000. The opportunity cost of E-V efficient portfolios. *Academy of Accounting and Financial Studies Journal* 4: 61–71.
49. Vrooman, John. 2009. Theory of the perfect game: Competitive balance in monopoly sports leagues. *Review of Industrial Organization* 34: 5–44. [CrossRef]

13

Howzat? The Financial Health of English Cricket: Not Out, Yet

Daniel Plumley *, Rob Wilson, Robbie Millar and Simon Shibli

Sport Business Management, Sheffield Hallam University, Sheffield S1 1WB, UK; r.j.wilson@shu.ac.uk (R.W.); r.millar@shu.ac.uk (R.M.); s.shibli@shu.ac.uk (S.S.)

* Correspondence: d.j.plumley@shu.ac.uk

Abstract: In 1997 a review of the financial health of English county cricket highlighted strategic weaknesses within the professional game, principally an over-reliance by clubs on the annual grants provided to them by the England and Wales Cricket Board (ECB). Without such grants the teams, in general terms, would be insolvent. Using the financial statements of the First Class Cricket Counties, this paper explores how the financial position and performance of the county game has changed, 20 years on from the seminal study. A series of structural changes to the game had been made, yet financial problems are still evident. Counties are as reliant on central grant income as they were in 1997, although there are cases where clubs have made strategic enhancements and are becoming self-sustainable as going concerns. Rather than the ECB directly funding county revenue it should be working in collaboration with individual clubs to achieve developments in the game from the grassroots upwards, in order to help clubs grow their own revenue streams.

Keywords: finance; financial health; cricket; professional team sport; profit maximisation; subsidy; grants

JEL Classification: G; Z2; Z23

---

1. Introduction

In 1997, just over 20 years ago, a paper published by Shibli and Wilkinson-Riddle in the Journal of Applied Accounting Research examined the financial health of English county cricket, specifically the finances of the 18 first-class counties. The article highlighted strategic weaknesses within the professional game, principally an over-reliance by clubs on the annual grants provided to them (to support income generation) by the England and Wales Cricket Board (ECB), essentially rendering the teams, in general terms, insolvent should the grants ever be removed. The grant money from the ECB remains and constitutes a distribution of international match-related revenues driven by the England National Team and is, therefore, dependant on the national team's sporting success and attractiveness to spectators, sponsors and broadcasters. Additionally, Shibli and Wilkinson-Riddle (1997) confirmed that an extremely low proportion of clubs' total revenue came from the paying public watching county cricket, that levels of debt at some clubs were unsustainable and that without the ECB hand-outs many clubs would cease to exist as a going concern.

To that end, we set out to examine the current financial health of the domestic game, 20 years on, in 2018. Cricket, from a participation perspective, is second only to football in England, yet the professional game has not seen the revenue growth, at the elite end, in line with football, yet there have been major developments in the domestic game during the last 20 years in terms of its changing format and structure. Indeed, in 2002, the ECB realised it had to open the game up to new audiences to reverse the trend of dwindling attendances and financial uncertainty affecting the 18 counties. The advent of Twenty20 (T20) cricket came in 2003 and it was a revolutionary step forward, as matches could take place after work and last for no more than three hours. Most importantly, the domestic

T20 season was scheduled to take place during the school summer holidays, making it particularly attractive to families. T20 was a ground-breaking success; matches were regularly played to sell-out crowds and have become an important revenue stream for counties. Stuart Robson former Head of Marketing at the ECB stated:

> "£200,000 of ticket revenue would have been double the amount derived from any other competition. It was a proper cash cow to those smaller grounds and a life saver. Without Twenty20 at a professional level the domestic game in this country would be in a very precarious state by now." (The Independent 2017)

This fundamental shift in the English cricket landscape can be seen around the world, with the introduction of various franchise-based competitions, most notably the Indian Premier League and Big Bash in Australia, which have become lucrative multi-million pound leagues (The Guardian 2017a). The ECB reacted and recently introduced a new franchise city-based T20 format due to launch in 2020 in an effort to maintain its market share (The ECB 2018).

The emergence in popularity of One Day Internationals (ODIs) has led to new broadcasting contracts being agreed with Sky and the BBC. These new arrangements provide broadcasting revenue totalling £1.1 billion over a five year period from 2020–2024 (The Guardian 2017b). Not only is this £220m-a-year deal worth nearly three times what Sky is paying for current exclusive rights (£75m-a-year) but it will also see live coverage return to free-to-air television for the first time since 2006—a statement that perhaps suggests that the move to a subscription only model might have removed the game from the eyes of the masses and impacted negatively on grassroots participation. This deal will also allow the ECB to meet its promise of providing central grant money to the 18 counties of £1.3 m each. However, as we have seen historically, counties have perhaps been over-reliant on this grant in the past (Shibli and Wilkinson-Riddle 1997).

The dichotomy between on-field and off-field performance in professional team sports, exacerbated by the commercialisation of sport during the last two decades, according to Wilson and Plumley (2017), and the need for clubs to balance both financial and sporting performance has led to a multitude of academic papers in the area of sport finance. Sport teams tend to be fairly unique entities with the majority strategically positioning themselves to maximise performance both on and off the pitch, whilst simultaneously satisfying a number of different stakeholders.

As previous research suggests, reconciling the "on-field/off field" equation in professional team sport is not easy and it has proved a highly contentious issue in recent years (Chadwick 2009). Often, discussion transcends towards what has been labelled the 'twin' objectives of professional sports teams (e.g., Plumley et al. 2017). One is financial, in relation to business operations, and the other is sporting, in relation to on-pitch performance and trophy success.

There is also substantial academic literature, which considers the relationship between financial and sporting performance in professional team sports (e.g., Kesenne 2000; Garcia-del-Barrio and Szymanski 2009; Sloane 2015; Szymanski and Kuypers 1999). Historically, much of the wider literature has pointed to these 'twin objectives' being at odds with one another and creating 'financial crises' at the club level as sporting objectives supersede financial decision making, plunging clubs into operational losses. Most notably, this literature has focused on European football across a number of different countries (e.g., Andreff 2007; Barros 2006; Buraimo et al. 2006; Dietl and Franck 2007). Notwithstanding this historical narrative, the financial problems in football, at least generally, appear to be abating, in part through stricter regulations aimed at financial sustainability and encouraging clubs to spend within their means (e.g., UEFA Financial Fair Play) although there are still some problems at individual club level. However, financial problems are not only exclusive to football in relation to professional team sports in the UK. Previous research has also highlighted financial problems in rugby union (e.g., O'Brien and Slack 1999, 2003; Williams 2012; Wilson and Plumley 2017) and rugby league (Wilson et al. 2015). However, aside from the paper by Shibli and Wilkinson-Riddle (1997), there is a lack of literature available on the financial health of county cricket in the UK.

Consequently, the primary aim of this paper is to analyse the current state of the UK County Championship and its member clubs in an attempt to understand the financial climate of the game in 2018. This will help determine whether each cricket county is an attractive product, within the UK professional sport system, and are capable of fulfilling the fundamental requirements of a league association. Our data focuses on the 18 first-class counties that take part in the County Championship. The financial information pertains to all business aspects of the clubs including their respective one-day and T20 teams and whether or not they host international matches or other events at their grounds. This approach allows for a holistic measurement of financial performance in respect of these clubs and helps to determine whether each club would meet a going concern requirement were central grants ever withdrawn. The remainder of this paper is structured as follows. First we consider the theoretical context of accounting theory and professional team sports before considering the literature available on the County Championship itself. Following this, the paper discusses the methods applied and the findings before concluding with the key challenges that the sport faces and highlighting the potential areas of growth for the sport in the future.

2. Theoretical Framework and Literature Review

2.1. On Truth and Fairness in Accounting Policies

We structure our theoretical framework on accounting policies and practice on the argument of the contested nature of a conceptual framework for accounting, a topic that is prevalent in much of the extant literature. We use this as a guide to state that whilst the analysis of financial information may still be debated in relation to the techniques used, and the figures contained within in annual reports, there is still a regulatory framework in place that companies have agreed to adhere to (especially in the UK). As such, we argue that despite the inconsistencies in the literature presented below, the measurement and analysis techniques used in this study are rigorous and appropriate based on the data we put forward.

Firstly, let us define the term 'conceptual framework'. International Generally Accepted Accounting Principles GAAP (International GAAP 2005) state that, in general terms, a conceptual framework is a statement of generally accepted theoretical principles which form the frame of reference for a particular field of enquiry. In terms of financial reporting, these theoretical principles provide the basis for both the development of new reporting practices and the evaluation of existing ones. Since the emphasis of financial reporting is on the provision of information that is useful in making business and economic decisions, a conceptual framework will form the theoretical basis for determining which events should be accounted for, how they should be measured and how they should be communicated to the user. Therefore, a conceptual framework for financial reporting must be substantially practical in its application (International GAAP 2005).

Much of the critique surrounding the conceptual framework of accounting centres on the struggle to distinguish the separation of accounting from societal happenings. Indeed, Hines (1991) suggested that the conceptual framework is elaborated around a highly problematic conception of the relationship between financial accounting and economic reality. The view of Hines that the meaning and significance of conceptual framework projects is not so much functional and technical, but rather social and cultural is shared by a number of other authors (see for example, Boland 1989; Burrell 1987; Hopwood 1990; Miller and O'Leary 1987; Richardson 1987; Tinker 1988; Willmott 1986). All of these authors argue that financial accounting practices are implicated in the construction and reproduction of the social world. Furthermore, the conceptual framework projects similarly play a part in the process of the social construction of reality (see for example, Booth and Cocks 1989; Hines 1991). One of the main arguments here is that accounts, and the numbers contained within them, can be manipulated subjectively.

This view is shared in a recent article by Sunder (2016) who states that conflicts among the claims of the shortcomings of financial reporting point to the political elements of the problem inherent in collective choice in society. Since 'better' in this context (the accounting policies) depends on the interest group whose perspective is chosen for analysis, politics lies at the heart of accounting policy. Thus, Sunder (2016) argues that any regulations should also consider social norms and market competition.

There has also been considerable focus in accounting literature on the transition from Historical Cost Accounting (HCA) to Fair Value Accounting (FVA) which occurred in 2005. For a more historical overview of both these policies, readers are referred to Georgiou and Jack (2011). The move to FVA appears to have been largely positive yet it is still difficult to detach the practice from societal influences. The move towards fair value measurement is frequently characterised as a shift in paradigms (e.g., Barlev and Haddad 2003, p. 383). Accordingly, with respect to financial reporting, a paradigm is defined as a set of shared beliefs on the objectives of financial reporting and on the accounting principles by which these can be achieved. It is grounded in elaborated assumptions, and characteristically requires a theoretical foundation or vindication. Once a financial reporting paradigm is adopted by regulatory bodies, it becomes the guiding principle for accounting regulation, that is, standard-setting (Hitz 2007).

Fair value accounting is, put simply, an income definition that anchors on changes in assets and liabilities rather than on the vague notion of 'nondistortion' (Bevis 1965, p. 104), which had increasingly been perceived as a pretext for discretionary definitions of balance sheet positions. Additionally, researchers and regulators felt uncomfortable with a balance sheet that had no informative purpose of its own (Hitz 2007). However, despite being the dominant practice in present day accounting, FVA is still not without its critics. It is argued that the concept of 'fair value' measurement emerged in financial accounting and was accepted in the abstract long before it was a subject of analysis and dispute (Bromwich 2007). Furthermore, 'fair value' is not, itself, a single measurement methodology, but encompasses a variety of approaches for the estimation of an exit value. Therefore, it is hardly surprising that many of the arguments which have been developed for and against the use of fair values in accounting are not well-supported by evidence (Laux and Leuz 2009); with disputants often talking past each other.

It is evident from the literature that throughout history the legitimacy of accounting practices and principles has been questioned. Furthermore, there are also implications and challenges based on the qualitative characteristics of accounting information, namely reliability, relevance, comparability and materiality. In the profession of accounting, the debate between FVA and HCA, it appears, is likely to be prolonged, as the unintended consequence of more firmly embedding an acceptance of the appropriateness of fair values for some balance sheet items has been to confer further pragmatic legitimation for mixed measurements in annual reports. It is possible that moral and cognitive arguments in favour of mixed measurement may emerge, or the debates on cost or value based accounting continue, as they have done for over a century. The emergence of new reporting forms should be carefully observed and recorded, as a basis for a longitudinal study of the diffusion of practice and processes of legitimacy (Georgiou and Jack 2011).

The authors acknowledge that accounting theory remains a contested issue, but accounts have to be prepared in line with accounting principles and the current standards in place. Furthermore, accounts are prepared with a 'true and fair' view and decision usefulness in mind and the supporting of financial figures with qualitative characteristics of accounting information provides a reliable and valid framework upon which analysis can be undertaken. In respect to English Cricket, clubs are subject to compliance with FRS 102 rather than international accounting rules, although there is overlap between the two.

2.2. The Economic Theory of Professional Team Sport

Professional team sports are intrinsically different from other businesses, in which a firm is likely to prosper if it can eliminate competition and establish a position as a monopoly supplier (Dobson and Goddard 2011), being profitable and responsible for earned revenue, in this context, naturally provides competitive advantage; you can afford to pay players higher wages for example. In sport, however, it does not pay for one team to establish such a position due to the joint nature of 'production' in sports. With this in mind, it is paramount for league organisers that their 'product' on the pitch is a contest between equally matched opponents. The practical economic problem with this notion, however, is that professional sport leagues form imperfectly competitive natural cartels where games are played between teams with asymmetric market power (Vrooman 2015). Sport teams might not be able to eliminate the competition, but they still try to be dominant over the rest. Ultimately, the 'biggest' clubs, often in respect of size, resources and fan base, tend to win more than they lose. As a result, professional sport teams operate in a uniquely eccentric environment and comparisons between the economic environment of professional team sports and that of more traditional commercial businesses have been well documented by sports economists (e.g., Dobson and Goddard 2011; Leach and Szymanski 2015).

Thus, a key priority for professional sport leagues is the economic concepts of uncertainty of outcome, competitive balance and profit and utility maximisation (e.g., Buraimo et al. 2015; Fort 2015; Kesenne 2015; Leach and Szymanski 2015; Sloane 2015; Vrooman 2015). Much of the historical literature surrounding professional team sports was developed by US sport economists and focused on North American team sports. Naturally, over time, the literature has evolved to compare the North American and European model of professional team sports (see Hoehn and Szymanski 1999; Andreff and Staudohar 2000; Sloane 2006; Szymanski 2003). There are distinct differences between the two models notably draft systems, revenue sharing, salary caps and closed league systems with no promotion or relegation between leagues (regulatory policies that are in place in North American team sports but not in the European model). Despite these differences, there has also been some convergence between the two models on certain features. In both Europe and the North America, sports leagues are joint ventures that can be viewed as a single entity. Clubs are separately owned with discretion to set prices, market the games, and adopt strategies to compete with other clubs. However, such strategies must be executed under the regulations of the league.

Precisely why such differences have arisen in the two continents has never been fully explained (Sloane 2015). However, Szymanski and Zimbalist (2005) contrast the development of baseball and soccer, with the latter spreading throughout the world, first under the influence of British expatriates and then by local elites, whereas baseball was much more inward looking and concerned with commercial development. Previous literature has argued that profit maximisation is the prime objective of North American leagues and team owners, so profitability is the main factor influencing decisions concerning the award of franchises and relocation (Dobson and Goddard 2011). Contrastingly, other authors have suggested that the European sports model is more closely related to utility or 'win' maximisation (see Sloane 1971; Kesenne 2000; Garcia-del-Barrio and Szymanski 2009).

3. The County Championship

The County Cricket Championship is unusual in many ways when compared against received economic theory. This is because it has historically taken elements of both models of professional team sport (European and North American) to structure its competition. It is also the only team sport in the UK where clubs receive central grant money from the governing body (England and Wales Cricket Board (ECB)). The origins of the competition can be traced back to 1890 but the present day format began taking shape around the mid-1960s when bonus points were introduced to the scoring system alongside the already established points system relating to wins and losses. Up until 2000, all member teams competed in one league with no promotion and relegation and entries to the league decided on an application basis. This mirrored the North American style model for professional team sport outlined in the previous section. However, post-2000 the league has been split into two divisions with promotion and relegation between them. Originally, there were three teams promoted and relegated between divisions although this has since been reduced to two teams since 2006.

In some respects, the County Championship bears some resemblance to rugby league's Super League in this regard. When the Super League was formed, it can be argued that the plan was to take elements from both models of professional team sports. Essentially, rugby league was attempting to replicate the English Premier League in football whilst maintaining American team sport principles of salary caps and no promotion or relegation (up until the 2014 season). Wilson et al. (2015) argued that Rugby League is, in global terms, a minority sport but has clearly been modernised in recent times through the advent of subscription television and other global processes. It could be argued that cricket is in a similar position in the UK as it battles with both rugby league and rugby union to be the second most popular sport behind football.

The challenges facing cricket's County Championship are not new. Indeed, Ammon (2017) began a media piece on the beginning of the County Championship season with the following quote:

> "The beginning of every new cricket season brings with it reports of county cricket in demise, accompanied by pictures of a solitary, cold supporter in a stand, surrounded by rows of empty plastic seats. It is the stereotypical image of county cricket watched by a man and a dog, and of its impending death - killed by public apathy and crippling financial issues. For as long as I can remember, people have been prophesying the death of county cricket" (Ammon 2017)

The article goes on to state that the clubs themselves still appear reliant on the central grant money from the ECB, that county game attendances are modest and that participation in the sport itself has been declining in recent years (Ammon 2017). Again, similarities can be drawn here with rugby league and the findings of Wilson et al. (2015) who outlined a similar picture in rugby league. This combination of factors appears unsustainable at league level but for as long as the county clubs are operating as going concerns, producing players for the international England team and producing entertaining cricket, is cricket just doing its job? The evidence in other sports is that the league and its member clubs would be better off becoming more self-sustaining entities, particularly if the financial position of the ECB was to weaken in the future and central grant money had to be cut.

One piece of positive news in relation to this is the recent broadcasting deal that has just been agreed with Sky Sports and BBC which will see live domestic cricket return to terrestrial television for the first time since the 2005 Ashes series (BBC 2018). Not only that, but the deal is worth a record total of £1.1 billion running for five years and commencing in 2020. However, as part of the deal, the ECB has stipulated that it will increase the central grant money to clubs. This is fine in principle but, again, highlights the issues facing the County Championship and its reliance on ECB central funding.

To that end, and given the context outlined in the introduction, now is a worthy time to study the financial state of play in respect of the County Championship and its member clubs. There have been a small number of academic articles in relation to cricket but these have historically focused on institutional change (Wright and Zammuto 2013), the globalisation of the sport (Gupta 2004), brand extensions and facility utilisation (Pritchard 2016) and the market valuation of cricket players (Saikia et al. 2013). To the authors' knowledge, this is the first paper of its kind to focus on the financial performance of English cricket clubs since the seminal paper by Shibli and Wilkinson-Riddle in 1997.

4. Methods

Data for this research was obtained by analysing the annual accounts of the 18 first-class counties for the last three years available at the time of writing, covering financial data from 2014–2016. Financial data was not available for two clubs in certain years (Worcestershire (2014) and Middlesex (2016)) whilst the accounts for Northamptonshire do not reveal the total figure of ECB grant income that they receive.

Analysis was performed using recognised industry techniques (see Wilson et al. 2013). Financial results were analysed in relation to the five key areas of financial performance—all relevant to professional sports clubs and investment. These were: growth, profitability, ROCE (return on capital employed), liquidity and defensive positioning. The first three indicators relate to an organisation's ability to generate profit and return for its owners and also to maintain a sustainable future. The latter relate to an organisation's ability to meet its liabilities as they fall due and also how certain organisations are financed and how much capital is made up of debt finance. Ratio analysis is a widely used technique to measure financial performance across a number of industries and organisations including, but not limited to, the airline industry (Feng and Wang 2000), power/energy industry (Sueyoshi 2005) and the manufacturing industry (Ponikvar et al. 2009).

Alternative models for analysing performance in professional team sports have been excluded on the basis of accessibility to data, particularly in relation to the financial statements of county cricket clubs. Chadwick (2009) outlined that performance measurement in sport has to include both the financial and the non-financial and it is important that this paper considered non-financial factors as well when analysing the current state of the game. It is this holistic approach to data collection and analysis that is the key benefit from a methodological perspective and it also provides a further robustness to the subsequent results and discussion.

5. Financial Health

In respect of turnover, there appears to be a polarisation between the counties that host international test cricket and those that do not (see Figure 1). This point is further underlined by the four highest average turnover figures relating to four counties who have historically regularly hosted test cricket (Surrey, Warwickshire, Lancashire and Nottinghamshire). Indeed, Surrey's average revenue of around £27 m for 2014–2016 is particularly impressive compared with the revenue profile of the 17 other counties. Although a regular spot on the Test match rota bolsters Surrey's finances, it has developed new revenue streams utilising its facilities to host conferences and events.

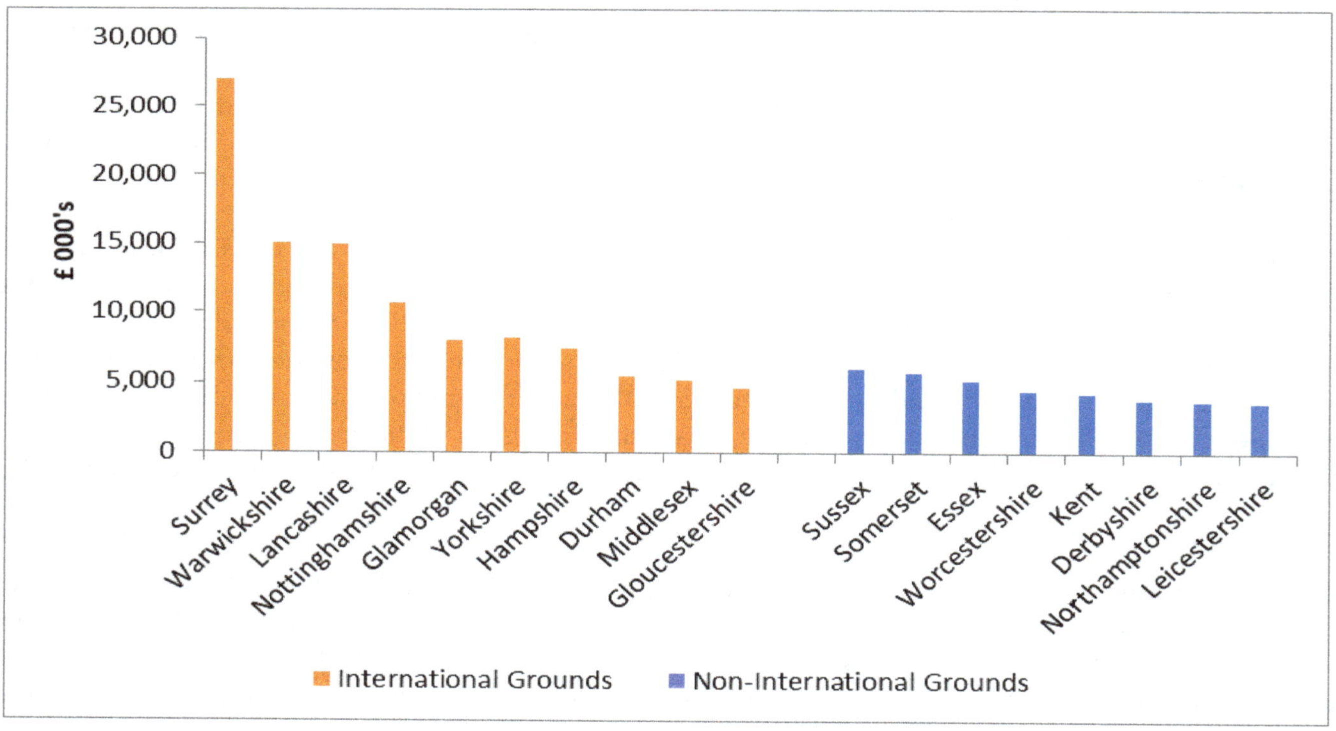

Figure 1. Average turnover in £000s (2014–2016).

Furthermore, of the counties that have relatively low revenue, a high proportion of this is attributable to the ECB grant income. In some cases, this ECB grant income accounts for over half of a club's total revenue (Middlesex, Worcestershire, Kent, Derbyshire, and Leicestershire) (see Figure 2).

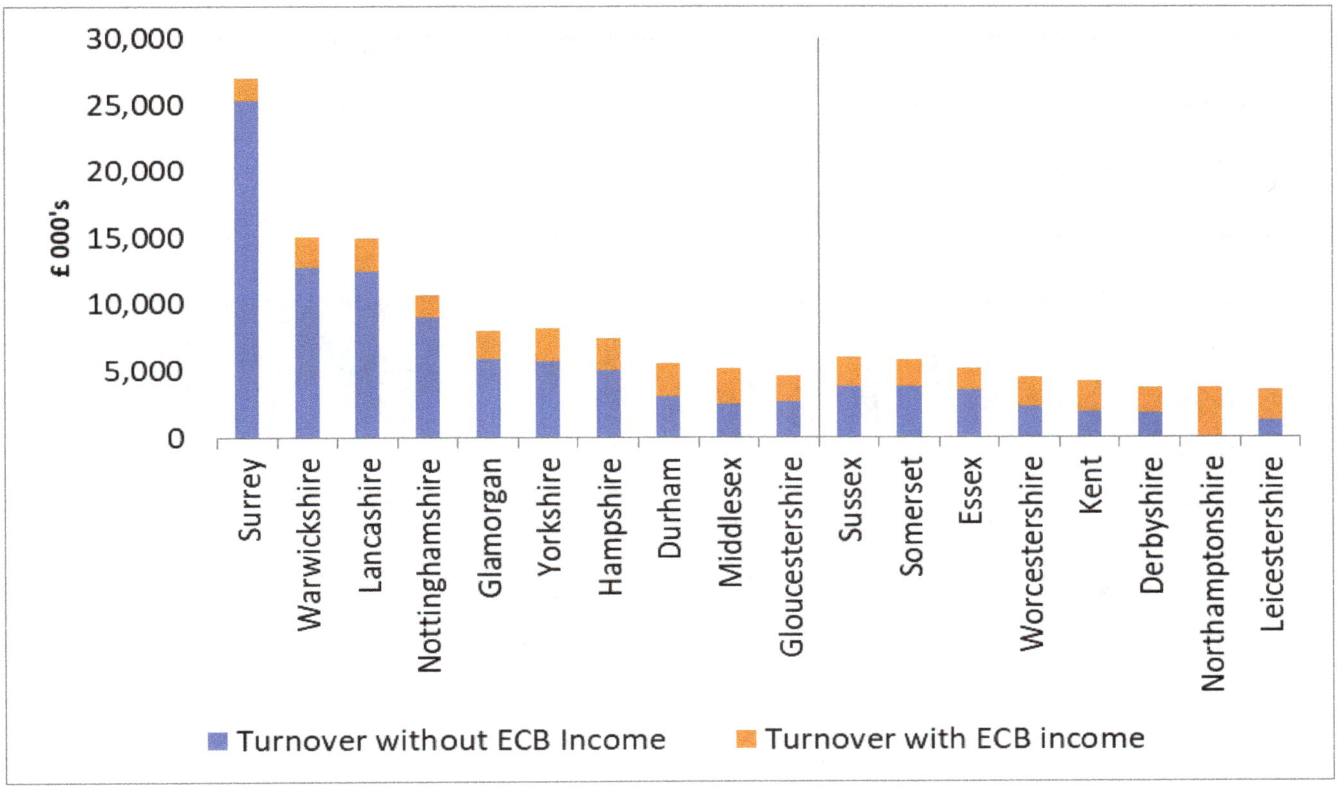

Figure 2. Average 'earned' vs. 'unearned' income in £000s (2014–2016).

This finding leads to further financial problems, in respect of general financial health, when considering profitability (see Figure 3). A number of clubs are just about breaking-even taking into account the subsidy from the ECB and if we were to hypothetically remove this income then only Glamorgan would still have posted a net profit overall for the time period studied. This point suggests that, from a revenue perspective at least, there is an over-reliance on 'unearned' income from the ECB.

The ECB continues to support the domestic game (and other aspects of the sport down to grassroots level), which is obviously a positive for the clubs. However, this relationship is dependent on two things; (1) that the clubs do not become over-reliant on this central grant (which it appears some are) and (2) that the ECB can continue to afford the central grant payments to the county network. At the present time, the ECB appears to be capable of doing this and plans its business activities on a four-year cycle to include lucrative home Test series against Australia (The Ashes) and India. However, the ECB states that the central grants is one of its largest areas of expenditure and in the most recent set of accounts (year ending January 2017) the ECB's administrative expenditure increased by £23.0 m during the year from £114.2 m to £137.2 m—attributable to the increased level of distributions made to the counties.

Overall, 11 of the 18 counties have a debt ratio of over 75% (a percentage that is considered a cause for concern when considering financial health). For two clubs, Yorkshire (110%) and Lancashire (108%) the debt ratio is over 100%. Indeed, the average balance sheet debt for the 18 first-class counties stood at £14.46 m for 2014–2016 although within this there was large individual debt figures attributed to Yorkshire (£33.7 m), Warwickshire (£35.8 m), Surrey (£36 m) and Lancashire (£53.5 m). Some clubs posted a much better figure in respect of average balance sheet debt with Sussex, for example, having a debt ratio as low as 14% and average balance sheet debt of £1.7 m.

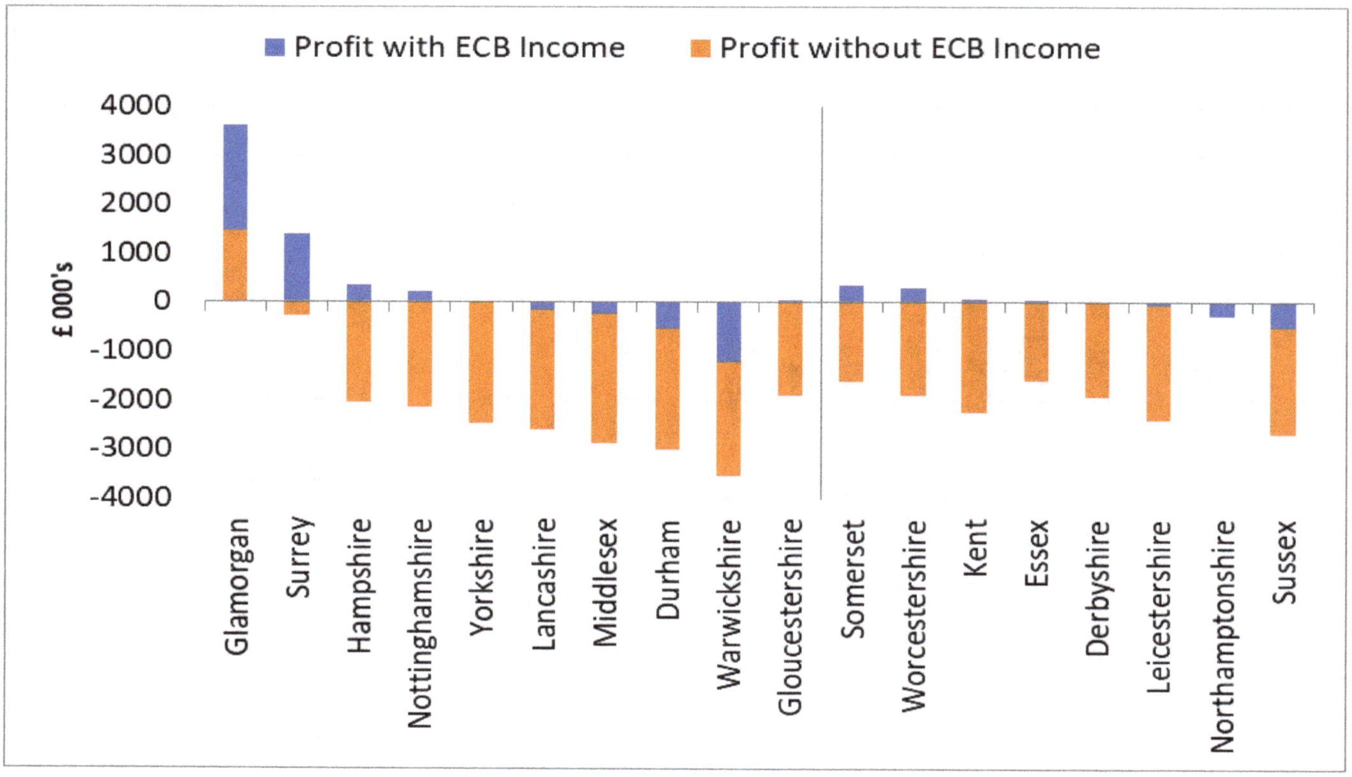

Figure 3. Average profit/(loss) in £000s (2014–2016).

5.1. Dominating the Game

In financial terms Surrey is leading the way, as shown in Figure 2 its average turnover over the last 3 years is almost twice that of its nearest rivals (Warwickshire and Lancashire). Surrey's fiscal dominance is built on the foundations of guaranteed international Test cricket, as it always hosts the last Test match of the summer, which is usually against a high profile opponent. Geographically, being based in London Surrey can charge a premium for international tickets and The Oval is the second largest cricket ground after Lords. International fixtures are typically sold out, which puts an added importance on one of the main benefits of being a Surrey member, as members gain priority access to international tickets.

Since the re-vamped domestic T20 competition has moved to Friday nights, Surrey has seized this opportunity to increase revenue. The club have marketed these T20 fixtures to families with family only sections, cheap tickets and child-friendly activities; as well as to young professionals as events for post-work socialising whilst watching the cricket. This new approach to marketing has resulted in a high-demand for tickets and the majority of Surrey's home T20 matches are sold out.

The area which sets Surrey apart from the other counties, is the revenue it gains through the use of its facilities to host corporate events and conferences. Figure 4 shows a breakdown of Surrey's revenue from the 2016 financial year, 46% of revenue came from 'Oval Events', which are these non-cricketing events. This sum is more than the revenue from the ECB Grant, international matches and domestic matches put together. To put this finding in to further perspective, this single revenue stream if set against other counties total revenue, would sit third behind only Lancashire and Warwickshire. These non-cricketing events are vitally important to counties as they bring in revenue all-year round, as grounds are not used for cricket between October and March.

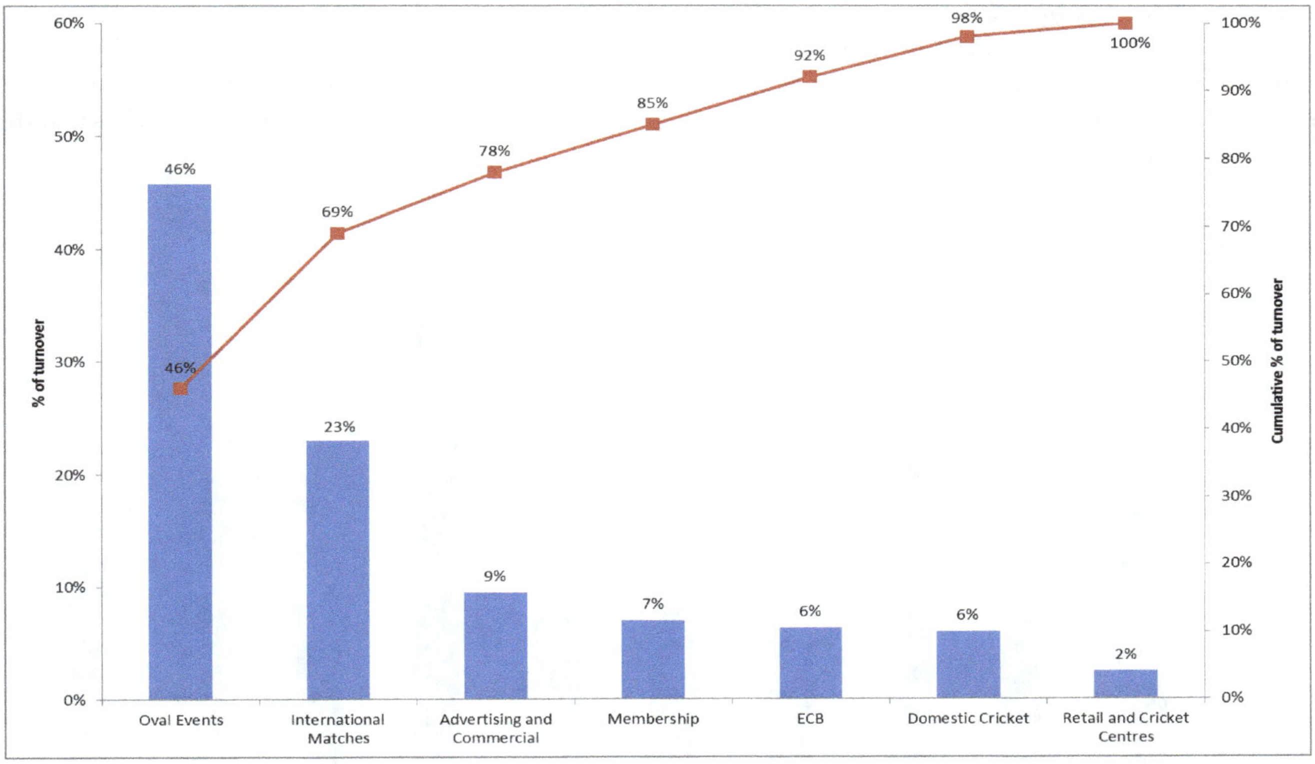

Figure 4. Breakdown of Surrey's 2016 turnover.

To develop this funding stream further and increase capacity of The Oval, planning permission has been granted to build new conference facilities and additional tiers on the adjoining stand, which will see capacity increase to just under 28,000 (Surrey CCC 2018). This capital investment will cost around £55 million, which when compared with other counties is a monumental sum. However, with a healthy balance sheet and revenue growth expected, this is a sensible venture for the club that will only increase the financial gap between itself and the other counties.

5.2. Contrasting Fortunes

In 1992, Durham County Cricket Club (DCCC) was accepted into first-class cricket to become the 18th first class county to compete in the County Championship. This was the first time a new county had been introduced into the County Championship since Glamorgan in 1921. Durham's vision was to bring cricket back to the North East of England, with a long-term ambition to regularly host international matches in the county. In 1996 the club moved to its new purpose built ground The Riverside. For the 1999 Cricket World Cup, Durham was awarded two group matches (Pakistan vs. Scotland and Australia vs. Bangladesh). The continued transformation of the ground was assured when the ECB awarded Durham its first England international, to host an ODI against the West Indies in 2000. The county received Test status in 2003 and hosted its first ever Test match when England faced Zimbabwe that summer. This was a landmark moment for the club as it was the first new Test ground since 1902 and signalled Durham's competency in hosting international matches, as it was placed on the list of grounds that would host at least one international match each summer.

With the guarantee of seemingly lucrative international cricket revenue, Durham began to invest more capital in facilities and upgraded The Riverside to increase capacity and improve the spectator experience. Figure 5 shows Durham's last 10 annual turnover figures, it is noticeable that the three years with the highest annual turnover are when it hosted a Test match (2007, 2009 and 2013). The year 2013 was ground-breaking as Durham was awarded an Ashes Test match; previously it had only hosted the 'lesser' Test matches. However, to secure the Ashes Test match, the club had to invest heavily in the bidding process to the ECB. As a result for the Ashes Test match the club had to charge a significant fee for tickets in order to see a return on its investment. Although the club saw record turnover in 2013 and achieved an operating surplus, this was a one-off year. Even though the staging of the Test match was successful, with the first three days being a sell-out, Durham was still down the pecking order below the established Test grounds and, therefore, not guaranteed a Test match every summer.

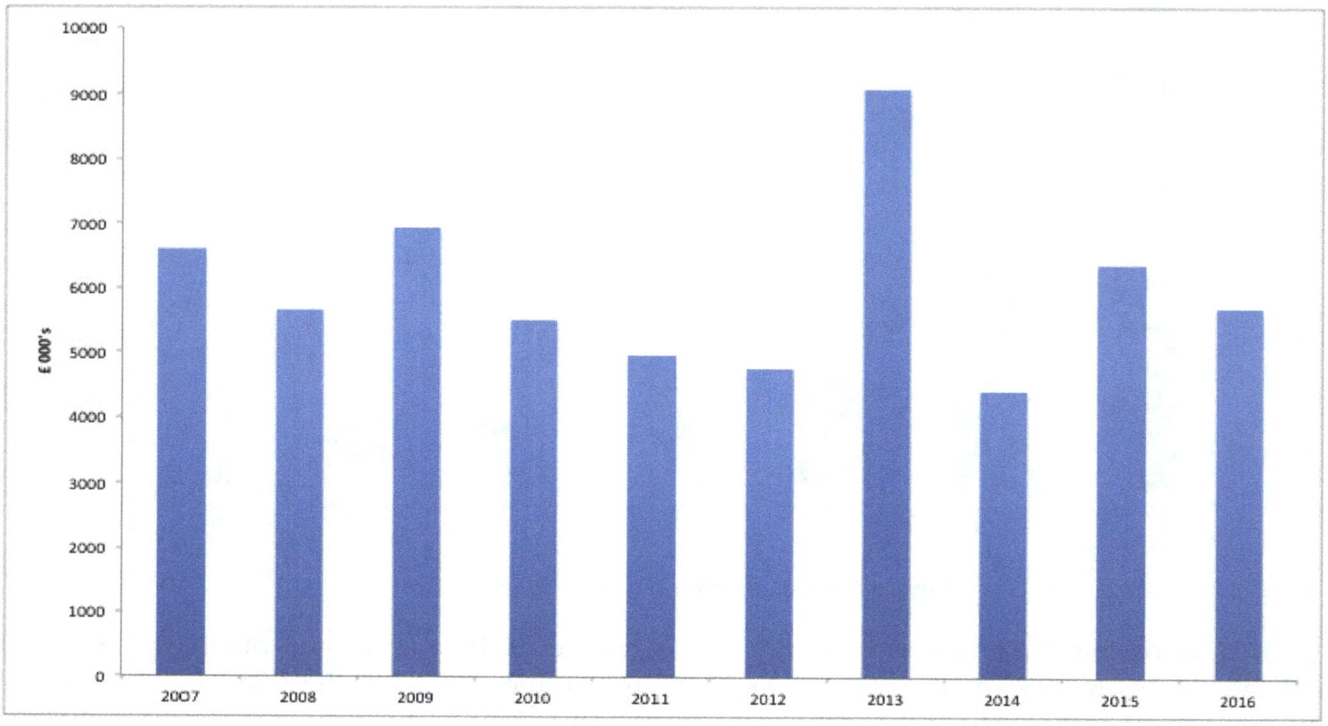

Figure 5. Durham's annual turnover 2007–2016.

In 2014, a year after the Ashes Test match, Durham hosted an ODI against Sri Lanka in May, which is not the premier slot in the English cricket summer. This step down in the prestige of its international cricket offer had a significant negative impact on the county's finances. Turnover halved compared with the 2013 Ashes year, which resulted in an overall £1.1 million deficit. The club knew it could not rely on the lucrative international fixtures as their main source of income, therefore focused on growing the revenue from T20 fixtures, which had moved to a more marketable Friday night slot during the 2015 season. Six permanent floodlights were installed to allow day/night matches to be played and the county's T20 team was re-branded to the 'Durham Jets'. In addition, the club sought to identify new revenue streams by planning to build a hotel and conference facilities on the site of The Riverside (DCCC Annual Report, Durham CCC 2015).

The last Test match Durham hosted was against Sri Lanka in 2016, which again was in the early part of the English cricketing summer. The result was the lowest turnover of the four Test match hosting years (2007, 2009, 2013 and 2016). Figure 6 displays Durham's debt ratio over the last 10 years. As previously stated anything over 75% is considered a cause for concern and Durham apart from 2009 and 2010 has consistently exceeded this figure. The club's growth has been reliant on external borrowing to fund capital investments, mainly from Durham County Council. However, the club's financial health demonstrates a lack of liquidity with their cash-flow focused on, and around, the cricketing summer (April to September). Unfortunately, with creditors calling in their debts, a financial restructure had to take place to stop the club being the first county cricket club to enter administration. In 2016 the ECB bailed out Durham, in order for the club to pay its creditors (The Telegraph 2018). However, the club faced stiff penalties (relegation and deduction of points). This is a prime example of the risk county cricket clubs face if creditors call in their debts. Ultimately the majority of clubs could not afford to pay their creditors if debts were called in and Durham was the first club to succumb to this pressure.

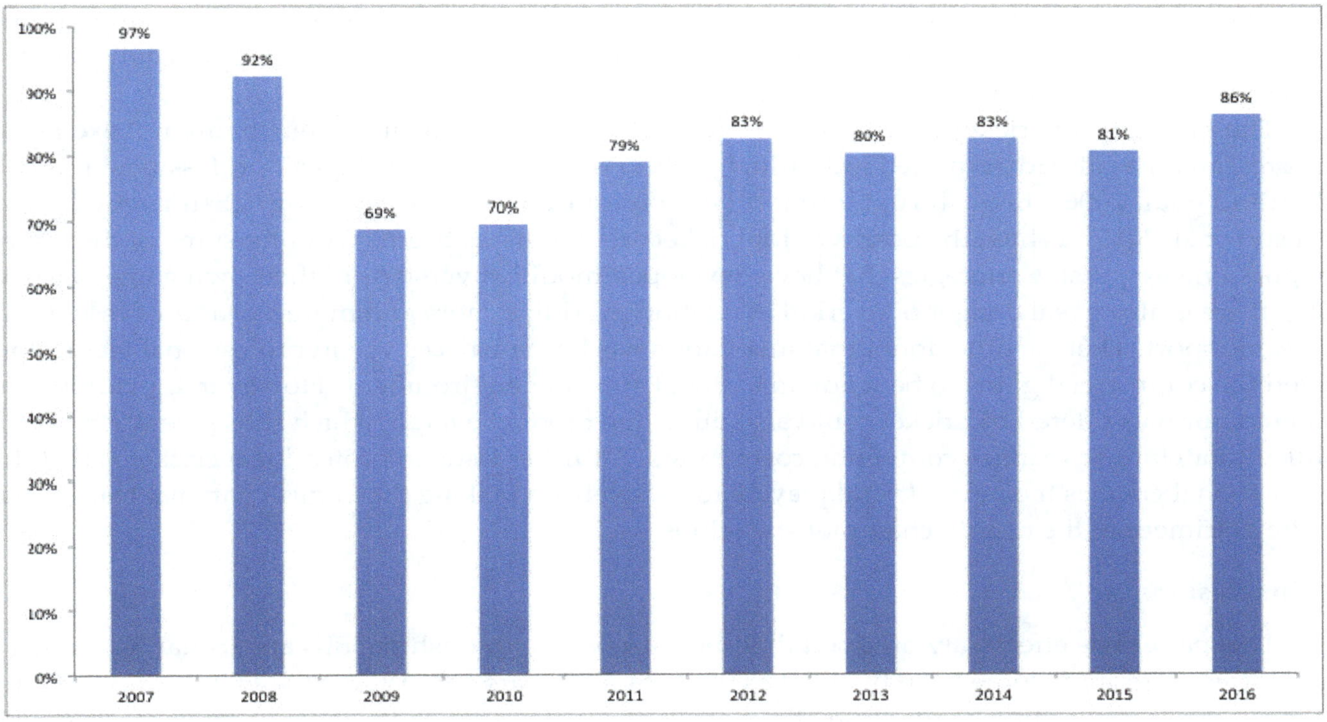

Figure 6. Durham's debt ratio 2007–2016.

5.3. How Does This Compare with 1997?

On the face of it, it appears as though the counties still have a problem with profitability and that debt (in relation to the absolute amounts on the balance sheets) has increased. The over-reliance on the ECB grant income is consistent if not more prominent now than it was in 1997, particularly for the 'non-international counties'. There have undoubtedly been positive developments in the game during the last 20 years such as the birth and growth of the T20 game and introducing the sport to younger people but there remains a problem with the financial health of some individual county clubs, particularly those that do not or cannot host Test cricket, which continues to be the pinnacle of the game from a sporting and commercial perspective.

5.4. What Can Cricket Do to Improve Its Position?

There are some positive developments taking place in cricket that can help the ECB and its county clubs to become financially sustainable including the new TV deal mentioned previously and the introduction of the new T20 franchise league due to begin in 2020. However, both of these come with *caveats*. If the TV deal allows the ECB to increase the central income to clubs, then is there a danger of clubs becoming more reliant on that than ever before. In relation to the T20 franchises, could such a system actually be of detriment to the 'smaller' non-international ground counties? The T20 city franchise will be positive for the counties who are going to host the teams, but could be negative for the ones that are not. For example, some of the small counties who rely on ECB income also rely on the income they generate through T20 matches. The new franchise league could take spectators away from the current T20 matches to the T20 franchise matches, starving the smaller counties of even more income and putting it in the pockets of the international ground counties.

It is not an easy problem to solve and the ECB will face challenges in the short and medium term in respect of county club finances. The county game still struggles with attendances and the best income stream for clubs at this point in time remains in hosting international Test match cricket. Indeed, the most recent figures released by Nottinghamshire for the year ending 2017 point to just this fact. The club made a pre-tax profit of £279,000 compared to a £741,000 loss in 2016 and chairman Richard Tennant stated that the change 'demonstrates the importance of hosting Test cricket at Trent Bridge' (BBC 2018). It is important that the ECB considers the financial situation of the non-international hosting counties alongside the international hosting ones to avoid a situation where the county cricket system begins to be dominated financially by a select number of clubs.

The problems of cricket and its clubs in respect of financial mismanagement are not exclusive. Past research has already outlined individual problems at club level in English professional football (Buraimo et al. 2006), English rugby union (Wilson and Plumley 2017) and English rugby league (Wilson et al. 2015). Whilst the positives for cricket are that it has tried to counter some of the issues by pursuing aggressive strategies that have developed modified versions of their own game (such as T20), there is also a real danger of overkill in relation to adding more and more variants of essentially the same sport. There is little doubt that innovation has become necessary in professional team sport given the commercial gains to be made in a global sporting environment. However, the number of different formats offered by cricket could also dilute the product overall, which subsequently makes it difficult for clubs to manage competing cost centres. A further issue in professional cricket is that the international game is the pinnacle and players focus solely on making the English national team, often to the detriment of the county championship clubs.

6. Conclusions

This paper has effectively outlined that the county championship clubs are arguably as reliant on the central grant income from the ECB as they were 20 years ago. Whilst the ECB is undoubtedly trying to do the right thing by providing the clubs with this funding, there is a clear financial argument that clubs must become 'self-sufficient' without this income, under the proviso that it may not always be available. As such, the ECB and the counties need to work more closely together and be more strategic in their approach to growing participation, which, in turn, can help support spectator growth and revenue generation. Counties can achieve this by incentivising clubs financially to improve their community schemes and outreach activity, thus engaging actively with the next generation of cricket players and observers. There is the requirement of the league and its governing body to maintain a sustained level of competition amongst its member clubs in line with the theoretical determinants of what makes an attractive sports league considering the 'joint' production nature of professional team sports (see Dobson and Goddard 2011; Hogan et al. 2013; Neale 1964).

Whilst the 'joint' production nature of professional team sports is of prime importance, there is a need for the member clubs individually to support the governing body to achieve its objectives and for them to operate in a more prudent financial manner. Of equal importance, is the need for clubs to be more autonomous with facility use, thus increasing the opportunity for secondary spend and additional revenue. Wilson et al. (2015) stated a similar point in relation to rugby league clubs and the same is true for cricket. Some clubs have made positive strides in respect of utilising their grounds better for other events such as conferences and concerts and this must become the business model of the majority in the future. Indeed the reliance on central grants or subsidy is not unique to English cricket and is replicated, in some way in other sports. English Football League Clubs receive a solidarity payment for example, stemming from the English Premier League TV deal which supports the solvency of its member clubs. These payments however, come from their 'mother' league rather than the governing body. Professional sport teams can only earn revenue through three main streams and one of those (in respect of broadcasting revenue) is effectively unearned. As such, the importance of maximising matchday and commercial income (through additional secondary spend activities) is of a paramount importance in county cricket where the broadcasting fees have historically been low in comparison with other sports. A further disconnect in cricket, as evidenced by this paper, is the status held by being Counties holding International Test Matches hosting ground. Clubs often overstretch themselves financially in an attempt to secure Test Match status and we have seen the issues that this can cause financially in the case of Durham. Consequently, there is an argument that clubs should not focus on securing Test Match status and instead attempt to generate secondary revenue through engaging more in the local area linked to community and outreach schemes. Despite this view, it should also be recognised that the four day game has a very restricted demographic appeal and exists mainly to provide a production line for the national team rather than a standalone sport in its own right. The national team then reinvests the proceeds of Test matches and one day internationals via the ECB. Clubs, quite rightly, may well see the grants from the ECB as a dividend for the work they put into player development.

This paper has provided a valuable contribution to the literature on the financial health of professional team sports and provides an update to the paper by Shibli and Wilkinson-Riddle in 1997. This paper also contributes to contemporary literature that has documented the issues in professional team sports in the UK in recent years such as football (e.g., Buraimo et al. 2006; Wilson et al. 2013), cricket (e.g., Shibli and Wilkinson-Riddle 1997), rugby union (e.g., Hogan et al. 2013; O'Brien and Slack 1999, 2003; Wilson and Plumley 2017) and rugby league (Wilson et al. 2015). The findings of this paper, in respect of poor financial health (by commercial standards) and the influence of governing body intervention are consistent with the findings of these authors.

The paper indicates that there remains a problem with the attractiveness of the county championship which is a product of questionable financial value at club level and reluctance by the ECB to force the clubs to become self-sustainable. The study focused on in-depth financial analysis of all county championship clubs and, unfortunately, the indicators outlined paint an austere picture. For example, in general terms, revenues are not high enough to generate sufficient growth within the game. Coupled with this is the fact that attendances, across all clubs, are stagnating in general terms. Furthermore, this reduced attendance does not encourage growth in revenue and therefore limits financial health, given that attendance figures are the main source of income generation for the majority of clubs.

In summary, with reference to cricket, the paper concludes that the county championship has not developed significantly, in business terms, since 1997. It would, however, be unfair to suggest that issues with financial performance are exclusive to county championship clubs and comparisons with other professional team sports will be evident. Indeed, other leagues do experience similar problems. Yet such comparisons to sports such as football are perhaps less relevant given that attendance figures and participation levels in that sport are the highest they have ever been. Additionally, the money associated with professional football in line with broadcasting deals and club income streams is a level far above county championship clubs at the present time. The results in this paper demonstrate that despite twenty years of history and a number of structural changes, in general terms, the clubs competing in the county championship are failing to generate profits, expand the supporter base or grow commercial revenues with a better national and international profile. The ECB and the clubs need to work closer together and the ECB should in actual fact be attempting to make the clubs self-sustainable rather than propping them up financially year-on-year.

Author Contributions: Conceptualization, R.W. and S.S.; methodology, D.P. and R.M.; software, R.M.; validation, D.P. and R.M.; formal analysis, D.P. and R.M.; investigation, D.P. and R.M.; resources, D.P. and R.M.; data curation, D.P. and R.M.; writing—original draft preparation, D.P. and R.M.; writing—review and editing, R.W. and S.S.; visualization, R.W. and S.S.; supervision, S.S.; project administration, D.P.; funding acquisition, N/A.

References

1. Ammon, Elizabeth. 2017. Available online: http://www.espn.co.uk/cricket/story/_/id/19064584/elizabeth- ammonstate-english-county-cricket (accessed on 21 December 2018).
2. Andreff, Wladimir, and Paul D. Staudohar. 2000. The Evolving Model of Professional Sports Finance. *Journal of Sports Economics* 1: 257–76. [CrossRef]

3. Andreff, Wladimir. 2007. French Football: A Financial Crisis Rooted in Weak Governance. *Journal of Sports Economics* 8: 652–61. [CrossRef]
4. Barlev, Benzion, and Joshua Rene Haddad. 2003. Fair value accounting and the management of the firm. *Critical Perspectives on Accounting* 14: 383–415. [CrossRef]
5. Barros, Carlos Pestana. 2006. Portuguese Football. *Journal of Sports Economics* 7: 96–104. [CrossRef]
6. BBC. 2018. Available online: http://www.bbc.co.uk/sport/cricket/43211323 (accessed on 21 December 2018). Bevis, Herman W. 1965. *Corporate Financial Reporting in a Competitive Economy*. New York: Macmillan.
7. Boland, Richard J. 1989. Beyond the objectivist and the subjectivist: Learning to read accounting as text. *Accounting, Organizations and Society* 14: 591–604. [CrossRef]
8. Booth, Peter, and Neil Cocks. 1989. Critical research issues in accounting standard setting. *Journal of Business Finance and Accounting* 17: 511–28. [CrossRef]
9. Bromwich, Michael. 2007. Fair values: Imaginary prices and mystical markets—A clarificatory review. In *The Routledge Companion to Fair Value and Financial Reporting*. Edited by Peter Walton. Oxon: Routledge, pp. 46–67.
10. Buraimo, Babatunde, Bernd Frick, Michael Hickfang, and Rob Simmons. 2015. The economics of long-term contracts in the footballers' labour market. *Scottish Journal of Political Economy* 62: 8–24. [CrossRef]
11. Buraimo, Babatunde, Rob Simmons, and Stefan Szymanski. 2006. English Football. *Journal of Sports Economics* 7: 29–46. [CrossRef]
12. Burrell, Gibson. 1987. No accounting for sexuality. *Accounting, Organizations and Society* 12: 89–102. [CrossRef] Chadwick, Simon. 2009. From outside lane to inside track: sport management research in the twenty-first century. *Management Decision* 47: 191–203. [CrossRef]
13. Dietl, Helmut M., and Egon Franck. 2007. Governance Failure and Financial Crisis in German Football. *Journal of Sports Economics* 8: 662–69. [CrossRef]
14. Dobson, Stephen, and John A. Goddard. 2011. *The Economics of Football*, 2nd ed. Cambridge: University Press. Durham CCC. 2015. *Annual Report and Accounts*. Durham: Durham CCC.
15. Feng, Cheng-Min, and Rong-Tsu Wang. 2000. Performance evaluation for airlines including the consideration of financial ratios. *Journal of Air Transport Management* 6: 133–42. [CrossRef]
16. Fort, Rodney. 2015. Managerial objectives: A retrospective on utility maximization in pro team sports. *Scottish Journal of Political Economy* 62: 75–89. [CrossRef]
17. Garcia-del-Barrio, Pedro, and Stefan Szymanski. 2009. Goal! Profit maximisation versus win maximisation in soccer. *Review of Industrial Organisation* 34: 45–68. [CrossRef]
18. Georgiou, Omiros, and Lisa Jack. 2011. In pursuit of legitimacy: A history behind fair value accounting. *The British Accounting Review* 43: 311–23. [CrossRef]
19. Gupta, Amit. 2004. The globalization of cricket: The rise of the non-West. *The International Journal of the History of Sport* 21: 257–76. [CrossRef]
20. Hines, Ruth D. 1991. The FASB's conceptual framework, financial accounting and the maintenance of the social world. *Accounting, Organizations and Society* 16: 313–31. [CrossRef]
21. Hitz, Joerg-Markus. 2007. The decision usefulness of fair value accounting—A theoretical perspective. *European Accounting Review* 16: 323–62. [CrossRef]
22. Hoehn, Thomas, and Stefan Szymanski. 1999. The Americanization of European Football. *Economic Policy* 28: 205–40. [CrossRef]
23. Hogan, Vincent, Patrick Massey, and Shane Massey. 2013. Competitive balance and match attendance in European rugby union leagues. *The Economic and Social Review* 44: 425–46.
24. Hopwood, Anthony G. 1990. Accounting and organization change. *Accounting, Auditing and Accountability Journal* 3: 7–17. [CrossRef]
25. International GAAP. 2005. *Generally Accepted Accounting Practices under International Financial Reporting Standards*.
26. London: LexisNexis.
27. Kesenne, Stefan. 2000. Revenue Sharing and Competitive Balance in Professional Team Sports. *Journal of Sports Economics* 1: 56–65. [CrossRef]
28. Kesenne, Stefan. 2015. Revenue sharing and absolute league quality: Talent investment and talent allocation. *Scottish Journal of Political Economy* 62: 51–58. [CrossRef]
29. Laux, Christian, and Christian Leuz. 2009. The crisis of fair value accounting: Making sense of the recent debate. *Accounting, Organizations and Society* 34: 826–34. [CrossRef]
30. Leach, Stephanie, and Stefan Szymanski. 2015. Making money out of football. *Scottish Journal of Political Economy* 62: 25–50. [CrossRef]
31. Miller, Peter, and Ted O'Leary. 1987. Accounting and the construction of the governable person. *Accounting, Organizations and Society* 12: 235–66. [CrossRef]

32. Neale, Walter C. 1964. The peculiar economics of professional sports. *Quarterly Journal of Economics* 78: 1–14. [CrossRef]
33. O'Brien, Danny, and Trevor Slack. 1999. Deinstitutionalising the amateur ethic: An empirical examination of change in a rugby union football club. *Sport Management Review* 2: 24–42. [CrossRef]
34. O'Brien, Danny, and Trevor Slack. 2003. An analysis of change in an organizational field: The professionalization of English rugby union. *Journal of Sport Management* 17: 417–48. [CrossRef]
35. Plumley, Daniel, Robert Wilson, and Simon Shibli. 2017. A holistic performance analysis of English professional football clubs 1992–2013. *Journal of Applied Sport Management* 9: 1–29. [CrossRef]
36. Ponikvar, Nina, Maks Tajnikar, and Ksenja Pušnik. 2009. Performance ratios for managerial decision-making in a growing firm. *Journal of Business Economics and Management* 10: 109–20. [CrossRef]
37. Pritchard, Adrian. 2016. It's not just cricket—The portfolios of the English/Welsh cricket teams. *Sport, Business and Management: An International Journal* 6: 19–35. [CrossRef]
38. Richardson, Alan J. 1987. Accounting as a legitimating institution. *Accounting, Organizations and Society* 12: 341–56. [CrossRef]
39. Saikia, Hemanta, Dibyojyoti Bhattacharjee, and Atanu Bhattacharjee. 2013. Performance based market valuation of cricketers in IPL. *Sport, Business and Management: An International Journal* 3: 127–46. [CrossRef]
40. Shibli, S., and G. J. Wilkinson-Riddle. 1997. The financial health of English Cricket—An analysis based upon the 1995 annual reports and financial statements of the 18 first class counties. *Journal of Applied Accounting Research* 4: 4–37.
41. Sloane, Peter J. 1971. The Economics of Professional Football: The Football Club as a Utility Maximiser. *Scottish Journal of Political Economy* 17: 121–46. [CrossRef]
42. Sloane, Peter J. 2006. Rottenberg and the economics of sports after 50 years. In *Sports Economics after 50 Years*. Edited by Placido Rodriguez, Stefan Kesenne and Jaume Garcia. Essays in Honour of Simon Rottenberg. Spain: University of Oviedo, pp. 211–26.
43. Sloane, Peter J. 2015. The economics of professional football revisited. *Scottish Journal of Political Economy* 62: 1–7. [CrossRef]
44. Sueyoshi, Toshiyuki. 2005. Financial Ratio Analysis of the electric power industry. *Asia-Pacific Journal of Operational Research* 22: 349–76. [CrossRef]
45. Sunder, Shyam. 2016. Better financial reporting: meanings and means. *Journal of Accounting and Public Policy* 35: 211–23. [CrossRef]
46. Surrey CCC. 2018. *Annual Report and Accounts*. Surrey: Surrey CCC.
47. Szymanski, Stefan, and Andrew S. Zimbalist. 2005. *National Pastime: How Americans Play Baseball and the Rest of the World Plays Soccer*. Washington: Brookings Institution Press.
48. Szymanski, Stefan, and Tim Kuypers. 1999. *Winners and Losers: The Business Strategy of Football*. London: Viking Books.
49. Szymanski, Stefan. 2003. The Economic Design of Sporting Contests. *Journal of Economic Literature* 41: 1137–87. [CrossRef]
50. The ECB. 2018. Available online: https://www.ecb.co.uk/news/623583/where-will-major-matches-be-played- from-2020 (accessed on 21 December 2018).
51. The Guardian. 2017a. Available online: https://www.theguardian.com/sport/2017/feb/20/ipl-auction-ben- stokes-sets-record-tymal-mills-indian-premier-league (accessed on 21 December 2018).
52. The Guardian. 2017b. Available online: https://www.theguardian.com/sport/2017/jun/30/live-cricket-return- bbc-twenty20-tournament (accessed on 21 December 2018).
53. The Independent. 2017. Available online: https://www.independent.co.uk/sport/cricket/t20-twenty20-new- tournament-natwest-blast-love-it-hate-domestic-game-back-from-brink-a8291796.html (accessed on 21 December 2018).
54. The Telegraph. 2018. Available online: https://www.telegraph.co.uk/cricket/2017/06/30/game-changing-tv- deal-sky-bbc-will-broaden-crickets-appeal-says/ (accessed on 21 December 2018).
55. Tinker, Tony. 1988. Panglossian accounting theories: The science of apologising in style. *Accounting, Organizations and Society* 13: 165–90. [CrossRef]
56. Vrooman, John. 2015. Sportsman leagues. *Scottish Journal of Political Economy* 62: 90–115. [CrossRef]
57. Williams, Peter. 2012. Any given Saturday: Competitive balance in elite English rugby union. *Managing Leisure* 17: 88–106. [CrossRef]
58. Willmott, Hugh. 1986. Organising the profession: A theoretical and historical examination of the development of the major accounting bodies in the UK. *Accounting, Organizations and Society* 11: 555–82. [CrossRef]
59. Wilson, Rob, and Daniel Plumley. 2017. Different shaped ball, same financial problems? A holistic performance assessment of English Rugby Union (2006–2015). *Sport, Business and Management: An International Journal* 7: 141–56. [CrossRef]
60. Wilson, Rob, Daniel Plumley, and David Barrett. 2015. Staring into the abyss? The state of UK rugby's Super League. *Managing Sport and Leisure* 20: 293–310. [CrossRef]

61. Wilson, Robert, Daniel Plumley, and Girish Ramchandani. 2013. The relationship between ownership structure and club performance in the English Premier League. *Sport, Business and Management: An International Journal* 3: 19–36. [CrossRef]
62. Wright, April L., and Raymond F. Zammuto. 2013. Creating opportunities for institutional entrepreneurship: The Colonel and the Cup in English County Cricket. *Journal of Business Venturing* 28: 51–68. [CrossRef]

14

The Effects of the Clock and Kickoff Rule Changes on Actual and Market-Based Expected Scoring in NCAA Football

Kenneth Linna [1], Evan Moore [1,*], Rodney Paul [2] and Andrew Weinbach [3]

[1] Department of Economics, Finance, and Marketing, Auburn University at Montgomery, P.O. Box 244023, Montgomery, AL 36124, USA; klinna@aum.edu

[2] Department of Finance, Syracuse University, 810 Nottingham Road, Syracuse, NY 13224, USA; rpaul01@syr.edu

[3] Department of Finance and Economics, Coastal Carolina University, P.O. Box 261954, Conway, SC 29528-6054, USA; aweinbac@coastal.edu

* Author to whom correspondence should be addressed; emoore1@aum.edu

Abstract: Clock rule changes were introduced in the 2006 season with the goal of reducing the average duration of the game; these changes were reversed in 2007. In addition, in 2007 the kickoff rule was changed to create more excitement and potentially more scoring. We examine what happened to actual and expected scoring during these National Collegiate Athletic Association (NCAA) football seasons. The clock rule change in 2006 led to lower scoring which was not fully encompassed in the betting market, leading to significant returns to betting the under. Multiple rule changes in 2007 led to volatility in the betting market that subsided by season's end.

Keywords: rule change; amateur sports; scoring; gambling; betting; market efficiency; prediction markets

JEL Classification: L83

---

1. Introduction and Literature Review

Regulation and rule changes are instituted in business and in sports for a variety of reasons. In some cases regulation is introduced to protect consumers or players. In other cases, changes in rules occur to simply increase revenues, lower costs, or achieve both simultaneously. When rules or regulations are changed, it provides a natural framework to perform a case study as to the financial ramifications of the changes to determine if they match the stated goals of the policy. Just as important and interesting is to study the market expectations of rule and regulation changes through financial markets. Understanding how financial markets performed before, during, and after rule changes provides insights into the thoughts and minds of investors and allows for testing of the efficient markets hypothesis.

The testing of stock price movements as they relate to accounting rules and regulation date back to the classic study of Fama *et al.* [1], where the role of new information on security prices was formally investigated. Over time, many research papers have investigated the role of regulation announcements and the implementation of regulations on stock prices (*i.e.*, Binder [2,3] and Schwert [4]). These studies on stock price movements relate back to the testing and further understanding of the implications of the efficient markets hypothesis (Fama [5,6]). Specific examples of where case studies of financial regulation on stock prices were performed include investigation of Sarbanes-Oxley (Jain and Rezaee [7];

Zhang [8]), Garn-St. Germain (Millon-Cornett and Tehranian [9]), Glass-Steagall Act: Section 20 (Cyree [10]) and reviews of bank regulation in general (Millon-Cornett [11] and Carow and Kane [12]).

Financial research into investor sentiment and feelings has been performed on a variety of fronts and is summarized in a literature review by Lucey and Dowling [13]. The role of investor feelings has been used to study stock market response to sporting events, where stock prices are examined and abnormal returns (if any) are calculated following sports contests. These findings have led to considerable debate in the literature surrounding market returns related to English football (soccer) on the London Stock Exchange (FTSE) (Ashton *et al.* [14,15] and Klein *et al.* [16]). Bell *et al.* [17] used a similar concept to study stock market returns of publicly-traded soccer clubs as it related to match results and expectations. Edmans *et al.* [18] studied sports sentiment and stock returns for major international sporting events such as the world cup and international cricket, rugby, and basketball.

It is also possible to study the expected and actual influences of rule changes on gameplay within a sport itself through the investigation of sports betting markets. Sport betting markets are simple financial markets which allow market participants to wager on the outcome of a game or the total number of points scored in a game through prices expressed as point spreads, totals, or odds.

Although sports gambling markets are simple in nature, they are quite popular, with estimates for annual sports wagering by the American Gaming Association being over $3 Billion in Nevada (legally) and $380 Billion illegally across the United States [19]. Rule changes that impact the style of play can be investigated through changes in betting market prices before games are actually played and changes to these prices can be tracked over time. In general, financial studies of sports wagering markets have been unable to reject market efficiency for large overall samples of games across sports. Sports betting markets were assumed to behave under the balanced book hypothesis, where point spreads and totals were assumed to be set to even the betting dollars on each side of the wagering proposition. If achieved, this would allow the sports book to profit without risk in this market, due to the commission charged on bets (a bet $11 to win $10 rule). Recently, Levitt [20] challenged the balanced book hypothesis showing that sports books are not balanced as bettors consistently prefer the favorite in data from a betting market tournament. Paul and Weinbach [21] confirmed this result with betting market percentage data on sides (wagers on a team compared to the point spread) and totals (over/under bets) through data from actual on-line sports books.

Two studies that investigated betting market expectations related to rule changes in sports were Paul *et al.* [22] and Paul and Paul [23]. When the National Football League introduced the two-point conversion rule, it was found that the frequency of posted point spreads increased around key numbers such as three (a field goal differential). The increase in frequency of these key numbers outpaced the frequency of game outcomes of three by a wide (statistically significant) margin [22]. This change in policy by the sports book likely helped them from the greater likelihood of being "middled" (losing both sides of a wager) in NFL games.

Another instance where the betting market adjusted to a rule change was in the National Hockey League. When the NHL eliminated ties in games by adding a shootout, the totals (over/under) market went through a major adjustment. Overall scoring increased by nearly a goal-per-game, but the betting market actually over-adjusted early in the season. This led to profitable returns for under bettors [23] in the totals market. By the end of the season, however, the market appeared to completely adjust to the new rule changes as expected scoring mimics actual scoring within the league.

Two significant rule changes were undertaken by the National Collegiate Athletic Association (NCAA) Football Rules Committee for the 2006 and 2007 seasons. In 2006, the clock rule was introduced to change the timing on plays and reduce the length of college football games. In 2007, this rule was reversed, but the committee also introduced a new kickoff rule to induce more returns by moving the kickoff spot back by 5 yards (from the 35 to the 30 yard line). The goal of our research is twofold. We examine the impact of these rule changes to determine how they impacted actual and expected scoring. We study if the rule changes had the anticipated impact on scoring by investigating total points scored (actual scoring) and the betting market total on the game (expected scoring). We aim to determine if the market anticipated the changes in scoring and how quickly it adjusted. When the 2006 rule was reversed and the new rule was introduced in 2007, we examine which effect had a bigger impact on scoring, the clock rule or the kickoff rule. The overall goal of this research is to determine how the NCAA football rule changes impacted on-field play and how the betting market reacted to these changes before, during, and after their initiation.

The NCAA is the governing body for major collegiate sports in the United States, with supervision of different sports for over 1200 colleges and universities. Major collegiate football is referred to as Division I, and this division currently has two subdivisions: the Football Bowl Subdivision (FBS) and the Football Championship Subdivision (FCS). The FCS uses a single-elimination playoff system to determine a champion; the teams participating in the playoffs are selected by an NCAA FCS committee. The FBS is significantly different from the FCS in two ways: (1) the FBS has a series of bowl games at the end of the regular season; and (2) the champion is not determined by the NCAA but rather by the Bowl Championship Series (BCS). While the authority of the BCS is sanctioned by the NCAA, this is the only NCAA sporting division that does not finish with an NCAA championship [24].

To expand upon the details of the rule changes and to obtain some semblance of the expectations related to these rule changes, consider the following details and quotes related to the rule changes in college football for the 2006 and 2007 seasons. Prior to the start of the 2006 college football season, the NCAA Football Rules Committee made "recommendations concerning the length of the game" in an attempt to shorten the duration of football games [25]. The recommendations included:

(1). Starting the clock on kickoffs when the foot touches the ball, not the returning team;

(2). Starting the clock when the ball is ready for play on a change of possession; and

(3). Shorten the halftime allowance from 20 to 15 minutes.

According to NCAA Football Rules Committee chair and football coach at Pittsburg State Charles Broyles, "We looked at quite a few proposals to shorten the game ... Starting the clock on the change of possession is probably our biggest change. We think this is a good change and that this will help reach our goals in this area [26]." Broyles was correct; Steve Wieberg wrote, "College football's rules makers got what they wanted: a faster, shorter game." He reports, of the opening week games, that in 2006 31 of the 72 games were completed in 3 hours or less, with four lasting as long as 3.5 hours. In 2005 only five of 52 games completed in 3 hours or less; 13 went 3.5 hours or longer [26].

Coaches noticed that these changes had an impact on play. West Virginia coach Rich Rodriguez stated, "Normally, in most games, you have 12 or 13 possessions. We had 10 on offense." He went on to say, "So you've really got to make things happen offensively." In a similar vein, South Florida coach Jim Leavitt noted, "People are very aware of the speed of the game right now [26]."

However, early in the season there did not appear to be many coaches viewing the changes as particularly problematic to game management. Texas Tech coach Mike Leach noted, "I don't think they're too hard to work around." However, he also added, "I just think it's dumb to shorten these games that have been a perfectly good length for years and years [26]."

Coach Leach's assessment was ultimately shared by other coaches. According to Steve Wieberg [27], "Coaches hated the moves (the clock rule changes)." The NCAA rules oversight panel voted to eliminate the clock rule changes " ... used last year that helped shave 14 minutes off of game times [28]." Additionally, the panel decided to change the kickoff from the 35 yard line to the 30 yard line beginning with the 2007 season. According to the football rules committee spokesman, Ty Halpin, the proposed justifications for changing the kickoff rule in NCAA football include creating " ... more opportunities for what the committee feels is one of the most exciting plays in a game, and we're not really sure, but it may increase scoring, too [29]." This was mirrored by Dave Parry, national coordinator of NCAA football officiating, who stated, "It will create a little more excitement, and we'll get a little more movement of the ball [30]."

A number of coaches have commented regarding this rule change on scoring. According to Kentucky head coach Rich Brooks, "It's going to be one of the most significant rule changes to come around in a decade .... You're going to see scoring averages go up because of this rule change." Auburn head coach Tommy Tubberville stated, "It will add more points to the scoreboard [31]." Mark Nelson, Louisville's special teams coach, made the following prediction: "Add about seven points to the total score of every game [32]."

Regardless of the sport, rule changes are usually made with specific intentions. Often, rules are changes with the goal of increasing interest in the game. Bannerjee and Swinnen [33] investigated FIFA's introduction of the golden goal rule, to "stimulate more attractive football" and Bannerjee *et al.* [34] noted that the NHL's rule change regarding overtime results was done "in an effort to stimulate a more exciting and entertaining style of play."

The effects of rule changes in sports have covered a variety of other topics as well. These include the effects of rule changes on competitive balance in Formula 1 racing [35], Japanese professional baseball [36], and across North American major sports leagues [37]. Still other works address the effects of rule changes on strategy and play style; Guedes and Machado [38] examine the effect of FIFA's increase in the number of points awarded to winning a game on offensive efforts and Moschini [39] finds that the change led to a statistically significant increase in the expected number of goals. Banjeree *et al.* [34] investigate the NHL's overtime rules change on play style during the both the regular and overtime periods. McCannon [40] investigates the effect of the three-point line being extended on men's NCAA basketball finding that the change led to a decrease in three-point shooting and scoring along with a decrease in the percentage of successful two-point shots. Regarding rule changes and penalties, Witt [41] evaluates the effects of FIFA's rule change regarding the increase in offenses qualifying as red-card worthy on the number of the number and types of penalties called.

This paper presents results concerning the effects of NCAA Football rule changes in 2006 and 2007 on total scoring, scoring margin, and competitiveness of the games. These results are then compared to what happened in the financial (betting) market for college football totals. The outcomes between actual and expected scoring due to the rule changes are compared. These results are then compared to the preseason predictions of the rules committee, the officials, and a variety of coaches. The next section provides analyses of the actual scoring data and findings. Section 3 presents the results from the totals betting market. Section 4 discusses the findings and concludes the paper.

2. Actual Scoring and Outcomes

The actual scoring data used in this study consists of the final scores from NCAA Division I football games in the 2005, 2006 and 2007 seasons. This includes all 2308 games involving at least one Division I Football Bowl Subdivision (FBS) team. The complete data set will be used in the overview provided in the next section. However, 364 matchups, totaling 1092 games, were played in each of the three seasons. To avoid dependence issues, most of the analysis was conducted using difference scores for these repeat matchups.

Table 1 presents summary statistics for the scores of the three seasons in six categories. In five of the six categories the total scoring decreased from 2005 to 2006 then increased with the 2007 season to a higher mean than that of the 2005 season. The exception was BCS bowl games as scoring in 2007 did not exceed that of the 2005 season.

Table 1. Summary scoring statistics for the 2005–2007 seasons.

		2005 Mean (StDev)	*2006 Mean (StDev)*	*2007 Mean (StDev)*			*2005 Mean (StDev)*	*2006 Mean (StDev)*	*2007 Mean (StDev)*
	Total score	52.60 (17.20)	47.53 (16.12)	55.41 (18.69)		Total score	56.61 (19.80)	51.44 (16.54)	57.69 (20.63)
All games	Winning score	35.11 (12.14)	32.51 (11.46)	36.46 (12.32)	**Bowl games**	Winning score	33.75 (10.32)	32.09 (8.917)	35.56 (13.06)
	Losing score	17.49 (9.852)	15.02 (9.448)	18.95 (10.99)		Losing score	22.86 (11.73)	19.34 (10.54)	22.12 (11.00)
	Margin	17.62 (13.90)	17.49 (13.47)	17.51 (14.00)		Margin	10.89 (9.814)	12.75 (10.37)	13.44 (12.55)
	N	718	792	798		N	28	32	32
	Total score	52.13 (16.92)	47.88 (15.37)	54.20 (18.05)		Total score	63.75 (14.5)	56.40 (17.60)	60.00 (12.27)
Non-conference games (reg. season)	Winning score	36.97 (13.33)	34.76 (12.19)	38.05 (13.28)	**BCS Bowl games**	Winning score	34.75 (6.500)	36.20 (8.044)	40.00 (10.08)
	Losing score	15.16 (9.484)	13.13 (9.381)	16.15 (10.56)		Losing score	29.00 (8.832)	20.20 (12.34)	20.00 (6.892)
	Margin	21.80 (15.77)	21.63 (15.39)	21.91 (15.81)		Margin	5.750 (5.550)	16.00 (11.14)	20.00 (12.15)
	N	239	303	316		N	4	5	5
	Total score	52.61 (17.18)	47.03 (16.57)	56.09(18.97)		Total score	55.42 (20.55)	50.52 (16.51)	57.26 (21.98)
Conference games (reg. season)	Winning score	34.22 (11.48)	31.06 (10.89)	35.40 (11.43)	**Non-BCS Bowl games**	Winning score	33.58 (10.92)	31.33 (9.000)	34.74 (13.54)
	Losing score	18.39 (9.661)	15.97 (9.186)	20.69 (10.89)		Losing score	21.83 (11.99)	19.19 (10.43)	22.52 (11.66)
	Margin	15.83 (12.46)	15.08 (11.47)	14.71 (11.78)		Margin	11.75 (10.19)	12.15 (10.34)	12.22 (12.46)
	N	451	457	450		N	24	27	27

The margin of victory was relatively stable for non-conference games over the period while the margin decreased in conference games. It was also relatively stable for non-BCS bowl games in both the 2006 and 2007 seasons. However, note that the margin of the BCS bowl games increased from 5.5 points in 2005 to 16 points in 2006, and then to 20 points in 2007. This coincides with the winning teams increasing scoring and the losers decreasing scoring in these games, on average.

These increasing scoring margins coincided with a decline in average BCS bowl game television ratings, from Nielson ratings of 13.98 in 2005–2006 to 9.52 in 2007–2008. This corresponds with the findings of Salaga and Tainsky [42] in their work on Neilson ratings for BCS games; their results indicate that increases in the margin at a given quarter decrease ratings. The previously mentioned study investigates the uncertainty of outcome hypothesis while Grimshaw *et al.* [43] examines TV audiences for the NCAA men's basketball Final Four games based on a consumer theory model. Future research into the factors affecting TV audiences for these games is warranted due to the financial stakes; the 2011–2014 television deal generates $155 million per season for the BCS while the upcoming contract is estimated at $470 million per year [42]. Given six BCS games in the upcoming season then the per-game figure is approximately $78.3 million. For the sake of comparison, the NCAA men's basketball tournament's television deal currently averages $771 million per year [43]. However, excluding any play-in games there are 63 games in this tournament resulting in a per-game figure of approximately $12.2 million. Table 2 presents summary statistics for each of the BCS automatic bid conferences. This summary information reveals that the margin of victory decreased for these conferences between the 2005 and 2007 seasons. In five of the six conferences this is driven by increases in the losers' scores.

Table 2. Scoring statistics for Bowl Championship Series (BCS) Automatic Bid Conferences.

		2005 Mean (StDev)	*2006 Mean (StDev)*	*2007 Mean (StDev)*			*2005 Mean (StDev)*	*2006 Mean (StDev)*	*2007 Mean (StDev)*
ACC	Total score	46.64 (15.05)	40.98 (16.82)	47.71 (13.93)	**Big Ten**	Total score	56.14 (13.78)	46.50 (17.59)	52.64 (17.97)
	Winning score	30.56 (11.21)	27.13 (10.36)	30.22 (9.150)		Winning score	37.05 (9.838)	31.68 (11.67)	33.30 (10.43)
	Losing score	16.09 (7.940)	13.84 (10.02)	17.49 (7.959)		Losing score	19.09 (9.215)	14.82 (9.848)	19.34 (10.27)
	Margin	14.47 (12.29)	13.29 (11.51)	12.73 (10.01)		Margin	17.95 (13.18)	16.86 (12.53)	13.95 (10.28)
	N	45	45	45		N	44	44	44
Big 12	Total score	54.35 (16.74)	52.02 (17.26)	62.18 (19.28)	**PAC-10**	Total score	59.25 (16.82)	44.84 (13.52)	53.47 (17.16)
	Winning score	37.10 (13.47)	33.02 (10.61)	41.00 (12.51)		Winning score	37.85 (12.20)	30.80 (9.236)	33.98 (10.96)
	Losing score	17.24 (9.013)	19.00 (9.314)	21.18 (11.13)		Losing score	21.40 (9.139)	14.04 (8.116)	19.49 (9.134)
	Margin	19.86 (15.65)	14.02 (10.03)	19.82 (13.75)		Margin	16.45 (13.48)	16.76 (10.93)	14.49 (10.62)
	N	49	49	49		N	40	45	45
Big East	Total score	49.54 (16.05)	49.21 (17.57)	53.36 (18.46)	**SEC**	Total score	43.88 (17.60)	42.20 (13.58)	53.90 (20.25)
	Winning score	34.39 (10.21)	31.68 (9.813)	33.89 (12.64)		Winning score	28.92 (11.18)	26.71 (9.115)	33.27 (11.93)
	Losing score	15.14 (9.679)	17.54 (9.879)	19.46 (9.693)		Losing score	14.96 (9.460)	15.49 (7.901)	20.63 (10.81)
	Margin	19.25 (11.76)	14.14 (8.902)	14.43 (12.92)		Margin	13.96 (10.93)	11.22 (10.32)	12.63 (10.40)
	N	28	28	28		N	49	49	49

Table 3 presents the results of two-tailed t-tests for the mean differences in each category from zero. The results from the repeated matchups are used in this analysis. The total, winning, and losing scores are all significantly lower at less than the 1 percent level in the 2006 season compared to the values for 2005. The total score decreased by 4.66 points per game. However, the margin of victory did not change significantly. This suggests that the implementation of the clock rule changes led to decreased scoring but did not have any statistically significant effect on the margin of victory. A comparison of the 2007 and 2005 seasons reveals that the kickoff rule changes led to total scoring increasing by 2.93 points per game, with this being driven primarily by increases in the losers' score by 1.77 points. This supports the results discussed in regard to Table 2. These results are statistically significant at the 5 percent level.

Table 3. Tests of significance for changes in scoring across the 2005–2007 seasons.

	t-statistic	*p-value*	*Mean Difference*
2006–05 total score	−3.858	0.000	−4.659
2006–05 winning score	−3.274	0.001	−2.571
2006–05 losing score	−3.036	0.003	−2.088
2006–05 margin	−0.569	0.570	−0.484
2007–05 total score	2.253	0.025	2.934
2007–05 winning score	1.421	0.156	1.168
2007–05 losing score	2.391	0.017	1.766
2007–05 margin	−0.693	0.489	−0.599

Degrees of freedom for all tests equals 363.

3. Financial Market Expectations and Outcomes

The next step in our analysis is to examine the financial (betting) market reaction to the rule changes in NCAA football. As was seen in the previous section, scoring declined in 2006 when the NCAA introduced rules aimed at shortening the length of the game. When these rules were reversed in 2007, the NCAA also introduced a change in the placement of the kickoff which was likely to result in better starting field position for the offense. The combination of these rule changes in 2007 led to increased scoring beyond the levels seen in 2006 and even in 2005 (prior to the rule changes).

Given that the betting market for college football is a simple financial market, it is possible to trace the rule changes in college football to their implications on prices. In the case of analyzing rules that impact scoring, the totals markets is the market we will investigate. The totals market is commonly known as the over/under market and is a simple financial market where bettors can wager on whether the combined score of both teams will be greater than or less than the posted number by the sports book. Previous studies of market efficiency in the college football wagering market has shown the market to be efficient in the aggregate, although simple strategies of wagering on the under at the highest totals has been shown to reject market efficiency [44].

The question pertaining to this study is if the betting market adjusted to these rule changes and, if it did, how quickly did the market adjust? Given that the rule changes were announced in advance, sports book managers and bettors alike were able to analyze and hypothesize about the impact of these changes before the season began. Even if the rule changes could not be incorporated immediately, it is likely if one assumes market efficiency (and the incentives present in the market) that the impact of the rule changes would quickly be realized and prices would adjust to their unbiased values.

To begin, we will examine the year prior to the rule changes, 2005, and then compare these results to 2006 and 2007. We examine what happened each season in the aggregate to allow for enough observations to perform possible meaningful tests on market efficiency. It is important to understand that small sample sizes in sports betting markets can reveal unreliable results as noted in Osborne [45].

Given that we are interested in specific years and are attempting to understand the speed of adjustment of the market in those seasons, we believe the relatively large number of games in a college football season (over four times as many games as an NFL season), we believe the data set is large enough to provide insight on the issues of interest. The following table shows the mean and standard deviation of the total for each season. For each year studied, the first four weeks of the season and the results for the season as a whole are presented.

Table 4. Descriptive statistics summarizing totals by season.

Week	2005 Season Mean Total (Standard Deviation)	2006 Season Mean Total (Standard Deviation)	2007 Season Mean Total (Standard Deviation)
Week 1	50.55(5.71)	47.52(4.96)	49.36(5.16)
Week 2	51.53(6.31)	47.71(5.91)	50.32(7.48)
Week 3	51.32(5.63)	47.68(5.08)	53.08(8.77)
Week 4	51.60(7.43)	47.05(6.37)	53.88(8.23)
Entire Season	51.96(7.08)	47.73(6.52)	54.50(8.27)

The results of Table 4 above illustrate that when the new clock rules were introduced in 2006, totals immediately fell. In Week 1, the mean total fell by 3 points. By Week 4, the mean total was around 4.5 points lower than it was at the same time in 2005. By the end of the season, the mean total was over 4 points lower than in 2005. The standard deviation of the total also fell by around a half point. Compared to the actual scoring results, where scoring on the average in 2006 was shown to decrease nearly 5 points compared to 2005, the average total fell, but not quite as much as actual scoring.

In 2007, with the change back of the clock rules and the movement of the kickoff from the 35 to 30 yard line, there appeared to be a bit more confusion in the totals market. Totals only rose slightly (compared to 2006) in Weeks 1 and 2, but jumped by Week 3 to levels beyond those seen in 2005. Overall, totals rose by about 7 points compared to 2006 and about 2.5 points compared to 2005. The standard deviation also rose in 2007. This compares quite closely to the actual change in scoring, which would be predicted under the efficient markets hypothesis, as actual scoring rose by nearly 8 points from 2006 to 2007 and was between 2.5 and three points greater than it was in 2005.

The next step in analyzing the market is to compare betting market results during these years to see how simple strategies of wagering on the over or the under-performed before and after the college football rule changes. The following three tables show the over and under record in the 2005, 2006, and 2007 seasons. For each season, individual week results for Weeks 1–4 and the overall season results are shown. Table 5 includes information on the number of overs, unders, and pushes, the under win percentage, and the log likelihood ratio test for a fair bet (win percentage equal 50%) from Even and Noble [46].

Before the rule changes, in 2005, overs and unders split nearly evenly in the totals betting market. With the introduction of the new clock rules in 2006, the under did considerably better than the over. The 53.16% win percentage of simply betting the under was great enough to reject the null hypothesis of a fair bet at the 10% level. This result is not overly surprising given the previous findings in this paper, as the actual amount of scoring fell by a greater amount than the betting market total, resulting in more wins on betting the under.

Table 5. Over/Under Records and Fair Bets by Season.

Week	Overs	Unders	Pushes	Under %	Log Likelihood Fair Bet
Week 1	20	25	1	56.56%	0.5567
Week 2	25	23	0	47.92%	0.0834
Week 3	23	21	0	47.73%	0.0909
Week 4	21	23	0	52.28%	0.0909
2005 Season	336	330	6	49.55%	0.0541

a. 2005 NCAA Football Season—Over/Under Record.

Week	Overs	Unders	Pushes	Under %	Log Likelihood Fair Bet
Week 1	23	21	0	47.73%	0.0909
Week 2	24	26	0	52.00%	0.0800
Week 3	21	29	0	58.00%	1.2855
Week 4	20	28	1	58.33%	1.3396
2006 Season	334	379	9	53.16%	2.8420*

b. 2006 NCAA Football Season—Over/Under Record.

Week	Overs	Unders	Pushes	Under %	Log Likelihood Fair Bet
Week 1	19	27	1	58.70%	1.3984
Week 2	32	18	1	36.00%	3.9729**
Week 3	21	27	2	56.25%	0.7520
Week 4	33	14	1	29.79%	7.9051***
2007 Season	339	370	12	52.19%	1.3559

c. 2007 NCAA Football Season—Over/Under Record.

Note: The log likelihood test statistics have a chi-square distribution with one degree of freedom. Critical values are 2.706 ($\alpha = 0.10$), 3.841 ($\alpha = 0.05$), 6.635 ($\alpha = 0.01$).

In 2007, multiple rule changes appeared to cause some confusion in the betting market. There was great volatility early in the season, with some weeks where the over dominated and other weeks where the under outperformed the over. In Weeks 2 and 4, scoring was so high that the over won enough to reject the null hypothesis of a fair bet at the 5% level in Week 2 and at the 1% level in Week 4. By the end of the season, however, unders did slightly better than overs, but not nearly as well as in 2006. It appeared that uncertainty reigned early in the 2007 college football season due to the multiple rule changes, but by the end of the season the total pretty well reflected the actual amount of scoring that happened in college football games.

Detailed betting data available from Sportsinsights [47] can shed further light in terms of what happened in the totals market during these seasons. Sportsinsights publishes the betting percentages on each side of the wagering proposition for college football and other sports. This information was used to test the balanced book hypothesis (the notion that sports books set prices to even the betting action on each side of the proposition). The balanced book was soundly rejected in college football [21] in addition to other sports. Although this study and more recent research illustrated that the book was not balanced, the point spreads and totals studied were still shown to serve as an unbiased forecast of game outcomes (despite clear betting biases toward the favorites and overs).

Table 6. Betting Public Perception: Betting Percentage on the Over.

Year	Average % on Over	Standard Deviation on Over
2005	63.12	16.25
2006	65.69	15.09
2007	64.08	13.75

Table 6 presents the mean percentage bet on the over for the 2005–2007 seasons. As is clearly seen in the table, bets on the over are much more popular than bets on the under. Wagers on the over received greater than 60% of the betting action throughout the sample period. In 2006, the percentage bet on the over rose to 65.69%, an increase of nearly 2.5% over 2005. Due to the clock rule changes, totals fell in 2006. These lower totals likely proved to be even more tempting to over bettors, due to their pre-existing bias that already existed for wagering on the over. This increase in betting percentage on the over also likely contributed to the under being a winning wager overall during the 2006 NCAA football season. In 2007, with the rise in the total due to the reversal of clock rules and the introduction of the kickoff rule, the percentage bet on the over fell by about 1.5% compared to where it was in 2007, which was slightly higher than it was in 2005, but the betting market went back to a more even split between overs and unders during that season.

Overall, the effects of the clock rules were anticipated by the book makers as they lowered totals, but bettors did not fully grasp the effects. This led to slightly higher totals than there should have been and a winning season for under bettors in 2006. The reversal of the clock rules and the introduction of the new kickoff rule in 2007 was met with some confusion in the early season by both bookmakers and bettors. By the end of the season, it appeared that the market adjusted to the new rules in place for college football.

4. Discussion and Conclusions

The results reveal that the clock rule changes instituted in the 2006 season and the kickoff rule change that began with the 2007 season had an effect on scoring in Division I Football Bowl Subdivision (FBS) games. Using 2005 as the base year, we found that the clock rule changes of 2006 decreased total scoring by 4.66 points per game, with the winners' scores decreased by 2.57 points and the losers' scores decreased by 2.09 points on average. These results are statistically significant at the 5 percent level or lower. The elimination of the clock rule changes for the 2007 season allowed us to compare the effects of the kick rule change against the scoring of the 2005 season. We found that total scoring increased by 2.93 points per game, with the losers' scores earning the bulk of the increase, receiving 1.77 points on average. Nevertheless, neither rule change had a statistically significant effect, at any generally accepted level, on the margins of victory during these seasons. It is not clear from the results that the games are more competitive on average. This suggests that other rule changes may be necessary to reduce the margin.

In the over/under market for college football, the total fell due to the clock rule changes in 2006. These lower totals spurred more betting action on the over during this season (due to the behavioral bias which already exists in this market where bettors prefer wagering on the over rather than the under) and led to under bets significantly outperforming over bets. The financial market for NCAA football totals betting showed much volatility early in the season in 2007, due to the reversal of the clock rules and the introduction of the kickoff rule. By the end of the season, however, market expectations and actual results meshed with general findings of market efficiency with the slight (but normal compared to previous studies) behavioral bias of bettors toward the over.

The predictions of the kick rule change by various coaches were generally correct; scoring averages increased with this rule. However, statements by coaches that it may have a "huge impact" or be one the "most significant" rule changes appear a bit strong, at least in regard to scoring. Our results suggest that the timing rule changes had a much stronger impact on scoring in these games.

Overall, rule changes in sports change the manner of play on the field, influence the way fans respond to the sport, and influence financial (betting) markets related to the game. The major rule changes which occurred in college football in 2006 and 2007 led to changes in scoring that were mostly predictable ex-ante by sports book managers, but still led to some biased results due to the behavioral preferences of market participants.

Acknowledgments: The authors thank the participants at the sports economics session of the 45th annual Academy of Economics and Finance conference for their helpful comments.

Author Contributions: All listed authors contributed equally to the research completed and writing of the paper.

References

1. Fama, E.; Fisher, L.; Jensen, M.; Roll, R. The Adjustment of Stock Prices to New Information. *Int. Econ. Rev.* **1969**, *10*, 1–21. [CrossRef]
2. Binder, J. Measuring the Effects of Regulation with Stock Price Data. *Rand J. Econ.* **1985**, *16*, 167–183. [CrossRef]
3. Binder, J. The Event Study Methodology Since 1969. *Rev. Quant. Finance Account.* **1998**, *11*, 111–137. [CrossRef]
4. Schwert, G. Using Financial Data to Measure Effects of Regulation. *J. Law Econ.* **1981**, *24*, 121–158.
5. Fama, E. Efficient Capital Markets: A Review of the Theory and Empirical Work. *J. Finance* **1970**, *25*, 383–417. [CrossRef]
6. Fama, E. Efficient Capital Markets II. *J. Finance* **1991**, *46*, 1575–1617. [CrossRef]
7. Jain, P.; Rezaee, Z. The Sarbanes-Oxley Act of 2002 and Capital Market Behavior: Early Evidence. *Contemp. Account. Res.* **2006**, *23*, 629–654. [CrossRef]
8. Zhang, I. Economic Consequences of the Sarbanes-Oxley Act of 2002. *J. Account. Econ.* **2007**, *44*, 74–115. [CrossRef]
9. Millon-Cornett, M.; Tehranian, H. An Examination of the Impact of the Garn-St. Germain Depository Institutions Act of 1982 on Commercial Banks and Savings and Loans. *J. Finance* **1990**, *45*, 95–111. [CrossRef]
10. Cyree, K. The Erosion of the Glass-Steagall Act: Winners and Losers in the Banking Industry. *J. Econ. Bus.* **2000**, *52*, 343–363. [CrossRef]
11. Millon-Cornett, M. Stock Market Reactions to the Depository Institutions Deregulation and Monetary Control Act of 1980. *J. Bank. Finance* **1989**, *13*, 81–100. [CrossRef]
12. Carow, K.; Kane, E. Event-Study Evidence of the Value of Relaxing Longstanding Regulatory Restraints on Banks: 1970–2000. *Q. Rev. Econ. Finance* **2002**, *42*, 439–463. [CrossRef]
13. Lucey, B.; Dowling, M. The Role of Feelings in Investor Decision-Making. *J. Econ. Surv.* **2005**, *19*, 211–237. [CrossRef]
14. Ashton, J.; Gerrard, B.; Hudson, R. Economic Impact of National Sporting Success: Evidence from the London Stock Exchange. *Appl. Econ. Lett.* **2007**, *10*, 283–785.
15. Ashton, J.; Gerrard, B.; Hudson, R. Do National Soccer Results Really Impact on the Stock Market? *Appl. Econ.* **2011**, *43*, 3709–3717. [CrossRef]
16. Klein, C.; Zwergel, B.; Heiden, S. On the Existence of Sports Sentiment: The Relation between Football Match Results and Stock Index Returns in Europe. *Rev. Manage. Sci.* **2009**, *3*, 191–208. [CrossRef]
17. Bell, A.; Brooks, C.; Matthews, D.; Sutcliffe, C. Over the Moon or Sick as a Parrot? The Effects of Football Results on a Club's Share Price. *Appl. Econ.* **2012**, *44*, 3435–3452. [CrossRef]
18. Edmans, A.; Garcia, D.; Nurli, O. Sports Sentiment and Stock Returns. *J. Finance* **2007**, *62*, 1967–1998. [CrossRef]
19. American Gaming Association. Available online: http://www.americangaming.org/industry-resources/research/fact-sheets/sports-wagering (accessed on 19 March 2014).
20. Levitt, S. Why are gambling markets organized so differently from financial markets? *Econ. J.* **2004**, *114*, 223–246. [CrossRef]
21. Paul, R.J.; Weinbach, A.P. Sportsbook Behavior in the NCAA Football Betting Market: Tests of the Traditional and Levitt Models of Sportsbook Behavior. *J. Prediction Markets* **2009**, *3*, 21–37.

22. Paul, R.J.; Weinbach, A.P.; Mahar, J. The Betting Market Response to the 2-Point Conversion in the NFL. *J. Bus. Econ. Persp.* **2007**, *33*, 98–110.
23. Paul, R.J.; Paul, K.K. Market Reaction to a Structural Change: The Totals Market of the NHL. *Bus. Res. Yearb.* **2007**, *14*, 53–59.
24. Wallace, R. FBS vs. FCS. Available online: http://www.differencebetween.net/miscellaneous/difference-between-fbs-and-fcs/ (accessed on 19 March 2014).
25. NCAA Press Release. Available online: http://football.refs.org/rules/NCAA2006pr.html (accessed on 19 March 2014).
26. Wieberg, S. Teams get adjusted to rules shortening game. *USA Today*, 4 September 2006.
27. Wieberg, S. NCAA rules committee proposes reworking football time-saving rules. *USA Today*, 14 February 2007.
28. NCAA Press Release. Available online: http://fs.ncaa.org/Docs/PressArchive/2007/Playing%2BRules/NCAA%2BFootball%2BRules%2BCommittee%2BVotes%2BTo%2BRestore%2BPlays%2BWhile%2BAttempting%2BTo%2BMaintain%2BShorter%2BOverall%2BGame%2BTime.html (accessed on 19 March 2014).
29. Associated Press. Available online: http://sports.espn.go.com/ncf/news/story?id=2835266 (accessed on 19 March 2014).
30. Brunt, C. College Football Changes Kickoff Rule. Available online: http://www.washingtonpost.com/wp-dyn/content/article/2007/08/16/AR2007081601365.html (accessed on 19 March 2014).
31. Hood, S. New Kickoff Rule Gets (Special) Teams Attention. Available online: http://sports.yahoo.com/ncaaf/news?slug=rivals-146383&prov=rivlas&typs=lgns (accessed on 19 March 2014).
32. Dodd, D. Kick Back and Enjoy as Returns Grow More Intriguing. Available online: http://www.sportsline.com/collegefootball/story/10323027 (accessed on 19 March 2014).
33. Banerjee, A.N.; Swinnen, J.F.M. Does a Sudden Death Liven Up the Game? Rules, Incentives, and Strategy in Footbal. *Econ. Theor.* **2004**, *23*, 411–421. [CrossRef]
34. Banerjee, A.N.; Swinnen, J.F.M.; Weersink, A. Skating on Thin Ice: Rule Changes and Team Strategies in the NHL. *Can. J. Econ.* **2007**, *40*, 493–514. [CrossRef]
35. Mastromarco, C.; Runkel, M. Rule Changes and Competitive Balance in Formula One Motor Racing. *Appl. Econ.* **2009**, *41*, 303–314.
36. La Croix, S.J.; Kawaura, A. Rule Changes and Competitive Balance in Japanese Professional Baseball. *Econ. Inq.* **1999**, *37*, 353–356.
37. Fort, R.; Lee, Y.H. Structural Change, Competitive Balance, and the Rest of the Major Leagues. *Econ. Inq.* **2007**, *45*, 519–532. [CrossRef]
38. Guedes, J.C.; Machado, F.S. Changing Rewards in Contests: Has the Three-Point Rule Brought More Offense to Soccer? *Empir. Econ.* **2002**, *27*, 607–630. [CrossRef]
39. Moschini, G. Incentives and Outcomes in a Strategic Setting: The Three-Points-for-a-Win System in Soccer. *Econ. Inq.* **2010**, *48*, 65–79. [CrossRef]
40. McCannon, B.C. Strategic Offsetting Behavior: Evidence from National Collegiate Athletic Association Men's Basketball. *Contemp. Econ. Policy* **2011**, *29*, 550–563. [CrossRef]
41. Witt, R. Do Players React to Sanction Changes? Evidence from the English Premier League. *Scot. J. Polit. Econ.* **2005**, *52*, 623–640. [CrossRef]
42. Salaga, S.; Tainsky, S. The effects of outcome uncertainty, scoring, and pregame expectations on Neilson ratings for Bowl Championship Series games. *J. Sport. Econ. 2013.* [CrossRef]
43. Grimshaw, S.; Sabin, R.P.; Willes, K.M. Analysis of the NCAA men's Final Four TV audience. *J. Quant. Anal. Sport.* **2013**, *9*, 115–126.
44. Paul, R.J.; Weinbach, A. Bettor Preference and Market Efficiency in Football Totals Markets. *J. Econ. Financ.* **2005**, *29*, 409–415. [CrossRef]
45. Osborne, E. Efficient markets? Don't bet on it. *J. Sport. Econ.* **2001**, *2*, 50–61. [CrossRef]
46. Even, W.E.; Noble, N.R. Testing efficiency in gambling markets. *Appl. Econ.* **1992**, *24*, 85–88. [CrossRef]
47. Sportsinsights. Available online: http://www.sportsinsights.com (accessed on 19 March 2014).

15

European Club Football after "Five Treatments" with Financial Fair Play—Time for an Assessment

Egon Franck

Department of Business Administration, University of Zurich, Affolternstrasse 56, 8050 Zurich, Switzerland; egon.franck@business.uzh.ch

Abstract: UEFA's Club Licensing and Financial Fair Play Regulations (FFP) have impacted European club football. After five distinct applications of the break-even requirement, which represents the cornerstone of these regulations, it is time for an assessment. How has the situation in European top-division football changed since the FFP regulation? The most recent financial data show that European club football is characterized by significant financial recovery and further polarization. How has the FFP regulation presumably affected this development? This article discusses plausible reasons why FFP has contributed to financial recovery but has not aggravated polarization. Understanding the drivers of polarization is essential before taking further regulatory steps.

Keywords: football; regulation; financial fair play; financial recovery; polarization

JEL Classification: L83; L49; L51

---

1. Introduction

European club football has been confronted with a major regulatory intervention, UEFA's Club Licensing and Financial Fair Play Regulations (FFP). Today, after five distinct applications of the break-even requirement, which represents the cornerstone of this intervention, it is time for an assessment: How has the situation changed since FFP first impacted European top-division football? Additionally, how has the regulatory intervention presumably affected this development?

In sum, the most recent data show that European club football is characterized by quick financial recovery and further polarization. While pre-FFP European club football was on a trajectory of ever-deepening financial distress until 2011, the data show a continuous improvement since financial year (FY) 2012, the first reporting period entering into a break-even assessment. Of course, the mere comparison of the financial indicators pre- and post-FFP does not prove that FFP is the (or the main) cause behind the financial comeback of the European football industry. Nonetheless, this article suggests a plausible economic story as to why FFP has had a significant impact on creating a more financially stable industry[1].

The newest data also show that financial recovery went hand in hand with further polarization. Absolute revenue growth has been much stronger at the top of the football pyramid, thereby further entrenching the sportive dominance of the "big clubs". However, the mere coincidence of FFP and further polarization does not imply that FFP is a (or the) cause for this development. This article discusses good reasons why polarization has not been aggravated by FFP. Clearly identifying the main drivers of polarization is of fundamental importance before embarking on a new regulatory exercise beyond the scope of FFP.

---

1 See Franck (2014) for a detailed explanation.

The remainder of this paper is organized as follows. Section 2 gives a short overview of the financial situation of European club football pre-FFP. Section 3 briefly explains the main pillars, the assessment periods, and the judicial process of FFP. Section 4 is devoted to the economic analysis of FFP: Where exactly does the regulation change the incentives of decision-makers in the football industry? Section 5 presents facts and figures about the financial situation of post-FFP European club football. Section 6 is devoted to the analysis of the polarization between the top-tier clubs and the rest. Section 7 provides some first reflections on the European "super league" project. Section 8 concludes.

2. The Financial Distress of Pre-FFP European Club Football

UEFA publishes a yearly Benchmarking report[2] covering the financial situation of approximately 700 first division clubs in 55[3] member associations. Figure 1 shows the aggregate "bottom line", country by country, for the FY 2011. While football operating profits focus on the contribution from core football activities, the "bottom line" gives the performance of the clubs after including transfer activity, financing and divesting results, non-operating items, and tax. The country by country result in Figure 1 sends a message of financial distress. The red columns show countries whose first division clubs had spent between €1.10 and €1.20 to gain €1.00 of revenue, whereas dark-red columns show countries where even more than €1.20 had been spent to gain €1.00 of revenue. The predominance of the red and dark-red colors indicates that, with rare exceptions, football was a largely unprofitable business in 2011.

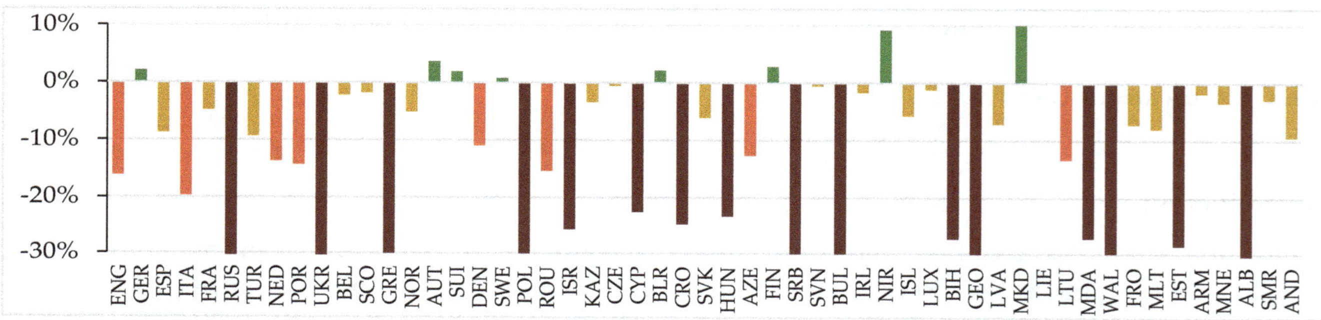

Figure 1. Aggregate "bottom line" (net profit/loss of the leagues in 2011). Source: UEFA (2013, p. 104). UEFA limited the chart at −30%. Maximum losses were significantly higher in single cases.

Figure 2 shows the development of the combined yearly net losses of all European top-division clubs from 2007 to 2011. The losses almost tripled from €0.6 billion to €1.7 billion.

The cause of increasing financial distress was that the clubs spent everything and even more than they could reasonably afford on players. While revenues had increased at an average rate of 5.6% per year[4], wages grew by 9.1% per year from 2007 to 2011.[5] The combined employee and net transfer costs to revenue ratio, which impacts bottom-line results, increased from 62% to 71%, meaning that the revenue increase between FY 2007 and FY 2011 had not been enough to cover the increase in combined employee and net transfer costs. As a consequence, the financial results of the clubs competing in European competitions were worsening year after year despite the fact that football as an industry was growing. The percentage of "financial zombies", i.e., clubs with negative net equity, reached 38%.[6] Meanwhile, in 2011, 63% of all top-division clubs reported an operating loss and 55% a net loss.[7] The reported liabilities of the top-division clubs reached €18.5 billion in 2011, and auditors expressed

2 All financial information in this section is taken from the UEFA Benchmarking Report covering the FY 2011. See UEFA (2013).
3 This is the actual number in 2018.
4 See UEFA (2013, p. 78).
5 See UEFA (2013, p. 80).
6 See UEFA (2013, p. 15).
7 See UEFA (2013, p. 8).

"going concern" doubts (i.e., doubts whether the club could still trade normally in 12 months' time) for one in every seven clubs.[8]

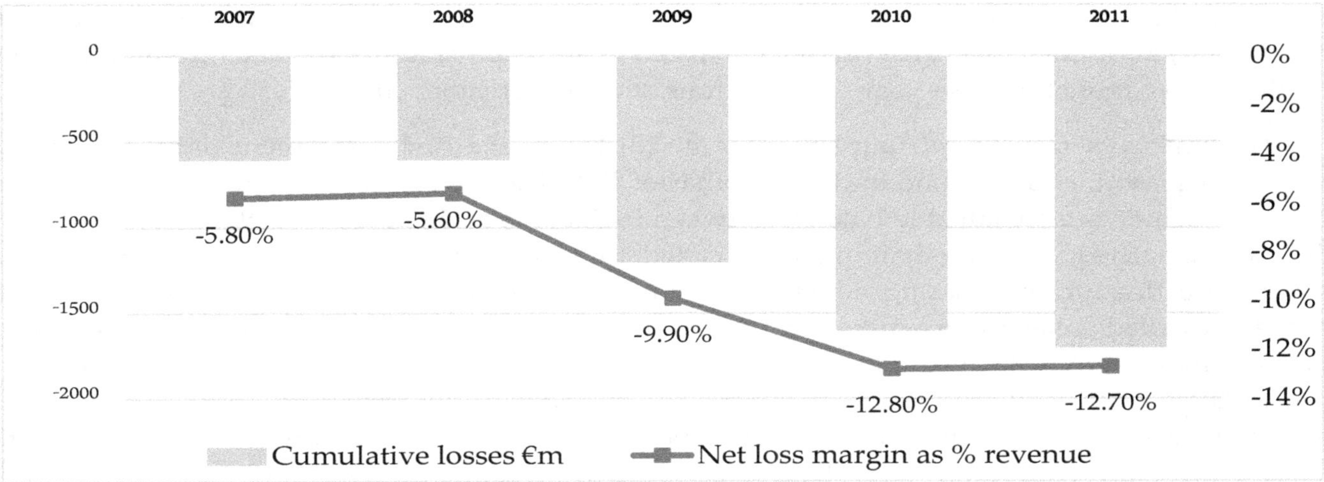

Figure 2. Combined net losses (€ Millions) of the European top-division clubs, 2007 to 2011. Source: UEFA (2013, p. 82).

As a reaction to this development, stakeholders in the football industry increasingly shared the perception that the long-term viability and sustainability of the entire system was being threatened by football clubs' ever-deepening financial crisis. As clubs are strongly interconnected through their peculiar technology of producing a team output, the "championship race"[9], if some clubs go out of operation in mid-season, the credibility of the entire product of "championship" is severely harmed. Financial domino effects get triggered because bankrupt clubs cannot fulfill their obligations from transfer deals. Several factors, such as the high percentage of clubs with negative equity, the high level of overdue payables, the exit of "normal" investors[10] from the industry, etc., jointly indicated that the system was "overheating"[11].

Alerted by these developments, UEFA gathered internal and external experts to work on a regulation that would restabilize the football industry without entering into conflict with European Union competition law. The first version of the UEFA Club Licensing and Financial Fair Play Regulations was approved by the UEFA Executive Committee in September 2009.

3. The Two Main Pillars, the Assessment Periods, and the Judicial Process of FFP[12]

UEFA designed the new regulations as an enhancement of UEFA's established "workhorse", the club licensing system, which was introduced at the start of the 2004/2005 football season. In order to be admitted to UEFA's club competitions, the Champions League and the Europa League, each club must fulfill a series of quality standards falling into five categories: Sporting, infrastructure, personnel, legal, and financial. With the introduction of the new FFP regulations, UEFA upgraded the financial standards by introducing two important new requirements, explained below. These requirements are monitored by a newly created body of independent experts, the Club Financial Control Body (CFCB).

8 See UEFA (2013, p. 15).
9 See Neale (1964) for the initial formulation of this basic insight. Neale wrote about an "inverted joint product".
10 "Normal" investors expect a competitive risk-adjusted return from their engagement.
11 These and other related developments were already highlighted in the Independent European Sports Review published in 2006. See Arnaut (2006).
12 All information included in this section is based on the relevant UEFA documents: The Procedural Rules Governing the UEFA Club Financial Control Body (see UEFA 2015a) and The UEFA Club Licensing and Financial Fair Play Regulations (UEFA 2015b).

The enhanced overdue payable rule, monitored from June 2011 onwards, is the first of the two new requirements. It demands that clubs playing in UEFA competitions must fulfill all their financial obligations towards other clubs, employees, and social or tax authorities punctually. While the established licensing system already assessed overdue payables, it only did so at one single date in the year, i.e., as of December 31. With the enhanced overdue payables rule, the CFCB monitors the fulfillment two more times per year, i.e., as of June 30 and September 30.

The break-even requirement, implemented in 2012 with the first assessment done during the 2013/2014 season, is the second and main pillar of FFP. The idea behind this requirement is that each club achieves a sustainable balance between its income and expenses in the football market. The income earned in the football market is called "relevant income" and consists mainly of gate receipts, broadcasting, sponsoring, advertising, and commercial income. The expenses in the football market are called "relevant expenses" and consist mainly of employee benefit expenses and player transfer amortization. Balancing these two factors means that clubs must be able to perform their core football activities without owner contributions and without incurring debt. At the same time, clubs can still invest and incur debt or expend owner contributions on infrastructure, youth development, and community activities. Because such investments are for the long-term benefit of the club, the corresponding expenses are not considered as "relevant" for the purpose of the break-even calculation.

Importantly, clubs must balance "relevant income" and "relevant expenses" not in one FY, but in monitoring periods usually consisting of three FYs. Table 1 explains the concept of the applied "rolling three-year assessment". The main consequence of the rolling three-year assessment is that every FY will be part of three break-even assessments until it drops out.

Table 1. The aggregate break-even result is assessed over three reporting periods (T, T-1, T-2).

	Monitoring Period		
Assessment #	**FY_T**	**FY_{T-1}**	**FY_{T-2}**
1	2013	2012	N/A
2	2014	2013	2012
3	2015	2014	2013
4	2016	2015	2014
5	2017	2016	2015

Source: UEFA (2015b).

The first genuine break-even assessment took place in spring 2014. The CFCB had to wait until the clubs with a December year end closed their books for the FY 2013. In its first assessment, the CFCB assessed only the FYs 2012 and 2013 as an exception. In spring 2015, the CFCB then looked at the first complete monitoring period consisting of the FYs 2012, 2013, and 2014. The bottom box indicates the most recent assessment of the CFCB.

Due to the huge influence of sportive results on financial results—consider, for example, the financial impact of qualifying or not qualifying for the next round in the UEFA Champions League—the regulations give some flexibility to the clubs. More precisely, a break-even deficit of €5 million over three years is considered to be an "acceptable deviation". Furthermore, the rules permit an additional deficit of up to €25 million over three years, provided that it is covered through the injection of equity by the owners. This gives some flexibility to redevelop mismanaged clubs into viable businesses[13].

---

13 Additional flexibility for new owners has been introduced through the concept of *voluntary agreements*. See UEFA (2015b, pp. 94–95).

Table 2 and Figure 3 provide a brief overview of the judicial process of FFP. The CFCB comprises two chambers. The investigatory chamber conducts the investigation, determines the facts, and gathers all relevant evidence. It decides on every case, taking one of the following options:

- Dismiss the case;
- Impose minor disciplinary measures;
- Conclude a settlement agreement;
- Refer the case to the second chamber, the adjudicatory chamber.

The adjudicatory chamber takes a final decision on the case, which is either a dismissal or the instruction of disciplinary measures. As Figure 3 shows, the disciplinary measures of the adjudicatory chamber reach from a warning to the exclusion from competitions and withdrawal of titles and awards. Clubs can appeal the decisions of the adjudicatory chamber before the Court of Arbitration of Sport in Lausanne (CAS).

Table 2. The judicial process of FFP.

Investigatory Chamber	**Adjudicatory Chamber**
• Conducts the investigation, determines the facts, and gathers all relevant evidence	• Takes the final decision on the cases referred by the CFCB investigatory chamber and eventually imposes disciplinary measures
CFCB's Chief Investigator may (in consultation with all members):	**Court of Arbitration for Sport (CAS)**
• Dismiss the case • Impose minor disciplinary measures • Conclude a settlement agreement • Refer the case to the adjudicatory chamber	• Appeals can be lodged before the CAS

Source: UEFA (2015a). CFCB: Club Financial Control Body, FFP: UEFA's Club Licensing and Financial Fair Play Regulations.

- Warning, Reprimand
- Fine
- Deduction of points
- Withholding of revenues from a UEFA competition
- Prohibition on registering new players in UEFA competitions
- Restriction on the number of players that a club may register for participation in UEFA competitions
- Disqualification from competitions in progress and/or the exclusion from future competitions

Figure 3. Disciplinary measures of the adjudicatory chamber. Source: (UEFA 2015a).

The experience of the last years clearly shows that the most important instrument in the daily practice of the CFCB is the settlement agreements concluded by the investigatory chamber with individual clubs. A significant number of clubs—28 until today, among them prominent ones, such as Paris Saint-Germain FC, Manchester City FC, Inter Milan, AS Monaco, AS Roma, FC Zenit, or FC Porto—entered into settlement agreements.

Instead of going through a lengthy judicial procedure, clubs with the clear potential to come back into compliance rather quickly sign settlement agreements voluntarily with the investigatory chamber. These agreements contain a detailed plan with annual and aggregate break-even targets that have to be reached and a set of "provisions" that, from an economic point of view, can be seen as sanctions and restrictions. For example, there have been very high (unconditional and conditional) withholdings of prize money, up to €60 million, and also strict limitations of player registration activities.

UEFA publishes on its website summaries of all settlement agreements and of all the decisions of the adjudicatory chamber[14].

4. The Economic Analysis of FFP[15]

Football championships are examples of a certain form of economic competition, which is known as a contest in the literature. Research on contests shows that under certain circumstances, a phenomenon of overinvestment emerges.[16] While this "arms race" or "rat race" effect[17] explains why clubs may dissipate some resources in their attempt to achieve sporting success, it does not suffice to explain the extreme dissipation of resources in football, which transformed many clubs into "financial zombies" (i.e., a situation where the value of their liabilities exceeds the value of their assets). In other words, the concept of a "rat race" seems too weak to characterize an industry in which such a substantial part of the participants was technically bankrupt. Therefore, in this context, the concept of a "zombie race" seems more appropriate.

Obviously, a "zombie race" requires that the "normal" threat of dissolution of the club in case of insolvency is not functioning as a hard constraint. This leads to the second element of the story, i.e., to the soft budget constraints (SBCs) of many football clubs before the regulation.[18] Football club managers could rationally expect that in case of a deficit, some form of "supporting organization", either the state or a private benefactor[19], would step in to relieve the club from the pressure to "cover its expenditures out of its initial endowment and revenue" (Kornai et al. 2003, p. 4).

What is wrong with SBCs, though? Normally, economists would immediately discuss the differences between burning public or private money in football. However, this diverts from the main problem of bailouts in this specific context: They distort the incentives of decision-makers in football clubs.

4.1. Runaway Demand for Talent and the Emergence of a "Salary Bubble"[20]

If a club has a perfect SBC, the own price–elasticity of demand for player talent becomes zero, meaning that the demand for talent is not determined by the price but rather by other variables (Kornai 1986, p. 9). It seems rational to assume that winning is desirable for club decision-makers and that talent contributes to winning. If the supply of talent is not sufficiently elastic, the direct consequence of the SBC is the formation of excess demand for player talent. Frank and Bernanke (2004) explain why the supply of talent is inelastic by definition: "Indeed, the most important input of all—highly talented players—is in extremely limited supply. *This is because the very definition of talented player is inescapably relative—simply put, such a player is one who is better than most others*" (Frank and Bernanke 2004, p. 113). Thus, talent, understood as the capacity of a few players to be better than most others, is extremely scarce and its price gets bid through the roof if enough clubs have SBCs and a very low price–elasticity of demand for talent as a consequence. The more clubs operate with SBCs, the more football becomes

---

14 See https://www.uefa.com/insideuefa/disciplinary/club-financial-controlling-body/cases/index.html.

15 This section is not original but entirely based on my previous work. Please refer to Franck (2014, pp. 195–206) and the following Franck (2015, pp. 230–33) for the original analysis.

16 See Dietl et al. (2008) for an in-depth treatment of this issue.

17 See Akerlof (1976).

18 The concept of soft budget constraints had been introduced and initially studied by Kornai (1980, 1986) in the context of post-socialist economies. It has received much attention in the sports economics literature and also in the media. See e.g., Andreff (2007, 2011, 2015), Storm (2012), Storm and Nielsen (2012), Franck (2014, 2015) or Kuper (2009).

19 See the detailed discussion of this mechanism in Franck (2014, pp. 197–201).

20 This section corresponds to Franck (2015, p. 231). See Franck (2014, pp. 202–3) for a more in-depth explanation.

a "talent shortage economy", resulting in a "salary bubble"[21], where the wages and transfer fees of the few talented players reach levels that are unsustainable without systematic money injections.

4.2. *Managerial Moral Hazard: Too Much Risk and Too Little Care*[22]

Another consequence of the declining price–responsiveness of football clubs operating with SBCs is risk escalation. The emergence of managerial moral hazard behavior in environments with SBCs is a standard result that has been studied in different contexts. A prominent example is the "too big to fail" problem in the financial sector[23], in which managers are inclined to take excessive risks because they can expect to be bailed out ex post. Franck and Lang (2014) analyzed money injections in football clubs based on a formal model. As soon as the option to be bailed out with a certain probability exists, club decision-makers are induced to make riskier investments.

Risk escalation is only one aspect of managerial moral hazard. In absence of what Kornai (1986, p. 12) called "'dead-serious' considerations of revenues and ultimately of supply", decision-makers do not invest enough of their own time and energy to end bad projects and develop good projects. Therefore, money "coming like manna" (Kornai 1986, p. 12) triggers waste and profuseness.

4.3. *Managerial Rent-Seeking*[24]

Managerial rent-seeking gives weak incentives to innovate and to develop the business, as Kornai (1986) explains: "Allocative efficiency cannot be achieved when input-output combinations do not adjust to price-signals. Within the firm there is no sufficiently strong stimulus to maximum efforts; weaker performance is tolerated. The attention of the firm's leaders is distracted from the shop floor and from the market to the offices of the bureaucracy where they may apply for help in case of financial trouble" (Kornai 1986, p. 10).

To the extent that rent-seeking behavior is systematically rewarded in SBC organizations, their managers invest less effort in developing competitive advantages by "improving quality, cutting costs, introducing new products or new processes" (Kornai 1986, p. 10). If productive efforts can easily be substituted by asking the "sugar daddy" to compensate for unfavorable developments, SBC organizations will be less innovative and their managers less entrepreneurial in a dynamic perspective.[25]

4.4. *Crowding Out of Incentives for "Good Management"*[26]

Clubs operating with hard budget constraints find themselves victims of the "salary bubble" produced by the clubs with SBCs. Maintaining their old level of playing strength by keeping their share of "star players" would require higher expenditure in the player market. At first sight, this could generate an additional incentive to further increase efficiency through "better management" in order to remain competitive on the pitch. However, what if the margin to further increase efficiency through "better management" becomes too small compared to the magnitude of the money injections of benefactors at their competitors?

---

21 The terms "shortage economy" and "salary bubble" are, of course, borrowed from Kornai (1980, 1986).
22 This section largely corresponds to Franck (2015, pp. 231–32) and to Franck (2014, p. 203).
23 See e.g., Stern and Feldman (2004).
24 This section largely corresponds to Franck (2015, p. 232). See also Franck (2014, p. 203) for the initial version.
25 Numerous hearings with "clubs in trouble" in the CFCB over the last years have personally convinced me of the relevance of this piece of economic theory about managerial rent-seeking. It is striking to see how commercially underdeveloped some "big clubs" of the past are, where "sugar daddies" wrote checks year after year to bail them out. They have no own stadia, no systematic international fan development, underdeveloped sponsorship and commercial rights, excess employment, lack of professional managerial competence, huge and inefficient player portfolios, etc. It is a true challenge for their new owners to turn around these clubs and make them catch up with their former peers in terms of commercial development.
26 This section corresponds to Franck (2015, pp. 232–33). See also Franck (2014, p. 204) for the initial version.

It seems that these clubs will have no choice but to accept sportive decline or to change sides and start gambling on success and invest more aggressively. If we consider that sportive decline generates disutility both for club decision-makers and fans, it seems plausible that the SBCs of some clubs should intensify the incentives of other clubs to overspend.

Thus, "unlimited" money injections have a tendency to crowd out business models based on "good management". More and more clubs tend to take more risk and chronically expend more than their earnings, hoping to be rescued by external money injections year after year if the gamble goes wrong. One might argue that this state of affairs had already been reached in the FY 2011, given the numbers presented in Section 2.

4.5. The Role of FFP

Against this background, FFP is an instrument to move from a state of affairs with SBCs to a state of affairs with harder budget constraints[27]. The message sent to football managers by the cornerstone of FFP, the break-even requirement, is that they should no more "hope for a bailout" when the payroll expenditures drive relevant expenses to a level that exceeds relevant income by more than the "acceptable deviation". Clubs will be sanctioned and, in extreme cases, not receive a license to play if they do not break even in the football market. Thus, the existence of benefactors that would be willing to donate additional money to cover excessive salary and transfer payments becomes irrelevant.

In theory, the FFP regulation should therefore mitigate the inefficiencies resulting from SBCs and reduce the systemic risk of a severe financial crisis in the football industry. Clubs that break even in the football market and pay their bills punctually are sustainable and do not produce any kind of negative externalities, which might bring other clubs in trouble.

5. The Financial Situation of Post-FFP European Club Football

"Will football revenues drop substantially post-FFP?" This "prosperity concern" was a major criticism when FFP was introduced[28]. "Will post-FFP football enter into a downward development if the money injections of benefactors no longer freely flow into the clubs?" The fear was that smaller money injections would lead to lower quality on the pitch, less attractive games, lower consumer interest, and lower sponsor interest, therefore driving clubs into a downward spiral.

However, Figure 4 shows that the post-FFP reality contrasted these criticisms. The post-FFP compound annual growth rate (CAGR) of revenues increased to an impressive 7.2%. There are at least two good reasons for this development.

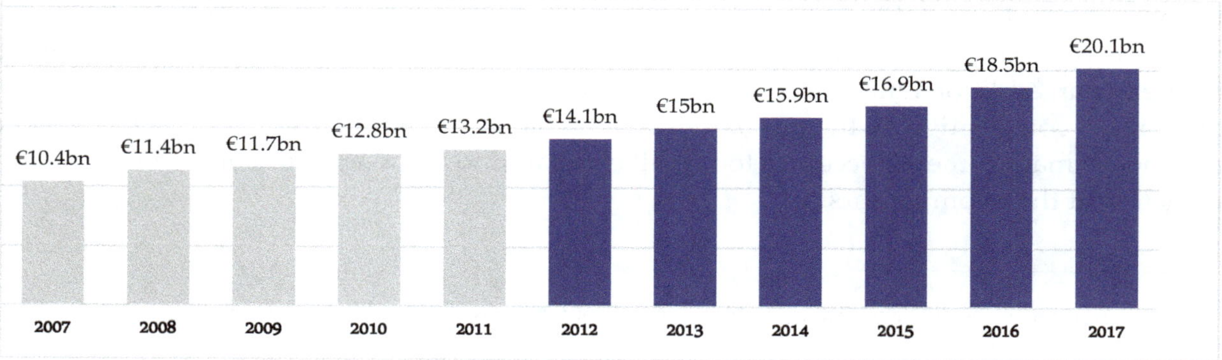

Figure 4. Long-term European club revenue growth (€ Billions). Sources: UEFA (2017, p. 56). The data for the FY 2017 have been provided by UEFA to the author in personal communication.

[27] See Franck (2015, p. 229) for a similar interpretation. See Franck (2014, pp. 204–5) for a more detailed analysis.
[28] See Madden (2015) for a theoretical analysis supporting the "prosperity concern".

5.1. First Reason[29]

Critics exaggerated the "prosperity concern" because they failed to precisely study the new regulations. In that case, they would have easily found out that the payments of owners made for the absorption of losses in the past would not entirely disappear post-FFP. A substantial part of them would simply become a fair market value transaction and continue to flow into football.

As an example, consider the German chemicals corporation Bayer AG, which is the 100% owner of the Bayer 04 Leverkusen football club. The question to be answered under FFP is how much would the Bayer AG have to invest in public relations (PR) activities per year in order to achieve a similar level of brand awareness as that produced by Bayer Leverkusen? The Bayer AG can continue to absorb losses of this level at its subsidiary club under FFP by simply concluding a sponsorship agreement and paying the fair market value sponsorship fee.

The major difference to the ex-post absorption of losses common in the past, is that such sponsorship deals have to be concluded ex ante. Because managers of football clubs have complete knowledge of the sponsorship revenues, which are a component of relevant income, they have no reason to develop any kind of SBC expectations with all the associated incentive problems. All the former money injections of club owners that constitute a fair market value compensation for transacted goods or services will therefore continue to flow into football, for example, by being transformed into sponsorships. However, they enter the system without creating SBCs.

Only payments that would constitute contributions above the fair market value of goods or services exchanged between the club and the owner will not be counted as relevant income under FFP. If, for example, the Bayer AG would pay more to its subsidiary club in a sponsoring agreement than a comparable amount of exposure/image transfer costs in the free market, this "sponsoring in excess of fair market value" would not count as relevant income.

Under FFP, the club can still take this money and spend it on infrastructure, youth development, or community activities. However, the club cannot use this money to cover relevant expenses, that is, for player salaries and transfer amortizations. For owners with a longer-term perspective, investments in infrastructure, youth development, etc. outside the direct payroll may still make good sense. These owners will not reduce their money injections to a "fair market value" level, but they will simply not use the "excess" to directly inflate payrolls in the club.

Thus, it could be expected that a substantial part of the owner injections seen in the past would still flow into football as fair market value transactions, and another substantial part would continue to flow into football as investment in infrastructure, youth development, and community projects outside the fair market value adjustment.

5.2. Second Reason

New revenue sources would emerge in a regime with different managerial incentives. A lot more money would be generated in the football market if managers facing hard budget constraints stopped playing moral-hazard and rent-seeking games and started doing "a good job", concentrating on productive efforts, taking adequate risks, and developing the business[30]. Taking all these reasons together, concerns that FFP would lead to decreasing revenues and to a downward spiral seemed unfounded.

Until 2011, growing revenues went hand in hand with deteriorating club finances. After the introduction of FFP, this is no longer the case. Figure 5 shows that the post-FFP overdue payables decreased by more than 90% compared to pre-FFP.

---

[29] See Franck (2014, pp. 205–6) for the short original treatment of this issue. See Franck (2015, pp. 236–38) for an in-depth discussion.

[30] See Franck (2014, p. 206) for stressing this main effect of hard budget constraints.

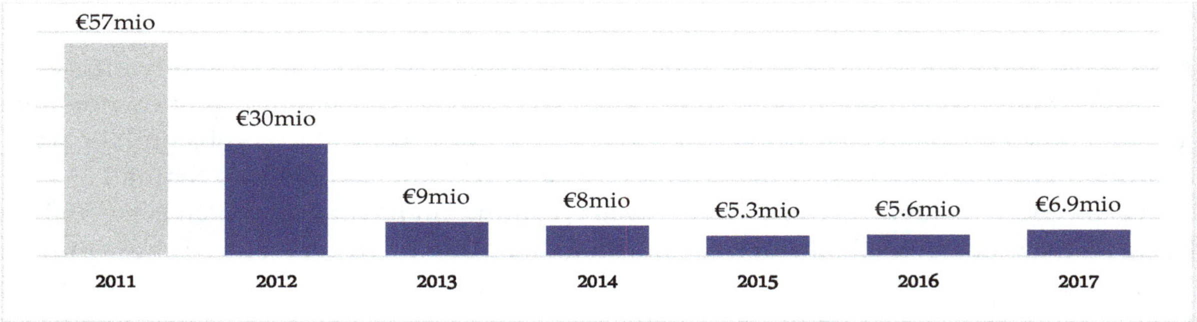

Figure 5. Overdue payables—Trend 2011 to 2017 (€ Millions). Source: The data have been provided by UEFA to the author in personal communication.

Figure 6 shows the aggregate operating results for the European top division clubs. For the first time, clubs reported decreasing operating losses in 2012, the first year entering into a break-even assessment. Since 2013, top-division clubs have reported positive operating profits: They generated €2.9 billion in operating profits over the 2015–2017 period.

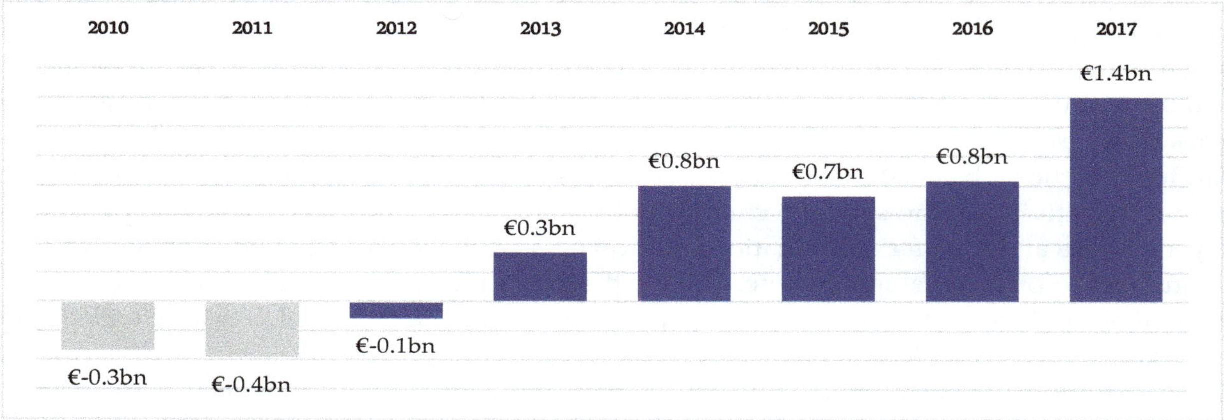

Figure 6. Aggregate European top-division operating profits. Sources: UEFA (2017, p. 101). The data for the FY 2017 have been provided by UEFA to the author in personal communication.

Figure 7 shows the aggregated net results after including transfer activity, financing, and investment/divestment and taxes. Since the FY 2012, a clear positive development in the aggregated net results is apparent. For the first time in 2017, European club football even reported an aggregate bottom line profit. This is remarkable when considering that European football clubs are generally not seen as "normal" profit-maximizing firms. Even after fixing the problem of SBCs through regulation, football remains a contest between win-maximizing participants. FFP does not force participants "to make profit", but only to break even in the football market by and large (with an acceptable deficit of somewhere between €5 and €30 million in 3 years, as long as the owner covers the difference through equity injections).

Figure 8 shows the evolution of top-division club net equity (assets less liabilities). A significant improvement of the balance sheets has taken place, meaning that the "zombie race" problem disappears. Net equity has more than tripled since the rules were approved in 2009.

The numbers presented in this section undeniably show the financial comeback of the European football industry.

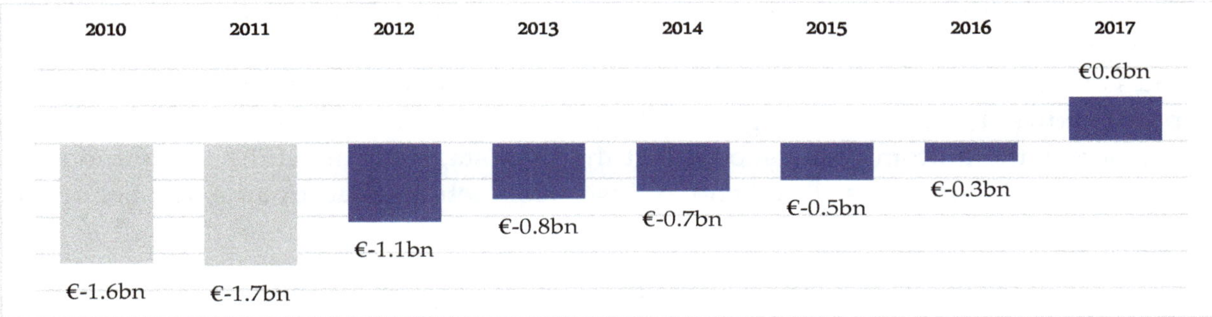

Figure 7. Aggregate European top-division net results. Sources: UEFA (2017, p. 102). The data for the FY 2017 have been provided by UEFA to the author in personal communication.

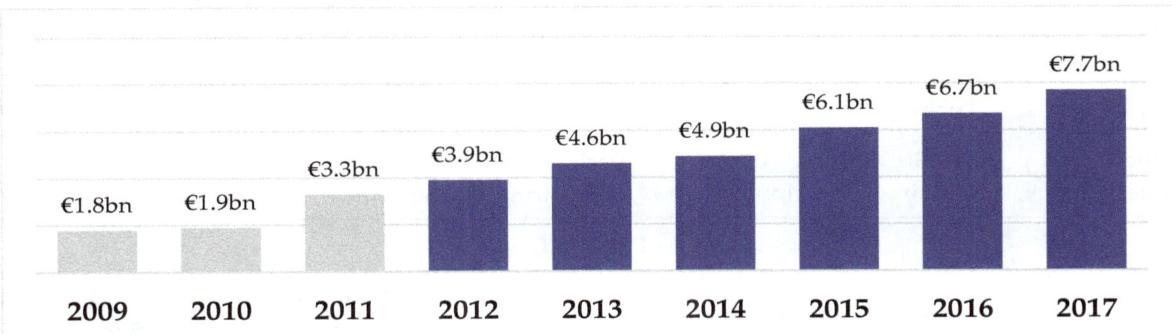

Figure 8. Evolution in European top-division club net equity (assets less liabilities) (€ Billions). Sources: UEFA (2017, p. 124). The data for the FY 2017 have been provided by UEFA to the author in personal communication.

6. Polarization: A Challenge Not Directly Addressed by FFP

The Deloitte Football Money League, a report produced annually by the accountancy firm Deloitte, ranks European football clubs based on their revenues[31]. Table 3 shows that in Season 2016/2017, the top 10 clubs in this ranking had revenues of €535 million on average, while the clubs ranked 11–20 had revenues of €255 million on average. In the Season 2011/2012, the revenues were €334 million for the top 10 and €150 million for the 11–20, whereas in the Season 2006/2007, the revenues were €251 million for the top 10 and €122 million for the 11–20.

Table 3. Top 20 clubs by revenue (€ Millions).

Year	Top 1–10 Clubs	Top 11–20 Clubs	Δ Top 10 vs. Top 11–20
2016/2017	535	255	+280
2011/2012	334	150	+184
2006/2007	251	122	+129

Sources: Deloitte (2007, 2012, 2018).

The last column exhibits the difference between the top 10 and the 11–20 clubs in the different seasons. The difference was €129 million in 2006/2007 and grew to €184 million in 2011/2012 and to a

[31] See e.g., Deloitte (2018).

€280 million in 2016/2017. These absolute numbers[32] show that in the last five years, the clubs at the top have literally "pulled away" away from the rest.

At the same time, these "big clubs" seem to become more dominant on the pitch. In Table 4, the top panel shows that the Bundesliga, the Serie A, and the French League 1 are dominated by one club, whereas the bottom panel shows that the final stages of the UEFA Champions League (UCL) look more and more like a closed and exclusive competition, because the number of different semifinalists decreased.

Table 4. Polarization in domestic leagues and in the UEFA CL.

Champions in Domestic Leagues						
League	**2017/2018**	**2016/2017**	**2015/2016**	**2014/2015**	**2013/2014**	**2012/2013**
German Bundesliga	Bayern Munich	Bayern Munich	Bayern Munich	Bayern Munich	Bayern Munich	Bayern Munich
Italian Serie A	Juventus Turin	Juventus Turin	Juventus Turin	Juventus Turin	Juventus Turin	Juventus Turin
French Ligue 1	Paris St. Germain	AS Monaco	Paris St. Germain	Paris St. Germain	Paris St. Germain	Paris St. Germain

UEFA CL			
Years	**Teams Reaching the Semifinals**	**Country of Origin of the Semifinalists**	**# Different Semifinalists**
2011/2012 to 2017/2018	Atletico Madrid, Barcelona, Bayern Munich, Borussia Dortmund, Chelsea, Juventus, Liverpool, Manchester City, Monaco, Real Madrid, Roma	England, France, Germany, Italy, Spain	11
2004/2005 to 2010/2011	Arsenal, Barcelona, Bayern Munich, Chelsea, Eindhoven, Inter Milan, Liverpool, Lyon, Manchester United, Milan, Real Madrid, Schalke, Villarreal	England, France, Germany, Italy, Netherlands, Spain	13
1997/1998 to 2003/2004	Barcelona, Bayern Munich, Bayer Leverkusen, Borussia Dortmund, Chelsea, Dynamo Kiew, Inter Milan, Juventus, Deportivo de la Coruña, Leeds United, Manchester United, Milan, Monaco, Real Madrid, Porto, Valencia	England, France, Germany, Italy, Portugal, Spain, Ukraine	16

In the period covering the Seasons 1997/1998 to 2003/2004, 16 different clubs reached the UCL semifinals. In the period covering the Seasons 2004/2005 to 2010/2011, the number of clubs in UCL

32 One could argue that in relative terms, not so much has changed over time: The ratio between the revenues of the top 10 and the revenues of the 11–20 was always around 2 (it was 2.057 in the season 2006/2007, 2.227 in the season 2011/2012, and 2.098 in season 2016/2017). However, what matters with respect to balanced competition is the absolute difference in revenues and not the relative difference. Carreras and Garcia (2018) look at the newly signed TV deals in England and Spain. They lead to smaller relative differences in revenues. However, absolute differences in revenues go up and competitive balance worsens as a result. This can be explained by the fact that wages and talent do not have a linear relationship but an exponential one.

semifinals decreased to 13. Finally, in the period covering the Seasons 2011/2012 to 2017/2018, only 11 different clubs entered the UCL semifinals.

In sum, the numbers suggest that a process of polarization has taken place:

- Absolute revenues have grown stronger at the "big clubs" and
- "Big clubs" have become more dominant on the pitch.

An important question is whether there is a causal relationship between FFP and polarization. Indeed, FFP has been at times attacked by pointing to the fact that it has not worked as an effective remedy against polarization. However, it is important to note that FFP was not designed as a remedy against polarization. For example, if Real Madrid and FC Basel follow the rules and balance relevant income and expenses, the consequence is not that they become equal competitors on the pitch. If "big clubs" and "small clubs" live within their own means, in line with the break-even requirement, this does not imply that they rely on equal means.

FFP has also been attacked with the argument that it contributed to further polarization[33] because even the richest "sugar daddies" have to compete based on payrolls largely financed through income generated in the football market. As a consequence, they will no longer be able to challenge the "bigger clubs" by spending more money on players. The idea that FFP might therefore entrench the dominance of already "big clubs" seems plausible at first sight. However, the key question is whether a mechanism exists that systematically allocates payroll injections according to a pattern that makes "small clubs" relatively more competitive[34].

First of all, FPP only caps "inflated" owner payments. A sponsoring agreement, where the owners pay a fair market price in exchange for the exposure/image transfer generated by the team for their other businesses, is in line with the regulations. In order to be affected by FFP, the owners must be willing to inject more money into payrolls than the publicity and image transfer generated through the success of their teams. In other words: Those owners that will be restrained by FFP in their "usual" spending behavior are "pure" success-seekers. "Pure" success-seekers by definition will try to spend their money where winning probabilities are the highest. As a consequence, they will systematically search for the clubs with the largest market potential available on the market.

It is widely accepted that the behavior of European football clubs is best described as "win maximization" subject to a budget constraint. Which is the likely result of a matching process between success-seeking benefactors and win-maximizing clubs? This article suggests that, in equilibrium, "money comes to money" because success-seeking benefactors look for the clubs with the largest market potential available and win-maximizing clubs by definition prefer the largest payroll injection. If unregulated, this simultaneous competition for money injections and market potential should converge to a state where the benefactors with the deepest pockets get allocated to the clubs with the largest market potential (the "favorites"), making them even more dominant.

One could argue that by preventing "pure" success-seekers from inflating payrolls, FFP is also preventing the deepest pockets from supporting clubs from the largest markets. Thus, FFP actually slows down the speed of polarization.

However, what else may be driving polarization? Polarization is likely the result of the concurrence of several factors, such as digital technologies, globalization, and the "winner-take-most" dynamic in many entertainment markets. The basic mechanism has been explained in the seminal paper of Rosen (1981).

New technology dramatically enlarges the market for producers of football entertainment. While before the advent of TV, the potential number of consumers of a football game was limited by the size of the stadium and the local population, later, with national TV rights, the national market became the

---

[33] See for example Dupont (2013) and, for a formal academic treatment, Sass (2016).

[34] See Franck (2014, pp. 209–10) for a short initial treatment of this question and Franck (2015, pp. 235–44) for a detailed discussion.

crucial limitation. Nowadays, with new technologies, such as high-speed internet and mobile digital platforms, potentially the entire world is the relevant market.

If consumers prefer higher to lower quality, the likely outcome is a sort of "superstar" development: The attention of consumers with a preference for quality migrates to the producers of top content. During the first phase of market enlargement, from local stadium to national TV markets, national "top clubs" emerge. These producers will attract more attention. To the extent that revenues are attached to attention, these producers can further increase their quality. The larger the national TV market is, the more these "top clubs" can increase their quality and revenues. They are in a favorable position to exploit the next phase of market enlargement, the development of global entertainment demand through new technologies. Quality-sensitive consumers from the all over the world will be attracted by the "best product" offered by these "top clubs" that were able to grow and develop in their "big national markets" in the past. As a consequence, they will attract even more quality-sensitive consumers and further increase their revenues. In the end, these winners will take most of the market. As a consequence, attention and correlated revenues concentrate at the top of the producer hierarchy.

Adler (1985) has added to this theory the insight that new fans tend to attach to the clubs that already have many fans. A person interested in football derives utility not only from watching games, but also from discussing and interacting with other likeminded people. The more popular the club in question is, the lower the searching costs to find fellow fans will consequently be.

To sum up, the very skewed distribution of attention, correlated earnings, and success are the result of the following two factors:

- First, new technology has dramatically enlarged the market for producers and quality-sensitive worldwide demand has migrated to the top of the producer hierarchy (i.e., the Rosen effect).
- Second, once a club has a large "installed base" of fans, "popularity effects" kick in. New fans patronize the superstar club because of the network externalities emerging from a large fan base (i.e., the Adler effect).

In order to capture their global profile, UEFA measured the traffic on clubs' websites in September 2016. Figure 9 shows that 5 European club websites had more than 5 million visitors. The large portion of foreign online visitors (in grey) clearly suggests that these clubs are "global brands" reaching out to a worldwide audience, just as the Rosen–Adler superstar theory would predict. The extreme case is FC Barcelona: 91% of the online traffic on the FC Barcelona website originates from outside Spain.

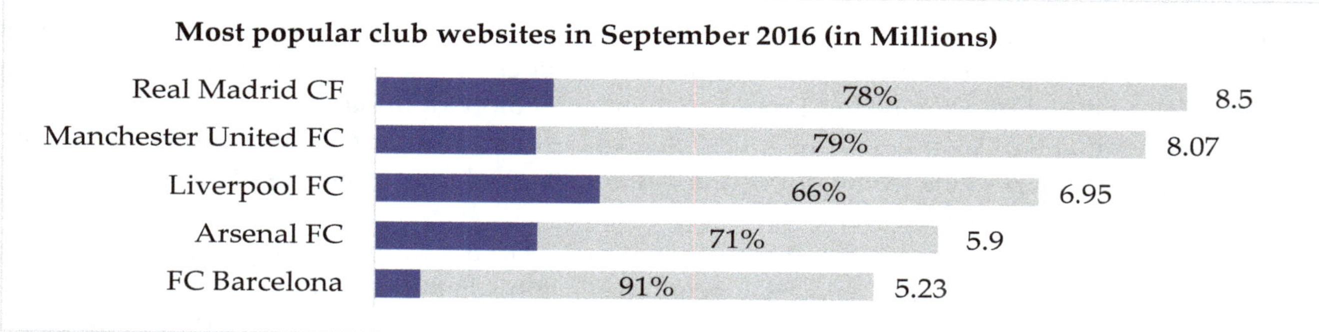

Figure 9. Global profile of largest clubs becomes clear from online traffic. Indicated in % (and in grey) is the proportion of foreign online visitors. Only the clubs with more than 5 million visitors were extracted from the original source. Source: UEFA (2017, p. 18).

Finally, an obvious consequence of polarization is the proliferation of "unequal pairings", i.e., matches between the "big clubs" and the rest. The "big clubs" literally dominate the other teams in domestic league games and the same happens in the group phase of the Champions League, where the "big clubs" encounter teams from much smaller domestic leagues. As a consequence, one may ask if in the future there will be sufficient suspense left in the system to attract fans, sponsors, or commercial partners. Should the preservation of sufficient suspense be addressed by changing the format of the competition? Is the European "super league" a possible solution?

7. Some Reflections on the Incentives of the "Big Clubs" in the European "Super League" Project

Discussions about the creation of a closed European league of "big clubs" recently gained new momentum[35]. A look at the current top-level format of the competition is helpful to clarify the incentives of the "big clubs". Two main characteristics stand out:

- Overlapping competitions, i.e., the "big clubs" play in the domestic leagues and in the Champions League simultaneously;
- Openness, i.e., access to the Champions League is mainly based on sportive qualification in the domestic leagues.

The overlapping competitions at the top of the football pyramid are an anomaly when compared to all other levels of the pyramid. Second division clubs, third division clubs, etc. normally only play in their respective divisions of the domestic competitions, if we abstract from cup games. A first approach to dealing with the problem of "unequal pairings" would be to abolish this anomaly of overlapping competitions and preserve openness by creating a European "super league" with promotion and relegation on top of the domestic leagues.

This "super league"[36] would replace the current European competitions, and its participants would no longer play and earn revenues in domestic competitions simultaneously. This model would be much more effective with respect to the avoidance of "unequal pairings" than the current format[37]. Teams that dominate domestically get promoted to the presumably stronger European level and teams that underperform at the European level "go back" to their domestic competitions. Of course, many details of this open "super league" model would have to be worked out properly before putting it into practice. In particular, the heterogeneity of domestic competitions is difficult to tackle in this context.

However, comparable problems have been solved in the past at other levels. For example, when the German Bundesliga was created in 1963, it was introduced as the "German super league" and the new "top" of the domestic football pyramid, which previously consisted of five different regional leagues ("Oberligen"). Why should the project of an open European "super league" be less successful today than the project of an open German "super league" was in 1963? If the Rosen–Adler superstar theory holds, games between strong teams attract quality-sensitive consumers. The current European competitions already show the existence of a supranational market for football entertainment. Moreover, travel time between the big European cities has become shorter than, for example, between provincial towns in Germany, thanks to modern transportation technologies. Why then do we not see any significant attempt to embark on projects that would further develop and implement this solution of an open European "super league" with promotion and relegation?

An important reason is presumably that the "big clubs" are not interested in this model. Their strategy seems to aim in the opposite direction, namely, to preserve overlapping competitions, and, at the same time, to put pressure on UEFA in order to increasingly "close" the final stages of the Champions League:

- The number of slots in the group phase of the Champions League has been increased to currently four for each of the "big" domestic leagues. Since the "big clubs" all come from the "big" domestic

---

35 See e.g., https://www.independent.co.uk/sport/football/european/football-leaks-european-super-league-manchester-city-manchester-united-uefa-a8619856.html.

36 Hoehn and Szymanski (1999) and Kesenne (2007), for example, provide much more sophisticated, welfare-oriented analyses of the "super league" problem. This article focuses on the incentives of the "big clubs" and not on welfare issues.

37 The focus is on the polarization problem here. I am not suggesting that there are no other disadvantages from a welfare perspective.

leagues, they have almost "safe access" to the Champions League. Even in less successful domestic seasons, their much more expensive squads will manage to finish on one of the first four ranks of the domestic league table;

- The group phase then systematically sorts out the "underdogs", which might win single games but cannot survive in a series of games against the star squads of the "big clubs";
- Finally, seeding ensures that the "big clubs" do not meet and sort out each-other in the first stages of the competition;

Thus, the final and most lucrative stages of the Champions League look more and more like a closed competition of the "big clubs".

Recently, the media have spread the idea that the "big clubs" intend to leave domestic competitions entirely to play only in a new hermetic self-operated European "super league". However, there is a difference between the threat, which the "big clubs" have systematically produced in the past in order to improve their own bargaining position in negotiations with UEFA, and the strategy they have pursued in reality. The threat to leave the football pyramid and the current system is a proven instrument to pressure UEFA into giving ever larger pieces of the Champions League "pie" to the "big clubs". By definition, the threat to leave "the current system" can only be the creation of a hermetic, self-operated league, because there is no other football pyramid, which the "big clubs" could target as their new "home". Therefore, the "big clubs" started to invest resources in what can be called the "perpetual hermetic super league project". This project goes back to at least the year 1998 and gained additional momentum in 2000 with the G14 initiative[38].

A closer look at the incentives of the "big clubs" suggests that the credibility of their threat is rather moderate for a number of reasons.

First, if they would make real their threat and break away, they would automatically lose the advantages stemming from the current system of overlapping competitions, e.g.,:

Multiple sources of income: The current modus of overlapping competitions at the national and the European level allows the "big clubs" to earn money in their domestic competitions and in the European competitions simultaneously. The more developed and prosperous the respective domestic competitions are, the higher the incentives of "big clubs" to preserve the link and play domestically.

Multiple chances to lift trophies: A detailed inspection of a letter written by clubs such as Real Madrid, Manchester United or Bayern Munich is helpful to see the point made in this section. Half of the space on the left side of the letter typically lists the trophies these clubs have won in the past. For such "big clubs", years with only one "minor" trophy (for example, a domestic cup title) are considered as failures. Overlapping competitions create multiple chances to lift trophies.

Second, if the "big clubs" exited the current system, they would exit the football pyramid and lose the advantages related to this pyramid, e.g.,:

Multiple sources of suspense: By preserving the link to the pyramid, the "big clubs" make sure that fan interest is fueled by several open questions that generate suspense. Instead of a single potentially open question such as "which team will win the closed league?", many questions are open in a multilevel contest format, such as "which team will win the championship race in every league of the system? Which team will get promoted to the next level? Which team will be able to avoid relegation? Which team will be demoted? Which team will be able to qualify for the UCL from a domestic league? Which team will qualify for the Europa League?", etc.

Multiple sources of surprise: Entertainment demand is not only driven by suspense, but also by surprise[39]. The rise and unexpected performance of underdogs fascinates people and attracts new fans to the game. The current system, the football pyramid, is open to "success stories". Consider the rise of RB Leipzig from the bottom to the top of the German football leagues within only seven seasons, or FC

---

[38] See, e.g., https://www.theguardian.com/football/2008/jan/16/newsstory.sport7.

[39] See Ely et al. (2015) for a theoretical treatment of this and Bizzozero et al. (2016) for an empirical proof in the tennis industry.

Leicester City winning the Premier League in 2016. Compared to that, the model of a closed, balanced "big club"-league leaves little room for surprise because "underdogs" are nonexistent by definition.

Third, "hermetic leagues" function according to a different logic, which would require a *complete redesign of the governance and incentives systems*. To make a closed league attractive, the "big clubs" would need to guarantee "openness of outcome" as long as possible in every season through revenue redistribution, salary caps, drafts systems, etc. Is it realistic to assume that the win-maximizing "big clubs" of today, which voluntarily engage in genuine arms races, will convert to an "egalitarian regime", where they share their resources and voluntarily respect "arms-control" regulations? Redesigning the governance and incentives systems would generate very substantial transaction costs, which the "big clubs" would then bear. In addition, if they really succeeded in creating such a league with 16 clubs, every club would lift a trophy only every 16 years, on average. It is hard to imagine that the owners and executives running these clubs at the moment and also their fans can really adapt to such a "trophy tax" situation.

8. Outlook

Football clubs are strongly interconnected because they jointly produce the championship race. If some clubs go out of operation in mid-season, the credibility of the entire championship is severely harmed through incomplete schedules. Financial domino effects get triggered because bankrupt clubs no longer fulfill their obligations from transfer deals, which brings other clubs in danger.

Clubs that manage to break even and live within the income generated in the football market are sustainable and do not produce this kind of negative externalities. In that sense, the clubs respecting the break-even requirement and the no-overdue-payables rule behave in a "financially fair" way. The FFP regulation derives its specific notion of "fairness" from this link to the overall goal of systemic financial stability. Given the numbers presented, it seems difficult to deny that the football industry has become financially much more stable since the introduction of FFP.

However, systemic financial stability is not the only concern among the stakeholders of the European football industry. Polarization raises new challenges. The "normal" solution for the problem of "unequal pairings" would be to abolish overlapping competitions and create a European "super league" with promotion and relegation on top of the domestic leagues. However, the strategy of the "big clubs" is not compatible with this model. Their "perpetual hermetic super league project" has been used as a threat to improve their bargaining power in negotiations with UEFA. So far, they succeeded to capture ever larger pieces of the Champions League "pie", while continuing to simultaneously play and earn money and lift trophies in their prosperous domestic leagues.

In conclusion, if this path continues into the future, polarization and the question of adequate regulation will presumably remain the hot topics of the coming years. Recently, UEFA has announced the reform of the Europa League and the introduction of a third level of club competitions[40]. In the context discussed here, this can be interpreted as a first "corrective move". Given that the "big clubs" already profit from overlapping competitions, the reform creates the chance for more football clubs in Europe to profit from simultaneous participation in domestic and European competitions, thus redirecting some revenues and attention to the lower levels of the pyramid.

Acknowledgments: The paper is based on a keynote lecture delivered at the II. International Conference on Economics of Football in Moscow, Russia, 9–11 July 2018. We thank the participants of the II. International Conference on Economics of Football in Moscow. Thanks go to Paolo Bizzozero, Philippe Meier, and Martje Timmermann for excellent research assistance.

40 https://www.theguardian.com/football/2018/dec/02/uefa-new-european-club-competition-2021.

References

1. Adler, Moshe. 1985. Stardom and talent. *American Economic Review* 75: 208–212.
2. Akerlof, George. 1976. The Economics of Caste and of the Rat Race and other Woeful Tales. *Quarterly Journal of Economics* 90: 599–617. [CrossRef]
3. Andreff, Wladimir. 2007. French football: A financial crisis rooted in weak governance. *Journal of Sports Economics* 8: 652–61. [CrossRef]
4. Andreff, Wladimir. 2011. Some comparative economics of the organisation of sports: Competition and regulation in North American vs. European professional team sports leagues. *European Journal of Comparative Economics* 8: 3–27.
5. Andreff, Wladimir, ed. 2015. Governance of professional team sport clubs: Agency problem and soft budget constraint. In *Disequilibrium Sports Economics*. London: Edward Elgar, pp. 175–227.
6. Arnaut, José Luis. 2006. *Independent European Sport Review*. Technical Report. Brussels: European Commission.
7. Bizzozero, Paolo, Raphael Flepp, and Egon Franck. 2016. The importance of suspense and surprise in entertainment demand: Evidence from Wimbledon. *Journal of Economic Behavior & Organization* 130: 47–63. Carreras, Miquel, and Jaume Garcia. 2018. TV rights, financial inequality and competitive balance in European Football: Evidence from the English Premier League and the Spanish LaLiga. *International Journal of Sport Finance* 13: 201–24.
8. Deloitte Football Money League. 2007. The Reign in Spain. Available online: https://www2.deloitte.com/ content/dam/Deloitte/uk/ Documents/sports-business-group/deloitte-uk-deloitte-football-money- league-2007.pdf (accessed on 15 June 2018).
9. Deloitte Football Money League. 2012. Fan Power. Available online: https://www2.deloitte.com/content/dam/ Deloitte/uk/Documents/ sports-business-group/deloitte-uk-deloitte-football-money-league-2012.pdf (accessed on 15 June 2018).
10. Deloitte Football Money League. 2018. Rising Stars. Available online: https://www2.deloitte.com/content/dam/ Deloitte/uk/ Documents/sports-business-group/deloitte-uk-sbg-dfml2018.pdf (accessed on 15 June 2018).
11. Dietl, Helmut M., Egon Franck, and Markus Lang. 2008. Overinvestment in team sports leagues: A contest theory model. *Scottish Journal of Political Economy* 55: 353–68. [CrossRef]
12. Dupont, Jean-Louis. 2013. Football's anticompetitive streak. *The Wall Street Journal*, March 25. Available online: http: //online.wsj. com/news/articles/SB10001424127887324077704578357992271428024#printMode (accessed on 15 June 2018).
13. Ely, Jeffrey, Alexander Frankel, and Emir Kamenica. 2015. Suspense and Surprise. *Journal of Political Economy* 123: 215–60. [CrossRef]
14. Franck, Egon. 2014. Financial Fair Play in European Club Football—What is it all about? *International Journal of Sport Finance* 9: 193–217. [CrossRef]
15. Franck, Egon. 2015. Regulation in leagues with clubs' soft budget constraints: The effect of the new UEFA Club Licensing Regulations on managerial incentives and suspense. In *Disequilibrium Sports Economics*. Edited by Wladimir Andreff. Cheltenham: Edward Elgar, pp. 228–49.
16. Franck, Egon, and Markus Lang. 2014. Theoretical analysis of the influence of money injections on risk taking in football-clubs. *Scottish Journal of Political Economy* 61: 430–54. [CrossRef]
17. Frank, Robert H., and Ben S. Bernanke. 2004. *Principles of Microeconomics*, 2nd ed. New York: McGraw-Hill/Irwin. Hoehn, Thomas, and Stefan Szymanski. 1999. The Americanization of European football. *Economic Policy* 14: 204–40. [CrossRef]
18. Kesenne, Stefan. 2007. The peculiar international economics of professional football in Europe. *Scottish Journal of Political Economy* 54: 388–99. [CrossRef]
19. Kornai, János. 1980. *Economics of Shortage*. Amsterdam: North-Holland. Kornai, János. 1986. The Soft Budget Constraint. *Kyklos* 39: 3–30. [CrossRef]
20. Kornai, János, Eric Maskin, and Gerard Roland. 2003. Understanding the soft budget constraint. *Journal of Economic Literature* 41: 1095–136. [CrossRef]
21. Kuper, Simon. 2009. Football Abandons the Fantasy that it is a Business. Available online: http://www.ft.com/ intl/cms/s/2/fd77a01c-aa07-11de-a3ce-00144feabdc0.html#axzz2GRMmCmGD (accessed on 15 June 2018).
22. Madden, Paul. 2015. Welfare economics of "Financial Fair Play" in a sports league with benefactor owners. *Journal of Sports Economics* 16: 159–84. [CrossRef]
23. Neale, Walter C. 1964. The peculiar economics of professional sports: A contribution to the theory of the firm in sporting competition and in market competition. *Quarterly Journal of Economics* 78: 1–14. [CrossRef]
24. Rosen, Sherwin. 1981. The economics of superstars. *American Economic Review* 71: 845–58.
25. Sass, Markus. 2016. Glory hunters, sugar daddies, and long-term competitive balance under UEFA Financial Fair Play. *Journal of Sports Economics* 17: 148–58. [CrossRef]
26. Stern, Gary H., and Ron J. Feldman. 2004. *Too Big to Fail: The Hazards of Bank Bailouts*. Washington: Brookings Institution Press.
27. Storm, Rasmus K. 2012. The need for regulating professional soccer in Europe: A soft budget constraint argument. *Sport, Business and Management: An International Journal* 2: 21–38. [CrossRef]

28. Storm, Rasmus K., and Klaus Nielsen. 2012. Soft budget constraints in professional football. *European Sport Management Quarterly* 12: 183–201. [CrossRef]
29. UEFA. 2013. The European Club Licensing Benchmarking Report Financial Year 2011. Available online: http://www.uefa.com/MultimediaFiles/Download/Tech/uefaorg/General/01/91/61/84/1916184_ DOWNLOAD.pdf (accessed on 15 June 2018).
30. UEFA. 2015a. Procedural Rules Governing the UEFA Club Financial Control Body, Edition 2015. Available online: http://www.uefa.org/MultimediaFiles/Download/Tech/uefaorg/General/02/28/72/ 46/2287246_DOWNLOAD.pdf (accessed on 15 June 2018).
31. UEFA. 2015b. UEFA Club Licensing and Financial Fair Play Regulations, Edition 2015. Available online: https://www.uefa.org/MultimediaFiles/Download/Tech/uefaorg/General/02/26/77/91/2267791_ DOWNLOAD.pdf (accessed on 15 June 2018).
32. UEFA. 2017. The European Club Footballing Landscape. Club Licensing Benchmarking Report Financial Year 2016. Available online: https://es.uefa.com/MultimediaFiles/Download/OfficialDocument/uefaorg/ Clublicensing/02/53/00/22/2530022_DOWNLOAD.pdf (accessed on 15 June 2018).

16

Country of Origin Effects on the Average Annual Values of NHL Player Contracts

Aju J. Fenn *, Lucas Gerdes and Samuel Rothstein

Economics & Business department, Colorado College, Colorado Springs, CO 80919, USA; L_gerdes@coloradocollege.edu (L.G.); Samuel.Rothstein@coloradocollege.edu (S.R.)

* Correspondence: Aju.Fenn@coloradocollege.edu

Abstract: Using data from 2005 to 2016, this paper examines if players in the National Hockey League (NHL) are being paid a positive differential for their services due to the competition from the Kontinental Hockey League (KHL) and the Swedish Hockey League (SHL). In order to control for performance, we use two different large datasets, (N = 4046) and (N = 1717). In keeping with the existing literature, we use lagged performance statistics and dummy variables to control for the type of NHL contract. The first dataset contains lagged career performance statistics, while the performance statistics are based on the statistics generated during the years under the player's previous contract. Fixed effects least squares (FELS) and quantile regression results suggest that player production statistics, contract status, and country of origin are significant determinants of NHL player salaries.

Keywords: NHL; KHL; country of origin; salary

---

1. Introduction

The Kontinental Hockey League (KHL) was founded in 2008. It comprises of 27 teams based in Belarus, China, Finland, Kazakhstan, Latvia, Russia, and Slovakia. The Swedish Hockey League (SHL) was founded in 1975. It comprises of 14 teams that play their games in Sweden. The existence of these two leagues may provide an alternative to the National Hockey League (NHL) for players who want to play professional hockey. We examine if players that may play in these leagues because of their country of origin now command a higher salary in the NHL.

Figure 1 plots the annual average value (AAV) for players by their country of origin. AAV is the total salary over the term of a contract divided by the length of the contract in years plus annualized performance bonuses. The data are taken from https://www.capfriendly.com. In the 2015–2016 season, the NHL consisted of players from all over the globe, with players of Canadian descent dominating the league at 49%. Second on the list were players from the United States at 24.6%. Players of Swedish descent came third, making up 8.6% of the league, followed by Russians at 4.1%. Players from Czech Republic and Finland each represented 3.9% of the league. Looking at Figure 1, it is clear that median Russian, Swedish, Finnish, and Czech salaries exceed those of American and Canadians for every given year. Is this because Russian and European players are more talented than their American and Canadian counterparts? Or is it because Russian and European players have more leverage in NHL salary negotiations because of the demand from the KHL and the SHL for their services? We use salary and NHL statistics from the 2005–2016 seasons to explore these questions.

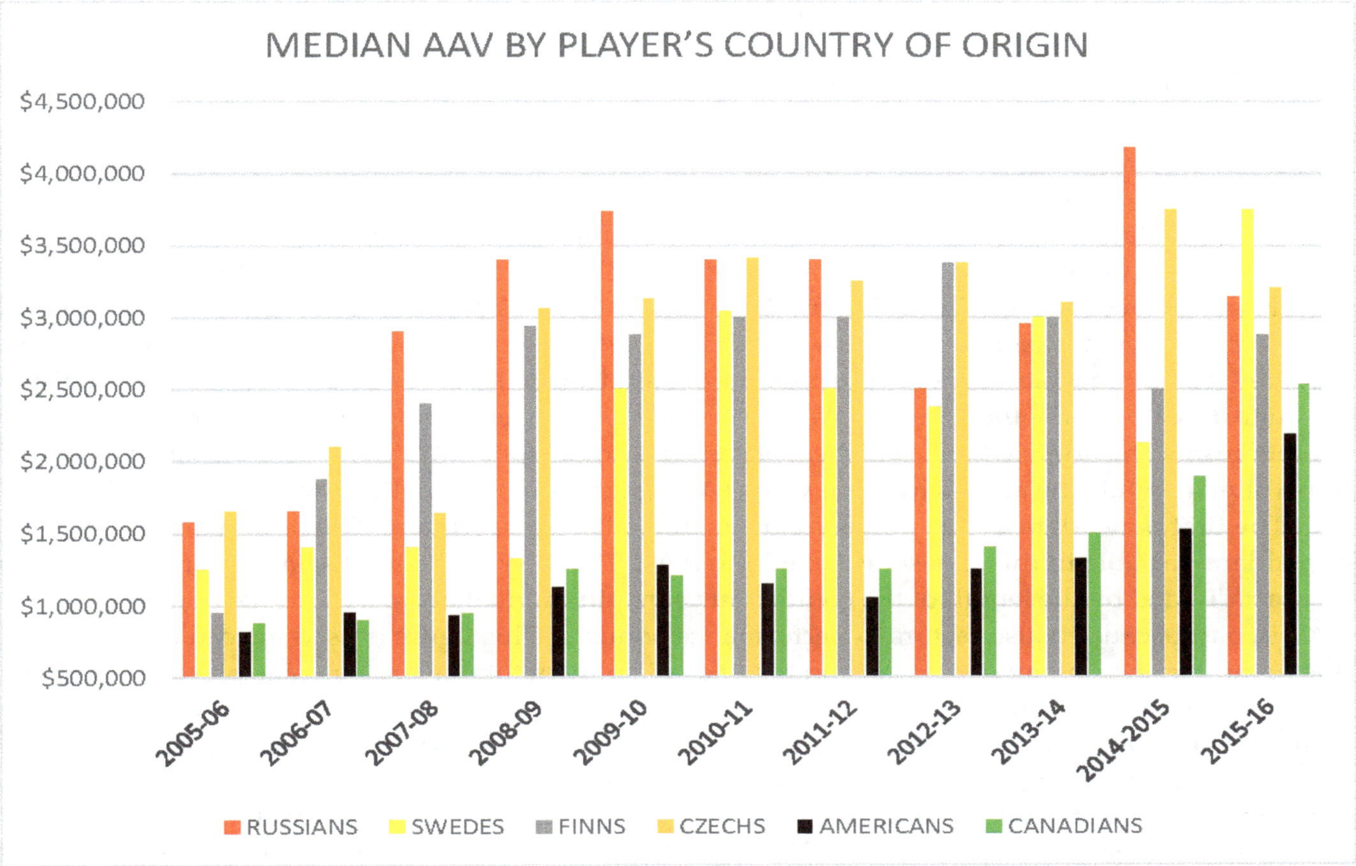

Figure 1. Review.

2. Literature Review

Salary discrimination and entry discrimination have both been studied extensively in North American professional sports (Kahn 1992; Holmes 2011; Yang and Lin 2012). Earlier studies focus on the discrimination against Francophones on Anglophone Canadian NHL teams (Lavoie et al. 1987; Jones and Walsh 1988). Previous studies on the NHL found salary discrimination against European players in the NHL (Bruggink and Williams 2009). Recently, Christie and Lavoie found discrimination against young Russian players in the NHL draft (Christie and Lavoie 2015).

There is also an established literature on salary and player performance in the NHL. There are many statistics that can determine what a player may be worth. The most common statistics used are points (for offensive production), penalty minutes (for defensive intensity), and a plus/minus statistic for a combination of both offensive and defensive skills (Idson and Kahane 2001). The impact of a player's statistics on their salary can be challenging due to the fact that players are paid based on statistics of their play in previous years (Kahane 2001). Kahane uses lagged career statistics to account for this fact. Brander and Egan use on-ice statistics from the year immediately prior to the contract that determines the player's salary in their dataset (Brander and Egan 2018). They also control for the type of player contract using dummy variables. We too use lagged on-ice statistics for the same reasons and dummy variables to control for the type of player contracts. Holmes studies the impact of performance on salary in Major League Baseball (Holmes 2011). He points out that ordinary least squares (OLS) models that employ a single dummy for ethnicity may fail to detect discrimination at various levels of the salary distribution. His approach is to use a quantile regression model, which detects the subtleties of discrimination at different quantiles. Vincent and Eastman also employ quantile regression to examine the impact of performance on salary at different quantiles of the NHL wage distribution (Vincent and Eastman 2009). They claim that the standard conditional expectations model employed by OLS misses some important subtleties of the earnings determination in the NHL, as opposing effects at different quantiles may cancel each other out in a single mean conditional expectations OLS model. We also present results from quantile regressions in addition to fixed effects ordinary least squares results (FELS).

3. Data

Two panel datasets, (N = 4046) and (N = 1717), are used in this study. The first dataset, called career lagged statistics data, uses player-years as the unit of observation. The second dataset, called previous contract statistics data, uses player contracts as the unit of observation. Both datasets include players that played in the NHL during the 2005–2006 to 2015–2016 seasons. Players must have played over 25 games in at least one season over the course of their career or their previous contract to be considered a full time player for the purposes of this study. Goalies are excluded because their statistics are quite different from other players. We also exclude any players that were traded during a season to another team. The original NHL statistical player data come from http://www.hockeyabstract.com and Rob Vollman, while the annual average value (AAV) data come from https://www.capfriendly.com.

The first panel dataset has player-years as the unit of observation. The nominal version of the dependent variable in this dataset is called the AAV. The AAV is the total salary over the term of a contract divided by the length of the contract in years plus annualized performance bonuses. We use AAV in part because it also factors in performance bonuses. This figure is used instead of total salary due to the variance in pay per season and the unavailability of total salary for some players. We obtain real AAV in year t by deflating nominal AAV in year t by the NHL salary cap in year t. AAV is expressed as a percentage of the NHL salary cap in a given year. Salary cap is used as the deflator instead of the consumer price index (CPI) because the salary cap rises faster than the CPI. We thank an anonymous referee for this helpful suggestion. As with Kahane, our first dataset uses lagged career statistics. In other words, player i's AAV in year t is a function of his career statistics accumulated until year $t-1$. The first dataset includes players on all types of contracts, including players on entry level contracts. We include a table of sample statistics by country of origin for this dataset in Table 1. We thank an anonymous referee for suggesting this table.

Table 1. Sample statistics by country (career lagged dataset)

	Averages with Standard Deviations Below										
	AAV	**Games Played**	**Goals per Game**	**Assists per Game**	**Plus-Minus**	**Penalty Minutes per Game**	**Shots per Game**	**Time on Ice per Game**	**Total Defensemen**	**Total Left Handed Players**	**N**
Canadians	$2,358,205	315.11	0.14	0.22	2.23	0.46	1.54	14.97	675	1388	2231
	1,975,705	269.03	0.11	0.14	35.69	0.40	0.72	4.27			
USA	$2,100,078	265.89	0.13	0.21	0.16	0.38	1.56	15.43	350	468	913
	1,713,163	235.43	0.10	0.12	24.65	0.29	0.68	3.87			
Russians	$3,977,614	375.47	0.22	0.33	21.24	0.32	2.05	17	54	117	148
	2,619,935	298.29	0.18	0.18	54.33	0.16	1.11	3.77			
Swedes	$2,662,338	282.59	0.13	0.24	23.55	0.26	1.64	17	103	185	226
	1,797,811	250.14	0.11	0.14	45.00	0.15	0.78	3.62			
Finns	$3,119,577	414.64	0.17	0.29	9.05	0.32	1.76	16	25	87	101
	1,912,461	339.72	0.11	0.13	32.19	0.15	0.63	3.92			
Czechs	$3,212,325	428.48	0.15	0.29	16.73	0.37	1.67	17.06	103	196	252
	1,820,973	280.99	0.10	0.13	50.47	0.27	0.58	3.85			
OTHERS	$2,773,339	317.11	0.16	0.26	3.17	0.31	1.73	16	55	140	175
	2,101,381	259.39	0.13	0.13	27.53	0.23	0.63	3.59			

AAV: annual average value.

The second panel dataset has contract-years as the unit of observation. The dependent variable in the second dataset (previous contract statistics) is the real AAV of a player in the first year of a new contract. Once again, we obtain real AAV in year t by deflating nominal AAV in year t by the NHL salary cap in year t. AAV is expressed as a percentage of the NHL salary cap in a given year for the reasons stated above. The player statistics in the second (contract lagged statistics) are the player's statistics averaged over the years of their last contract. After excluding observations for missing data, this reduces the number of data points from 4046 to 1717. Both datasets contain dummy variables to control for the type of player contract. We thank an anonymous referee for this excellent suggestion. The previous contract dataset does not have players on entry level contracts; therefore, in keeping with Brander and Egan, restricted free agents (RFA) are the default comparison group. Both datasets also contain dummy variables for the player's country of origin, team, and annual fixed effects. The second dataset does not have players on entry level contracts, as they have no previous NHL contract on-ice statistics. For the most part, academic researchers in the literature use lagged career statistics, while NHL executives tend to look at more recent measures of player performance, such as their statistics from their last few years. A notable exception is Brander and Egan, who use statistics from the year prior to the current contract. It is interesting to compare and contrast the results from the career lagged statistics dataset and the previous contract statistics dataset.

4. Empirical Model

The first empirical model, given by Equation (1), is applied to all players in both datasets. The second model, given by Equation (2), is estimated separately for defensemen and forwards in both datasets. We thank an anonymous referee for this suggestion. We employ dummy variables to capture the effects of nationality on salary. In addition, we also employ team specific and annual dummy variables to control for team and annual effects.

$$\begin{aligned}\text{Real AAV} =&\ \beta_1 + \beta_2 \text{ Games played} + \beta_3 \text{ Goals per game} + \beta_4 \text{ Assists per game} + \beta_5 \text{ Plus-minus} \\ &+ \beta_6 \text{ Penalty minutes per game} + \beta_7 \text{ Shots per game} + \beta_8 \text{ Time on ice per game} \\ &+ \beta_9 \text{ Defenseman Dummy} + \beta_{10} \text{ Defenseman Dummy X Time on ice per game} \\ &+ \beta_{11} \text{ Left Handed Player Dummy} + \beta_{12} \text{ RFA Dummy} + \beta_{12} \text{ UFA Dummy} \\ &+ \beta_{13} \text{ TFP35 Dummy} + \beta_{14} \text{ UFA Years Lost Dummy}\end{aligned} \tag{1}$$

$$\begin{aligned}\text{Real AAV} =&\ \beta_1 + \beta_2 \text{ Games played} + \beta_3 \text{ Goals per game} + \beta_4 \text{ Assists per game} + \beta_5 \text{ Plus-minus} \\ &+ \beta_6 \text{ Penalty minutes per game} + \beta_7 \text{ Shots per game} + \beta_8 \text{ Time on ice per game} \\ &+ \beta_9 \text{ Left Handed Player Dummy} + \beta_{10} \text{ RFA Dummy} + \beta_{11} \text{ UFA Dummy} \\ &+ \beta_{12} \text{ TFP35 Dummy} + \beta_{13} \text{ UFA Years Lost Dummy}\end{aligned} \tag{2}$$

Real AAV is nominal AAV expressed as a percentage of the NHL salary cap in a given year. UFA stands for unrestricted free agents.

The on-ice variables are taken from (Kahane 2001). Games played is the total amount of games a player has played in during his career in $t - 1$ years or during his last contract, depending on the dataset. Each of the on-ice performance statistics is averaged over the entire course of the player's previous years in the NHL for the lagged career statistics dataset and over the course of the years of his last contract for the previous contract statistics dataset. Goals per game is the amount of goals a player scored per game. Assists per game represents the amount of assists per game a player made divided by the number of games that he has played. Points are left out of the study because they are made up of goals and assists, both of which are already counted for. Plus-minus represents a player's career plus/minus figure, a measurement describing the amount of times a player is on the ice for a goal or a goal against. If a player is out for a goal, then he gets a +1 rating, and if he is out for a goal against, he gets a −1 rating. Penalty minutes per game is the amount of penalty minutes taken per game during the time period in question. According to a referee, this is a good indicator of toughness for a player, and teams are willing to pay more for that player characteristic.

The literature finds that salary is influenced positively with goals and assists per game, plus-minus, and penalty minutes (Bruggink and Williams 2009). Shots per game is given by the total number of shots taken divided by the total number of games played. It is used as an indicator of offensive play other than goals and assists. Time on ice per game represents average time on ice per game for a player during his career. This indicates how much a player was on the ice for his team and usually shows if the player was used in special team situations.

In keeping with Coates (2017), we control for left handed players using the left handed player dummy that takes on a value of one if the player is left handed and zero otherwise. Coates finds that left handed players are paid a premium.

Defensemen play more minutes than forwards, thus we estimate the model separately for each group using Equation (2). The defenseman dummy takes on a value of one if the player is a defenseman and takes on a value of zero otherwise. At the suggestion of a referee, we account for the extra time played by defensemen by interacting the defensemen dummy with the time on ice variable when estimating (1) over both groups of players. This allows the slope of the time on ice variable to differ between defensemen and forwards. Our maintained hypothesis is that defensemen are usually paid less than other players but that they are paid more for their time on ice than forwards. We also include dummy variables to control for the player's country of origin. We classify players into seven groups: Canadian, American, Russian, Swedish, Finnish, Czech, and Other. We include dummy variables for all groups except Canadians. Thus, all country dummies are in reference to the AAVs earned by Canadian players in the NHL.

Following Brander and Egan, we also include contract type dummies in both equations to control for the types of contracts and their impact on AAV. We thank an anonymous referee for this excellent suggestion. The reader is referred to Brander and Egan (page 86) for an excellent discussion of the different types of contracts and their impact on a player's AAV. Most players start their careers on an entry level contract. This is the type of contract that we omit from the regression. Therefore, all contract dummy coefficients are to be interpreted relative to the impact of an entry level contract on player earnings. The RFA dummy takes on a value of one if the player is on a restricted free agent contract and zero otherwise. The UFA dummy takes on a value of one if the player is on an unrestricted free agent contract and zero otherwise. The TFP35 dummy takes on a value of one if the player is on a 35 plus TFP contract and zero otherwise. The UFA Years Lost variable is the number of years above the age of 27 that a player continues to play on as an RFA. According to Brander and Egan, UFAs have much more bargaining power than RFAs. TFP35s can also sell their services to the highest bidder but have some salary cap implications that reduce their bargaining power compared to UFAs. Brander and Egan find that players who play on beyond the age of 27 as RFAs receive a slight premium relative to other RFA players in order to do so. They capture this effect using the UFA years lost dummy variable.

5. Empirical Results

We employ fixed effects OLS estimators and quantile regression estimators for Equations (1) and (2) in both datasets. Table 2 contains the FELS results for Equations (1) and (2) for all players. At the suggestion of an anonymous referee, we also estimate Equations (1) and (2) separately for forwards and for defensemen. Columns (1) to (3) are estimates of Equations (1) and (2) from the career lagged statistics dataset. Column (1) is the estimate of Equation (1), while columns (2) and (3) are the estimates of Equation (2) applied to defensemen and forwards, respectively, for the career statistics lagged dataset. Similarly, columns (4) to (6) contain the FELS estimates of Equations (1) and (2) estimated from the contract lagged dataset. We also employ Newey-West robust standard errors for the FELS models, because White and Breusch-Godfrey tests indicate the presence of both Heteroskedasticity and Serial Correlation, respectively. In keeping with Brander and Egan, we use a linear functional form instead of the semi-logarithmic functional form proposed by Mincer (1958).

Table 2. Fixed effects ordinary least squares (FELS) regression results.

Dependent Variable	Lagged Career Statistics			Previous Contract Statistics		
Real AAV	All Players Column (1)	Defensemen Column (2)	Forwards Column (3)	All Players Column (4)	Defensemen Column (5)	Forwards Column (6)
Independent Variables	Coefficient (*t*-Statistic)	Coefficient (*t*-Statistic)	Coefficient (*t*-Statistic)	Coefficient (*t*-Statistic)	Coefficient (*t*-Statistic)	Coefficient (*t*-Statistic)
Games played	0.003 (10.228) *	0.005 (8.560) *	0.003 (7.026) *	0.009 (3.588) *	0.017 (3.662) *	0.005 (2.189) **
Goals per game	3.982 (3.906) *	3.016 (1.835) ***	2.840 (2.382) **	4.669 (3.478) *	4.815 (2.382) **	3.802 (2.346) **
Assists per game	5.230 (7.734) *	3.853 (3.839) *	6.581 (8.070) *	5.240 (7.787) *	2.949 (2.723) *	6.489 (7.384) *
Plus-minus	0.007 (4.458) *	0.007 (2.981) *	0.007 (3.395) *	0.040 (5.314) *	0.043 (3.829) *	0.033 (3.227) *
Penalty minutes per game	0.710 (4.663) *	0.876 (2.877) *	0.652 (4.229) *	0.665 (6.540) *	0.515 (2.137) **	0.723 (6.108) *
Shots per game	0.680 (5.047) *	0.425 (2.352) **	0.918 (5.603) *	0.747 (4.770) *	0.431 (1.579)	0.976 (5.675) *
Time on ice per game	0.146 (5.597) *	0.225 (8.030) *	0.110 (3.532) *	0.157 (4.961) *	0.282 (7.823) *	0.125 (3.146) *
Defenseman	−0.795 (−1.92) ***			−1.198 (−2.356) **		
Defenseman X Time on ice	0.063 (2.265) *			0.087 (2.373) *		
Left Handed player	0.089 (0.976)	0.105 (0.693)	0.018 (0.174)	0.039 (0.419)	0.070 (0.411)	0.009 (0.0826)
USA	−0.139 (−1.374)	0.004 (0.022)	−0.203 (−1.693) ***	−0.083 (−0.766)	−0.146 (−0.853)	−0.030 (−0.232)
Russia	0.723 (3.27) *	0.750 (2.296) **	0.654 (2.350) **	0.809 (3.057) *	0.766 (1.90) ***	0.832 (2.384) *
Sweden	0.129 (0.787)	0.457 (1.775) ***	−0.179 (−0.890)	0.192 (0.859)	0.627 (2.009) **	−0.163 (−0.606)
Finland	0.298 (0.639)	0.079 (0.108)	0.374 (0.714)	−0.348 (−0.984)	−0.188 (−0.215)	−0.374 (−0.919)
Czechoslovakia	0.214 (1.103)	0.407 (1.349)	0.071 (0.356)	0.370 (1.601)	0.629 (1.72) ***	0.209 (0.772)
Other Country	0.188 (0.763)	−0.005 (−0.012)	0.334 (1.186)	−0.121 (−0.425)	−0.357 (−0.803)	0.098 (0.301)
RFA Dummy	0.526 (4.198) *	0.379 (1.953) ***	0.621 (3.925) *			
UFA Dummy	0.464 (2.986) *	0.417 (1.636)	0.513 (2.672) *	0.280 (3.161) *	0.446 (2.771) *	0.146 (1.397)
TFP35 Dummy	−2.126 (−8.967) *	−1.868 (−5.599) *	−2.333 (−7.646) *	−0.780 (−3.805) *	−0.618 (−1.626)	−0.830 (−3.203) *
UFA Years Lost Dummy	0.046 (0.644)	−0.173 (−1.440)	0.157 (2.196) **	−0.109 (−0.635)	−0.241 (−1.472)	0.140 (0.554)
Adjusted R^2	0.69	0.65	0.72	0.70	0.64	0.74
F-stat	150.64	45.33	118.32	68.63	19.21	57.31
N	4046	1365	2681	1717	579	1138

* Significant at the 1% level, ** Significant at the 5% level, *** Significant at the 10% level. Newey-West robust standard errors are employed.

The FELS results, columns (1) through (6), in Table 2 support all of the maintained hypotheses about player statistics and salary. All of the performance measure—games played, goals per game, assists per game, etc.—are statistically significant across both datasets, and the coefficients of the various performance statistics have the expected positive signs for all three groups of players (all players, defensemen, and forwards). A unit increase in a given continuous independent variable is interpreted as a percentage change of real AAV equal to the coefficient of the given variable. In column (1), an increase in one game played results in a 0.01 percent increase in a player's salary, where salary is expressed as a percentage of the NHL salary cap, and so on. Penalty minutes per game are positive and significant in both datasets. The dummy variable for defenseman is negative and statistically significant in both datasets, indicating that defensemen get paid less than forwards. However, defensemen do play more minutes, and the positive and significant sign on the defensemen and time on ice interaction variable has a positive and significant sign. The dummy variable for left handed players is insignificant in both datasets. Both Russian and Swedish players command a higher salary over their Canadian counterparts (the omitted player category). The adjusted R-squares from both datasets are pretty close in magnitude. The difference in the magnitude of corresponding on-ice coefficients between both datasets is also quite small. Therefore, as a practical matter, the FELS results suggest that using one year lagged career statistics or statistics from the player's last contract does not make much of a difference in the findings. The dummy variable for left handed players (Left Handed player) is insignificant across all three groups of players in both the career lagged and the contract lagged statistics datasets.

Country of origin effects are captured by the dummy variables named for the players' countries of origin (USA, Russia, Sweden, Finland, Czechoslovakia, and Other). The comparison group is Canadian players. Players of Russian origin have positive and significant coefficients across all models in both datasets. This indicates that Russians are paid more than their Canadian counterparts. The dummy variable coefficient for Swedish defensemen is positive and significant in both the lagged career and the previous contract datasets (columns (2) and (4)), indicating that some Swedish players also command a premium. Czech defensemen command a higher AAV but only based on the previous contract dataset. Finally, USA forwards get paid less than their Canadian counterparts based on the career lagged dataset alone. The reader may refer back to Table 1 to compare and contrast sample statistics by player's country of origin.

We include contract status dummy variables in all of our models, because a player's contract status impacts their bargaining power and consequently their AAV. We are thankful to an anonymous referee for suggesting this improvement. Compared to entry level players, players who are restricted and unrestricted free agents command a premium. The contract status dummy variables, RFA, UFA, and TFP35, have the expected signs and are significant in most of the models. The comparison group in the career lagged statistics dataset is players on entry level contracts, while the comparison group in the previous contract dataset is restricted free agents. Both the RFA and the UFA dummies are positive and significant in the majority of the regression estimates. TFP35 players command a slightly lower premium than other UFAs because of certain salary cap rules. This is consistent with the negative sign on the TFP35 dummy. Finally, the UFA years lost dummy is positive and significant only for forwards in the career lagged dataset. Brander and Egan suggest that this is because RFAs that give up some years of unrestricted free agency are expected to receive slightly larger RFA contracts to compensate them for the delay to becoming unrestricted free agents.

We turn next to the quantile regressions estimates of Equation (1) from both the career lagged statistics dataset and the previous contract statistics dataset. We use Huber-White robust standard errors. As Vincent and Eastman point out, different variables have varying impacts at different quantiles of the wage distribution. Quantile regression estimates allow us to estimate these impacts at different quantiles of the wage distribution. The quantile regression results for the career lagged dataset are displayed in Table 3, while Table 4 gives the quantile regression results based on the player's previous contract statistics. The career lagged dataset contains players on all types of contracts. The comparison group is players on entry level contracts. The previous contract dataset only contains players that are RFAs, UFAs, and TFP35s, thus the default comparison group in Table 4 is RFAs. We employ robust Huber-Sandwich standard errors and covariances for the quantile regressions. Once again, we do not report the annual and the team specific dummy variables for the sake of brevity.

The coefficient on games played is positive and significant across the 10th, the 25th, and the 50th quantiles in both datasets. Goals and assists per game are significant and positive across all quantiles in both datasets. The plus-minus variable is significant and positive up to the 75th quantile in the lagged career statistics dataset (Table 3) and across all quantiles in the previous contract dataset (Table 4). Penalty minutes per game is significant across all quantiles in the lagged career statistics dataset and is significant and positive up to the 75th quantile in the lagged contract statistics dataset (Table 4). Shots per game and time on ice per game are significant across all quantiles in both datasets.

Defensemen are paid less than forwards at the 50th, the 75th, and the 90th quantiles across both datasets. However, this effect is lessened when the defensemen time on ice interaction dummy has a positive and significant coefficient at the same quantiles in both datasets. The net effect of the defensemen dummy coefficient plus the defensemen time on ice interaction dummy coefficient is still negative at the 50th, the 75th, and the 90th quantiles. Once again, the dummy variable for left handed players is insignificant across all quantiles in both datasets.

Table 3. Quantile regression results based on lagged career statistics.

Dependent Variable	**Real AAV**				
Regression Level	**10th Quantile**	**25th Quantile**	**50th Quantile**	**75th Quantile**	**90th Quantile**
Independent Variable	**Coefficient** ***t*-Statistic**	**Coefficient** ***t*-Statistic**	**Coefficient** ***t*-Statistic**	**Coefficient** ***t*-Statistic**	**Coefficient** ***t*-Statistic**
Games played	0.003 (15.416) *	0.004 (19.826) *	0.004 (13.218) *	0.003 (10.377) *	0.003 (6.679) *
Goals per game	1.257 (3.287) *	2.907 (4.106) *	4.559 (5.94) *	4.931 (5.768) *	7.443 (7.185) *
Assists per game	1.191 (3.06) *	3.110 (6.72) *	4.933 (9.246) *	7.361 (13.895) *	8.609 (8.753) *
Plus-minus	0.010 (6.11) *	0.012 (9.03) *	0.009 (7.016) *	0.006 (4.92) *	0.003 (0.921)
Penalty minutes per game	0.225 (4.249) *	0.490 (5.614) *	0.692 (6.731) *	0.719 (6.26) *	0.550 (3.872) *
Shots per game	0.295 (4.209) *	0.427 (4.143) *	0.648 (5.956) *	0.728 (7.137) *	0.463 (3.67) *
Time on ice per game (TOIPG)	0.036 (2.323) **	0.077 (3.357) *	0.107 (5.569) *	0.102 (5.415) *	0.104 (4.05) *
Defenseman	−0.567 (−1.119)	−0.689 (−1.311)	−1.378 (−3.593) *	−1.116 (−3.884) *	−1.060 (−3.253) *
Defenseman X TOIPG	0.040 (1.252)	0.052 (1.489)	0.104 (4.33) *	0.108 (5.852) *	0.123 (5.551) *
Left Handed player	−0.023 (−0.55)	0.046 (0.79)	−0.002 (−0.024)	0.124 (1.745)	0.032 (0.294)
USADUMMY	0.030 (0.624)	0.034 (0.565)	−0.180 (−2.554) **	−0.149 (−1.878) ***	−0.126 (−0.967)
RUSDUMMY	0.441 (2.088) **	0.827 (5.571) *	0.902 (3.566) *	0.753 (4.427) *	0.418 (1.782)
SWEDUMMY	0.316 (3.048) *	0.300 (2.493) **	0.136 (0.905)	0.087 (0.631)	0.088 (0.374)
FINDUMMY	0.144 (0.942)	0.155 (0.679)	0.202 (0.877)	0.344 (1.573)	0.360 (0.747)
CZEDUMMY	0.409 (3.348) *	0.436 (3.446) *	0.121 (0.904)	0.046 (0.288)	−0.120 (−0.528)
OTHERDUMMY	−0.008 (−0.072)	0.057 (0.364)	0.122 (0.624)	0.066 (0.378)	0.506 (1.237)
RFA Dummy	0.272 (2.74) *	0.405 (3.699) *	0.273 (2.394) *	−0.034 (−0.285)	−0.529 (−2.726) *
UFA Dummy	−0.111 (−0.969)	0.021 (0.145)	0.158 (1.141)	0.175 (1.257)	−0.142 (−0.612)
TFP35 Dummy	−1.737 (−4.729) *	−2.085 (−8.97) *	−1.837 (−9.042) *	−2.020 (−11.206) *	−1.837 (−6.818) *
UFA Years lost	0.316 (2.805) *	0.139 (1.878) ***	0.093135 (1.646) ***	−0.045358 (−0.754)	−0.150418 (−1.198)

* Significant at the 1% level, ** Significant at the 5% level, *** Significant at the 10% level. Robust standard errors are employed.

The country of origin dummies show that Russian players are paid more than Canadian players at all quantiles except the 90th quantile in both datasets. Swedes and Finns are paid more at the 10th and the 25th quantiles according to the estimates from the lagged career statistics dataset. However, according to the regressions based on the contract lagged statistics dataset, they are paid more only at the median quantile. American players are underpaid relative to the Canadian group of players at the 50th quantile based on the lagged career dataset in Table 3.

Table 4. Quantile regression results based on previous contract statistics.

Dependent Variable	**Real AAV**				
Regression Level	**10th Quantile**	**25thQuantile**	**50th Quantile**	**75th Quantile**	**90th Quantile**
Independent Variable	**Coefficient *t*-Statistic**	**Coefficient *t*-Statistic**	**Coefficient *t*-Statistic**	**Coefficient *t*-Statistic**	**Coefficient *t*-Statistic**
Games played	0.011 (8.733) *	0.012 (7.203) *	0.004 (1.783) ***	−0.004 (−1.071)	−0.007 (−1.394)
Goals per game	1.244 (2.539) **	4.005 (5.902) *	6.344 (6.076) *	6.417 (4.54) *	9.556 (4.03) *
Assists per game	0.894 (2.42) **	2.693 (4.839) *	5.127 (7.122) *	7.804 (7.851) *	8.740 (8.147) *
Plus-minus	0.022 (4.197) *	0.027 (4.115) *	0.030 (4.225) *	0.030 (3.318) *	0.031 (2.635) *
Penalty minutes per game	0.269 (4.554) *	0.491 (6.902) *	0.686 (5.8) *	0.606 (3.846) *	0.476 (1.669)
Shots per game	0.202 (2.553) **	0.482 (4.773) *	0.592 (3.981) *	0.733 (5.315) *	0.630 (2.444) **
Time on ice per game (TOIPG)	0.069 (3.984) *	0.096 (4.574) *	0.118 (4.589) *	0.107 (4.085) *	0.073 (2.26) **
Defenseman	−0.209 (−0.397)	−0.996 (−1.16)	−2.332 (−4.522) *	−1.696 (−4.363) *	−2.043 (−3.423) *
Defenseman X TOIPG	0.009 (0.259)	0.064 (1.136)	0.166 (4.861) *	0.155 (5.885) *	0.202 (4.705) *
Left Handed player	−0.015 (−0.278)	0.068 (0.957)	0.040 (0.428)	−0.076 (−0.733)	0.043 (0.314)
USADUMMY	−0.031 (−0.514)	0.021 (0.266)	−0.004 (−0.035)	−0.140 (−1.235)	−0.051 (−0.269)
RUSDUMMY	0.454 (1.982) **	0.592 (1.753) ***	0.671 (2.816) *	0.839 (2.254) **	0.517 (1.39)
SWEDUMMY	0.190 (1.283)	0.182 (0.915)	0.563 (2.645) *	0.373 (1.564)	0.212 (0.748)
FINDUMMY	−0.019 (−0.094)	−0.258 (−0.799)	0.008 (0.023)	−0.082 (−0.232)	0.420 (0.485)
CZEDUMMY	0.219 (1.131)	0.483 (2.997) *	0.470 (2.544) **	−0.076 (−0.366)	−0.336 (−0.988)
OTHERDUMMY	−0.034 (−0.258)	−0.154 (−0.79)	−0.284 (−1.238)	0.090 (0.326)	−0.212 (−0.505)
UFA Dummy	−0.052 (−0.863)	0.110 (1.347)	0.335 (3.632) *	0.460 (4.423) *	0.452 (2.879) *
TFP35 Dummy	−0.053 (−0.334)	−0.360 (−1.68)	−0.605 (−2.597) *	−0.799 (−3.411) *	−0.752 (−2.642) *
UFA Years lost	−0.165 (−1.132)	0.003 (0.043)	−0.024 (−0.1)	−0.040 (−0.141)	−0.538 (−5.854) *

* Significant at the 1% level, ** Significant at the 5% level, *** Significant at the 10% level. Robust standard errors are employed.

The RFA contract status dummy is positive and significant in Table 3 up to the median quartile. Table 4 does not contain the RFA dummy because RFAs make up the comparison group in the contract lagged dataset. The UFA dummy is insignificant at all quantiles in the career lagged statistics dataset in Table 3. However, it is significant and positive at the 50th, the 75th, and the 90th quantiles in the contract lagged statistics dataset. This is in keeping with the logic that unrestricted free agents have more bargaining power and are likely to secure higher AAVs. The TFP35 dummy is negative and significant across all quantiles in the career lagged statistics dataset, while it is negatively significant at the 50th, the 75th, and the 90th quantiles in the contract lagged statistics dataset. This is in keeping with the reasoning that more restrictive salary cap rules make teams less likely to award high TFP35 contracts. The contract status dummies tend to perform better in the contract statistics lagged dataset than the career lagged statistics performance dataset. General managers are more likely to base their decisions on a player's recent productivity from their last few years rather than on their career statistics. For older players, such as those in the TFP35 category, there could be a significant difference in those statistics.

6. Conclusions

The purpose of this paper is to examine if the country of origin influences a player's average annual contract value in the NHL after controlling for on ice performance, contract status, and position. We use two different sets of on-ice statistics to control for on-ice performance. The first dataset contains players' average annual values of their current contract in each year and a lagged career average of their various on ice statistics. This is the type of data used in most academic studies. The second dataset looks at player's real average annual value in the first year of a new contract as a function of their average on-ice statistics during their last contract. This is the type of data that most NHL teams are likely to use when making contract offers.

The FELS results for on-ice production statistics are quite similar across both datasets. We find that players annual average values increase with their on-ice performance measured by games played, goals per game, assists per game, their plus-minus statistic, penalty minutes per game, shots per game, and their time on ice per game. However, the FELS results suggest that defensemen get paid less than forwards. The FELS results from both datasets do not support the idea that left handed players are paid more for being left handed. After controlling for on-ice productivity, contract status, and position, we find that Russian players are paid more than others in the NHL across the board in all FELS regressions based on both datasets. We also find that Swedish and Czech defensemen get paid more than their Canadian counterparts.

The quantile regression results are a little more nuanced and insightful. These results for both datasets show that on-ice productivity, for the most part, is related positively to NHL salaries. In general, goals per game, assists per game, plus-minus, penalty minutes, and shots per game are related positively and significantly to player salary. However, according to the estimates from the contract lagged statistics, games played is not significant in determining salary at the 75th and the 90th quantiles. This suggests that NHL general managers view the relationship between games played and higher end salaries differently than the results from academic studies, which find games played and salary to be related at all quantiles.

We find that defensemen are paid less than forwards at the 50th, the 75th, and the 90th quantiles in both datasets. However, when accounting for the time on ice played by defensemen, we find that defensemen are paid a little more than forwards for their time on ice. This allows us to understand why past FELS results in the literature found that defensemen get paid less than forwards. However, this slight increase is not enough to offset the negative differential in pay between forwards and defensemen, and defensemen still get paid less than forwards at the middle to upper quantiles of the distribution. These results are consistent with previous findings by Kahane (2001). However, unlike Coates (2017), we do not find any significant salary differential for left handed players.

The results from the contract lagged statistics dataset show that Russians get paid more at every quantile up to the 75th quantile. Players from other countries do not see additional compensation above the median quantile. There is also a country of origin effect on compensation for Swedish and Czech players from the lower to the middle quantiles, depending on the dataset used. Given that the KHL and the SHL cannot outbid NHL teams for the very top talent, it makes sense that country of origin dummies are insignificant beyond the median quantile (for the previous contract dataset). The only exception is Russia, which is significant at the 75th quantile. These country of origin effects are observed after controlling for on-ice performance, contract status, team effects, annual effects, and player position. Given that NHL teams are trying to win subject to a hard salary cap, the only plausible explanation is that some of these Russian, Swedish, and Czech players have leverage in negotiations due to the availability of options to play in other leagues such as the SHL and the KHL.

According to the dataset based on lagged career statistics, Russians get paid more in the NHL at every quantile. However, NHL teams are more likely to award contracts based on recent performance as measured by the previous contract dataset.

In closing, this study suggests that, while the statistical significance of most on ice performance variables on AAV are very similar between career lagged statistics and previous contract lagged statistics datasets, there may be differences in the magnitude of the coefficients. Academics may be missing nuances of salary studies by just focusing on lagged career statistics instead of statistics generated during the player's most recent contract. In addition, the use of quantile regression produces interesting results at different points of the wage distribution that are masked by the use of a simple ordinary least squares estimator.

Author Contributions: All authors contributed equally to this work.

Acknowledgments: We are grateful for the comments from two anonymous referees from this journal, Neal Rappaport from Colorado College, Dennis Coates and other session participants and the Southern Economics Meetings. Any remaining errors are our own. We would also like to thank Andrew Farny, Jacob Miller, Rae Conlon and Alan Fox for their outstanding work as our research assistants.

References

1. Brander, James A., and Edward J. Egan. 2018. Seniority Wages in the National Hockey League. *Eastern Economic Journal* 44: 84–96. [CrossRef]
2. Bruggink, Thomas H., and Daniel Williams. 2009. Discrimination against Europeans in the National Hockey League: Are Players Getting Their Fair Pay? *American Economist* 54: 82–90. [CrossRef]
3. Christie, Tom, and Marc Lavoie. 2015. Entry Discrimination in the NHL: Evolution and the KHL Effect. *Eastern Economic Journal* 41: 214–29. [CrossRef]
4. Coates, Dennis. 2017. Returns to Handedness in Hockey. In *Breaking the Ice: The Economics of Hockey*. Edited by Bernd Frick. Berlin and Heidelberg: Springer, pp. 41–56.
5. Holmes, Paul. 2011. New Evidence of Salary Discrimination in Major League Baseball. *Labour Economics* 18: 320–31. [CrossRef]
6. Idson, Todd, and Leo Kahane. 2001. Team Effects on Compensation: An Application to Salary Determination in the National Hockey League. *The Economics of Sport* 1: 583–95. [CrossRef]
7. Jones, J. C. H., and William Walsh. 1988. Salary Determination in the National Hockey League: The Effects of Skills, Franchise Characteristics, and Discrimination. *Industrial and Labor Relations Review* 41: 592–604. [CrossRef]
   Kahane, Leo H. 2001. Team and Player Effects on NHL Player Salaries: A Hierarchical Linear Model Approach. *Applied Economics Letters* 8: 629–32. [CrossRef]
8. Kahn, Lawrence M. 1992. The Effects of Race on Professional Football Players' Compensation. *Industrial and Labor Relations Review* 45: 295–310. [CrossRef]
9. Lavoie, Marc, Gilles Grenier, and Serge Coulombe. 1987. Discrimination and Performance Differentials in the National Hockey League. *Canadian Public Policy* 13: 407–22. [CrossRef]
10. Mincer, Jacob. 1958. Investment in Human Capital and Personal Income Distribution. *Journal of Political Economy* 66: 281–302. [CrossRef]
11. Vincent, Claude, and Byron Eastman. 2009. Determinants of Pay in the NHL: A Quantile Regression Approach. *Journal of Sports Economics* 10: 256–77. [CrossRef]
12. Yang, Chih-Hain, and Hsuan-Yu Lin. 2012. Is There Salary Discrimination by Nationality in the NBA?: Foreign Talent or Foreign Market. *Journal of Sports Economics* 13: 53–75. [CrossRef]

How the Economic and Financial Situation of the Community Affects Sport Clubs' Resources: Evidence from Multi-Level Models

Pamela Wicker * and Christoph Breuer

Department of Sport Economics and Sport Management, German Sport University Cologne, Am Sportpark Muengersdorf 6, Cologne 50933, Germany; breuer@dshs-koeln.de
* Author to whom correspondence should be addressed; p.wicker@dshs-koeln.de

Academic Editor: Brian P. Soebbing

Abstract: In many Western countries, local community sport clubs are important providers of leisure, sport, and social programs. These sport clubs are nonprofit organizations, which operate in an increasingly challenging environment. This study considers a club's direct local environment, *i.e.*, the community the club is located in. The open systems model and the resource dependence represent the theoretical framework. The purpose of this research is to examine the effect of the financial and economic environment in the community on the resource situation of sport clubs (human, infrastructure, and financial resources). The empirical evaluation is undertaken using data from a nationwide survey of non-profit sport clubs in Germany (organizational level; n = 19,345), which are combined with secondary data on community characteristics (community level; n = 3153). Given the hierarchical data structure, multi-level analyses are applied. The results show that volunteer problems are smaller among clubs in communities with high unemployment. Facility and financial problems are greater in large communities. Sport clubs located in communities that could break even were also more likely to break even themselves. The findings show that resource problems are not necessarily due to poor club management, since higher-level (community) factors significantly affect the resource situation of sport clubs too.

Keywords: Environment; community; finance; nonprofit sport club; multi-level analysis; resources

---

1. Introduction

In many Western countries, local community sport clubs are important providers of leisure, sport, and social programs (e.g., [1–3]). Members join the club and pay a membership fee, which allows them to use all programs of the club. By their legal form, these sport clubs are nonprofit organizations. Recent research shows that these organizations operate in an increasingly challenging environment [4], which may impact their functioning. Following Foster and Meinhard [5] "the environment plays a significant role in the creation and survival of organizations" (p. 44). External influences can relate to the political environment (e.g., changes in policies and public funding), but also to the economic environment [6]. Generally, the research focus has been on the social-political environment and the relationship with the government, and how this affects the behavior, structure, and development of non-profit organizations [7,8]. However, the environment of a non-profit organization includes more than the government and funding relationships [9].

For many non-profits operating at a local level, the community the organization is located in represents the direct environment. Within the community, the economic and financial situation is critical to the organization [6]. Specifically, the labor market situation and resulting income distribution of the population may be critical for membership based non-profit organizations. In communities with high unemployment rates and low income, residents may not have the resources to become a member. Moreover, the labor market situation affects the financial situation of the community's government in the sense that it has high social spending while generating low revenues from income taxes. When the community has financial difficulties, its support of local non-profit organizations in terms of providing financial or infrastructure resources may be limited. However, not much is known about community effects on non-profit resources.

The purpose of this study is to examine the effects of the financial and the economic situation in the community on organizational resources of local non-profit organizations. The research context for this examination is the non-profit sport club sector in Germany. Human, infrastructure, and financial resources are the focus of this research [10]. Although German sport clubs have more members and provide programs in more sports compared with clubs in other countries, they report similar challenges in terms of human, infrastructure, and financial resources [1–3]. The aim of this study is to analyze how external community-related factors influence these resources since intra-organizational factors have already been examined in previous research [11]. In doing so, this study advances the following main research question: How do community factors affect organizational resources of non-profit sport clubs?

When examining the relationship between nonprofits and their environment, it must be considered that this relationship has a multi-level structure [12], which has methodological implications. There are two levels in this study, the community level and the organizational level (sport clubs). These levels are hierarchical in nature, *i.e.*, sport clubs are nested within communities and clubs in the same community share the same community characteristics. This hierarchical structure must be considered in empirical examinations by using multi-level analyses, which represent the appropriate method [13]. Thus, this study contributes to the body of research on the relationship between non-profits and their environment by applying multi-level analyses, which have largely been neglected in non-profit research with a few exceptions (e.g., [14]).

2. Theoretical Framework and Literature Review

2.1. Open Systems Perspective and Resource Dependence Theory

At least two theoretical approaches are relevant to frame the proposed research; the open systems model [15] and the resource dependence theory [16]. Following Scott [15], organizations can be regarded as rational, natural, or open systems. While the first two systems relate more to intra-organizational aspects, the last perspective is critical when examining the relationship between organizational behavior and the external environment. Organizations should be seen as open systems whose performance is the result of interchanges between the organization and its environment [15,17]. Since no organization disposes of all the resources it needs for survival, all organizations are in an exchange with their environment to some extent [15]. Therefore, it is important to understand the context in which the organization operates.

The resource dependence theory (RDT) [16] is rooted in the open systems perspective [15]. Following this theory, organizations seek scarce resources from external stakeholders in the environment [16]. Typically, organizations do not have all the resources they need for their operations; they are incomplete systems [17]. Therefore, they compete for scarce resources in their environment [7]. However, organizations may lose autonomy when external stakeholders exert power and control over the organization as a result of resource dependence [16]. In summary, organizations depend on their environment for acquiring resources, seeking legitimacy, and guaranteeing survival [15]. In the present research, the type of external environment which is considered is the local community; *i.e.*, the municipality where the sport club is located.

Following Oliver [18], this need for external resources is one of the determinants of inter-organizational relationships. This determinant is referred to as necessity—the others are asymmetry, reciprocity, efficiency, stability, and legitimacy. She further states that relationships driven by necessity can be voluntary or mandatory in nature. In the present research context where the community represents the direct environment, the relationships can be considered mandatory. Although a sport club can be founded wherever the founding members wish to, it must be located in a community. Typically, clubs are founded in communities where the founding members live. Thus, the external environment cannot be voluntarily chosen. Yet, it is likely that the perceptions of the mandatory environment are reduced by organizations [19]. For this reason, it is important to sharpen perceptions by examining potential influences of this environment on organizations.

Importantly, the exchange between the organization and its environment is not restricted to resources. In addition to resource inputs from the environment, organizations also try to secure legitimacy and provide outputs to various stakeholders such as members, clients, and the general public [15]. Both aspects—resource inputs and the provision of organizational outputs to various stakeholders including potential members and customers—are critical in the present research.

While the assumed relationships between organizations and their environment within RDT are widely accepted, it was pointed out that the proposed relationships should be tested more rigorously in empirical studies [20]. Although it is not possible to empirically test RDT in its entirety, it was widely analyzed as summarized by Nienhueser [21]. Yet, this summary also indicates that most studies looked at for-profit organizations. This study adds to the body of literature on RDT by examining non-profit sport clubs.

2.2. Research on Nonprofit Organizations and the Environment

The influence of the environment on organizational behavior has been examined to a lesser extent than intra-organizational dimensions [17]. Specifically, the body of research on the effects of community factors is relatively scant. Since non-profits are strongly linked with government authorities, probably more than with any other type of institution [8], the majority of studies looked at the link between the government and the non-profit organization (e.g., [8,22,23]). One reason for the neglect of other external factors could be the availability of adequate data and measures. Oftentimes, the share of government income is used as a measure to proxy government influence [22,24]. One study used the field of activity, the percentage of funding from various sources, and the presence of a state audit requirement as measures for external environmental characteristics [9]. However, these characteristics do not seem to be characteristics of the external environment; instead these are internal characteristics that are influenced by the environment. This example illustrates the methodological difficulties associated with an examination of environmental factors.

In summary, several studies analyzed the relationship between non-profit organizations and the external environment. Nevertheless, some shortcomings can be observed. First, most studies focused on the political environment and specifically the government as an external entity (e.g., [23]). Yet, the economic and financial environment is also important and should not be omitted [6]. Probably due to issues regarding data availability, economic and financial factors have been largely neglected in previous research. Second, most studies were qualitative in nature (e.g., [17,25,26]), while the chosen measures on the community level could be improved in quantitative approaches [9]. Therefore, the body of research would benefit from quantitative studies that apply adequate measures and allow generalizations and predictions. Third, community measures have not been adequately integrated into statistical analyses; they were treated like characteristics on the organizational level [11,27]. As will be seen in the data analysis section, the multi-level analysis is the appropriate statistical test in the case of hierarchical (nested) data. This study attempts to address these shortcomings.

2.3. Community-Level Effects on Organizational Resources of Sport Clubs

This study extends the perspective of previous research and considers the economic and financial environment. Based on the open systems model [15] and the resource dependence theory [16] it is assumed that organizational resources of non-profit sport clubs are affected by the environment. In the next paragraphs, it is explained what community factors may be relevant to organizational resources and how they could potentially affect those resources. Yet, it is difficult to find related studies because research looking at the role of community factors is relatively scarce.

First of all, the size of the community is associated with the resources of sport clubs, specifically human and financial resources. The community size is relevant when looking at organizational outputs such as programs and services that are provided to a variety of external stakeholders (e.g., donors, corporate sponsors, customers participating in sports courses). While club members are *obvious* stakeholders, also customers (non-members), donors, and the wider community such as businesses engaged as sponsors may be interested in the clubs' services. For example, some clubs also offer sport courses for non-members against a service fee [28], while corporate businesses may be interested in showcasing social corporate responsibility by sponsoring and supporting local sport clubs. From the output perspective sport clubs may have more opportunities to provide their services in larger communities, simply because more potential stakeholders are present.

However, it could also be argued that there is more competition for resources in large communities because there are also more clubs and other fundable organizations and, thus, stakeholders have different opportunities to spend their money on. Since environmental resources are often limited, there is competition among organizations for scarce resources [26]. The level of competition increases with an increasing number of competitors and is thus higher in large communities [28]. To successfully compete for scarce resources, organizations may feel more pressure to adapt programs to the preferences of stakeholders in an effort to please more stakeholders [25]. This change in programs may in turn negatively affect potential members and volunteers working for the club.

The few studies analyzing effects of community size showed mixed findings. In a study on Finnish sport clubs, Koski [11] detected a negative correlation between town size and organizational effectiveness: Clubs in larger communities were less effective. A German sport club study [27] revealed that clubs in larger communities had significantly greater financial problems, while the effect of community size on problems related to members and volunteers was not significant. A different German study [28] showed that clubs in larger communities charge higher membership fees, which may be a result of the evident higher competition in large communities. The clubs receive less support from the community and have to charge their members higher fees to compensate for missing income in other areas. The study also showed that problems regarding infrastructure resources (sport facilities) are bigger for clubs in large communities. Given the above evidence, it is assumed that clubs located in large communities experience greater resource problems.

Second, the financial environment is relevant for the sport clubs' resource situation. While the focus of previous research was on the effect of public funding on aspects like program design [25] and organizational autonomy [23], this research looks at the financial situation of the community, which is critical for the support of sport clubs. Research showed that organizational performance is affected by environmental resources [17], specifically financial resources [26]. This also applies to the sport club sector [29].

The community's financial situation is particularly relevant for infrastructure resources (like investments in public sport facilities that can be used by clubs) and for direct financial support. Clubs located in communities with financial difficulties should be less likely to receive public funding, because expenditure on culture and sport are typically cut in case of financial difficulties [30]. The reality is that many German communities have debts and are far away from breaking even at the end of the financial year [31]. The community's financial difficulties are mirrored in the public funds provided to clubs: Only approximately half of the clubs in Germany receive funds from the community [28]. Based on the above explanations, it can be assumed that the better the financial situation of the community, the smaller the resource related problems of sport clubs.

Third, the economic environment affects the resource situation of sport clubs. The focus of this research is on the employment and income situation of the local population. Recent evidence documents that the labor market situation and the resulting income distribution of the population is problematic in many countries [32]. Although the unemployment rate and income disparity are lower in Germany than in other countries [32], there are nevertheless many people who are working full-time, but still receive low wages. In 2010, 23% of the employed people received low wages and therefore needed additional money from the employment office as compensation [33].

The employment and income situation should be important for human, financial, and infrastructure resources of sport clubs. The income situation of the resident population is associated with the community's financial position; the higher the income of the resident population, the higher the revenues the community generates from income taxes. Those revenues should improve the community's financial situation and capacity to financially support clubs and invest in public sport facilities. Thus, economic and financial aspects are interrelated. The relationship between the employment situation and human resources (*i.e.*, volunteers) is probably the topic that has received most academic attention. Andreff [34] conceptualized that there is a possible relationship between unemployment and voluntary work. He recommended that unemployment could be reduced when sport organizations replace voluntary labor by paid labor. Following his idea, high unemployment would lead to volunteer problems because volunteers are replaced by paid staff. However, it is also likely that in this case clubs would not perceive a shortage of volunteers because all tasks are completed.

When examining the relationship between employment and voluntary work, the opportunity costs of time must be considered. Opportunity costs refer to the income people forego by spending time on other activities (e.g., volunteering) rather than work [35]. Following the opportunity cost approach [35], unemployed people have zero opportunity costs (when a *pure* approach is considered) and should be more likely to volunteer because opportunity costs are lower. On the other hand, employed people have higher opportunity costs and are, therefore, expected to be less likely to volunteer. These arguments were supported in previous research documenting a negative relationship between working time and volunteering: individuals working full-time were less likely to volunteer than individuals without employment or those only working part-time [36,37]. However, once the decision to volunteer was positive, full-time work was positively associated with volunteering hours, *i.e.*, individuals working full-time were volunteering more hours [36]. Another study also showed that volunteers are typically highly skilled [38]. Although these findings may look contradictory, Freeman [38] argued that people with high opportunity costs of volunteering carefully reflect their decision to volunteer and only volunteer when asked to do so. Taking the arguments of the opportunity cost approach into account, volunteer problems should be smaller for sport clubs located in communities with high unemployment. The effects of community factors are examined empirically using comprehensive sport club data from Germany.

3. Method

3.1. Data Sources

A combination of primary data (organizational level; sport clubs) and secondary data (community level) is used for this research. Primary data were collected with a nationwide online survey of German non-profit sport clubs in 2009. The clubs' email addresses were provided by the state sports confederations; altogether 63,468 email addresses of a total of approximately 91,000 clubs were made available. All clubs with a valid email address received an invitation email including a personalized link to the online questionnaire that allows logging in and out. After controlling for drop-outs (5399), 58,069 clubs were invited to take part in the survey. The survey was online from October to December

2009 with n = 19,345 clubs participating (response rate: 33.3%). The sample is representative for German sport clubs in terms of size and state. Since 2009, the year of the data collection, no major changes were observed in the German sport club system.

In a second step, secondary data on the characteristics of communities were made available. The Federal and Regional Statistical Offices release those data every year, but the included variables are inconsistent. While community size is always included, figures on unemployment and the community's finances (e.g., tax income) are not available in all years. For 2008, most community figures are available. The club survey is part of a wider sport club project where data are collected every two years since 2005 [28]; however, due to the restricted availability of data on the community level, the third wave from 2009 was used for the analysis since the financial and membership data from the club survey refer to the year before the survey (because 2008 is the last completed household year). The secondary data include information about all communities in Germany [39]. They are provided with community codes. Based on the postcode and the club's community name the respective community code was assigned to every club in the primary dataset. Clubs from the same community received the same community code. Altogether, the clubs in the sample are located in n = 3153 different communities. The community code is the key variable that links both datasets.

3.2. Measures and Variables

The variables used in this study are summarized in Table 1, the descriptive statistics are provided in Table 2. Human, infrastructure, and financial resources of sport clubs are examined and operationalized with five variables. Four variables capture the perceived severity of organizational problems related to those resources. These are the recruitment and retention of (1) members (P_MEM) and (2) volunteers (P_VOL); (3) the availability of sport facilities (P_FAC); and (4) the financial situation of the club (P_FIN). In sport club research it is common to ask for problems or challenges (e.g., [1–3]). Also, the subjective problem items are not biased by club size like other potential resource measures. The financial resources are enriched with one objective measure capturing whether the club could at least break even at the end of the financial year (BREAKEVEN_O). These five variables serve as the dependent variables in the models.

Independent variables are available on two levels (Table 1). The community level variables are community size (SIZE), which proxies market size and the level of competition for resources as explained in the theoretical part. BREAKEVEN_C captures the financial situation of the community. The profit of the community could have also been used in the analysis; yet, local governments are non-profit organizations and thus a profit measure is not adequate given that they are only required to break even. The economic environment is captured with two variables. The labor market situation is covered with UNEMP, which is obtained by dividing the number of unemployed people by the number of inhabitants in the community. Figures on the potential total work force, which is normally used for the calculation of the unemployment rate, are not available. LN INC_TAX reflects the income situation in the community and is also adjusted for community size. Another opportunity would be to use income from business taxes; however, these variables are highly correlated ($r = 0.989$; $p < 0.001$) causing multicollinearity problems in the models. We decided to use the income tax variable because most communities generate revenue from income taxes, while there are some (particularly smaller) communities, which do not generate revenue from business taxes, as they do not have any corporate businesses. Therefore, the business tax variable is excluded from the analysis.

Table 1. Overview of variables.

Variable	Description	Scale
	Dependent variables	
P_MEM	Recruitment/retention of members (1 = *no problem*, 5 = *a very big problem*)	Ordinal
P_VOL	Recruitment/retention of volunteers (1 = *no problem*, 5 = *a very big problem*)	Ordinal
P_FAC	Availability of sport facilities (1 = *no problem*, 5 = *a very big problem*)	Ordinal
P_FIN	Financial situation of the club (1 = *no problem*, 5 = *a very big problem*)	Ordinal
BREAKEVEN_O	Club could at least break even (=total revenues-total expenses $\geq$ 0; 1 = *yes*)	Dummy
	Independent variables: Community level	
SIZE	Community size (=number of inhabitants in the community/1000)	Metric
BREAKEVEN_C	Community could at least break even (=total revenues-total expenses $\geq$ 0; 1 = *yes*)	Dummy
UNEMP	Unemployment (=number of unemployed people/number of inhabitants)	Metric
LN INC_TAX	Logged per capita revenues from income taxes	Metric
	Independent variables: Organizational level	
MEMBERS	Number of members in the club	Metric
VOL_ENG	Share of voluntary engagement in % (=number of core volunteers/number of members $\times$ 100)	Metric
SEC_VOL	Share of secondary volunteers (in %)	Metric
PAID_STAFF	Club has paid staff (1 = *yes*)	Dummy
PUB_FAC	Club uses public sport facilities (1 = *yes*)	Dummy
OWN_FAC	Club possesses its own sport facilities (1 = *yes*)	Dummy
STRATEGY	Our club has a strategy (from 1 = *do not agree at all*, 5 = *totally agree*)	Ordinal

Table 2. Descriptive statistics.

	Mean	SD
	Organizational Level	
P_MEM	2.70	1.16
P_VOL	3.14	1.20
P_FAC	2.22	1.36
P_FIN	2.27	1.19
BREAKEVEN_O	0.63	0.48
MEMBERS	394.44	1546.01
VOL_ENG	12.47	23.91
SEC_VOL	23.74	22.21
PAID_STAFF	0.38	0.49
PUB_FAC	0.59	0.49
OWN_FAC	0.55	0.50
STRATEGY	3.56	1.06
	Community Level	
SIZE	17.70	50.74
BREAKEVEN_C	0.51	0.50
UNEMP	0.04	0.02
LN INC_TAX	0.00	0.01

On the organizational level, this study controls for the organizational capacity of sport clubs that may also affect resource problems [27]. These are MEMBERS capturing club size, VOL_ENG measuring the share of core volunteers (*i.e.*, those with a formal position), SEC_VOL measuring the share of secondary volunteers (*i.e.*, those who only help sporadically in the club), and PAID_STAFF reflecting whether the club employs paid staff. PUB_FAC captures whether the club uses public sport facilities (that are provided by the community) and OWN_FAC whether the club possesses its own facilities (including a club house). These variables capture the two main types of facilities German sport clubs rely upon. Hiring or leasing facilities from other stakeholders like a private operator, a trust or charity, and a church are less relevant in Germany compared with the UK [3]. Importantly these are not two categories of the same variable. It is likely that some clubs use both public facilities (in Germany, school sport facilities are also owned by the community and are, thus, public facilities) and their own facilities, while there may be other clubs, which do not rely on any type of facility at all (e.g., in road cycling clubs, members may train on the street). STRATEGY is a measure for the club's planning and development capacity, which was found to influence the perceived severity of organizational problems [27]. The independent variables on the organizational level serve as controls and are not the focus of this research.

3.3. Statistical Analysis: The Multi-Level Analysis

For the statistical analysis the hierarchical (or nested) structure of the data must be considered, *i.e.*, sport clubs are nested within communities. Thus, sport clubs located in the same community share the same community-level characteristics. The adequate statistical procedure to analyze hierarchical (nested) data is the multi-level analysis (also referred to as hierarchical linear model; HLM). Following Tabachnick and Fidell [40], "analyzing data organized into hierarchies as if they are all on the same level leads to both interpretational and statistical errors". One of the common errors of interpretation is referred to as the *ecological fallacy*, *i.e.*, applying higher-level results to the lower level [40].

Multi-level analyses require two different datasets because the number of cases differs between the levels. If this is not the case, another misleading interpretation occurs referred to as the *atomistic fallacy*, *i.e.*, lower-level analyses are interpreted at the higher (group) level [41]. Applied to this research, multi-level models allow predictions of club parameters adjusted for community scores and predictions of community scores adjusted for club differences within communities. When higher-level variables are simply included in the lower-level dataset and treated as lower-level variables in the analyses, the degrees of freedom are too high leading to an inflated Type I error [40]. As a result of the nested structure there are fewer cases on the higher level, *i.e.*, several clubs are located in one community. In some communities there is only one club in the data; this is not problematic as long as there are communities with more clubs [42]. The two levels are linked in the analysis with the key variable, community code. The different levels are mirrored in the equations which, consequently, have two-sub-indexes (*i* for organizational level and *j* for community level). In line with Todd *et al.* [43], the initial model in this study is in the form of a general linear model:

$$Y_{ij} = \beta_{0j} + \beta_{1j}\,XO_{ij} + r_{ij} \tag{1}$$

where Y_{ij} is the outcome of interest for club *i* in community *j*; β_{0j} the intercept for each community; β_{1j} the expected change in the outcome of interest (Y_{ij}) with a one-unit increase in XO_{ij}; and r_{ij} the residual.

Within multi-level analysis, every organizational-level estimate is calculated in separate community-level equations, which are of the following form:

$$\beta_{0j} = \gamma_{00} + \gamma_{01}XC_j + u_{0j} \tag{2}$$

$$\beta_{1j} = \gamma_{10} + \gamma_{11}XC_j + u_{1j} \tag{3}$$

where β_{0j} is the intercept from the organizational-level equation; β_{1j} the slope; XC_j the community-level variable; γ_{00} and γ_{10} the community-level intercepts; γ_{01} and γ_{11} the community-level slopes; and u_{0j}

and u_{1j} the community-level residuals. The community-level Equations (2) and (3) can be substituted into the organizational-level Equation (1) yielding the multi-level model.

Altogether, five multi-level models are estimated. A hierarchical *non-linear* model is run for the dependent dummy variable BREAKEVEN_O, while hierarchical *linear* models are estimated for the organizational problems. The four problem variables are assessed on five-point Likert scales. Following Wittenberg and Cramer [44], an ordinal variable with at least five categories can be treated as a metric variable when the interval distances are similar (which is the case in Likert scales). Bortz [45] states that when these requirements are given, all statistical tests for metric variables can be applied in research practice. All independent variables from Table 1 are entered in the models. Fixed-effects models are preferred because they provide the constant for all groups (communities). Models with robust standard errors are estimated [46]. Other specifications of the multi-level models (e.g., least-squares estimates, models without robust standard errors) were tried, but the results were not materially different.

The analyses are performed using specific multi-level software (HLM 7.1) [47].

Multi-level models require large sample sizes, particularly on the higher level (here: community level). Following Tabachnick and Fidell [40], at least 20 cases should be available on this level. Multi-level analyses were only rarely applied in non-profit research [14,37]. One likely reason for this shortcoming could be the need for many higher level units combined with the lack of available data at that higher level. The present study is based on 3,153 higher-level units and, thus, meets the required sample size [40].

4. Multi-Level Results and Discussion

The results of the multi-level models for resource problems of sport clubs are summarized in Table 3. Since the focus of this study is on community-level effects, no attention is paid to organizational-level factors in the discussion of results, also because they have already been discussed in previous research [27,48]. Regarding human resources, only unemployment has a significant effect on the dependent variable in model 1: The higher the unemployment in the community, the bigger the organizational problem of recruiting and retaining members. This finding can be explained by the costs associated with club participation and the income needed for club membership. Although sport clubs charge relatively low membership fees compared with commercial sport providers like fitness centers [28], income is a positive driver of club membership [49] and unemployed people may not have the financial resources to afford club membership. Consequently, clubs in communities with high unemployment experience problems of recruiting members.

Table 3. Results of the multi-level analyses for organizational problems regarding human and infrastructure resources.

	Model 1: P_MEM		Model 2: P_VOL		Model 3: P_FAC	
	icient	*t*	*Coefficient*	*t*	*Coefficient*	*t*
			Community Level			
Constant	3.660791	45.082 ***	3.930460	51.574 ***	2.091705	24.328 ***
SIZE	0.000124	1.015	0.000052	0.658	0.000468	4.289 ***
BREAKEVEN_C	0.002454	0.076	−0.044889	−1.456	−0.000975	−0.029
UNEMP	2.198204	2.416 **	−1.545328	−1.898 *	−1.671486	−1.902 *
LN INC_TAX	0.484344	0.146	6.631643	1.609	−6.880648	−1.748 *
			Organizational Level			
MEMBERS	−0.000036	−1.752 *	−0.000015	−3.641 ***	0.000018	0.581
VOL_ENG	0.003547	1.964 **	−0.001669	−1.837 *	−0.000536	−0.899
SEC_VOL	−0.002985	−3.725 ***	−0.009652	−13.269 ***	−0.004131	−5.248 ***
PAID_STAFF	−0.075336	−2.345 **	0.119982	3.576 ***	0.153535	3.802 ***
PUB_FAC	−0.263328	−7.482 ***	0.146998	4.333 ***	0.741956	18.814 ***
OWN_FAC	−0.024832	−0.746	0.246436	7.586 ***	−0.462229	−11.691 ***
STRATEGY	−0.224910	−14.505 ***	−0.203595	−12.867 ***	0.004163	0.248
$R^2_{\text{comm. level}}$	0.058		0.111		0.162	
$R^2_{\text{org. level}}$	0.058		0.111		0.162	

*$p < 0.1$; **$p < 0.05$; ***$p < 0.01$; displayed are the unstandardized coefficients; robust standard errors reported.

Model 2 shows that unemployment has a significant negative effect on the problem of recruiting and retaining volunteers. Thus, the finding is in accordance with the literature conceptualizing a relationship between unemployment and voluntary work [34]. However, this study is among the first to provide empirical evidence of this relationship using data on the organizational and community level since previous research was limited to the individual level and identified drivers of individual volunteering [36]. The negative effect implies that the higher the unemployment in the community, the smaller are volunteer problems among clubs. This negative effect is in line with the opportunity cost approach suggesting that the opportunity costs of time are lower for unemployed people, which is why those people should be more likely to volunteer [35,38]. Consequently, clubs in communities with high unemployment can mobilize volunteer resources more effectively.

Concerning infrastructure resources, model 3 shows that the problem related to the availability of sport facilities is significantly determined by community size, unemployment, and revenue from income taxes. The larger the community, the bigger are facility problems. This finding is in line with the previous assumption that competition for scarce resources is higher in large communities because of more competitors. The community provides a limited number of facilities for schools that are also used by clubs in the afternoon and evening hours. Since there are typically more clubs in larger communities, the facilities have to be shared by more clubs leading to increased facility problems.

The results also show that problems related to the availability of sport facilities are smaller in communities with high unemployment and high revenues from income taxes. While high unemployment may lead to fewer club memberships and thus fewer people needing facilities, the effect of revenues from income taxes is more associated with the community's or the local government's financial position. Communities that are in a good financial position can afford to invest money in building and maintaining sport facilities which can then be provided to sport clubs, while communities that have financial difficulties spend most of their money on education and child care facilities leaving no money for sport facilities. This situation is not specific to Germany since clubs in other countries also report facility issues [1,3].

Turning to financial resources (Table 4), model 4 reveals that the perceived financial situation of the clubs is worse in large communities with high unemployment. In large communities competition for financial resources from the local government, local businesses, and other stakeholders is higher [28] leaving fewer resources for each club. Also, the potential contribution of individuals is lower when inhabitants are unemployed and, thus, have fewer financial resources at their disposal that can be used for memberships and/or donations.

Table 4. Results of the multi-level analyses for financial resources.

	Model 4: P_FIN		Model 5: BREAK EVEN_O	
	Coefficient	*t*	*Coefficient*	*t*
		Community Level		
Constant	2.046551	25.576 ***	0.428219	2.288 **
SIZE	0.000255	3.214 ***	−0.000236	−1.084
BREAKEVEN_C	−0.035742	−1.138	0.188273	2.447 **
UNEMP	4.819861	5.454 ***	−2.446856	−1.183
INC_TAX	0.258572	0.068	−4.737284	−0.478
		Organizational Level		
MEMBERS	−0.000014	−1.785 *	0.000039	0.598
VOL_ENG	0.000890	0.841	0.000390	0.293
SEC_VOL	−0.000374	−0.498	0.005485	3.109 ***
PAID_STAFF	0.173759	5.137 ***	−0.051557	−0.631
PUB_FAC	0.031933	0.957	−0.015956	−0.198
OWN_FAC	0.244443	7.152 ***	−0.042499	−0.546
STRATEGY	−0.066732	−4.484 ***	0.019394	0.563
$R^2_{\text{comm. level}}$	0.057		0.170	
$R^2_{\text{org. level}}$	0.057		0.216	

* $p < 0.1$; ** $p < 0.05$; *** $p < 0.01$; displayed are the unstandardized coefficients; robust standard errors reported.

Model 5 analyses the determinants of whether a club could at least break even (BREAKEVEN_O). The only significant community-level factor is whether the community could at least break even. This means that clubs located in communities with solid finances are also more likely to have solid finances. This significant relationship could be a result of the exchange of financial resources between the local government and the sport club in the sense that a financially healthy government is capable to provide more resources for clubs that are then also financially healthier. However, a different explanation can be advanced, too: The community could serve as a *role model* for clubs, in a positive and negative way. When people running clubs are used to an environment where financial problems are common, they are also more likely to run the club in a way that it has financial problems. More generally speaking, people adopt the characteristics, behavior, and attitudes of people in their environment, a phenomenon that is referred to as *social contagion* [50]. While previous research focused on obesity, smoking, and happiness [50], this phenomenon may also apply to managing financial resources. Altogether, the results showed that not only the mere size of the community is relevant to sport clubs [11,37], but also other community-level factors.

Comparing the community-level effects in Model 4 and Model 5 shows that different variables are significant. Yet, the direction of effects is similar. Recall that negative effects in Model 4 mean that this factor reduces the severity of the problem (which is beneficial), while positive effects in Model 5 indicate that the likelihood of breaking even increases (which is also beneficial). Nevertheless, these differences—although only in the significance of variable—are interesting because both models examine the financial situation. Yet, Model 4 is based on a subjective measure (*i.e.*, the perceived of the problem *financial situation of the club*) and Model 5 on an objective measure (*i.e.*, whether the club could at least break even; calculated based on the reported revenues and expenditures). Previous research showed that both variables are positively correlated [51]. Thus, it is unlikely that clubs tended to over- or underestimate their financial situation in the subjective judgment. Yet, the scale allows a more nuanced judgment, while the breakeven measure is a dummy variable with less variation.

In summary, the regression results reveal that the R^2s on the community level are (almost) as high as on the organizational level indicating that community-level factors are equally important for the resource situation of sport clubs. It also stands out that—despite the large sample size on both levels—some variables have no significant effect and some significant effects are based on relatively low t-values (e.g., the effect of UNEMP on P_VOL). The difficulty of observing relationships, which are statistically significant and can, thus, be applied to all clubs may be explained by the heterogeneity of German sport clubs in terms of members and volunteers (as evident by the standard deviations in Table 2). The heterogeneity of clubs together with the cross-sectional character of the sample may also explain the relatively low R^2s—a problem shared by previous research [27].

This study has implications for club management and policy makers. The finding that community factors (as an area of an organization's direct environment) influence organizational resources has implications for the management of non-profit organizations in general and specifically for non-profit sport clubs which are important providers of local leisure and sport programs in many countries (e.g., [1,3]). On the one hand, the findings imply that organizations should not only manage their internal processes, but also take steps to actively engage with their environment [6]. One form of managing the financial environment would be advocacy, which was found to be positively correlated with an organization's government income [22]. While the results support previous research stating that governance is critical to the effectiveness of nonprofit sport organizations [52], they also draw attention to the importance of an organization's environment. Thus, on the other hand, the results indicate that resource problems of sport clubs are not necessarily only due to poor club management, since higher-level effects (here: community factors) significantly affect the resource situation of sport clubs too. In addition to management implications, this study has practical implications for policy makers. The results highlighted that not only the internal, but also the external situation affects the resources of sport clubs and their effective functioning. This has implications for the distribution of public funding: public subsidies may not be effectively directed at sport clubs when the economic and financial situation is critical. Policy makers should ensure to also support the communities because a sound economic and financial environment is important to the functioning of sport clubs. This is particularly relevant in Germany where many communities have serious financial debts [53], which inarguably affect the situation of the local sport clubs.

5. Conclusions

The environment is important for organizational behavior and the resource situation of non-profits. The focus of this study was on the direct environment of organizations, *i.e.*, the community the organization is located in. Community-level effects on the resources of non-profit organizations were examined using the example of non-profit sport clubs in Germany. This study was among the first to integrate the community level into statistical models using multi-level analyses and to consider the economic and financial environment. The results show that not only community size, but also the financial situation of the community, the level of unemployment, and the revenue from income taxes significantly affect club resources. While these results are not unexpected, this study is among the first to provide quantitative evidence of these relationships. Given that resource problems are similar among sport clubs in other countries [2,3] and that the chosen community-level factors are also relevant to communities and clubs in other countries, the findings of this study should be relevant to sport clubs in other countries and non-profit organizations in other industries.

This study has some limitations that represent avenues for future research. First, this study is only based on cross-sectional data. While panel data would have been available on the organizational level, the availability of community-level data is problematic, specifically when consistent measures are needed over time. Given the evident importance of community-level factors and the limited empirical evidence particularly regarding quantitative approaches, this study calls for more research in this area and the application of multi-level analyses. Future research should also examine how the economic and financial situation of the community affects sport clubs in other countries, which—as noted earlier—share similar problems regarding human, infrastructure, and financial resources [1–3]. Another limitation refers to the measures used on the community level. While it would have been interesting to also examine the effects of other financial and economic indicators like debts, gross domestic product, and the number of potential competitors, this study is restricted to the measures that were available. Third, this study only provides evidence that the environment in the form of the community affects the resources of sport clubs. Future research should examine the power relations between the community and sport clubs, which result from resource dependence and external impacts. Fourth, this study is limited to two levels of analysis. Future research may add another layer like the state level or the individual level (*i.e.*, club members) to the multi-level analysis.

Acknowledgments: The authors would like to thank the Federal Institute for Sports Sciences (BISp), the German Olympic Sports Confederation (DOSB), and the 16 federal state sports confederations (LSBs) for supporting the research into sport clubs in Germany (Sport Development Report).

Author Contributions: Christoph Breuer is the head of the project Sport Development Report from which the sport club data (organizational level) were taken. Pamela Wicker conducted the data analysis and wrote the final manuscript.

References

1. Lamprecht, M.; Fischer, A.; Stamm, H.P. *Die Schweizer Sportvereine: Strukturen, Leistungen, Herausforderungen [Sport Clubs in Switzerland: Structure, Performance, and Challenges]*; Seismo: Zurich, Switzerland, 2012.
2. Lasby, D.; Sperling, J. *Understanding the Capacity of Ontario Sports and Recreation Organizations*; Imagine Canada: Toronto, ON, Canada, 2007.
3. Sport Recreation Alliance (SRA). Sports Club Survey 2013. Available online: http://www.sportandrecreation.org.uk/policy/SSC (accessed on 12 December 2013).

4. Enjolras, B. A governance-structure approach to voluntary organizations. *Nonprof. Volunt. Sect. Quart.* **2009**, *38*, 761–783. [CrossRef]
5. Foster, M.K.; Meinhard, A.G. Diversifying revenue sources in Canada. *Nonprofit Manag. Lead.* **2005**, *16*, 43–60. [CrossRef]
6. Scott, W.R. Reflections on a half-century of organizational sociology. *Annu. Rev. Sociol.* **2004**, *30*, 1–21. [CrossRef]
7. Lammers, J.C. The effect of competition on labor management in nonprofit organizations. *Nonprof. Volunt. Sect. Quart.* **1990**, *19*, 171–186. [CrossRef]
8. Neal, R. The importance of the state: Political dimensions of a nonprofit network in Oaxaca, Mexico. *Nonprof. Volunt. Sect. Quart.* **2008**, *37*, 492–511. [CrossRef]
9. Ostrower, F.; Stone, M.M. Moving governance research forward: A contingency-based framework and data application. *Nonprof. Volunt. Sect. Quart.* **2009**, *39*, 901–924. [CrossRef]
10. Wicker, P.; Breuer, C. Scarcity of resources in German non-profit sport clubs. *Sport Manag. Rev.* **2011**, *14*, 188–201. [CrossRef]
11. Koski, P. Organizational effectiveness of Finnish sports clubs. *J. Sport Manag.* **1995**, *9*, 85–95.
12. Stone, M.M.; Sandfort, J.R. Building a policy fields framework to inform research on nonprofit organizations. *Nonprof. Volunt. Sect. Quart.* **2009**, *38*, 1054–1075. [CrossRef]
13. Bryk, A.S.; Raudenbush, S.W. *Hierarchical Linear Models*; Sage Publications: Newbury Park, CA, USA, 1992.
14. Rotolo, T.; Wilson, J. State-level differences in volunteerism in the United States: Research based on demographic, institutional, and cultural macrolevel theories. *Nonprof. Volunt. Sect. Quart.* **2012**, *41*, 452–473. [CrossRef]
15. Scott, W.R. *Organizations. Rational, Natural, and Open Systems*, 5th ed.; Prentice Hall: Upper Saddle River, NJ, USA, 2003.
16. Pfeffer, J.; Salancik, G.R. *The External Control of Organizations: A Resource Dependence Perspective*; Harper and Row: New York, NY, USA, 1978.
17. Cadena-Roa, J.; Luna, M.; Puga, C. Associational performance: The influence of cohesion, decision-making, and the environment. *Voluntas* **2012**, *23*, 993–1013. [CrossRef]
18. Oliver, C. Determinants of interorganizational relationships: integration and future directions. *Acad. Manag. Rev.* **1990**, *15*, 241–265.
19. Whetten, D.A.; Leung, T.K. The instrumental values of interorganizational relations: Antecedents and consequences of linkage formation. *Acad. Manag. J.* **1979**, *22*, 325–344. [CrossRef]
20. Hillman, A.J.; Withers, M.C.; Collins, B.J. Resource dependence theory: A review. *J. Manag.* **2009**, *35*, 1404–1427.
21. Nienhueser, W. Resource dependence theory—How well does it explain behavior of organizations? *Manag. Rev.* **2008**, *19*, 9–32.
22. Moulton, S.; Eckerd, A. Preserving the publicness of the nonprofit sector: Resources, roles, and public values. *Nonprof. Volunt. Sect. Quart.* **2012**, *41*, 656–685. [CrossRef]
23. Verschuere, B.; de Corte, J. The impact of public resource dependence on the autonomy of NPOs in their strategic decision making. *Nonprof. Volunt. Sect. Quart.* **2014**, *43*, 293–313. [CrossRef]
24. Vos, S.; Breesch, D.; Késenne, S.; van Hoecke, J.; Vanreusel, B.; Scheerder, J. Governmental subsidies and coercive isomorphism: Evidence from sports clubs and their resource dependencies. *Eur. J. Sport Soc.* **2011**, *8*, 257–280.
25. Hetling, A.; Botein, H. Positive and negative effects of external influences on program design. *Nonprofit Manag. Lead.* **2010**, *21*, 177–194. [CrossRef]
26. Mulroy, E.A. Community as a factor in implementing interorganizational partnerships. *Nonprofit Manag. Lead.* **2003**, *14*, 47–66. [CrossRef]
27. Wicker, P.; Breuer, C. Understanding the importance of organizational resources to explain organizational problems: Evidence from non-profit sport clubs in Germany. *Voluntas* **2013**, *24*, 461–484. [CrossRef]
28. Breuer, C.; Wicker, P. *Analysis of the Situation of Sports Clubs in Germany*; Sports Development Report 2009/2010; Abbreviated Version; Sportverlag Strauß: Cologne, Germany, 2011.
29. Misener, K.; Harman, A.; Doherty, A. Understanding the local sports council as a mechanism for community sport development. *Manag. Leis.* **2013**, *18*, 300–315. [CrossRef]

30. Wagner, B. Budgetsanierung auf Kosten der Kultur? [Budget Improvement at the Expense of Culture?]. Available online: http://kulturrisse.at/ausgaben/022010/kosmopolitiken/budgetsanierung-auf-kosten-der-kultur (accessed on 11 December 2013).
31. Schlenk, C.T. Der große Schuldengraben [The Big Debt]. Available online: http://www.zeit.de/wirtschaft/2013--09/schulden-statistik-kommunen-oberhausen (accessed on 11 December 2013).
32. Mackintosh, E. Report: Income Inequality Rising in Most Developed Countries. Available online: http://www.washingtonpost.com/blogs/worldviews/wp/2013/05/16/report-income-inequality-rising-in-most-developed-countries/ (accessed on 21 May 2013).
33. Oechsner, T. Jeder vierte Beschäftigte erhält nur Niedriglohn [Every fourth employee only earns a low wage]. Available online: http://www.sueddeutsche.de/wirtschaft/2.220/studie-entfacht-neue-gerechtigkeitsdebatte-jeder-vierte-beschaeftigte-erhaelt-nur-niedriglohn-1.1308326 (accessed on 21 May 2013).
34. Andreff, W. Voluntary work in sport. In *Handbook on the Economics of Sport*; Andreff, W., Szymanski, S., Eds.; Edward Elgar: Cheltenham, UK, 2006; pp. 219–224.
35. Salamon, L.M.; Sokolowski, S.W.; Haddock, M.A. Measuring the economic value of volunteer work globally: Concepts, estimates, and a roadmap to the future. *Ann. Public Coop. Econ.* **2011**, *82*, 217–252.
36. Burgham, M.; Downward, P. Why volunteer, time to volunteer? A case study from swimming. *Manag. Leis.* **2005**, *10*, 79–93.
37. Schlesinger, T.; Nagel, S. Who will volunteer? Analysing individual and structural factors of volunteering in Swiss sports clubs. *Eur. J. Sport Sci.* **2013**, *13*, 707–715.
38. Freeman, R.B. Working for nothing: The supply of volunteer labor. *J. Labor Econ.* **1997**, *15*, S140–S166. [CrossRef]
39. Federal and Regional Statistical Offices (Ed.) *Statistik lokal. Daten für die Gemeinden, kreisfreien Städte und Kreise Deutschlands [Local Statistics. Data of the Communities, Country Boroughs and Districts in Germany]*; Landesamt für Datenverarbeitung und Statistik Nordrhein-Westfalen: Düsseldorf, Germany, 2008.
40. Tabachnick, B.G.; Fidell, L.S. *Using Multivariate Statistics*; Allyn & Bacon: Boston, MA, USA, 2007.
41. Hox, J.J. *Multilevel Analysis*; Lawrence Erlbaum Associates: Mahwah, NJ, USA, 2002.
42. Snijders, T.A.B.; Bosker, R. *Multilevel Analysis: An Introduction to Basic and Advanced Modeling*; Sage: London, UK, 1999.
43. Todd, S.Y.; Crook, T.R.; Barilla, A.G. Hierarchical linear modeling of multilevel data. *J. Sport Manag.* **2005**, *19*, 387–403.
44. Wittenberg, R.; Cramer, H. *Computergestützte Datenanalyse [Computer Assisted Data Analysis]*, 2nd ed.; Lucius & Lucius: Stuttgart, Germany, 1998.
45. Bortz, J. *Statistik für Human- und Sozialwissenschaftler [Statistics for the Human and Social Sciences]*, 6th ed.; Springer: Heidelberg, Germany, 2005.
46. White, H. A heteroskedastic-consistent covariance matrix estimator and a direct test for heteroskedasticity. *Econometrica* **1980**, *48*, 817–838. [CrossRef]
47. Raudenbush, S.; Bryk, A.; Cheong, Y.; Congdon, R.; du Toit, M. *HLM 6: Hierarchical Linear and Nonlinear Modeling*; Scientific Software International, Inc.: Lincolnwood, IL, USA, 2004.
48. Wicker, P.; Breuer, C.; Lamprecht, M.; Fischer, A. Does club size matter? An examination of economies of scale, economies of scope, and organizational problems. *J. Sport Manag.* **2014**, *28*, 266–280.
49. Nagel, M. Die soziale Zusammensetzung der Sportvereinsmitglieder. In *Integrationsleistungen von Sportvereinen als Freiwilligenorganisationen [Integration Achievements of Sport Clubs as Voluntary Organisations]*; Baur, J., Braun, S., Eds.; Meyer & Meyer: Aachen, Germany, 2003; pp. 409–448.
50. Christakis, N.A.; Fowler, J.H. Social contagion theory: Examining dynamic social networks and human behavior. *Stat. Med.* **2013**, *32*, 556–577. [CrossRef] [PubMed]
51. Coates, D.; Wicker, P.; Feiler, S.; Breuer, C. A bivariate probit examination of financial and volunteer problems of non-profit sport clubs. *Int. J. Sport Financ.* **2014**, *9*, 130–148.
52. Yeh, C.M.; Taylor, T. Issues of governance in sport organisations: A question of board size, structure and roles. *World Leis. J.* **2008**, *50*, 33–45. [CrossRef]
53. Schäfers, M. Überschuldete Kommunen: Die Krise vor der Haustür [Overindebted Communities: The Crisis in Front of the Entry Door]. Available online: http://www.faz.net/aktuell/wirtschaft/ueberschuldete-kommunen-die-krise-vor-der-haustuer-11619334.html (accessed on 13 January 2015).

Permissions

All chapters in this book were first published in MDPI; hereby published with permission under the Creative Commons Attribution License or equivalent. Every chapter published in this book has been scrutinized by our experts. Their significance has been extensively debated. The topics covered herein carry significant findings which will fuel the growth of the discipline. They may even be implemented as practical applications or may be referred to as a beginning point for another development.

The contributors of this book come from diverse backgrounds, making this book a truly international effort. This book will bring forth new frontiers with its revolutionizing research information and detailed analysis of the nascent developments around the world.

We would like to thank all the contributing authors for lending their expertise to make the book truly unique. They have played a crucial role in the development of this book. Without their invaluable contributions this book wouldn't have been possible. They have made vital efforts to compile up to date information on the varied aspects of this subject to make this book a valuable addition to the collection of many professionals and students.

This book was conceptualized with the vision of imparting up-to-date information and advanced data in this field. To ensure the same, a matchless editorial board was set up. Every individual on the board went through rigorous rounds of assessment to prove their worth. After which they invested a large part of their time researching and compiling the most relevant data for our readers.

The editorial board has been involved in producing this book since its inception. They have spent rigorous hours researching and exploring the diverse topics which have resulted in the successful publishing of this book. They have passed on their knowledge of decades through this book. To expedite this challenging task, the publisher supported the team at every step. A small team of assistant editors was also appointed to further simplify the editing procedure and attain best results for the readers.

Apart from the editorial board, the designing team has also invested a significant amount of their time in understanding the subject and creating the most relevant covers. They scrutinized every image to scout for the most suitable representation of the subject and create an appropriate cover for the book.

The publishing team has been an ardent support to the editorial, designing and production team. Their endless efforts to recruit the best for this project, has resulted in the accomplishment of this book. They are a veteran in the field of academics and their pool of knowledge is as vast as their experience in printing. Their expertise and guidance has proved useful at every step. Their uncompromising quality standards have made this book an exceptional effort. Their encouragement from time to time has been an inspiration for everyone.

The publisher and the editorial board hope that this book will prove to be a valuable piece of knowledge for researchers, students, practitioners and scholars across the globe.

List of Contributors

Benjamin Baumer
Program in Statistical and Data Sciences, Smith College, Northampton, MA 01063, USA

Andrew Zimbalist
Department of Economics, Smith College, Northampton, MA 01063, USA

Ruud Koning
Department of Economics and Econometrics, Faculty of Economics and Business, University of Groningen, 9700 AV Groningen, The Netherlands

Victor Matheson, Anil Nathan and James Pantano
Department of Economics and Accounting, College of the Holy Cross, One College Street, Worcester, MA 01610, USA

Paul Gift
Pepperdine Graziadio Business School, Los Angeles, CA 90045, USA

Rodney J. Paul
Department of Sport Management, David B. Falk College of Sport and Human Dynamics, Syracuse University, 810 Nottingham Road, Syracuse, NY 13224-8165, USA

Andrew P. Weinbach
E. Craig Wall Sr. College of Business Administration, Coastal Carolina University, Conway, SC 26195, USA

Mercedes Mareque
Department of Financial Economics and Accounting, Faculty of Business and Tourism, University of Vigo, Campus Universitario, s/n, 32004 Ourense, Spain

Angel Barajas
Department of Finance, School of Economics and Management, National Research University Higher School of Economics, 194100 St. Petersburg, Russia

Francisco Lopez-Corrales
Department of Financial Economics and Accounting, Faculty of Social Sciences and Communication, University of Vigo, Campus A Xunqueira, s/n, 36005 Pontevedra, Spain

Svenja Feiler
Department of Sport Economics and Sport Management, German Sport University Cologne, Am Sportpark Muengersdorf 6, Cologne 50933, Germany

Wladimir Andreff
Scientific Council at the Observatory of the Sports Economy, French Ministry for Sports, 75013 Paris, France

Kelly M. Hastings and Frank Stephenson
Department of Economics, Berry College, Mount Berry, GA 30149, USA

Nick Riccardi
Department of Sport Management, Syracuse University, Syracuse, NY 13244, USA

Andrew Weinbach
Department of Finance and Economics, E. Craig Wall Sr. College of Business Administration, Coastal Carolina University, Conway, SC 29528, USA

Panagiotis E. Dimitropoulos and Konstantinos Koronios
Department of Sport Organization and Management, University of Peloponnese, Sparta 23100, Greece

Benjamin Waggoner, Daniel Wines, Brian P. Soebbing, Chad S. Seifried and Jean Michael Martinez
School of Kinesiology, Louisiana State University, Baton Rouge, LA 70803, USA

Duane Rockerbie
Department of Economics, University of Lethbridge, Lethbridge, AB T1K3M4, Canada

Stephen Easton
Department of Economics, Simon Fraser University, Burnaby, BC V5A1S6, Canada

Daniel Plumley, Rob Wilson, Robbie Millar and Simon Shibli
Sport Business Management, Sheffield Hallam University, Sheffield S1 1WB, UK

Kenneth Linna and Evan Moore
Department of Economics, Finance, and Marketing, Auburn University at Montgomery, Montgomery, AL 36124, USA

Rodney Paul
Department of Finance, Syracuse University, 810 Nottingham Road, Syracuse, NY 13224, USA

Egon Franck
Department of Business Administration, University of Zurich, Affolternstrasse 56, 8050 Zurich, Switzerland

Aju J. Fenn, Lucas Gerdes and Samuel Rothstein
Economics & Business department, Colorado College, Colorado Springs, CO 80919, USA

Pamela Wicker and Christoph Breuer
Department of Sport Economics and Sport Management, German Sport University Cologne, Am Sportpark Muengersdorf 6, Cologne 50933, Germany

Index

www.ingramcontent.com/pod-product-compliance
Lightning Source LLC
LaVergne TN
LVHW082141200926
848484LV00008B/2086